FREEDOM'S COST
The Story of
General Nathanael Greene

Janet Uhlar
(2/17/12)

FREEDOM'S COST

The Story of General Nathanael Greene

A Novel

Janet Uhlar

First published by Dog Ear Publishing
4010 W. 86th Street, Ste H
Indianapolis, IN 46268
www.dogearpublishing.net

ISBN: 978-145750-306-1

This book is printed on acid-free paper.

Printed in the United States of America

Dedicated to the memory of,
David Charles (Uhlar) Tinney, my precious child who excitedly joined me
in discovering Nathanael Greene on field trips to Rhode Island and beyond.
Dave, have you met the general? Introduce me when I arrive!

And to Nancy Atkins Aldrich, my gentle editor, source of encouragement,
and dear friend.
Nancy, it's finally in print! Thank you!

David C. Tinney   Nancy Atkins-Aldrich
December 4, 1983—September 12, 2001   August 18, 1951—November 14, 2010

"Since the Episcopalian and the Congregationalist won't, I suppose the Quaker must."
(Nathanael Greene)

CHAPTER ONE

"DUPLICATE COPIES, TRIPLICATE copies, quadruplicate copies! The writing never ends!" The young man, barely more than a boy, mumbled as he dipped the quill pen into the ink well and reluctantly returned its well-lubricated point to the paper before him. He stopped the movement of the quill in mid-stroke bringing an abrupt halt to the graceful letter being formed. Then looking at the many piles of paper on the desk he sighed. "I think I am already developing rheumatiz!" He complained, hearing the roll of distant thunder. In response, he lifted his left hand and placed it upon his painful right shoulder, rubbing it aggressively. "I just want to fight—trade in the quill for a musket and fight! 'No, no, Johnny' they tell me. 'Your abilities are needed elsewhere at present.' What abilities I ask? Any fool can take a quill and make quadruplicate copies!"

"Excuse me, son." A voice sounded, coming from behind Johnny.

Startled, the young man jumped, and then quickly turned to face the intruder, dragging a long line of ink as the quill grazed the paper before him. "May I help you, sir?" Johnny asked looking up at the sturdy six-foot frame, which filled the doorway. The imposing figure was adorned in a bright red coat faced with green, and a white waistcoat and breeches with black gaiters, which identified his militia unit as that of Rhode Island's Kentish Guards. The black plume on the tricorne, which he held in his hand, signified that he was an officer. The epaulets on his shoulders distinguished his rank of brigadier general.

"I am General Nathanael Greene. I have been summoned to meet with the Committee," the officer explained, in a soft, non-threatening tone. He held out the dispatch he received.

Johnny's initial embarrassment and tension fled as he looked upon the kind expression of this militia officer. His blue eyes sparkled out from an oval face, with a thin nose, full lips and a coarse, blond, head of hair. His eyes caught the young man's attention.

Johnny, who served as secretary to the Committee, appeared confused by the dispatch. He glanced at the paper and shrugged. "The Committee adjourned more than an hour ago, sir, but the chairman is still here. Perhaps he is waiting for you. You will find him down the hall to the left. Raining yet, sir?" Johnny asked, as a clap of thunder sounded.

"No, not yet."

"We could use the rain—" Johnny looked down at the line of ink on the quadruplicate copy, and picking up the paper crumbled it in his hand.

"Yes, we could use the rain," Nathanael Greene agreed. "And, quite honestly, lad, I do not think you have to worry about developing rhuematiz—you are much too young for that." He said with a grin, turned and walked away.

As he came to the end of the hall, Nathanael noted that the door on the left was open. He stepped over the threshold and paused. Alone at the head of the large, rectangular table was the Committee chairman, Dr. Joseph Warren. He sat motionless, his head buried in his hands. Papers were scattered before him; a quill lay flat, slowly dripping its rust colored liquid onto the wood beneath.

Nathanael hesitated, not sure if the doctor's silent posture indicated distress, quiet prayer, or both. Warren's positions as chairman of the Committee of Safety, president of the Provincial Congress of Massachusetts, and head surgeon of the newly established military hospital brought with them immense responsibility and strain. *In truth,* Nathanael thought as he stood there, *Warren is possibly the most influential patriot in Massachusetts—perhaps throughout the colonies. It is no wonder that the British commander declared the death of Warren equal to 500 ordinary colonials.*

Slowly, Dr. Warren lifted his head, as if sensing Nathanael's presence, and looked straight at the officer. In an instant, the agonizing stress upon his countenance transformed. His blue eyes twinkled as a warm, genuine smile came to his face. "Come in, General Greene. Please have a seat," the doctor said, standing and extending his hand to greet Nathanael.

Nathanael returned the handshake and placed his hat on the table as both simultaneously sat down. The doctor picked up the quill pen and blotted the ink from the table with his handkerchief. Another clap of thunder sounded.

"How are your men faring, General?" Dr. Warren asked with what appeared to be genuine concern.

"As well as can be expected, sir."

"We have a job on our hands, General Greene, the monumental task of feeding, clothing and sheltering the thousands who have come to our aid since the battles of Lexington and Concord; never mind trying to supply them with the proper equipment that befits an army." He made the last comment with distress as he looked down and placed his hand upon a pile of papers on the table. Nathanael assumed the papers must have something to do with the supplies they didn't have.

"Ah," Dr. Warren continued, gazing intently at Nathanael and suddenly cheerful again. "But we will properly supply the men, for we must!" He paused a moment in reflection.

"We in Massachusetts are immensely grateful for the support of the Rhode Island regiments. I have been keeping tabs on your 3000 men, General," Dr. Warren continued. "You have reason to be proud of them. They are, without a doubt, the most disciplined regiments represented."

"Thank you, Doctor," Nathanael responded.

Dr. Warren smiled. "You are a paradox, General Greene, and I have been eager to find time to speak to you privately."

"A paradox, sir?"

"It has been reported that you are a Quaker." The doctor had a whimsical gleam to his eyes.

"Ah, yes—and you'll discover for yourself my Quaker upbringing, for I am told that when the pressure about me intensifies I quickly revert to the form of speech I am most accustomed to," Nathanael said with a weak smile, referring to the Quaker dialect.

"I was admonished by the Society of Friends for my interest in the militia. It was a difficult decision, whether to remain loyal to my religious training of pacifism, or aid in the defense of my Country," Nathanael confessed.

"Please forgive me, General, I didn't mean to pry," Dr. Warren apologized.

"I am not offended, sir. My decision was made and I will stand by it."

Dr. Warren studied Nathanael in silence for a moment. "—You could not be any older than I, thirty-three, thirty-four?" the doctor asked.

"Thirty-three." Nathanael acknowledged with a nod.

"Those in Rhode Island must place a great deal of confidence in you, sir; from Quaker to brigadier general and only thirty-three years-old."

Nathanael chuckled. "Actually I think they sought out an Episcopalian for the commission; and, when he turned it down, they tried a Congregationalist. Neither one wanted it so they enticed the newly fallen Quaker!"

Dr. Warren laughed in response.

"It is known that I have been an ardent reader of military writings. I suppose that may have had some bearing on their decision. I purchased my books from Henry Knox, the Boston book merchant. I purchased a brown Bess from Mr. Knox as well," Nathanael smiled as he recalled this particular purchase. "It was a bargain, for with the musket I received a British deserter. He came back to Rhode

Island with me to drill the militia. We had a time smuggling both the musket and the deserter out of Boston."

Dr. Warren returned the smile. "I am glad Mr. Knox put our British friend to such good use—and as for the musket, if the British only knew how many have passed through Boston. Mr. Knox's shop certainly helped move a few."

"Then you know Henry?"

"Yes, we are well acquainted. Tell me, General, do you have a family in Rhode Island?" Dr. Warren asked.

"Yes—at least the start of one. My wife is expecting our first child. And you, sir?"

Dr. Warren's smile faded. He paused before responding. "My family is trapped in Boston," he said, instinctively turning his head in the direction of the town he spoke. Then returning his gaze to Nathanael, he sensed the discomfort, and the unspoken questions, his response had caused. "I failed to move them out before the battle at Lexington. It has been almost two months since I have seen them, and the British do not intend to let them go. They, and a few other family members of noted patriot leaders, are being held as security so that we will not attack the town. As long as our army lays siege to Boston, my family will be held as hostages—" Dr. Warren paused, looked blankly at the table before him and took a deep breath. Then turning to Nathanael, he continued, "We have reason to believe the British will be making an offensive move. Our supplies have been depleted. We need lead, powder, guns—I would like you to go back to Rhode Island and make our needs known to your Congress. It is imperative that supplies be furnished by the sister colonies if we are to continue in this fight."

"I understand, sir. When shall I leave?" Nathanael asked.

"Tomorrow—and you must be back within the week."

Nathanael was keenly aware of the urgency of this mission. "You will have your supplies, Doctor," his tone was assuring as he stood up. "By your leave, Dr. Warren. I must prepare my officers for my absence."

"Of course. Godspeed to you, General Greene."

"Your servant, Doctor," Nathanael said with the nod of his head. He picked his hat up off the table and walked toward the door.

"Is that a recent injury?" Dr. Warren called after him, noting the limp in Nathanael's gait.

Nathanael turned to face him, momentarily confused by the question. "Sir?"

"The leg."

"Happened years ago—never healed properly," he answered.

"Have you had it checked? Perhaps there's something that could be done," the doctor offered, ever ready to help one in need of his skill.

"I have been assured that it is a permanent condition, but I thank you for your concern, sir."

The doctor nodded, "Please notify me immediately upon your return. Your servant, General."

The rain was falling when Nathanael left headquarters. It was a slow, steady rain that soaked through his jacket. He hardly noticed the dampness, for his mind was preoccupied with the meeting that just had transpired. There were rumors circulating that Joseph Warren was to be commissioned a major general. This would come as no surprise to Nathanael. The provincial army of ragtag soldiers needed a man in command whom they trusted. Warren was that man.

Though Warren, himself, had urged the Continental Congress in Philadelphia to commission a commander in chief, no word had been received to indicate that a commander had been decided on. And, as Dr. Warren pointed out, the British were ready to make a move. This ragtag army would be forced to face them with or without a Commander in Chief.

He and Dr. Warren were very much alike, Nathanael decided. He had no doubt that within time they would develop a strong friendship. Even now, Nathanael felt the sense of devotion such affection brings.

"Caty!" Nathanael beckoned for his twenty-year-old bride as he stepped into the foyer. "Caty, I am home!" he cried out again, removing the riding gloves. He smiled as the silence within the house was immediately disrupted by the sound of running feet on the floor above.

"Nathanael! Is it really you?" she cried as she flew down the narrow staircase, holding her skirt up to her knees in her haste. Before he had time to warn her to slow down, she was upon him, her arms tight around his neck.

"Thank God you are home!" she exclaimed breathlessly, kissing him upon the cheek repeatedly.

"Caty!" he said with a chuckle. After loosening her strangling hold, he kissed her tenderly on the lips. He gazed intently into her violet eyes; her black curls fell loosely about small shoulders. Caty's petite figure felt good in his strong arms, and her lips invited him back for a more passionate kiss.

"Has the trouble passed, Nat?" Jacob Greene asked from the threshold of the study.

Nathanael heard his brother's question, but was too mesmerized to respond immediately. Reluctantly releasing his wife, he turned to his brother. Caty kept hold of his arm.

"How are thee, Jacob?" Nathanael asked with a warm smile, extending his free hand to his Quaker brother. "No, the trouble has not passed," he said, looking from Jacob to Caty. "The situation remains as I have stated in my letters. I have been sent back to round up supplies for the army. I will only be here a few days."

"Oh, Nathanael!" Caty moaned. "Certainly you can stay more than a few days. You have been gone so long already!"

Nathanael smiled tenderly at his young wife as he softly caressed her cheek. "Angel, it has only been three weeks."

"It seemed an eternity!" she replied softly taking hold of his other hand.

"I wish I could stay longer, Angel, but I cannot. The army is in desperate need. The few days I am home will be busy with the work at hand. I am afraid I will not even be able to stay in Coventry except for tonight. We will stay in Potowomut," Nathanael said, referring to the town where the family homestead was located.

"How are things here, Jacob?" he asked his brother, who had been left in charge of the Coventry forge in Nathanael's absence.

"Work continues unhindered," Jacob replied, casting a peculiar glance at Caty. "The household chores run smoothly enough—" He stopped abruptly. Nathanael felt certain he had more to say, but thought it best not to pursue the matter.

"Tell me, Nathanael, do you like this gown?" Caty asked in her attempt to quickly change the subject. She let go of him and slowly turned to model the dress, of rose brocade. The delicate lace bodice dropped in a flirtatious curve below her creamy neck. The soft lace fell daintily about her elbows.

"It is quite becoming," he replied, distracted by the fact that there was obviously trouble between Caty and his brother.

"You can hardly tell I am in a family way, can you? That's why I bought them—to hide it for as long as possible."

"Bought them?" Nathanael repeated.

"Nathanael, thee must be hungry. Why don't I go see what I can find in the kitchen," Jacob interrupted, seemingly anxious to excuse himself.

Nathanael nodded in response to his brother's suggestion.

"It is good to have thee home," Jacob said, patting Nathanael on the arm as he moved past.

"Caty, where is Peggy?" Nathanael asked referring to Jacob's wife.

"Off doing something or other. She is so confoundedly efficient." Caty pouted.

"What's wrong, Angel?"

"She makes me feel inadequate. I cannot cook well enough, so Peggy cooks. I cannot regiment the household chores to suit her schedule so she does them. She has taken over and I am just in the way!"

Nathanael sensed from his wife's appearance that she was on the verge of tears. He pulled her into his arms in an attempt to comfort her. "Peggy seems to have forgotten what it was like to be a new bride."

"I am sure she was never as inefficient as I. Her mother thoroughly taught her all the tasks necessary to manage a home."

"It is certainly not your fault that you weren't taught such things, now is it?" Nathanael asked, placing his finger under her chin and gently pushing her head back. "And you are not inefficient; you are simply inexperienced. There is a vast difference. With Jacob acting as master of the house in my absence, I suppose it seems only natural for Sister Peggy to fill the role as mistress. I am sure she does not realize how uncomfortable this makes you."

Nathanael's years of familiarity with Peggy led him to make this observation; an observation that Caty's expression clearly communicated that she did not appreciate.

"I will talk to Jacob about it," he quickly added.

"Your brother does not like me, neither does his wife," Caty complained.

"Why do you say that? Of course they like you. They love you," Nathanael assured her.

Caty threw back her head and let out a short, sarcastic laugh. "They certainly do not love me!" she protested. "I am not a Quaker and they simply cannot get over the fact that you married me!" She laughed again, "Can you see me dressed in one of those ugly gray sacks they call dresses—And you!" she exclaimed, looking Nathanael up and down in his bright red and green uniform. "I remember so well how horrid you appeared in those drab, shapeless suits—I am delighted you have come out of that," she said, throwing her arms about his neck again. "But I do wish you would stop imitating their odd way of talking when you are around them."

Nathanael stood stiffly despite her embrace. "We have discussed this before, Caty; and, whether you like it or not, I will continue to speak thusly to the Friends out of respect," he said authoritatively. "I was a member of the Society for thirty-one years and except for their doctrine regarding pacifism, I still hold to my Quaker beliefs."

"Oh, really?" Caty said with the tilt of her head and a twinkle to her eyes. "Then why is there a bureau upstairs full of finely tailored suits that belong to you? And I get the distinct impression that you like all the lace and frill on my colorful gowns!" She paused for a reply.

"On two points I differ in my beliefs," he affirmed coolly, his gaze fixed straight ahead.

"Really? I recall that you took an oath when you were commissioned. And the title of general must certainly be considered a title of respect.

"And it is a known fact that you enjoy dancing and spend much of your leisure time entertaining yourself by reading books—and many of them are not related to the Scripture! How do you account for that?" she teased. Disregarding his coldness, she kissed his cheek.

"On six points I differ—" he said with a hint of a smile.

"Only six points, Quaker Nathanael? Then why did you marry such a worldly woman as me? Why, you had your eye on me before the Quaker's dismissed you." She kissed him again.

"Seven points," he said looking down at her this time. There was a definite twinkle in his eyes.

"Are thee mad at me, husband?" Caty asked with the tilt of her head. Her huge eyes widened even more in a flirtatious attempt to make him forget his anger. It always worked.

Nathanael sighed as he lifted his arms and wrapped them about her waist. "Nay! Try as I might, I cannot remain mad. You are my weakness, Catherine Littlefield Greene."

"And you are my strength, General," she whispered as he bent to kiss her.

"Given time the Mother Country would have come to see the folly in her treatment of the colonies—" Kitt Greene began.

"Time? How much time should we have given her?" Nathanael asked. This was a discussion the Greene brothers, now assembled at the dining room table of the old homestead, had on many an occasion in the past. Nathanael knew that the outcome would be the same, their four pacifist views against his. He could predict their responses verbatim. Rather than being aggravated, he found he was growing bored, and tired. Comfortably leaning back in the dining room chair, Nathanael clasped his hands behind his head.

"That is not the question," Kitt responded. "For what does it matter? Patience is needed in such matters. Certainly taking up arms against the Mother Country is not the answer."

Nathanael decided to abandon the former script and try a different approach. He leaned forward, looking at each brother assembled. "Thee is right, Kitt. What is wrong with me that I have failed to see the soundness in it? What does it matter how long it takes the King to see his folly? What does it matter if he decides to tax the colonies to the point of interfering with a man's ability to feed and cloth his family? What does it matter if the colonies have no representation in Parliament? What does it matter if the ports of Boston are closed, forcing ruin and possible starvation on the people? What does it matter if British troops are sent to police the streets of Boston, and the townspeople are forced to house them? And, as thee have pointed out in the past, God turned His back on those in Boston and allowed them to suffer—we cannot question His will. So why should we, such God-fearing men, involve ourselves in the sufferings of Boston? Thee are right. Let them starve. Let them live in fear of being shot down by British soldiers as those in the Boston Massacre were. Let their sons be beaten by the British troops as they go about their business in broad daylight. Let their daughters be raped, and bear the scars of such horror for life. God's will be done."

"One cannot oppose violence with violence, brother. And one cannot deny that God has allowed this to come about in Boston." Kitt's bristled reply came.

Nathanael no longer tired or bored, became frustrated. "Certainly God has allowed this, but not as punishment for those in Boston! Nay! It was a means of forcing them to do what many men throughout these colonies knew must be done, but lacked the fortitude to do—to reclaim their God-given rights by opposing the abuses of Great Britain—to face her might with the courage—and faith—to throw off the shackles!"

"God has not turned His back on those in Boston, and anyone who holds to that belief is a fool—" Jacob began, glancing at Kitt and the two silent brothers sitting on either side of him. Then placing a calming hand on Nathanael's arm he continued. "Nat is right, the abuses must be opposed, but *he who lives by the sword shall die by the sword*."

Nathanael looked his elder brother in the eye and somberly replied. "And perhaps that will be my fate. But, Jacob—we all have to die somehow."

A loud knock on the front door distracted the brothers.

"Late for a caller," Jacob remarked.

Nathanael walked to the door.

"General Greene, my apologies for disturbing you at this late hour," a militia captain greeted Nathanael with a quick salute. "We just received word from headquarters that the King's troops have made an attack, sir."

"Details, Captain," Nathanael ordered as he motioned for the captain to enter.

The brothers came into the hallway to hear what was being said. Caty, dressed only in her nightgown, a blanket draped about her shoulders, suddenly appeared on the winding staircase.

"There are not many details, sir. The Provincial Army occupied a piece of land referred to as Bunker Hill or Breed's Hill—there is confusion as to which it was. British troops drove them from it. Word is that the British suffered heavy casualties."

"And our men?" Nathanael asked.

"Few in comparison, sir. That's all I know."

"Was the Rhode Island militia called to battle?" Nathanael asked, alarmed that his men may have been forced to face the enemy without him.

"No, sir. They were posted elsewhere."

"Thank God!" Caty cried as she slowly descended the stairs.

"Captain, saddle my horse," Nathanael ordered.

"Yes, sir."

"Nathanael! You are not going back to Massachusetts!" Caty cried as she grabbed his arm.

He turned to her, "I have to go back, Caty. Surely you can see that."

"No! I cannot see it at all—you have not even had time to accomplish what you were sent to do!" she argued.

"The supplies are being rounded up. I will stop by the governor's on my way out and see that he has them sent to Massachusetts at once," he assured her.

"But you do not know what the situation is there—It may be dangerous!" She grabbed hold of both his shirtsleeves. The tears ran freely down her smooth cheeks.

"Caty, that's exactly why I have to go," he said tenderly, placing his hands on her shoulders. "I am commander of the Rhode Island forces. I must be there to command."

The brothers, sensitive to Nathanael and Caty's need to be alone, quietly made their way back into the dining room.

Nathanael wiped the tears from Caty's cheeks and pulled her close. "I promise you, if my stay in Massachusetts proves lengthy, I will send for you as I am able."

"Will you?" Caty asked looking up at him. There was a glimmer of hope in her tear-stained eyes.

"I do not know what our living conditions will be—"

"I do not care; I just want to be with you!" She cried, tightening her hold on him.

He kissed her softly on the lips. "I have to put on my uniform and get ready to go."

She tightened her hold even more.

The lights burned brightly at Cambridge headquarters as the early morning hours wore on. Nathanael could see familiar figures through the open windows as he approached the house. Members of the Committee of Safety, officers, secretaries and couriers could be seen scratching notes at the table, moving about the rooms and going to and from the house to deliver the latest intelligence.

"General Greene, you missed the fireworks." the gruff voice of the French and Indian War veteran, General Israel Putnam, greeted him from behind as he dismounted.

"I headed back as soon as I heard. You have been trying to get the Committee to agree to take that hill for weeks. Did you finally get a chance to fight?" Nathanael asked.

"Yeah—and we should have been able to hold it." Israel was obviously troubled.

"What went wrong?"

"The men were green—never faced enemy fire before—" he said in reply, but offered nothing more.

Nathanael was anxious to know what happened. "—The men didn't hold up in battle?" he asked, not at all surprised that this was the case, for many of the militia companies were unruly.

"No. The men in battle fought bravely. Twice they forced those bloody-backs to retreat. It was the third attack that drove our men from the hill. We ran out of ammunition." He stopped again.

Nathanael was confused by the blatant contradiction of Israel's statements, and his confusion was evident.

"Forgive me, General, I am a very tired man—" Israel apologized for his inability to communicate clearly. "The reinforcements failed us. There were 2000 men under orders to reinforce those on the hill. They watched the entire battle from a safe distance, refusing to march forward."

Nathanael shook his head, disturbed by the scene Israel Putnam had described. "I heard the British suffered many casualties—"

"If the victor were determined by casualties, this camp would be in glorious celebration," Israel replied. "They had at least 1000 killed or wounded against our 400. It was a gruesome sight, the likes of which I have never seen."

"I would like to sell them another hill at the same price—" Nathanael remarked.

"Yeah, the price was certainly too steep for that piece of ground. But we paid dearly for trying to hold it as long as we did," Israel patted Nathanael's horse as he spoke. "We had one casualty that has deeply affected the morale of the men—" he paused and looked straight at Nathanael. "Joseph Warren fought with us, but never came off the hill. He was engaged in hand-to-hand combat in an attempt to hold the enemy back as we made our retreat—it has been reported that he was shot down."

The impact of Israel's words came as a hard blow to Nathanael. "Warren's dead?" He could not manage more than a whisper.

"He is dead, and it is a loss that we will not quickly overcome. He was elected major general just two days ago, but he has had command of this army from the start—probably the only man that could hold the New England militia units together. The Continental Congress had better move fast to send us a man who can take his place and command this army, or they're going to find themselves hanging from the gallows right alongside us, my friend.

"I hope God will preserve me in the bounds of moderation, and enable me to support myself with proper dignity, neither rash nor timorous, pursuing a conduct marked by manly firmness, but never bordering on frenzy.
(Nathanael Greene to brother)

CHAPTER TWO

July 12, 1775

My Dear Caty,

As you have probably heard by now, our Commander in Chief has finally arrived. General George Washington is as grand as all the tales that have circulated since the French and Indian War claim him to be.

The army is no longer divided into separate militia companies, with confusion as to who commands what. We are now the Continental Army and the Congress in Philadelphia has graciously reaffirmed my commission as brigadier general. I am the junior of Washington's generals. To be truthful, I am in awe of the lot of them.

You are, no doubt, waiting for me to give you a detailed description of the men who will lead this army of 16,000 souls. Yet time will not permit me to indulge you. I will say that His Excellency is a tall man of six-feet, with a rugged frame. He is in his mid-forties, I would guess, with keen gray eyes. His face is pleasant to look upon, though scarred by the pox. He grooms himself to perfection, so I cannot report the color of his hair as it is always neatly powdered, though I suspect it to be brown, as are his brows.

As you can imagine there is no small amount of murmuring from the New Englanders with regard to an outsider being given the command. However, I do not think His Excellency is the least bit offended, for he commented to me that he is not too keen on the New Englanders—present company excepted. (You know the affection I feel for those of New England. Given time, General Washington will come to admire their qualities as well.)

Our second in command is Major General Charles Lee, a veteran officer of the King's army. This fact has caused a bit of suspicion and uncertainty. Nevertheless, the Continental Congress sings his praise.

General Lee, though expert in military matters, has a most abrasive personality. He is the opposite of General Washington in manners and grooming, and is perhaps the ugliest man I have ever seen.

Would that you could come to me, but General Washington is hesitant to have our families join us just yet. He is hoping for a quick and peaceful end to this nightmare. I am aware that he informed his own wife of his plans to be home before winter sets in. If this is the case, and pray God it is, I shall be with you for the birth of our child.

My prayer is that of yours, that I shall return to you shortly and peaceably live my life out as a Rhode Island iron master.

Adieu my love,

Nathanael

"How can we fight a war with no army?" General Charles Lee's words thundered through the large house, which served as his headquarters. "I will not stand idle and watch those men walk off. Sissies, that's what they are—" The general continued with one of his profane tantrums for which he was noted.

Nathanael witnessed Lee's rage from the other end of the house. He sat quietly in a safe, darkened corner of the kitchen, slowly sipping a steaming cup of coffee. The elderly woman, who had been hired to cook meals for the soldiers occupying Lee's headquarters, glanced at Nathanael from her place at the kitchen hearth. Her expression plainly revealed her horror at Lee's offensive language.

Nathanael threw her a sympathetic smile. He, too, found Lee's behavior unbearable at times—the very reason he was delaying to report.

He told himself that this delay was totally justified, for the cold air had caused his asthma to act up. A cup of coffee usually helped restore normal breathing. He would report just as soon as the coffee was gone. He took another sip.

Lee's ranting suddenly stopped. "I will just take the cup with me," Nathanael whispered to himself, preparing to stand.

"—We are expected to fight with virtually no heavy artillery, no engineers, no—" The screaming began again.

Nathanael decided to finish his coffee in the kitchen.

"Mrs. Parker, what magic are you working over this fire today?" Lee's aide-de-camp, Colonel Sutton, asked the elderly woman upon entering the kitchen.

"Venison stew, deary," She said with a warm smile.

Sutton moved closer to the pot in order to savor the aroma. As he turned his head to again address Mrs. Parker, he spotted Nathanael out of the corner of his eye. "General Greene. Excuse me, sir. I did not realize you were here. General Lee has been expecting you, sir."

"I am on my way," Nathanael replied as he stood up, grabbing his hat and cape. "Thank you for the coffee, Mrs. Parker."

"Did it help?" she asked with concern.

"Yes, ma'am, it did," he replied with a warm smile. "Come along, Colonel; I have news that will be pleasing to General Lee."

"Ah, Greene." Charles Lee exclaimed when Nathanael entered the room. "You better tell me you have convinced the Rhode Island troops to reenlist. Two entire colonies' enlistment's up at the same time—3000 men!"

Nathanael sat down next to General John Sullivan and made himself as comfortable as possible while Lee continued to rant. General Lee's constant companions, two bear-like dogs, came over to Nathanael and General Sullivan and began sniffing their boots. The dogs were as big, mean and as ugly as their master, which proved to be a bit unnerving. Sullivan looked at Nathanael apprehensively. The dogs soon became bored and returned to their master, lying contentedly at his feet.

"—Connecticut is a lost cause—they are even threatening to walk out before their term is up. Mutiny! It is out and out mutiny! Will Rhode Island join them?" he hollered at Nathanael, though he did not wait for a reply. "His Excellency expects a report of the situation tomorrow. It is up to you, Greene, as to whether or not it is a good report."

"The bulk of the Rhode Island forces will reenlist, sir," Nathanael remarked coolly.

"The bulk? Then you have lost some?"

"Some have no choice but to leave, for reasons of illness or family matters that warrant their attention. And there are some that I did not encourage to stay—"

"You what!" Lee bellowed.

"Men who have been trouble from the start—the ones who are constantly being disciplined and do indeed have it in them to become mutineers, sir," Nathanael shot back. Lee remained silent. "Then there are some who will reenlist only if they are guaranteed a furlough in order to get their houses in order and gather appropriate clothing for the winter."

"And what did you tell them, General Greene?" Lee asked with forced civility.

"That I thought General Washington would allow them furlough, sir."

"And, no doubt, you believe you can convince His Excellency to do this?" There was a hint of jealousy in Lee's tone, for George Washington had become quite fond of his youngest general.

"I hope so, sir."

A knock at the door prevented Lee from responding. "Come in!" he shouted.

A young soldier, barely more than a boy, timidly entered the room. He nervously saluted Charles Lee.

Nathanael's heart leaped upon seeing the soldier, for he had been given the duty of watching on the outskirts of town for the coach carrying Caty to camp. Nathanael had been worried the entire day, knowing this trip would be long, cold, and uncomfortable for a woman in her condition. Yet she insisted on coming.

"I—I have a message for General Greene, sir." The soldier addressed Lee.

"I am the senior officer here, mister, so you tell me!" Lee commanded loudly.

The frightened, though devoted, soldier looked at Nathanael, who smiled at him and nodded his approval.

"Mrs. Greene's coach is about three miles from Prospect Heights, General Lee." Turning to Nathanael, he grinned happily, "If you hurry, General, you could beat her to the house!"

"Permission to leave, General Lee," Nathanael said politely as he picked up his hat and cape.

"I am not finished yet, Greene. We happen to have a crisis on our hands!" Lee shot back.

"I am aware of that, sir, but I have done all that I can today to alleviate it."

"And what of Connecticut?" Lee roared

"I have not been asked to negotiate with the Connecticut troops. I do not claim any influence over them, but I will be happy to attempt it should His Excellency ask it of me tomorrow. So, therefore, I again ask your leave, sir."

Lee glared at him defiantly.

"May I remind the general that my term of enlistment is over with that of the Rhode Island troops—?" Nathanael said with stubborn determination.

"Are you threatening to resign your commission, Greene?"

"I have not seen my wife for five months—I have done exceedingly above what was expected of me in negotiating with my troops. I am simply asking for leave of one evening to spend with my wife."

Lee hesitated, meeting his gaze. "—You may leave, General Greene," he finally conceded.

In a flash, Nathanael was out of the room without taking time to even put on his cape. The trembling young soldier was at his heels.

At a full gallop, they traveled the road out of Prospect Heights, intercepting Caty's coach within a few minutes.

The driver of the coach pulled the horses to a gentle halt. Nathanael came up alongside him. Extending his hand to his friend from home, he inquired, "Did thee have a safe trip, Isaac?"

"We went nice and slow as thee instructed, Nat. I believe the lady inside is anxious to see thee," he said with a smile turning his head toward the coach.

Nathanael dismounted and handed the reins to the young soldier. "Take my horse back to headquarters, Mr. Perkins."

He opened the coach door and climbed in. Caty's huge eyes considered his entire form. With a smile, she approved his appearance in the uniform of the Continental Army. His dark blue coat with buff facings and under dress was smartly adorned with full epaulets and bright buttons. A pink sash draped across his chest, beneath his jacket, identified him as a brigadier general. A lock of powdered hair was fashionably curled above each ear; the remainder was pulled back in a neat queue. His lively blue eyes, shaded by a jet-black tricorne hat, met hers as she completed her appraisal.

Caty's cheeks were rosy from the cold air. Ringlets of black hair poured out from beneath a stylish bonnet. A wool blanket was draped around her disproportional body. "Am I to be honored in having the general personally escorting me into camp?" she asked sweetly, her face aglow.

"The honor is mine, my lady," he said, taking hold of her hand and kissing it in a most chivalrous manner.

"We can only wait for their arrival and pass the time as pleasantly as possible," Martha Washington commented, comfortably seated in an easy chair directly facing Caty. "I think, Mrs. Greene, we shall do a lot of waiting for them in the months to come." She took a sip of her tea.

From her position on the settee, Caty quickly inspected the Lady Washington while her attention was diverted. She appeared to be in her early forties, with a hint of gray contrasting the dark hair about her temples. A slender, graceful neck supported an oval face, pleasantly adorned with high cheekbones and soft brown eyes. Mrs. Washington returned her cup to its saucer, catching the unaware Caty's investigative check. As Caty's eyes moved upward on her subject, she saw Mrs. Washington's smile of amusement.

The older woman did not say a word, but graciously took another sip of tea. Caty turned her full attention to her own cup, humiliated at being so obvious. The uneasiness she had felt since her arrival at the Washington home suddenly intensified. Was it that Lady Washington was not much of a conversationalist, Caty wondered, or did she simply dislike her from the start? And why, Caty wondered, why she could not overcome this awkward silence herself? Nathanael had such great respect for the Washingtons; she so much wanted to make a good impression.

"Have you had the opportunity to inquire about a midwife?" Mrs. Washington asked.

Caty shifted her attention from her teacup and looked up. "—Actually, ma'am, General Greene has made arrangements for one of the army doctors to attend me."

"Are you comfortable with a physician attending you?" The older woman inquired.

"My husband has been assured that there is a group of young Boston physicians expert in attending births."

Martha Washington raised a skeptical brow.

"Were I in Rhode Island, I would assuredly entrust myself to the care of the local midwife. But I am not in Rhode Island," Caty said with a shrug of her small shoulders. "And, my time being so close, I must entrust myself to the physician General Greene has chosen."

"What a blessed event. You must be getting excited." Mrs. Washington placed her cup and saucer on the small table beside the chair.

All Caty could offer in reply was a weak smile. She was not excited and could not even pretend to be. She had been miserable throughout her pregnancy and anticipated labor with a sense of dread.

Martha Washington took note of Caty's reaction. "How old are you, dear?"

"Twenty-one, ma'am."

Mrs. Washington nodded. It was as she suspected. This young woman was about the same age as her own daughter, Patsy, would have been had she lived. And Caty's dark hair and eyes seemed so close to the color of Patsy's. "Then you are quite a bit younger than General Greene?" Martha asked while continuing to make the comparison in her mind.

"Twelve years," Caty informed her.

"Have you been married long?"

"A little more than a year, ma'am."

Mrs. Washington smiled sympathetically at the younger woman. "And you have spent a good portion of that time apart."

Caty nodded.

"It is not easy for a young bride, especially with the constant uncertainty of your husband's safety," Martha commented with compassion. "Do your parents live in Rhode Island?"

"My mother died when I was young—"

Martha Washington's heart latched on to Caty's words—her own daughter dead and this girl, so much like Patsy, without a mother.

"I lived with my aunt and her husband, William Greene. They were kind enough to rear me along with their own children. That is where I met General Greene—Uncle William and Nathanael are cousins." Caty paused, uncertain of how to read the older woman's steady gaze. "Do you have any children, Mrs. Washington?"

"A son—"

The front door opened, distracting Martha Washington from her maternal thoughts. "It seems our men have arrived," she said with a smile.

The women listened as question after question was directed to General Washington from his aides and secretaries who came out of an adjoining room that served as their office. Finally, the barrage of questions ceased, and General Washington entered the room followed by a black male servant.

"Well, this must be little Catherine Greene!" He exclaimed with a warm smile as he walked into the parlor.

"I am, sir. And you?" Caty returned with a teasing grin, knowing whom she was addressing.

"George Washington, my dear. I am commanding officer outside of this house, but within these walls, you will find Mrs. Washington wears the epaulets," he said sensing the disapproving look Martha had for him. "I failed to remove my sword, Mrs. Greene. I lose favor with Mrs. Washington if I wear my sword to the dinner table." He smiled affectionately at his wife.

"General Greene has not arrived?" he asked as he unfastened his sheath.

"No," Martha replied.

He raised his eyebrows in a thoughtful manner then handed his sword to the awaiting servant. "Thank you, Billy," he said to the servant, who took the sword and left the room.

"General Greene did such a fine job with the Rhode Island enlistment's that I sent him over to assist in the negotiations of the Connecticut troops. I suppose he will be here momentarily," he added, noting the disappointment on Caty's face. General Washington occupied a seat next to his wife's. "When I first arrived in Cambridge, General Lee and I toured the lines to appraise our situation. It was most disheartening. However, one encampment stood out in contrast to the rest. The tents were neatly pitched in proper military fashion. The soldiers were well drilled with the necessary equipment. The discipline of that camp was evident.

"Then their commander came forward," General Washington paused and smiled affectionately. "—with that limp of his that only adds to his character. He addressed me with proper military protocol, welcoming me to camp. I have grown quite fond of your husband. He is a remarkable man."

"I quite agree, General," Caty said with a proud smile.

"He takes a fair amount of joking from the senior officers in regard to his being a Quaker—Charles Lee in particular," General Washington said, turning to his wife.

Judging from Martha Washington's reaction, Caty determined she had no great affection for Charles Lee.

"He stands up to it well, though. I think they will leave him alone once they see they are not ruffling his feathers."

A knock on the front door sent a servant scurrying to answer it.

"General Greene has arrived," the servant announced, then quickly left the room.

In a moment Nathanael appeared, his sword removed. He acknowledged General Washington, and had a "good evening, ma'am" for his lady. Then, fixing his gaze on Caty, a brilliant smile came to his lips.

"Have a seat, General," George Washington offered.

"Thank you, sir." Nathanael sat on the settee next to his wife.

"How did things go this afternoon?" General Washington asked.

"The are a stubborn bunch of Yankees, sir," Nathanael said with frustration, bringing an instant smile to General Washington's lips. How often had he listened to his young, gentle brigadier general recite the many qualities of his fellow New Englanders? "I will try again tomorrow, if you want."

"Were any persuaded to stay?"

"A few—"

George Washington shook his head. "Connecticut leaves in less than two weeks, and then we have Massachusetts and New Hampshire to contend with."

"Why?" Caty asked.

Nathanael turned to her. "Their term of enlistment is up at the end of December."

"If we cannot get them to reenlist, we will not have an army," George Washington said matter-of-factly.

"The Continental Congress has to come up with better terms of enlistment," Nathanael stated.

"Congress is complaining to me that we are exceeding the expenses they projected to keep the army thus far," George Washington commented.

The men became silent, both searching their minds for a way to solve this formidable problem.

"Can't the militia companies be called upon to make up the numbers you will be lacking?" Caty asked.

George Washington smiled at her inquisitiveness. "Many of the militia companies are only required to sign on for a few weeks at a time," he began to explain with
great patience. "They come to us with no sense of discipline or proper training and
leave virtually the same. Two or three months are not long enough to instill any
true form of military expertise. Those enlisting in the army, the regulars, as we call
them, are the strength we will depend on when the fighting begins."

"Certainly Massachusetts cannot walk away from this war." Martha Washington
exclaimed.

"No, I imagine we will have close to full reenlistment with them," her husband
assured.

"And New Hampshire? It has been my observation that they're committed to
aiding their Massachusetts neighbors to the bitter end," she added.

"There is a sense of commitment there, yes," George Washington agreed.

"Then why are we becoming melancholy over what Massachusetts and New
Hampshire probably will not do?" she asked with a smile.

"Connecticut is enough to bring on this mood," Nathanael said, staring intently at the Commander in Chief. They had been faced with this situation for weeks,
and both knew how vital it was to the cause of liberty that they somehow make up
the numbers they were about to lose with Connecticut—before the British realized
how diminished their army was.

"I simply refuse to discuss it anymore. Tomorrow is a new day. Perhaps
Congress will come to their senses. But for tonight we are simply going to pretend
there is no war to concern us." Martha Washington exclaimed. Then turning to
Caty, she added with a smile, "we will just have to ignore the gold braids on their
jackets."

General Washington reached over and patted his wife's hand; there was a grin
on his face. Then looking at Caty he said, "I told you she wears the epaulets in the
house."

"Dinner is ready, whenever you are, Mr. Washington," Martha addressed her
husband, pretending to ignore his teasing remark.

"By all means, let us eat!" his hearty reply came as he rose to his feet. "Ladies
first." He gestured with his arm for his wife and Caty to go before them.

When they were a few paces away, he turned to Nathanael. "You continue negotiating with them, but I am afraid we will have to depend on new recruits to replace
much of Connecticut—and it will take a miracle to get them to enlist. Look what we
have to offer: scant amounts of food; no warm clothing; virtually no pay; and they
will be fighting, always in short supply, the best trained army on the face of the
earth."

"George Washington!" his wife scolded.

"We are coming, dear."

The lights of Boston illumined the blackened night. Their warm glow instilled a sense of homesickness in the many soldiers who viewed the town in silence from the cold heights of Prospect Hill. A biting March wind blew continuously over the mile wide expanse of river, which separated the town from the men on the hill. It was a wind that intensified in strength every few minutes, stealing the breath from everyone in its path.

"I am half frozen," a soldier complained as Nathanael and his aide, Major William Blodget, came up behind him on horseback. "It is hard to believe spring is less than three weeks away."

"Things are bound to warm up in just a few minutes," Nathanael assured him. "Stand ready, lads. The word will be given shortly," he called to the artillery detachment along the hill. This would be the third night the cannons would harass the British. However, tonight's show would be of greater intensity.

No damage on the town was intended. It was simply a diversionary tactic in order to protect the men on Dorchester Heights who, some eight miles away, under cover of darkness, had orders to build a fortification.

A smile came to Nathanael's face at the thought of British General Howe being awakened in the morning with the news that General Washington had outsmarted him. By dawn's first light a number of large cannon, sufficient to do great damage, would be directly aimed at the occupied town of Boston.

If the British were to discover Washington's plan during the night, Nathanael's orders were clear. He and General Sullivan were to transport their 4,000 troops in the waiting boats to the other side of the river and make a direct attack on the town.

Henry Knox's successful transport of the heavy artillery from Fort Ticonderoga had made possible this attempt to drive the British out of Boston. *Would that the recent attempt of the American forces to invade the British in Canada had met with such success,* Nathanael thought. The distressing news of the disastrous battle still lingered—especially the fact that his close friend, Captain Sam Ward, who volunteered for the Northern campaign, was taken prisoner.

General John Sullivan rode up alongside Nathanael. "Are we ready?" he asked.

"We are ready, sir."

"You are a man of prayer, aren't you, General Greene?" John Sullivan asked.

"—I have spent a good many hours on my knees, sir," Nathanael's hesitant reply came. His Quaker upbringing seemed to be ever present in the minds of his fellow officers.

"The thought of attacking that town, with as many civilians in it as there are, disturbs me a great deal," General Sullivan confessed. "Nat, say a prayer if you would, that this diversion works."

"I already have, and I trust thee have done the same," he replied with a smile. General Sullivan returned the smile and nodded.

"Major Martin," General Sullivan called to the officer in charge of artillery. The major brought his horse up close to Sullivan's. "Yes, sir."

"Get your guns roaring!"

"Right away, sir!" The major rode off in the direction of the cannon that would begin the bombardment.

The startled horses reared upon hearing the first cannon fire. Soon another sounded, then a third. Within a few minutes, the British returned the threat, as they had the previous night.

"That is the music I want to keep hearing," General Sullivan said. "As long as they are busy with us, they will not be concerning themselves with Dorchester Heights. It certainly is cold up here," he commented as he directed his horse away from the cannons and headed back toward the waiting troops.

Nathanael stayed in position, pulling his collar up around his neck. He thought of Caty, snug in their warm bed. She was not asleep though, he was certain of that. The cannons had interrupted her sleep the past two nights, but tonight she would consider it a serenade. For as long as the cannons sounded, Caty would know that Nathanael was safe.

Caty's report of their newborn son, George Washington Greene, sleeping soundly through the thunderous explosions the previous night was received with a sense of pride, by not only his papa, but the Commander in Chief as well. "A true soldier in the making." General Washington commented of his namesake, sharing Nathanael's proud smile.

Though his own son could sleep undisturbed, he knew the children in Boston would not. It grieved him to think of their small arms clinging to their equally frightened mothers, who themselves had no way of knowing what terror the night may hold.

He thought of Joseph Warren's family, hoping against hope throughout the ten months of their captivity to be released—now caught directly between two opposing armies.

"As much as I want to face those bloody-backs on the field, do not let it be tonight, Lord, not here—" he whispered another prayer.

"Sir?" Major Blodget asked.

"Let's go back to our men, Billy. It is going be a long, cold night." He said to his aide and close friend as he turned his horse about. The major followed.

After climbing out of bed, Caty went to the door, opened it a crack and listened. She heard them again—Nathanael and his officers were downstairs!

Her body shivered from the cold. She went to the fireplace and threw a log on the dying embers, poking them until the log was ignited. She slipped on a dress, and then hurriedly pulled on her stockings and clumsily laced up a pair of shoes. There was no time to waste on her hair. Quickly running a brush through it, Caty let the long black curls flow freely down her back.

George was still asleep. She gently tucked his blanket along the cradle's edge. Then leaving the door open so she could hear his cry, Caty raced down the stairs and into the kitchen.

"What's happening? Did they get the fort built? Are the King's troops going to attack? Are you all right?" Caty asked without taking a breath.

Nathanael, surrounded at the table by his military family, stopped eating and looked up.

"Good morning, Mrs. Greene," he said, his expression blank. A barrage of greetings followed.

"Morning, ma'am."

"Mrs. Greene."

"Ma'am."

"Did you sleep well?" Nathanael asked, knowing by the fact that she did not take the time to fix her hair that she was very eager for him to answer her questions.

"You know I did not," she replied, aware that he was toying with her. "Now stop teasing and tell me what happened!" she demanded her expression full of anticipation.

"The fort is up; the British are preparing their fleet for an attack from the bay. And we are just fine, thank you."

"Preparing for an attack?" Caty walked behind him, laying her hands on his shoulders. "Then you will not be involved," she said with relief, assuming that because they were eating their breakfast in a leisurely manner at home, that they were not anticipating any personal danger.

"If there is a fight, I hope to be in it." Nathanael exclaimed. "We are heading over to Headquarters now." He motioned for his officers to move out. Again, they acknowledged Caty.

"Mrs. Greene."

"Your servant, ma'am."

"Caty, sit down," Nathanael said after the men were gone. He placed his hand on hers and gently directed her to the seat beside him. "I want you to pack anything you might need for yourself and the baby. You are going to spend the night with Lady Washington."

The color drained from Caty's cheeks. Could this battle actually last all day and through the night as well? Or was it that he did not expect to return? "Why—?" she whispered.

"There's talk of a storm coming in from the ocean. It may do considerable damage. Since I cannot leave any of the men behind to watch out for you, I will feel better knowing you are with Lady Washington."

Caty took a deep breath, wishing it were only a storm she had to fear.

"I will leave one of the men long enough take you to the Washington's." He stood up. "This storm may prove to be the finger of God. If the winds pick up, the British fleet will not be able to form an attack. This will give us more time to strengthen our position. Howe would be a fool to move against us by sea or land when our position is secure. If he attempts a frontal attack, he will lose more men on Dorchester Heights than he did on Bunker Hill."

Caty acknowledged his statement with a nod, though the fear for his safety remained.

"Is the baby asleep?"

She nodded again.

"I will look in on him before I go." Nathanael leaned to kiss her, then stood and left the room.

She sat alone—motionless, listening to his footsteps on the stairs. Soon, he came back down and she heard the front door close behind him.

Caty and the baby were escorted to General Washington's Headquarters. The storm, which started out as heavy rain, increased in strength. The violent winds pounded against the house, rattling windows and doors, adding to the restlessness of its inhabitants.

The violent winds pounded against the British fleet as well, scattering the British men-of-war in confusion. Their plan of attack was aborted.

On the morning of March 17, 1776, the British troops evacuated Boston. Not a shot had been fired. Swarms of scarlet figures were transported to the waiting ships in a most disorderly fashion. Twelve hundred Tories were to sail with the British as well.

George Washington watched from Dorchester Heights. His general officers were surrounding him—the commander of artillery at his side.

"Where are they headed?" Colonel Henry Knox verbalized the question each of them contemplated. It had been the subject of their councils of war ever since the British showed signs of evacuating.

"If they head to the Carolinas, General Lee will greet them with four thousand troops. And if New York is their destination, we will be their welcoming committee, gentlemen." General Washington sat tall in the saddle with a look of confidence, which inspired his officers. "Colonel Knox, I suppose you are anxious to ride into Boston."

"It has been almost a year since I have seen my home and book shop, sir."

"General Greene," the commander called out.

"Yes, sir," Nathanael answered from behind.

"Lead those from Boston into the town. Take a medical detachment and a detachment to patrol the streets. Make certain the British, or any misguided Tory, have not left any surprises."

A joyful cheer arose from the inhabitants who swarmed the streets to welcome the victorious troops. The effect of the eleven-month siege was reflected in the gaunt appearances of the townsfolk. Their clothing was worn; their faces pale and drawn.

Tears began to flow as soldier-husbands spotted their wives and children in the crowd, running to them for a tender embrace. Some of the men were called out of line by a mother or father, others, like Henry Knox, by the need to discover what had become of his property.

The town had been pillaged. Many buildings were damaged. Furniture in the evacuated homes had been used for firewood. Puritan meetinghouses had been turned into riding stables and military barracks. Food, medical supplies, hay, blankets and military equipment had been destroyed.

Though many Tories had evacuated, a few brave souls, prepared to throw themselves on the mercy of the victors, remained. It was reported to Nathanael that two, who apparently could not bear to leave their home or face their offended countrymen, had taken their own lives.

Nathanael rode through the town offering words of hope and encouragement to the people. Yes, firewood and food would be brought in from the countryside, he assured them. Yes, assistance would be given to repair the homes of the aged and infirm. Yes, the needs of the sick would be met—many of who were American prisoners taken at Bunker Hill.

"Papa! Papa!" a small boy ran alongside Nathanael's horse, crying out to him.

A young girl, no more than ten-years-old raced after him grabbing the boy by the arm. "That's not our papa, Dick! Don't you remember? He is gone to Heaven! Come on now," she said, putting a comforting arm around her little brother's shoulders and leading him away from Nathanael.

"Child." Nathanael called out to her. Both children turned to face him, surprised that he had addressed them. They seemed so familiar to Nathanael, though he could not remember where he had seen them. "What's your name?" he asked the little girl.

"My name is Betsey Warren, sir," she timidly replied with a slight curtsey.

Their eyes were the exact shade of blue and their hair just as blonde as that of their father. Nathanael stared at them, but did not say a word. In a moment, the small boy ran off again, sending his sister in flight after him. Nathanael watched until they had disappeared from view.

"Good God! What brave fellows I must this day lose!"
(George Washington)

CHAPTER THREE

Camp at Long Island,
June 29, 1776

My dear Caty,

The long wait has ended with the appearance of one hundred British vessels in New York's harbor this morning. I cannot adequately relate the feeling their appearance effected in me. We have wondered since our arrival here: where they were? When they would form? For we had no way of knowing if the colonies of Canada were their sole aim, or perhaps the Southern colonies would gain their full attention. General Washington had the most hazardous duty of forming a defense in Canada, South Carolina and New York. Therefore, it was with a sense of relief that we received our answer, yet it is mixed with such apprehension for what is to come.

New York is virtually indefensible against the numbers the British have. Nevertheless, defend it we must, for the Continental Congress has ordered it. The area consists of three large islands or peninsulas. The harbor and rivers surrounding us are fully navigable to the British men-of-war. Our work in building defenses is continuous.

Your last letter assured me that little George's health has greatly improved. How worried I was and so helpless being at such a distance, though my pleas to Heaven were constant.

You must not come now, my angel. I am aware of your being upset, having barely arrived in New York only to be called back to Rhode Island to tend to George's illness. You patiently nursed our son to health, knowing that your presence here was sorely missed by all, and anticipating joining me again upon his recovery. Yet no wives are to remain here. It has been reported to me that Lady Washington departed for Philadelphia today.

His Excellency, I am told, has even ordered the evacuation of all the women, children and infirm from New York, fearing for their safety in the event of an attack on that town— though the first attack, in all likelihood, shall be against my men on Long Island. There has been a council of war called this evening concerning it.

You must not be fearful, my dear. My safety rests in the hands of God. Keep us in your
prayers. Be assured that you and our son are in mine. Tell George of his papa's love for
him, and his mother must never doubt my love for her.
   Your devoted and affectionate husband,
   Nathanael

The splashing waves sprayed cool drizzle on Nathanael's face as the oarsman
hastily made his way across the East River. The June sun was intense, and the occasional spray welcomed.

The crossing brought to mind the many trips Nathanael had made on Rhode
Island's Narragansett Bay as a boy, with his father's powerful arms effortlessly glid-
ing the boat atop the water. *It all seems but a dream now—another era—a different*
world, Nathanael thought.

His father, Nathanael, Sr., had become dependent on his namesake, placing the
bulk of the responsibility for the family businesses on him. For not only was he
aware that his fourth-born son was an exceptional worker, but also realized the
unique quality in the lad of having a need to understand all aspects of the business.
Such inquisitiveness, he knew full well, would lead to diligence and thoroughness.

Nathanael looked out upon the boat's portside, his face hidden from the oarsman and his aide, as he smiled at the remembrance of his father's remarks about
his curiosity. He was inquisitive; there was no denying that—inquisitiveness only
appreciated in relation to the mechanisms of the machinery at the mills and forge
or dealing with legal matters regarding the family businesses. When it came to
questioning some of the doctrines he had been reared on, or desiring to further his
own basic education, then his inquisitiveness was deemed worldliness, and any
interest in studying subjects other than Holy Writ frowned upon.

Nathanael was finally able to persuade his father to let him at least study geometry and Latin. Study he did—often retiring to the solitude of the unheated storage
room located above the activity of the warm kitchen.

As an adult, he still regretted his lack of formal education. He turned his gaze
to his aide-de-camp and friend, Colonel Thomas Paine, who was unaware of his
commander's attention.

Thomas Paine's ability to stir the American spirit was profound; especially
when one took into account the fact that this young man had only recently emigrat-
ed from Great Britain. English born and reared, he joined the American cause with
fervor and conviction.

Paine, too, was reared a Quaker. He, too, had educated himself with little support from family members. Yet, in Nathanael's opinion, Thomas Paine had

excelled in his studies. A recent pamphlet, written by him, entitled *Common Sense* was proof enough. It had circulated throughout the colonies, inspiring the multitudes to continue their stand against the tyranny of Great Britain.

Thomas was suddenly aware of Nathanael's gaze. His dark, penetrating eyes met those of his commander's. He waited for Nathanael to speak, Thomas' perpetual, whimsical expression giving the appearance that he would break into a smile momentarily. Nathanael did not say a word, but turned again toward the passing water.

Nathanael and Thomas had been good for one another. His arrival at camp, volunteering to serve as an aide, was now viewed as a Godsend. Occasional bouts of guilt and doubt about their present stand in the face of violence sometimes haunted both of them, along with feelings of intense disdain for participating in the bloodshed. Only a former Quaker could understand the turmoil within, and only with a former Quaker could one share such feelings.

Pacifism was deeply ingrained in them. Yet they could not find the strength, or was it weakness, to take a path other than that which they were.

What would their saintly fathers think of their inquisitive sons now, were they still alive, Nathanael wondered. How would they view their sons—epaulets on their shoulders; swords fastened to their belts; on their way to attend a council of war that would hopefully better prepare them to bring down the enemy—an enemy who was, in fact, their own countrymen.

As they neared the river's bank, Nathanael spotted Colonel Henry Knox sitting upon his horse, with two more horses in tow. Henry was a huge man in stature as well as weight, and always had a piece of cloth wrapped around his left hand to cover the fact that his thumb was missing—the result of a hunting accident a few years before.

"General Greene, Colonel Paine, how are you this evening, gentlemen?" Henry asked, saluting Nathanael. He then let loose into each one's hand the reins of the horses behind his own.

"Things could be better, Henry, much better." Nathanael remarked, mounting one of the horses. "And you?"

"I will be honest, gentlemen. When the alarm was sounded this morning and I viewed those masts on the horizon for myself, I was frightened." Henry confessed as the men began to ride toward Headquarters.

"It appears that all of London is afloat." Thomas Paine interjected.

"Henry, you would be more than human if that scene didn't frighten you," Nathanael responded.

Henry turned to face his friend. "Then I certainly am only human."

"Did Mrs. Knox and the baby get off?" Nathanael asked, aware that Henry's wife and son were evacuated with the other women and children.

"They are well on their way to Boston—I am so upset at how I handled the entire situation. No doubt she will be crying all the way home."

"What did you do?"

"—She was frantic when the alarm sounded. Bells were ringing, soldiers running here and there, civilians screaming—She needed me to comfort her and personally see her to safety, yet I had my own fears to overcome and duties to attend. I cannot tell you how torn I was with my wife so distraught and my country calling to me at the same time. I could not let her know of my own fears—she would have been worse off had she known. So I did what seemed sensible at the moment." Henry stopped speaking.

Nathanael turned to him questioningly. Henry appeared uncomfortable. There was not a trace of the usual jovial expression Henry wore. His gray eyes revealed his distress. "What did you do, Henry?"

"The only thing I could think of. With all the pretense of anger I could muster, I ordered her to pull herself together and leave, making it clear, God forgive me, that it was her fault to be in such danger, for she insisted on staying so long."

"She will understand when you explain it to her," Nathanael assured his friend. Henry and Lucy Knox often engaged in loud, verbal brawls—witnessed by all that were within earshot. Such domestic quarrels were always mended, with the Knox's emerging from their quarters, to the delight of an anxious audience, more in love than ever. "She will understand" Nathanael repeated.

"But will I get the opportunity?" Henry replied solemnly.

They continued their ride in silence.

At Headquarters, the generals and their aides sat around a table, conversing in quiet tones. George Washington stood at the head of the table with his back toward his men. A map of New York and its surrounding landmasses was his focus.

"General Greene, his aide and Colonel Knox, your Excellency," an aide standing beside him announced as the men entered the room.

George Washington turned to face them and returned their salute. "Sit down, gentlemen."

Nathanael sat next to Israel Putnam and whispered a quick greeting to him. Thomas Paine handed Washington's aide an accounting of the troops on Long Island before taking a seat next to his commander.

"Our situation is critical," General Washington began. "I have received intelligence that General Howe has 9,000 men ready to land."

"How many of our men are fit for duty, sir?" General Putnam asked.

"Did you tally General Greene's men in?" General Washington asked his aide.

"I did, sir. We have 8,300 fit for duty."

"I can see by your expressions, gentlemen, that you are comfortable with the ratio—do not be. Howe is, by all reports, expecting reinforcements from Great Britain."

"How many, sir?" General Lord Stirling asked.

"A vast fleet led by General Howe's brother, Admiral Lord Richard Howe. The numbers are estimated as high as 30,000 troops."

"Lord, help us!" General Benjamin Lincoln cried out with all earnestness. The men around the table began to murmur to one another.

General Washington took a deep breath. "I want you fully informed, gentlemen. There are rumors—only rumors at this point, that Hessian troops have been hired by Great Britain."

There was dead silence as each man contemplated the disheartening and somewhat terrifying rumor. Everyone's attention quickly focused on the Commander. His countenance revealed his own distress.

"Their aim is to take both New York and New Jersey, thus gaining control of the Hudson River." General Washington turned to the map and moved his finger along the area of which he spoke. "As you can see, this will divide the colonies in half. A counter movement is planned as well. The British troops now occupying Quebec are to march downward, with orders to cut off New England."

"Any word from General Lee, sir?" Nathanael asked.

"No. The enemy in the southern colonies may have already engaged him. We still have no word. I cannot recall our troops from Canada or the South at this point. Yet we are grossly undermanned here. We must prepare our 8,000 for battle and pray God for more recruits."

"The Hudson is their aim. They have more than fifty men-of-war anchored off Staten Island. How do we keep such ships from sailing past us and boxing us in from the north?" General Joseph Spencer asked.

"We block the waterways with vaunted batteries," Israel Putnam suggested. "We can sink the hulks of vessels at the entrance to threatened areas. Hopefully it will be enough to hold back their men-of-war."

"Have you seen it done?" General Washington asked.

"I have, sir."

"Good. Get on it right away. The engineers and labor needed to accomplish it are at your disposal. Long Island will most likely be the focus of the enemy's first attack. If they can gain control of Brooklyn Heights, they will have a clear view of New York and within artillery bombardment of it. What's the situation of your defense, General Greene?"

"A series of redoubts and forts form a defensive barricade before the town, extending a mile and half. The banks of the river behind the town are too steep to gain access, though a man-of-war may do substantial damage," he said, looking at Israel Putnam.

"I will take care of that for you, my friend," Israel smiled.

"I have thoroughly reconnoitered the island with the help of Colonel Knox," Nathanael said, motioning for Colonel Paine to hand General Washington the maps he had prepared. As the map was rolled out on the table, the officers stood to get a better view.

"The enemy has four roads from which to approach the town." He informed them; pointing to the roads on the map. "A twenty-four hour patrol on each road will alert us to any advance and give sufficient time to form a formidable defense."

"This road is hardly worth patrolling," General John Sullivan remarked pointing to Jamaica Road. "The British will not march on a road like this when they have easier access on one of the others."

"They may if they know we are not patrolling it. A surprise attack will do us infinite damage," Nathanael replied.

"You have 2,000 men on the island?" General Washington asked, looking from Nathanael to his own aide for verification of the number.

"I do, sir."

"Have 500 more sent to strengthen his force," he said to his aide, quickly naming off the regiments that would be assigned the duty. "I do not know when Admiral Howe will arrive, but until he does—until the last possible moment, we will continue building for our defense.

"Now, you will all stay for dinner, gentlemen," General Washington said, matter-of-factly, motioning for the servants to prepare the table.

The gravity of the situation prevented this gathering from becoming a relaxed occasion. Nathanael considered the mood to be more that of The Last Supper than a social gathering of fellow officers.

Expressions were somber. Talk was of defense tactics and strategies. Advice and encouragement were generously offered Nathanael. Through it all, the bond that united them because of their shared convictions to stand for this liberty they held so dear was strengthened even more. Though so diverse in their backgrounds and personalities, together they would face the enemy or die in the attempt. With such feelings of apprehension and brotherly support, they shared the meal at the Commander's table.

"Excuse me, your Excellency," General Washington's personal servant said as he stepped into the dining room. He sounded confused. Many of the officers responding to his tone focused their attention on the aide.

"Billy, what is it?"

Billy hesitated, then looking directly at Nathanael he said, "—General Greene's wife is here—"

"Nay!" Nathanael's response was immediate. His face blanched as Caty appeared in the doorway. Her brilliant smile went unnoticed by him. All became silent.

Nathanael placed his napkin on the table and slowly rose to his feet, never taking his eyes from his wife. Suddenly remembering his position, he turned to General Washington. "—By your leave, sir?" he asked.

The Commander nodded.

He walked across the room, not knowing which of the many emotions stirring would take control once he reached her. He was fearful for her safety with the enemy threatening to unleash their wrath. He was angry that she had failed to heed his constant warnings to remain at home until he gave word that all was safe. In addition, the humiliation he felt in the presence of his peers, because of her refusal to be in subjection to his authority, intensified his anger. Yet, he was, at the same time, delighted to see her.

Fear would be the victor he realized, as he drew close to her. Caty seemingly misunderstood the dumfounded expression upon his face, for her smile remained.

"What are thee doing here?" he whispered with intense emotion as he took hold of her arm and began to lead her out of the room.

"General Greene," George Washington called out.

Nathanael stopped and turned to face him. "Sir?"

"After you have had a moment to speak privately with your wife, please extend to her my invitation to dine with us. She must be hungry after her long trip."

"Thank you, sir. I shall."

When they were alone in the foyer, Caty reached up, having to stand on her toes, and threw her arms around his neck. "No generals are watching us now!" she whispered, prepared for him to kiss her.

He did not take her in his arms, but placed his hands on her arms, loosening her hold, and gently pushed her back. "Caty, do thee have any idea of the danger thee have walked into?"

She appeared confused, but did not reply.

"I made it clear in my letters that thee were to inform me of any plans to come here, and then wait for my reply."

"I saw no sense in it!" she replied rather pertly. "By the time your response comes back, weeks may have passed—or perhaps the letter would not even get through with so many Tories intercepting the mail."

"Thee saw no sense in it?" his voice was strained. "Caty, thee purposely defied my instructions?"

"I thought you would be happy to see me," she said lowering her head.

"Where's the baby, Caty?" He suddenly realized George was not there.

"I left him with Jacob and Peggy."

"Thank God! Do thee know that the British are only a few short miles away, preparing for an attack?"

"I do not care!" She looked up at him, tears pooling in her eyes. "I need to be near you!"

Nathanael sighed, melting at the sight of her tears. "Oh, Caty, do not cry," he pleaded, taking her into his arms. "If circumstances were different I would be delighted to have thee here." He softly kissed her perfumed hair. "I love thee more than my own life. It is simply too dangerous. I just posted a letter to thee this afternoon telling thee that the wives have been evacuated. I will arrange for thee to be taken to Philadelphia if thee would like. Lady Washington is there—"

"You cannot just send me away after I have traveled so far to be with you!" Caty pushed away from him.

Nathanael took hold of her hand and led her away from the dining room, certain that his colleagues had heard her outburst. "I must!" he insisted. "Thee can spend some time with Lady Washington before thee return home."

"And will you send me off just as soon as I have eaten dinner?" she asked, her lower lip quivering. "Thanks to His Excellency's kindness, I will at least be able to stay a few minutes!"

Moved by her tears, and the fact that she had traveled so far to be with him; yet fearful for her safety, Nathanael struggled with his need to protect her and his own desire to be with her.

"I am spending the night at Henry's quarters," he began hesitantly. "It does not appear the British are prepared to move just yet. Thee can stay with me, but come morning I must return to Long Island, and thee will head either homeward or south to Philadelphia."

He pulled her back in a comforting embrace. Placing his finger under her chin, he gently forced her head back. "I am happy to see you," he said with a most affectionate smile as he lowered his head to kiss her.

The light flickered and dimmed as the wick slowly began to disappear below the oil's surface. Nathanael stopped writing and adjusted the wick, quickly restoring the flame's brilliance.

He set his quill pen in its holder and massaged his left eye. Scar tissue on this eye as a result of a smallpox inoculation became annoyingly painful when over-tired. The bustling activity of the camp had long ceased. All but those on guard or hospital duty were asleep—a well-deserved sleep, he thought. They had accomplished a great feat in their work on the defenses around Brooklyn Heights.

A sudden, overpowering itch on the back of his neck distracted him. He slapped the spot, in the hope of killing the menacing mosquito, but soon saw it buzzing around his head. "Blasted insects. Agents of Satan himself, I suspect," Nathanael muttered as he scratched his neck.

Picking up the pen, he returned to his correspondence neatly addressing the letter to Rhode Island's governor.

"Permission to enter, Commander," Brigadier General Lord Stirling called from the threshold of Nathanael's office. Nathanael looked up from his work, surprised by the disturbance at such a late hour. A pleasant smile accompanied Lord Stirling's request. At his side was Henry Knox.

"Perhaps you will be pleased to know that His Excellency has ordered half of my brigade over," General Lord Stirling added, stepping into the room before Nathanael had a chance to respond to his request. The distinguished fifty-year-old, whose true name was William Alexander, had been granted the title, Earl of Stirling by the Scottish court. He had proven his ancestral claim to the title and inheritance that accompanied it, yet the British House of Lords refused to acknowledge his lineage. William Alexander was born and reared in the colony of New York—the only reason the House of Lords needed to deny William Alexander his heritage and the vast land holdings that went with it. His colonial countrymen acknowledged the title.

"Half your brigade? Tell me it is the Maryland regiment."

"It is." Lord Stirling's smile revealed his pride in the hard-fighting Marylanders.

"Praise be! You stay with them?"

"Only for the night."

"And what are you doing here at this hour?" Nathanael directed his question to Henry.

"Too hot to sleep. A ride across the river appealed to me," he responded with a smile.

"This is for you," Lord Stirling pulled a folded, sealed paper from his jacket and handed it to Nathanael.

He immediately recognized Caty's writing, but hesitated to open it.

"Do not let us keep you from reading a letter from home. We know you will be wondering about its contents," Henry said, as both men sat down at the table.

Nathanael broke the seal and anxiously scanned the letter. Folding it, he slipped it into his pocket for a more attentive reading later.

"Is she all right?" Henry asked.

"Safe in Coventry."

"Glad to hear it. My wife was none too happy to hear about Mrs. Greene's presence at camp after the other wives were sent away. Jealousy bars all sense of reason. She suspects I sent her off only to be rid of her, with no regard for the enemy's arrival, which she witnessed with her own eyes."

"Did you assure her that Caty was sent off almost as soon as she had arrived?"

"I did, but I do not know if she believes me."

"Here is a letter from His Excellency," Lord Stirling interrupted the conversation, pulling another sealed letter from his pocket.

"I wonder if General Washington would approve of the order in which you delivered his correspondence to Nat." Henry asked with a grin.

Lord Stirling smiled back.

"What is this about an offer of peace?" Nathanael asked, looking up from General Washington's letter. "His Excellency said to ask you for details, Henry."

"Admiral Howe had the gall to send an emissary, under a flag of truce, to deliver a letter of pardon to General Washington. His Excellency told the emissary that he understood Admiral Howe had come to offer a pardon, but the Americans had done nothing to offend; therefore, we were not in need of a pardon. He assured the emissary that we are fully committed. How can we not be after the Congress' recent Declaration of Independence?" Henry paused, looking at Lord Stirling, "Nat's been trying to convince the Congress to declare our independence since the beginning of this year."

"Have you? Maybe you should turn in your commission for a seat in Congress," Lord Stirling suggested with a smirk.

Nathanael grunted. "Nay, we should insist that each member of the Congress spend a few weeks with the army. I guarantee they will be more sympathetic to our needs."

"Because of this declaration, the world is now eagerly awaiting the outcome," Lord Stirling said. "Great Britain will no longer welcome us back as misguided subjects, should we be defeated, but as conquered foes."

"I do not think they will welcome us at all." Henry remarked, referring to the fact that officers would probably be executed for treason.

"Then we cannot let them defeat us, can we?" Nathanael's tone was encouraging.

"But what are they waiting for?" Henry sounded anxious. "They now have 290 ships in the harbor; the Hessians have arrived; an estimated 30,000 soldiers are ready to fight; and yet they sit, day after day, week after week—it is maddening."

"The delay has been advantageous to us." Nathanael was optimistic. "We have brought our enlistments up to 23,000. Our defenses have been strengthened. The men are eager to fight. We are now prepared to greatly reduce their numbers."

"That is if this putrid fever does not drastically reduce ours beforehand. How many of your men are down with fever?" Henry asked.

"Enough for me to justify a hospital right here on the island. Nevertheless, we have enough men to face them. If they move soon, and they must, we will prove ourselves worthy opponents."

"It is a good thing Nat's as confident as he is," Lord Stirling remarked to Henry with a smile. "He will be the first to face them head on."

"Ah, but your Lordship, you'll be right by my side," Nathanael held up General Washington's letter and returned the smile. "His Excellency promises me a total of 5,000 men, including the rest of your brigade. Where your men go, you go."

"With pleasure, General, with pleasure." Lord Stirling's immediate response came. He paused and suddenly appeared disturbed, searching the pockets of his jacket.

"—Henry, do you have the other letter?"

"Why, I do not think so, I thought you picked it up." Henry began checking his own pockets.

"What letter? From whom?" Nathanael's eyes darted between the men who seemed quite alarmed over the missing letter.

"Oh, it was not anything important, I am sure," Henry said, though his expression was not at all reassuring.

"What is it?"

"A Congressional document of some sort, addressed to you."

"Congressional?" Now Nathanael sounded alarmed.

"I found it." Lord Stirling announced, pulling the paper from an inner pocket and handing it to Nathanael.

"This isn't from Congress. It has General Washington's seal," Nathanael commented, noticing the smirks on the faces of his friends. "What is it?"

"Just open it—sir," Henry ordered.

There were two pages folded together. The first page was a note of congratulations and praise from George Washington—the second was a commission from the Continental Congress declaring Nathanael's promotion to major general. When he looked up, his friends were grinning.

"Congratulations, General," Lord Stirling said. Both men rose to their feet and saluted.

"And this belongs to you," Henry said, pulling the purple sash from a small package he had carried with him. Nathanael would wear the sash as part of his uniform, draped across his chest under his open jacket. The color identified his new rank.

"This calls for a toast!" Lord Stirling exclaimed.

"All I have to offer is water," Nathanael replied.

Lord Stirling had tasted the water on Long Island. "—Then we will forgo the refreshment—To Major General Nathanael Greene: may wisdom guide you, valor inspire you, and honor follow you throughout this campaign and in the days of peace and prosperity to come!"

"This end of the trench needs to be widened," the military engineer pointed out to Nathanael as they inspected the most recent portion of the Brooklyn Heights' barricade. "That wall needs reinforcement as well. They are cutting back, General. They will be sorry if such a poorly constructed wall is all that separates them from British lead." He made certain he commented loud enough for the men to hear.

Nathanael observed the reaction of his men. Some appeared to be angry. Others lowered their heads, seemingly preparing for their commander's verbal disapproval.

"My men have proved themselves to be diligent workers, Colonel," Nathanael said to the engineer, loud enough for the men to hear. "They've accomplished wonders in building the defenses we have. It is the blasted heat, coupled with the lack of fresh meat and produce that's caused them to lose their stamina, not to mention the rancid drinking water." He said with definite irritability as he walked over to a barrel filled with water and cupping some in his hand, let the murky fluid run slowly through his fingers. "It is no wonder the men are plagued with dysentery, and the fever that daily claims its victims."

A disturbance among the ranks brought Nathanael's outburst to a halt.

"What's wrong?" he called out.

"Private Mullens has collapsed, sir."

The men made way for Nathanael as he walked toward the fallen soldier. Two other soldiers stood over the ill man. One loosened his collar while the other fanned him with his own hat.

"Bring me some water," Nathanael ordered. A ladleful was speedily handed to him. He pulled his handkerchief from his pocket and poured the water over it. Kneeling beside Mullens, Nathanael gently wiped his forehead and neck with the cool, wet cloth.

"Sunstroke or the fever?" One of the soldiers asked.

No one answered. It would be up to the doctors to determine.

Mullens slowly opened his eyes. "Gen—General Greene—" he whispered. "—I—I am sorry, sir—"

"You have nothing to be sorry for, private," he replied.

"I am so thirsty, sir—"

"I know—Get a wagon over here," Nathanael called out as he began to remove Mullens' jacket. "We will get you to the hospital. They have a supply of fresh drinking water."

Nathanael watched as Mullens was placed on the wagon. There was a heavy silence as the wagon pulled away. Everyone present knew that, if it were the fever, Mullens' chances for survival were less than if he were to participate in a major battle.

"Let's get back to work, lads." Nathanael called out, removing his own jacket and waistcoat as he spoke. He tossed his clothing to the engineer and rolled up his shirtsleeves. "Throw me a shovel."

The men watched in awe as their commander began to dig the trench. His large, powerful arms, strengthened by so many years of hard work in the forge, effortlessly tore at the earth and tossed the soil aside. The physical labor felt good, as much for his body as for his mind. Working in the trench dismissed all thoughts of the impending battle and the great responsibilities he held.

The fast approach of an oncoming horse caught Nathanael's attention. When he recognized the rider to be Thomas Paine, he threw down the shovel and made his way toward his aide.

"Where is General Greene?" Colonel Paine called out to one of the soldiers as he reined in his horse to a dead halt.

"In the trench, sir."

The colonel dismounted, walked hastily toward the trench, and met the approaching Nathanael.

"What's afoot, Colonel?" Nathanael was alarmed.

Thomas hesitated a moment, taken aback by the general's appearance. His commander stood before him looking no different from any of the enlisted men: his shirt was drenched with perspiration, his arms and face smudged with dirt. "The British are moving, sir. The ships are being loaded. Some have already begun to sail toward the eastern side of the island."

Nathanael rolled down his shirtsleeves and fastened them as Thomas spoke. His jacket and waistcoat were handed to him. An officer assisted him in putting them on. "Finally. Merciful Heaven, be our defense!" he exclaimed, mounting his horse, which was brought alongside him.

Back at headquarters, final preparations for battle were made. Patrols were sent out on the four roads, which connected Brooklyn Heights to the eastern shore of Long Island. Dispatches were forwarded and dispatches arrived.

The hectic activity continued as the night wore on, permitting none to indulge in the luxury of even an hour's sleep.

Nathanael's body began to ache and the pounding in his head intensified with each passing hour. The continuous fluctuation of chills and excessive sweating were hardly noticed. Though he ignored his symptoms throughout the night, as the dawn approached his condition became evident.

"Ah—"

The officers in the room turned from their work in response to Nathanael's deep, mournful groan.

"Nat, what's wrong?" Lord Stirling asked with alarm.

There was no reply. Nathanael's eyes were closed as he held his head with his hands. He then let out another groan.

"General Greene!" Thomas Paine called out. He and Lord Stirling quickly rose to their feet and went to his side.

"He is burning with fever." Thomas announced. "Should we get him to the hospital, sir?"

"Nay." Nathanael shouted, forcing himself to overcome the agonizing pressure in his head. "I—must—remain here."

"Let's get him into bed," Lord Stirling said. "Can you walk with our assistance, Nat?"

"I will—try," came the breathless reply. As he stood, his legs immediately buckled. Two more officers ran to the aid of Lord Stirling and Thomas, helping them to carry him up the stairs to his bedchamber.

"Send for a physician," Lord Stirling ordered. One of the aides hastily departed.

"I will be—fine," Nathanael whispered. "A few—hours sleep—I will be fine."

"Colonel, send word to His Excellency of General Greene's condition." Lord Stirling began undressing Nathanael as he spoke.

"I will be fine—" Nathanael's feeble protest was barely audible.

Lord Stirling placed a comforting hand on his friend's shoulder. "Colonel, inform His Excellency of the general's condition, but tell him that General Greene insists on remaining in the hope of a rapid recovery. Assure him that we will keep him posted."

"Yes, sir."

Thomas' reply sounded strangely distant to Nathanael as Lord Stirling's tug on his clothing suddenly stopped.

General Washington was dependent on Nathanael's familiarity with the troops on Long Island, as well as the layout of the land itself. There was not sufficient time for a new commander to adequately prepare for the impending battle. As the British continued their mysterious delay, the Commander in Chief hesitated to replace his chosen general.

Though racked with pain, burning with fever, and at times fighting to remain conscious, Nathanael continued to receive reports, give orders and dictate dispatches to Headquarters. Eventually the fever took its toll. When General Washington received a dispatch, dictated in a state of semi-delirium, instructing the Commander in Chief in matters unassociated with the crisis at hand, General Washington ordered Nathanael to be temporarily replaced by General Sullivan.

Nathanael drifted into a state of semi-consciousness as he clung to life. Pain was constant, whether induced by the fever itself or inflicted by the physicians that came and went. He heard their voices and felt their presence as the razor sharp blade was applied to his forearm.

When the cannons were firing, he heard Henry Knox and General Washington. Loud and intense, the cannons' roar continued for what seemed like hours.

"Colonel Paine!" Nathanael yelled above the roar. "Get Colonel Knox over here immediately! We do not have enough artillery power to put up a defense against the men-of-war!"

"Nat, it is all right. It is thunder you hear." It was Henry's voice. Nathanael felt Henry's large hand rest upon his arm. Another thunderous roar sounded. It was close.

"Henry!" Nathanael took a weak hold of Henry's arm with his free hand. "Set up the twenty-four pounders! They are destroying the heights from the river. Good God! Are they bombarding New York as well?"

"New York is safe, General Greene. It is only thunder you hear." George Washington's voice assured him.

There was another roar.

"Your Excellency! The men-of-war have destroyed Brooklyn Heights—Forgive me, I have failed—They have destroyed Brooklyn Heights—" Then the cannons' roar ceased.

A female's voice now—he heard it again. Was it Caty? He struggled to open his eyes to see if it were his wife. She spoke again, encouraging him to take a sip of water. It was Caty's face he saw, but her voice was that of another.

"Caty! Thee must go home! The enemy may attack again!"

She gently lifted his head with one hand and brought a cup to his lips with the other, seemingly ignoring his words.

"Go home, Caty! 'Tis not safe here!" He took hold of her wrist, causing her to spill what felt like ice-cold water on his chest.

"General Greene," the voice was soothing, but it was not Caty's. He became confused. "Your wife is safe in Rhode Island. Please take another sip, General."

" 'Tis not safe here! Send her home, Major Blodget—Billy, please send her home—" His words drifted off as he slipped into unconsciousness once more.

A warm breeze softly caressed Nathanael's clean-shaven face. The fresh scent of a summer rain shower lingered, pleasantly accompanied by the harmony of the blue birds outside.

Nathanael struggled to open his eyes, and then looked toward the windows. The sunlight was blinding. Through squinted eyes, he studied his unfamiliar surroundings. It was a plain room, quite small and sparsely furnished. He attempted to get up, but he found himself too weak even to lift his shoulders from the mattress. He noticed that the door was ajar.

"Colonel Paine." he called though it came out as no more than a whisper. "Colonel Paine. Major Blodget." he tried again, though not much louder.

A woman appeared at the door. "What a blessed sight!" she exclaimed with a beaming smile. She stepped out of Nathanael's view and called out, "Colonel Knox. General Greene is awake!"

"A sip of water, General?" she asked, walking to his bedside.

"Please—" he whispered, his hands already extended, anxious to receive the cup.

She supported his head and held the cup to his lips as she had done so many times in the past week.

"Thank you. Could I trouble thee for something to eat?"

A hearty laugh from the doorway announced Henry Knox's arrival. "He is hungry. Isn't it wonderful?"

"That it is, Colonel Knox! Excuse me while I fetch him some broth."

"Nat, you certainly gave us a scare. Do you have any idea how close you came to the grave? The doctors didn't offer any hope." Henry pulled a chair up beside the bed and sat down. "The nurse sent word that the fever finally broke. His Excellency was delighted to hear it, though he was worried that—well—the doctors feared that, with such a raging fever for so long—" Henry stumbled over his words. Nathanael waited. "—They feared you might not have your wits about you if you came to— You do, don't you?"

Though Henry wore a smile, Nathanael suspected it was forced. He could only manage a slow nod in response.

"Of course you do." Henry patted his friend on the shoulder. "You'll be on your feet again in no time. His Excellency sent an express to your family about your condition. We received word back today that your brother Christopher is on his way to take care of you."

"Kitt? —Coming here?"

Henry nodded, assuming Kitt was his brother's nickname.

"What of Caty?"

"She wanted to come herself, but your brothers thought it too dangerous."

"Where? —Where am I?"

"New York."

"How long?"

"About a week."

"A week? Long Island? My men?" Though his voice was weak, his alarm was great.

"Here is the nurse with your broth. You need to eat, Nat. I will come back in a few minutes and answer all your questions." Henry stood intending to leave.

"Colonel Knox! My men?" The authority was clear through the weakened voice.

Henry hesitated.

"Shall I leave the broth, Colonel?" The nurse asked.

Henry nodded.

She placed the bowl on the nightstand, threw a sympathetic smile at Nathanael and left the room, closing the door behind her. Henry sat back down, but seemed at a loss for words.

"Did the British—attack—Long Island?" Nathanael agonized with each word, bracing himself for the news that Henry was having such difficulty relating.

"—Yes, they made their attack."

"Stirling in command?"

"No—Putnam had command. Sullivan was there as well."

"Good—good. All three there. Good." Nathanael became hopeful.

"Nat—your men fought valiantly, but—the British took them by surprise. They were driven back to Brooklyn Heights. By what seemed no less than a miracle, His Excellency was able to bring them to safety across the river to New York under the cover of a heavy fog."

"The island abandoned?"

"There was no choice."

"Our patrols—should have spotted the advance—"

"Putnam called back the patrol from Jamaica Road."

"Putnam? What?" Nathanael's expression became contorted as he absorbed Henry's words.

"He and Sullivan didn't believe the British would be aware of that back road. Lord Stirling paid a few men, out of his own pocket, to patrol the road during their free time. Though Putnam and Sullivan ridiculed him, he continued. But he could not keep them on a twenty-four-hour patrol. The British came during the night—"

"Stirling told thee this?"

'No—One of those paid to patrol the road did. Lord Stirling—" Henry stopped speaking.

"Lord Stirling? What of Lord Stirling?"

"He was taken prisoner—"

Nathanael lay motionless, staring blankly at the ceiling.

"His Excellency and I watched from the Heights as His Lordship engaged the British and Hessians. He fought like a wolf, Nat. You should have seen him. And his men stayed with him until they could no longer fight. It went on for close to four hours. Finally, they were surrounded. The Hessians were giving no quarter, and brutally cut our men down as they tried to surrender. Thank God, Lord Stirling was spared. He refused to surrender to the British generals, and instead forced his way through the enemy troops surrendering his sword to the Hessian commander."

"Casualties?" Nathanael asked as tears began to flow freely toward the back of his head.

"—There are 2,000 men unaccounted for. Both Lord Stirling and Sullivan were among the prisoners."

"No!" Nathanael cried out in despair, covering his face with his hands. "My men—my men!"

His strength was slow in returning. With Kitt's encouragement and care, a diet of gruel and broth gradually advanced to solid foods. Complete bed rest progressed to sitting and, eventually, to short walks in the warm, invigorating sunshine.

Military friends came and went with news of the army's present situation and detailed accounts of the Battle of Long Island. Colonel Paine related how General Washington watched the battle from the heights, having strengthened the force on Long Island to 11,500 men. He had warned his officers of the two loaded pistols he carried in his jacket, and how he would not hesitate to use them on any man that ran from the enemy. With quick assurance, he told them that he would not ask any man to go further than he would. "I will fight as long as I have a leg or an arm!" he exclaimed.

The retelling of the slaughter of his men again brought tears to Nathanael's eyes. The Hessians, it was learned, were told by the British commanders that the Americans had vowed no quarter for the mercenaries. Their brutality was the result of this lie.

The massive casualties coupled with the stormy weather brought about the evacuation of the island. The day following the battle it poured. The army was forced behind the fortifications at Brooklyn Heights. There were no tents—absolutely no shelter. They stood knee deep in the muddy trenches. Fires for cooking were extinguished by the downpour. Muskets became useless as the powder took on moisture.

As darkness fell, a dense fog blanketed the East River and Brooklyn Heights. General Washington speedily took advantage of this Godsend situation. Boats were gathered along the river's edge. Throughout the night, he managed to transport 9,500 men, their baggage, field guns, horses, and all provisions to the safety of New York. As the sun appeared and the last boat landed, the fog rose.

"Providential care," was General Washington's response to Nathanael's praise on the successful evacuation. And with that, the Commander went on to describe another event, equally awe-inspiring, though fearfully so.

The New York encampment was hit by a fierce storm just prior to the battle. "Some say it was a tornado," General Washington related. "I do not know what it was for certain, but it hung above this town for three hours as lightning bolts bombarded us and thunder shook the ground. Torrents of rain fell, and the thunder was like a hundred cannon discharged at once—"

Nathanael suddenly remembered the sound of the cannon-like thunder and his Commander's comforting voice.

General Washington nodded his head in response to Nathanael's expression. "It is no wonder you thought it was the men-of-war. Ten of our men were killed by a single bolt— Familiar as I am with death; it has a most startling effect when sent directly from the Hand of God."

"The storm of nature and the storm of the town exhibited a scene that filled the mind during the action with passions easier conceived than disturbed."
(Nathanael Greene to Caty Greene)

CHAPTER FOUR

"WELL, LOOK WHOSE Back." Hugh Mercer greeted Nathanael with a wide grin and a pat on the back as he sat down beside him. The middle-aged, Scottish born brigadier general greeted the other officers assembled at the table in his familiar, Americanized burr.

"Where is everyone?" he asked, noting the many empty seats.

"There was not enough notice given," General Heath commented.

Nathanael's eyes were drawn to the seats that Generals Sullivan and Lord Stirling usually occupied.

"It is good to see ya up and about again," Hugh Mercer continued as he directed his attention back to Nathanael. "I went by to care for ya myself a few times, I must admit, I gave ya up for dead." The physician-turned-warrior confessed. "Are ya sure yar feeling all right? You look a bit pallid to me."

Nathanael gave his friend a blank stare accompanied by a grunt. "Of course I look a bit pallid," he said as he unfastened the cuff of his shirtsleeve and rolled it up enough to expose the three scars left by bloodletting. "Which one is your handy work, Doc?" he asked with a playful stare. "Or perhaps you used this arm." He extended his fully covered arm.

"None of them are mine, laddie. I do not leave scars." Hugh Mercer's fatherly mannerisms extended him the liberty to be so casual with this superior, though younger, officer. "Nasty, nasty work," he said shaking his head as he ran his fingers over the scars on Nathanael's forearm.

"Then you admit you bled me?"

"Of course I did, but mine was only a surface laceration for minimal bleeding."

"It makes no sense to me," Nathanael commented as he fastened his cuff.

Hugh chuckled, patting Nathanael on the back. "Ya should be in the grave and here ya are questioning our treatment."

"Is he well enough to resume command?" General Spencer asked Hugh.

"I do not think so."

"I am ready, whether or not I am well enough. Three weeks' recuperation is all I can tolerate."

"A night will come, one of those endless, cold, suspenseful nights that we've all experienced, when you'll fondly remember your three weeks of leisure." Israel Putnam said with a chuckle.

Nathanael smiled at the older man. Israel's prior confession to Nathanael of his poor judgment on Long Island had done much to alleviate the hostility Nathanael felt toward him. Moreover, the passivity he showed during Nathanael's verbal lashing which followed softened the former iron master's heart, restoring the affection he held for "Old Put."

"I have been told ya suffer with asthma. Is it so?" Hugh Mercer asked Nathanael.

"Unfortunately it is."

"I will prepare ya a tea that'll take care of that problem."

"What kind of tea?" Nathanael asked as General Washington entered the room with his servant and an aide by his side.

"Remain seated, gentlemen," George Washington instructed the men at the table as each one prepared to stand and formally salute their Commander. "Not a very good attendance," he commented. "The others probably did not receive the dispatch in time. Regardless, we must proceed." He sat down at the head of the table.

"Gentlemen, I have called this council to inform you of the Continental Congress' desire that we defend New York."

"Desire, sir?" Israel Putnam asked.

"The Congress is leaving it up to my discretion, but has made it clear that they prefer we stay and fight. What is the opinion of this council?"

The men began to freely discuss the possibility of holding New York as General Washington listened. Nathanael remained silent, mulling over the comments in his mind. He had been out of action for so long that he felt a bit awkward about expressing his opinion.

General Washington's expression was blank, Nathanael noticed, which led him to believe that the Commander had no strong inclination either way and would decide this matter on the council's vote. As it now stood, most were in favor of holding the town; and Nathanael disagreed. He could remain silent no longer.

"This town cannot be defended. It is preposterous to think it could be." Nathanael finally blurted out in response to what he considered an outrageous remark to the contrary.

The officers at the table became silent, surprised by his sudden outburst.

"Go on, General Greene." It was the first time General Washington had spoken since the council convened.

"The waterways surrounding the island of Manhattan are fully navigable to the British men-of-war. All they have to do is sail north of us, unload their troops and box us in. We know they're able to sail past our vaunted batteries," Nathanael pointed out, referring to the fact that two British ships had done just that only to prove to the Americans, so it seemed, that it could be done. "A successful defense of this city can only be attained with a naval fleet. A fleet we do not have."

"Then you are suggesting we evacuate New York?" General Washington said.

"I am of the strongest opinion, sir, that we should not only evacuate New York, but that we should burn it as well."

The men began to murmur amongst themselves.

"That is somewhat drastic." General Heath protested.

"I have shared this with you already, your Excellency."

"Yes, General Greene, you have. And I already told you that I submitted the plan to Congress. They will not allow us to burn the town."

"Burn the town?" one of the officers called out in apparent disbelief at what he was hearing.

"Yes," Nathanael nodded. "It will prevent the British from establishing themselves here. Once that happens, they will not be moved."

"How can you know that?"

"The geography, gentlemen. Look at it." he exclaimed, pointing to the map of New York which was hanging behind General Washington. "It provides a perfect harbor for their fleet; a town large enough to quarter them in comfort. The majority of the inhabitants are Tories and thus sympathetic to them; and our Congress is close by, a definite incitement. You can be sure the Congress knows it as well. That is why they want us to hold this town."

"How can we justify burning the homes of civilians?" another cry arose.

"Militant Tories, sir. The vast majority of those in New York are militant Tories—Your Excellency, it was done during the campaign of the King of France against the invading army of Charles V."

"You mentioned reading it while recuperating," General Washington commented. "And I am aware that it was an effective tactic during that campaign, yet the Congress will not allow us to incorporate it here. My hands are tied."

"Of course, sir. I understand. I am sorry, your Excellency—gentlemen," Nathanael apologized, looking around the table. "I hope that my good intentions will excuse my zeal. But if a vote is to be taken, I firmly hold to an immediate evacuation."

"A vote is to be taken, General," George Washington said, his eyes intent upon Nathanael. "And what of the rest of you?" He made his way around the table as his aide wrote each officer's answer down.

The result affirmed that New York should be held.

"General Greene!" Captain Alexander Hamilton announced the general's appearance to those in the room with proper military protocol. All except Henry Knox responded in like manner.

The colonel looked up from his ledger. "General." He acknowledged Nathanael's presence with a nod.

"Captain Hamilton, I am surprised you are still here," Nathanael remarked.

"Yes thanks to you I am losing an excellent artillery officer," Henry complained. "He loves those guns as much as I do, Nat. He belongs here with me."

Captain Hamilton smiled in response to Henry's words.

"All I did was introduce him to General Washington—"

"Over dinner. Giving His Excellency plenty of time to discover his military genius."

"I am sorry, Henry," Nathanael said as he sat down.

"As much as I have appreciated serving under you, Colonel Knox, and I truly have, I am grateful to General Greene for introducing me to His Excellency. It is an honor to serve as his aide," Hamilton said. His blue eyes were gleaming with the excitement of this appointment. The young man's confidence was evident, and that, coupled with his obvious intelligence and extreme attractiveness had a drawing affect.

Henry held a steady, blank stare on Nathanael. "What do you say to that, General?" he asked playfully.

"I am sorry, Henry."

"You are dismissed, gentlemen," Henry said to his officers, who immediately left the room, closing the door behind them.

"What's this about defending New York?" Henry asked, holding up the dispatch Nathanael had sent informing him of the council's vote. "I am sent north to reconnoiter for the army's possible evacuation, and I come back to this. New York cannot be defended. Have they gone mad?"

"The majority of the field commanders were not at the council."

"Who voted to stay?"

Nathanael rattled off the names.

"I find it hard to believe that His Excellency is standing by that vote."

"He hoped for a larger turn out."

"What happened?"

"Not enough notice was given. Most of those I have spoken to are shocked by the decision, and rightfully so. It is insanity. The defense of New York will be military suicide."

"Has His Excellency restored your command?" Henry asked.

"No—Though I volunteered to take a division for this battle. I would rather go out fighting."

Henry had no response. After a moment's silence, he remembered a letter he had just received from home.

"My wife informs me that she is been corresponding with Mrs. Greene."

"Good. I am sure they will find pleasure in writing to one another."

"Have you heard from Caty recently?" Henry asked.

"Just the other day."

Henry waited for him to say more, but he remained silent. "Did she tell you?" Nathanael looked at him questioningly.

"I mean—your wife told my wife that—that—This is rather awkward," he said. "Do you know that—as a result of your brief encounter—did you know that your wife is with child?"

"Yes, I know," Nathanael, responded with no visible emotion.

"Oh." Henry appeared even more awkward. "—One of those letters, hey?" Henry said with a sympathetic smile. Complaints from home were most disheartening.

"She is young and lonely. It is certainly understandable," Nathanael came to her defense. "Somehow we have to persuade His Excellency to reconsider—"

His sudden change of subject confused Henry for a moment.

"With a better attendance, I believe we can turn the vote around." Nathanael reached for a quill pen and a fresh piece of paper from the table and began writing.

"How are you going to persuade His Excellency?"

"A petition signed by all general officers who oppose the council's vote. Here," he handed the paper to Henry, dipped the pen into the ink and held it out to him. "Sign under my name."

"I am only a colonel. This is a petition for generals; you said so yourself," Henry argued with a smile.

"You are commander of artillery and vote at every council of war. Why Congress hasn't promoted you to brigadier general is beyond my comprehension." Nathanael's disapproval of many of Congress' decisions concerning military matters was common knowledge to Henry. The portly commander of artillery appreciated his friend's concern over the fact that he had not been promoted.

"If His Excellency is offended by this petition, then we will face his wrath together, Henry. Now sign it."

"Is that an order?" Henry asked with a chuckle.

"Yes." Nathanael snatched the paper as soon as Henry's signature was complete. He quickly dusted it. Then folding it, he carefully placed it into the pocket of his jacket. "Come on, Henry," he said, jumping from his seat and grabbing his hat.

"Where to?"

"St. Clair's brigade is close by. We will start there."

"Do you intend to get every signature tonight?" Henry called as he followed Nathanael out the door.

"I do."

"It will take half the night. You will be waking most of them from a sound sleep."

"There is no time to waste. If we do not turn this decision around immediately, they will be losing plenty of sleep in the nights to come as they watch their men cut down before their very eyes!"

The petition was presented to General Washington the following morning. A second council of the war was called. The order was given for an immediate evacuation of New York. However, precious time had been lost. The British were already forming an attack. As the evacuation of the ill and injured, as well as supplies, continued, the main force of the army prepared for the imminent attack.

General Washington called for the immediate formation of a defensive line extending from New York to Harlem Heights, some sixteen miles in length. Nathanael was given command of the center, which was made up of 5,000 men, mostly raw militia. Because of their lack of experience in battle, the center was vulnerable—a fact, Nathanael hoped, would not be relayed to the enemy.

Cannons from the British men-of-war were heard just before sunset as they fired upon New York. Throughout the night, Nathanael kept his men in the line, lying in ditches along the bank of the East River.

With the morning light came the shocking realization that four British war ships had laid anchor within cannon range of Nathanael's line. Transport boats were already making their way to shore.

A sudden peal of cannon fire from the British ships was more than the shaky militia companies could stand. With no way to speedily get orders to the men, Nathanael watched helplessly as hundreds rose from the safety of the ditches and ran.

As they retreated down the road, thinking they were headed for safety, they came head long on a party of Hessians. Immediately the fleeing men changed direction.

Nathanael set out at a full gallop, hoping to get them to safety before all of them were cut down.

At the same time, General Washington came galloping toward them, shouting commands. "Take the walls!" he yelled, pointing toward the fences. They did not listen. "Take the cornfield!" he shouted trying to get them off the open road. They were not to be rallied, but continued past him in terror.

Nathanael came up alongside the Commander in Chief as Washington dashed his hat to the ground and called after them, "You dastardly sons of cowardice!" Turning to Nathanael, he cried, "Have I got such troops as these?"

The two watched helplessly as the frightened men encountered the enemy further up the road. Surrounded only by their aides, the generals failed to realize their own danger.

"General Washington, General Greene," an aide cried, "You must get to safety!" Neither one responded.

"Your Excellency, the enemy is approaching!" The aides boldly took hold of the bridles on the generals' horses and quickly led them away.

A forced, shameful retreat of the Continental Army followed. Then turning his attention north along the Hudson River, General Washington ordered General Greene to take command of the American Forts Lee and Washington. From this strategic location, British activity could be observed along the river, as well as upon the roads leading to the rich farmland north of New York.

"You failed me, Greene! You failed this Country!" General Washington shouted, his face crimson with rage. "All of America would have been better off had you stayed in your Quaker meeting-house!"

There was no defense Nathanael could give, nor did he try. For the Commander was right. He turned, shoulders drooping; his head hung low, and limped toward the door.

"I intend to call for a court-martial!" General Washington's words, filled with such vehemence, caused Nathanael to stop momentarily. Without looking back, he opened the door, only to face the stares of his fellow officers in the hall.

Nathanael's eyes popped open. A cold sweat sent a shiver through his body, as he lay fully clothed upon the bed. Slowly he sat up. "Only a dream," he whispered as he rested his forehead upon his hand and allowed himself a moment to recover.

Thomas Paine began to stir. "Is something wrong, General?" Thomas' drowsy words came from the other side of the bed.

"No, Colonel. Go back to sleep."

Nathanael stood up and carefully stepped over the sleeping forms of his officers positioned close to the hearth. He quietly placed a log on the dying embers, and walked over to the desk. He picked up the letter he had been drafting to Henry Knox, and by the light of the hearth, he began to read.

Camp at Newark, New Jersey
November 23, 1776

My Dear Friend,
Your favor of the 14th reached me in a melancholy temper—
The words became a blur as the overwhelming grief of the previous week haunted him. Henry, temporarily encamped north of the main army, was sorely missed by his friend.

The shameful retreat on Manhattan Island did not compare to the disgraceful surrender and losses of the past few days. Though his command of the militia on Manhattan Island could not be questioned because of its short duration, some were certainly scrutinizing his command at Forts Lee and Washington.

Was Washington himself questioning his ability to command? Nathanael wondered. If dreams had any bearing on future events, he had no doubt of it.

He stood up and walked to the window nearest the desk. Leaning his hand against the pane, he peered out through the glass. The night was dark, not a star could be seen. The campfires below blazed ferociously, offering the only warmth for those forced to sleep in the open air.

Nathanael considered the men—a shadow of the army that assembled in Massachusetts eighteen months before. An army of 3,000 disheartened men with virtually no supplies, including blankets and tents to protect them from the cold November air.

This, too, was his doing, Nathanael lamented, resting his head on his outstretched arm. His thoughts drifted back to his first meeting with General

Washington after the attack on Manhattan Island. Though deeply distressed over the retreat, the Commander's response to Nathanael was one of encouragement.

His Excellency personally related to Nathanael the news of New York's being set aflame after the British had comfortably settled in. With a definite glimmer in his eyes, he lay his hand on Nathanael's shoulder and said, "It was the Hand of Providence, or some good honest fellow that did for us what we could not do ourselves." Though five hundred buildings were destroyed, the British managed to remain in the town.

General Washington went on to confirm his confidence in his young general by honoring him with the command of New Jersey. He was to establish his 5,000 men in the Hudson River forts. Fort Washington lay on Manhattan Island along the river's bank. Fort Lee was opposite it on the New Jersey shore.

The forts possessed great natural strength due to their location. Flanked by steep cliffs, they not only overlooked the Hudson, but also the roads leading to upstate New York as well. Thus, they were in a position to harass any British vessels that might attempt to pass, or any land movement to the rich farmland around the forts.

Constantly on guard and communicating with General Washington who was located twenty miles north of the forts, Nathanael watched for any enemy activity. For three weeks, all remained quiet.

In the meantime, supplies were restocked. Food, ammunition, entrenchment tools, blankets and tents—items that the army was ever in want of—were in excess. Comfortably situated and ready to take action, General Nathanael Greene waited.

British vessels began moving up the Hudson in early November. Though the cannons fired incessantly from the forts, the ships continued.

Alarmed by the news, General Washington sent word to Nathanael that, because of the forts' inability to hold back the ships, he thought it might not be prudent to put the men and supplies in danger.

Nathanael read the dispatch. There was no direct order by His Excellency to evacuate.

Immediately taking a pen in hand, Nathanael had sent his evaluation of the situation to the Commander stating that he believed the fort could be held.

"Thee are a fool." Nathanael now whispered to himself with intense emotion as he remembered his hasty reply.

Upon receiving the response, Generals Israel Putnam and Hugh Mercer were sent to assist Nathanael. Before long, it was apparent that Fort Washington would become the enemy's aim.

"They agreed it could be defended," he whispered again, and shivered at the thought of Putnam's order to reinforce Fort Washington with five hundred more men.

General Washington came to assess the situation. "The men are eager to make a stand," Israel Putnam assured him. The General accepted his statement without question.

The morning to follow brought with it such misery as to bring into question the command of the Continental Army. Nathanael watched alongside Generals Washington, Putnam and Mercer, as the fort was quickly overrun.

The British attack was a military masterpiece, developed; it was later learned, with the aid of an American deserter who was well informed of the fort's defenses.

"Would that was the end of it." Nathanael lamented, shaking his head in despair as he relived the events.

Three days later the British moved against Fort Lee. There was no time to douse the fires or strike the tents. Only the ammunition was saved as the men made a quick retreat.

The casualty figures from the recent defenses ran through Nathanael's mind—haunting numbers that he could not escape no matter how desperately he tried—4,429 men taken prisoner, 600 men dead or wounded. Then there were the thousands who had deserted, spreading the word that the Americans' fight for liberty was a lost cause.

The sound of the British buglers playing *Tally-ho!* the traditional tune for a fox-hunt, which brought such disgrace to the Americans after the fiasco on Manhattan Island, seemed rather appropriate to Nathanael now.

They were all but defeated. The fact that Generals Sullivan and Lord Stirling had rejoined the army after a recent prisoner exchange brought little hope now. Nor did the fact that General Lee had returned from the Southern campaign.

The independence for which they had risked their fortunes, their very lives, was not to be, so it seemed. Their children's future was to be that of subservience to the might of Great Britain.

Returning to the desk, Nathanael sat down and picked up the quill pen.

"My dear friend," he whispered the salutation and silently read to where he had stopped writing. He paused to consider what to say next. '*I feel mad, vexed, sick, and sorry,*" he wrote, tears pooling in his eyes. "*Never did I need the consoling voice of a friend more than now—*'

The general officers stood upon hearing General Washington's dismissal from the council. Nathanael gathered his notes.

"General Greene. You will remain." It was George Washington's voice

This was the first time His Excellency had spoken directly to him since the disaster at the forts. Nathanael laid his papers back down and remained standing until the others were gone. Even General Washington's aides were dismissed, Nathanael noted, wondering, with a sense of dread if his nightmare were about to become reality.

"Sit down," General Washington said, seating himself at the head of the table. He paused as though unsure of how to proceed. "—You and I have become the subject of many a conversation. Some of those in Philadelphia have become verbal about their feelings on our recent defeats. And there are those among us who have joined them."

"I still believe if we had better officers to lead the men. If we had less militia and more regulars. If we—"

"But we did not have the officer caliber needed, nor enough regulars, nor an adequate water supply to withstand a siege," General Washington interrupted. There was tenderness in his expression, a tenderness that somehow eased Nathanael's inner turmoil. Yet behind George Washington's compassionate gaze was revealed the deep sense of agony he, too, was experiencing.

The Commander briefly placed his hand on Nathanael's arm. "Hind sight is always so very illuminating," he said with a forced smile. "You erred in your judgment, that is true. But I have the greater sin."

"Sir?"

"I allowed you to err. May God forgive me for not countering your orders though I had my doubts. I have come to depend on your advice—your knowledge of military science—your ability to quickly size up a situation and come to a logical conclusion. I was in awe of your military genius, and momentarily forgot you are but human," he said with a weak smile. "I am to blame, and I am prepared to take full responsibility should Congress call for a hearing."

"Certainly not, sir!" Nathanael protested. "It was my command, and I—"

"No, General. I was present. I should have acted on my own judgment. And, to be honest, the prospect of removal from this position is welcomed. I would not wish this job on my worst enemy. I have never been so miserable." Pausing, he took a deep breath.

"—Even our trusted friends and colleagues are calling for our removal."

"Who, sir?"

"General Lee and General Reed."

Lee's name came as no surprise, for his attitude had been insubordinate to General Washington's authority since the capture of the forts. But Reed? He had been the trusted adjutant and confidant of the Commander since the start of the war. Nathanael, too, had considered him a friend.

"I accidentally opened a letter from Lee to General Reed. I mistakenly assumed it was intended for me—I wish I had never seen it. Reed, it seems, believes me to be too indecisive, and too easily swayed by your counsel. Lee is of the opinion that he could do a much better job of commanding. He believes my fatal indecision of mind disqualifies me. Perhaps it does. Perhaps he would do better. His recent victory in South Carolina compared to my numerous defeats has certainly raised the question in the minds of many."

"Lee's lust for glory will be the destruction of this army!" Nathanael exclaimed.

"Maybe. But my indecision may prove as fatal."

"Your Excellency, you must not even consider resigning. The confidence of the men will be lost. Lee will not have an army to command should you resign."

"The confidence of the men is already lost, my friend," was General Washington's solemn reply. He stood and walked to the window, watching the activity of the camp outside. "We have an army of only 3,000, and the enlistment of half that number is up in a few short weeks. They will not reenlist. Why would they?" he asked, turning his head to face Nathanael.

"Because the men that remain truly believe that a man's freedom—and that of his posterity—is worth dying for. They have confidence in your ability to lead them; or they, too, would have deserted."

"They may not desert for the very reasons you give, but they are not going to reenlist just the same."

"We still have a few weeks to convince them otherwise."

General Washington smiled at Nathanael's enthusiasm. "How? We are in no shape to defend ourselves. The British need only wait for the river to freeze, then march across and destroy us. How shall we convince the troops to stay, General Greene?"

"Perhaps the British will not wait for a freeze. Word is that Howe plans to set up camp in New York for the winter."

"If I were he, I would wait for the freeze and end it here," General Washington commented as he stared out the window.

"And I. However, Howe is notorious for delaying when the odds are so much in his favor. He could have ended this war already had he continued his attack on Long Island. Providence has shown its protection when we are most vulnerable. If Howe should retreat, could there be an offensive move on our part that might prove advantageous?"

General Washington's thoughts were apparently occupied with the possibility. He walked to the map of New Jersey and New York, silently studying it for a few minutes.

"—I will not keep you any longer, General Greene," he said, without taking his eyes off the map.

Nathanael picked up his papers, hat and cape, and walked toward the door.

Coryells Ferry, Pennsylvania
December 16, 1776

My Dear Caty,

Your favor of the 2nd reached me today. My spirits were lifted to hear that you and George are in good health.

By now, you have heard of the disastrous losses of our defenses on the Hudson. I cannot fully relate my upset over the situation, but the needs of the present day prevent one from dwelling on what is past—a merciful fact of life. How my friends in Rhode Island view me now, I wonder.

Oh, Rhode Island! The recent news of Newport being occupied by the enemy has reached us. I have appealed to His Excellency time and again to assign me command of the troops marching to my state's defense. He refuses me the command, though he assures me that it is not a judgment against my ability.

Oh, my plight! To be torn between the need to protect my family and friends and to yield to the authority of a man I so respect. Know that my absence is not my choice.

Generals Spencer and Arnold shall be in Rhode Island shortly. General Spencer, you are acquainted with. General Benedict Arnold is an able officer. His courage in the campaign in Canada is noteworthy. No doubt, his praises are sung there as well as here.

I am confident that your distance from Newport shall keep you safe. The occupation does not appear to be much of a threat at present. For the winter they will remain dormant, not going beyond Newport, I am sure. Word is that many of their numbers are invalid, having been previously wounded and presently not fit for duty.

On the 13th instant, General Charles Lee was caught off guard by a small detachment of the enemy and taken captive. His loss is a great blow to America.

We remain in a state of astonishment over the news of General Howe's retreat to New York. Our fate, so it seemed, was in his hands. However, mortal eyes are so often blind to the dispensation of Heaven.

Despite the fact that the British have gone into winter quarters, General Washington has not called us off the field. Therefore, I am not yet at liberty to summon you to myself.

Moreover, even if I were, the present state of the army is so deplorable that I could not ask you to suffer our want for basic necessities, though I long for your companionship.

I expect to relate better news as to the condition of the army in my next letter. The fact that we remain on active duty gives us cause to suspect that something is afoot, though His Excellency has confided in no one. Pray for us. Pray for America, as her future hangs in the balance.

Adieu, my second self,

Nathanael

"Well, bless my soul!" Colonel Tilghman greeted General Greene, General Sullivan, and Colonel Knox with a casual salute as they entered Washington's headquarters. "Summoned to a council of war and all prompt in arriving. You will probably never witness it again, Captain Hamilton." He addressed the newest of General Washington's aides, who stood at full attention.

"It is not for want of trying," Henry Knox replied to the jest with a friendly smile. "At ease, Captain. Tell me, Hamilton, are they treating you well here?"

"Yes, sir."

"I was afraid of that. But, should the situation change," he said laying a hand on Hamilton's shoulder, "you are always welcome back."

"Have the others arrived?" General Sullivan asked in response to Colonel Tilghman's remark.

"No one else has been summoned."

"Peculiar," Sullivan commented, looking at his companions.

"Here you are on time, and His Excellency is tied up. He is in conference with Dr. Rush. The doctor arrived an hour ago from Philadelphia."

"Benjamin Rush?" Nathanael asked.

"Yes, sir."

"Had I known a distinguished Congressman was visiting the camp, I would have put on my good uniform." Nathanael's tone was sarcastic.

"I thought that was your good uniform, General," Henry commented.

"It is my only uniform," he said, examining the worn jacket, waistcoat and breeches. "I left the other one at Fort Lee."

"Well, here is the perfect opportunity to petition Congress for an allowance on a new uniform," Colonel Tilghman suggested, gesturing toward the paper and quill pen on his desk for Nathanael to make his written request.

Nathanael grunted in reply as the door to General Washington's office opened. Dr. Rush stepped out, closing the door behind him. His elegant suit of fine black virgin wool and sparkling white ruffles beneath, was in sharp contrast to the worn uniforms of the officers in the room.

With a smile, he greeted each officer by name. "General Washington informed me that a British informer escaped imprisonment last night. I hope such irresponsibility on the part of the guards does not cause the enemy to gain advantage due to weaknesses he will report."

"Rest assured, Doctor, the British are well aware of our weaknesses and already have full advantage," General Sullivan, himself a former delegate to the Continental Congress, replied matter-of-factly.

Dr. Rush seemed surprised by Sullivan's blunt statement. He turned to Nathanael and Henry, and said, "Congress has received the letters you have sent, gentlemen. They are almost identical in content, and very much like General Washington's as well. I have often wondered if you discuss what to write in advance."

"No, sir, we do not," Nathanael said. "If our letters are similar, it is simply because we are all faced with the problems we address to Congress. Problems, sir, which seem to fall on deaf ears."

"Congress is always eager to hear from our general officers and Colonel Knox, of course." Dr. Rush replied nodding in Henry's direction.

"Eager to hear, but slow to respond."

"I do not know what you mean, General Greene. If you have something to say, sir, speak your mind."

Nathanael ignored Henry's quiet moan. "We have half our remaining forces walking off the field come December 31st."

"And Congress is to blame for this, General?"

"Most certainly. If Congress would increase the ridiculously short term of enlistment, we would not be faced with the frightful task of having to round up such large numbers of new recruits. And even in this we are ignored."

"Sir?"

"We have little incentive to attract recruits. And those that do enlist are certain not to reenlist for want of pay, clothing, shelter, and food. Look at our men as you leave, Dr. Rush. Take the image of what you see back to Philadelphia and the gay social events. Remember; as you dine at the tables overlade with food, the men out there who are surviving on meager rations. Remember when elegantly dressed at your balls, the rags they wear, and their shoeless feet on the frozen ground. Remember, as you sleep in your warm bed, that a campfire is their only warmth."

"And is not much of that your own doing, General?" Dr. Rush asked with a strained voice, his eyebrows cocked.

Nathanael met Rush's gaze, his jaw set. "This army would be much better off had the stores at the forts been saved. I will not deny that. However, let me make one thing clear, sir, most of those supplies were not provided by the Continental Congress. They were gathered from the countryside by my men, under my instruction."

"The Quartermaster General advanced you the funds, funds raised by Congress," Dr. Rush said with a satisfied smile.

"No, they did not," Nathanael's quick reply came. "The Quartermaster's Department is virtually worthless, sir."

General Washington loudly cleared his throat, interrupting the conversation. Nathanael was surprised to see him standing at his office door. "Dr. Rush, if you would excuse us, I have matters to discuss with my officers."

"Of course, your Excellency. Your servant, gentlemen." Dr. Rush extended his hand to each one. Nathanael was last. "General Greene, I intend to tour the camp." He draped his cape about his shoulders and left.

"It sounds as though you gave the honorable Congressman food for thought," General Washington said to Nathanael as the men gathered around the table.

"I hope so, sir."

General Washington gestured for his servant Billy Lee to place a scroll on the table before them. "In the hope of inspiring the support of the people once more," he began, looking from one man to the other, "I have decided to form an attack on the Hessian camp at Trenton." He assisted Billy in rolling the scroll open and revealed a detailed map of the area he spoke.

"Billy, would you please get me a cup of tea." General Washington said.

"Is your throat still bothering you, sir?" the servant asked.

The General nodded.

"Did you think to have Dr. Rush look at it, sir?"

"It is but a mild throat pain, Billy."

"But, sir—"

"The cup of tea, Billy, please." As the servant turned to leave, General Washington threw him a weak, though affectionate smile then focused his attention on the map.

"The Hessians expect a comfortable winter rest, as is the custom of European warfare. However, our form of warfare is not that of Europe. We are fighting for our survival.

"The Germans, it has been reported to me, are planning for a grand celebration on Christmas Day. I trust, gentlemen, that you have no objection to disturbing their celebration," George Washington smiled at his New England officers. New Englanders, he had discovered during the siege of Boston, gave little regard to Christmas festivities.

They politely smiled in response, each of them eager to hear their Commander's plan.

"We will move across the Delaware River as soon as darkness falls the night of the twenty-fifth. We will travel the nine miles to Trenton under the cover of darkness, reaching the Hessian Camp before dawn. They will not be prepared for our attack, nor will they be in any condition to make a defense, for their celebration includes ingesting a great quantity of liquor."

"How can you be certain they will be celebrating being so far from home as they are?" General Sullivan asked.

"The British informer who was imprisoned was assisted by me in his escape. He is, in truth, an American spy. He came from Trenton, where he has managed to establish himself as a British sympathizer. The intelligence he related to me is invaluable; including the fact that a large quantity of local brew has been put up for the celebration."

Satisfied by the Commander's answer, the officers listened in earnest as details of the attack were addressed. Each man was informed of the major role that he was to play in this desperate move.

Colonel Knox was to be in charge of transporting the men, horses and artillery safely across the Delaware River. When Trenton was reached, he would see to his cannons.

Generals Greene and Sullivan would divide the troops, Nathanael taking his men on the road, which approached Trenton from the northeast. General Sullivan would approach, hopefully within minutes of Nathanael's appearance, from the south.

Greene, Sullivan and Knox related the details of the attack to the officers within their divisions. Preparations were quickly underway.

The night of December 25th swept upon the camp with piercing winds and drifting snow. Nevertheless, a firm determination of spirit motivated the ragged troops as they fell into line and awaited the orders of their officers.

Henry Knox had gathered a number of bulky, canoe-like craft, measuring forty feet in length by eight feet in width. The invaluable service of the Massachusetts fishermen, turned soldiers, who had safely maneuvered the boats used during the secret retreat from Long Island, was again to be put to use in transporting the 2,400 men, eighteen field pieces and officers' horses across the ice-packed river.

Through the howling wind, Henry's steady commands were heard. He was in complete control of the situation—as calm in overseeing this treacherous passage as if he were ordering the placement of books in his shop.

Generals Washington, Greene and Sullivan watched the activity from the river's bank. The Commander was unusually quiet. The moderate throat pain of the previous day had fully erupted. A woolen scarf was wrapped securely about his neck to protect it from the cold.

"Colonel Knox is ready for you to board, your Excellency," an officer addressed General Washington through the howling wind. He then led the three generals to the awaiting boats. They would be among the first to chance the trip. Henry wisely placed each of them in separate vessels. Should they be together and the boats capsize, all would be lost. To send them across separately would protect the command.

The floating ice in the river made the passage appear impossible. The water was unusually high and the current running swiftly. Chunks of ice crashed against the boats, threatening to push the bulky, overloaded vessels downstream.

The men groped in the darkness as the huge chunks of ice jarred the boats. The officers' attempts to reassure them were drowned out by a mixture of prayers and cussing. The horses, too, loudly squealed their protest as anxious soldiers held tight to their bridles, as terrified as the frightened animals that rocked the cumbersome vessels.

The able Massachusetts seamen managed to force the packed vessels across the river. On the opposite shore, their passengers gratefully disembarked, and the seamen returned repeatedly to continue the hazardous transport of men, horses, and finally the artillery.

By 2:00 A.M., the men were ready to march. General Washington appeared calm even though the planned attack was now three hours behind schedule. He pulled his pocket watch out, ordering Nathanael and John Sullivan to set their watches by his. The countersign for the operation, he informed them, was "Victory or Death."

"Have your men fall in," the command was given. Generals Greene and Sullivan relayed the order and countersign to their aides, who carried it to the brigadier generals.

Each man was keenly aware that the nine-mile march would prove more difficult than formerly anticipated due to the delayed start and fierce wind. Yet, despite the time pressure, despite the lack of proper apparel and being exposed to such severe weather, the men obediently began to march without so much as a murmur.

General Sullivan's division, along with Colonel Knox and much of the artillery, followed the road, which ran along the river's edge.

"I will accompany your division, General Greene," the Commander informed Nathanael as he prepared to split from Sullivan's force. Nathanael caught the Commander's concerned gaze.

"Are you feeling all right, General?" George Washington asked, hearing him wheeze, and noting the familiar yawning that accompanied his asthma attacks in response to his body's need for oxygen.

"I will be fine, sir," Nathanael replied, taking a swig of lukewarm coffee from his canteen.

In profound silence, the march wore on as the driving snow turned to a cutting sleet. General Washington ordered a halt to allow the men the opportunity to eat the rations they had prepared. He and Nathanael separated, riding through the line, to encourage the men. Coming upon Lord Stirling, Nathanael stopped. "How are they doing?" he asked.

"Better than I thought possible. Look at them, Nat." He exclaimed, viewing his huddled brigade from the saddle. "Exposed to this blasted storm, half have no winter coats, the other half no shoes."

Nathanael watched a few soldiers nearby, crowded on a fallen log, vainly rewrapping their numb and bloody feet in rags.

"Keep them moving, Nat. That is my advice. This cold may kill them if we do not keep them moving."

"I will tell His Excellency."

"Have you eaten anything?" Lord Stirling asked, holding out a piece of bread, his hand visibly shaking from the cold.

"I am not hungry."

"Force yourself," he insisted, pushing the bread into his friend's hand.

Nathanael smiled, wheeled his horse around and rode down the line in search of General Washington, stuffing the stale bread into his mouth as he went.

George Washington agreed with Lord Stirling's assessment. Nathanael was ordered to get the column moving while he remained back with the men.

"Soldiers, keep by your officers! For God's sake, keep by your officers!" The Commander in Chief's voice called out, deep and solemn.

Moving down the line of march, the Commander's horse's hind legs slipped on the icy road. To the horror of those close enough to witness it, the horse threatened to topple down the steep bank. George Washington grabbed the horse's mane with his hand, and pulled the animal's head erect, forcing it to regain its balance.

Nathanael approached Trenton around 8:00 A.M. and immediately sent word for General Washington to join him at the head of the line. The Commander quickly came to Nathanael's side just as the column was ordered to halt. The town was now in clear view.

"Any sign of Sullivan?" General Washington asked, hesitating to engage the enemy without Henry Knox's big guns to back the attack.

"Not yet, sir, but we are going to have to move forward, and pray God that Sullivan is close upon the town!" Nathanael said, pulling his sword from its scabbard and pointing to a group of Hessian guards off in the distance who had already spotted his men.

"Der Feind! Der Feind! Heraus!" the Hessian's cry was heard from a distance.

"What are they saying?" General Washington asked an aide who served as interpreter.

"The enemy. The enemy. Turn out."

As the aide spoke, the beat of drums and the sound of a bugle were heard. Then from the opposite side of the town came a cannon's boom.

"Sullivan!" Nathanael exclaimed as he and General Washington exchanged a quick glance.

"Take them in, General Greene," the Commander ordered.

Nathanael turned in his saddle to face the men. He held the sword high above his head, and brought it down, leading the men forward in battle formation. They rushed to the head of the two main streets going into Trenton, while Sullivan's men moved up from the opposite end.

Henry's cannons raked the streets as the troops began to seize the houses, blasting the Hessians with musketry. The Hessians, half-naked, abandoned the houses in fear and confusion. Frantically they ran down the streets in the hope of reaching the safety of the woodlands about the town, and came headlong on the cannon. The cannons boomed, hurling fragments of grapeshot into the bodies of those closest. Some fell without a sound, while others writhed in agony, their free-flowing blood steaming in the frozen air.

Stepping over the mauled bodies, the Americans charged the enemy as they sought out protection from the cannons behind the houses.

Muskets were aimed and triggers pulled. Many failed to fire—the powder being wet. "To the bayonet!" was Nathanael's order, as he lunged forward on his horse to take down as many as he could with the edge of his own sword.

A thirst for revenge gripped the exhausted American force. Boldly they attacked the stunned Hessians with the bayonet. The gruesome screams of their own compatriots being mercilessly cut down while begging for quarter in the previous battles echoed through their minds.

For an hour the chaotic battle continued, intensified by the swirling snow and cutting sleet, which greatly limited visibility. In a pathetic attempt to escape, the Hessians fled to a nearby apple orchard where Lord Stirling's brigade was able to take them captive.

General Washington rewarded Lord Stirling with the honor of receiving the sword of surrender from the Hessian commander. It was only a few months before that His Lordship was forced to offer his own sword to a Hessian general.

The triumphant soldiers cheered their victory, throwing their hats high into the air. Generals Washington, Greene, and Sullivan sat tall upon their steeds, joining in the joy and jubilation of their men.

General Washington ordered Lord Stirling to find a suitable barracks for the prisoners, and assign a detail to guard them.

"See that our men enjoy the spoil. We should find enough food here for a hearty breakfast. Then gather shoes for the men, shirts, breeches, capes and blankets." The Commander said to an aide.

"Yes, sir."

"I want an accounting of all military supplies and an accurate casualty count for both sides," he said to another aide, who quickly rode off.

Reports began to pour in as the generals made plans for the army's next move. Extra blankets, tents, and clothing were scarce. Food and military supplies were found in amounts that were a bit more encouraging.

Colonel Tilghman entered the room and went to General Washington's side. "Excuse me, your Excellency." General Washington acknowledged him with a nod

"The casualty figures are in, sir."

Every man at the table listened intently.

"There were 106 of the enemy killed or wounded. We have taken 868 prisoners. About 400 escaped during the battle."

"And our casualties, Colonel?" General Washington asked.

"Two of our men died as a result of exposure, sir. Four received minor injuries in the battle. Two of these were wounded in a heroic attempt to seize the German cannon. One was your cousin, Captain William Washington."

"And the other?"

"A young lieutenant, also from Virginia. Perhaps you know him; sir—let me see—" Colonel Tilghman looked at the casualty list in his hand. "Munroe is his name, Lieutenant James Munroe."

"Munroe—no, I do not believe I know him. I will be sure to speak to them."

"Sir, the Hessian commander, Colonel Rall, is among the wounded. He is not expected to make it through the night. He has asked to speak to you."

"I will see to it, Colonel. Thank you."

General Washington requested Nathanael to accompany him. With haste, they went to the wounded commander's bedside.

The semi-darkened room was filled with the harsh smell of antiseptics and the gloomy anticipation of certain death. Colonel Rall acknowledged General Washington's arrival from his deathbed by slowly lifting his bandaged arm in a pitiful salute of respect and defeat.

General Washington responded with his own silent salute, then pulled a chair beside the bed and sat down. Nathanael stood behind the chair, as one of General Washington's aides positioned himself at the foot of the bed, prepared to translate the conversation.

"I beg you, sir," Colonel Rall began. A choking cough violently gripped him as blood seeped into his lungs through the internal wounds. "Please have mercy on my brave men. It was not their choice to come to this place." Again, he began to choke.

"Perhaps you should not exert yourself so," General Washington said with concern.

"I must—I must—" he protested through the interpreter. General Washington laid a comforting hand on the dying man's arm. "We were sold by our prince into this service. This is not our war. God forgive us. Be merciful to my men, your Excellency—I beg you to be merciful—"

General Washington waited through another spasm of coughing. "I promise you, Colonel, that your men will be treated with human decency as is our Christian duty."

The dying commander grabbed hold of General Washington's arm with a trembling hand. Unable to verbalize his appreciation, he smiled at the American general, tears flowing down his cheeks.

A few short hours of rest was all the victorious Continentals were allowed. The risk of a counterattack was too great. General Washington ordered the men, along with the newly acquired stores and prisoners, to march back to the ice-filled river and cross to the safety of the Pennsylvania shore.

Thomas Paine, eyes half closed, was sprawled out on the overstuffed chair in the bedchamber he shared with General Greene. His worn boots were tossed on the floor, exposing stockings, which had been mended repeatedly. A dark blue jacket with the sheathed sword was fastened hung over the jacket. A blazing hearth was the only source of light in the darkened room.

The weary man lifted a pewter spoon from the bowl resting on his lap. With great effort he slowly brought it to his mouth then dropped his hand back to the bowl as though tugged by a heavy weight. There his hand remained, tightly clenching the spoon.

The opening of the bedchamber door failed to affect a response in Thomas. The sight of his aide's condition concerned Nathanael. Quietly, he closed the door behind him, trying not to disturb the half-conscious man.

"Forgive me, General, but I do not seem to have the energy to move," Thomas muttered.

Nathanael turned from the door and faced him. "Believe me, Colonel, I fully understand." He unfastened his sword and removed his worn jacket and waistcoat, laying them neatly upon a small table in the corner of the room.

After rinsing his hands and face at the washbasin, he walked to the bed and sat on the edge. "What's that you are eating, Common Sense?" Nathanael asked, revealing his high-spirits with the use of this nickname he had for his aide.

"Tis hasty pudding, friend. Would thee care for some?" Thomas asked, seemingly unaware that he had, in his exhaustion, reverted to the speech of his youth.

Nathanael grinned at him as he yanked off his boots. "Nay, friend Thomas." he began, reaching over and slapping his aide on the thigh. "Nay, but tis generous of thee to offer, brother."

Thomas' eyes popped open. He appeared confused by his commander's laughter.

"Are you planning to sleep in that chair?" Nathanael asked with a smile pulling the blankets back on the bed.

"No, I am just going to finish this pudding."

As he stretched out on the soft feather mattress, the dull ache in Nathanael's back momentarily intensified. An involuntary moan was his reaction. "I have never been so tired in my life."

"With good cause, sir. We've been on the move for over thirty hours."

Nathanael comfortably folded his arms behind his head. His tense muscles began to relax. In silence, he stared at the shadow of the dancing flames on the ceiling for a few minutes, as he listened to the clanking of Thomas' spoon against the bowl. "I was told that you wrote your last paper during the retreat from Fort Lee. Is it so?"

"Do you mean *The American Crisis*, sir?"

"Yes."

"It came to me during our retreat." He stopped and chuckled. "I used a drum-head for my desk."

"You did?" Nathanael asked with a smile.

"Yah—"

" 'These are the times that try men's souls,' " Nathanael began to quote the piece. "How does it go, Common Sense?"

"It is quite lengthy, sir. I cannot recite it all from memory," Thomas said drowsily.

"Recite as much as you can."

Thomas cleared his throat. His eyes were still closed and his fingers wrapped around the handle of the spoon. "These are the times that try men's souls," he began slowly. "The summer soldier and the sunshine Patriot will, in this crisis, shrink from the service of his country; but he that stands it now deserves the love and thanks of man and woman. Tyranny, like Hell, is not easily conquered. Yet we have this consolation with us, that the harder the conflict, the more glorious the triumph—" Thomas' voice drifted off, and Nathanael heard the spoon fall from his hand to the wooden floor.

" '—The harder the conflict the more glorious the triumph,' " Nathanael whispered. "How true, friend Thomas, how true." He rolled onto his side and watched the crackling flames in the hearth. Soon, he too was sound asleep.

"It's a fine for chase my boys!"
(George Washington)

CHAPTER FIVE

FROM THE PROTECTION of the wooded thicket to the cover of the houses, which lined the well-traveled road, Nathanael positioned his men. The day wore on as the American detachment harassed the enemy with musketry in an attempt to slow them down.

The Continental Army was encamped just outside of Trenton, vulnerably positioned between the Delaware River and the Assunpink Creek. Though their numbers were increased to 5,000, the sudden march of 7,000 British troops was more than the smaller, ill-equipped army was prepared to defend itself against. Nathanael's assignment was to keep the British from reaching the American encampment before nightfall, thus providing General Washington the precious time needed to decide his next move.

The winter sun began to sink into the western sky as the enemy neared the quiet Quaker village of Trenton. His task completed, Nathanael hurried his hard fighting men across the creek with the British fast on their heels. When safely within the boundary of the American camp, Nathanael left the work of keeping the British off the bridge to the artillery detachment standing ready for action.

The sudden boom of the cannon brought the newly appointed Brigadier General Henry Knox from his tent. Quickly mounting his horse, he raced toward the creek, encountering Nathanael and his men as they ascended the hill where the main body of soldiers was encamped.

Henry pulled his horse alongside Nathanael's and scanned the situation at the bottom of the hill. "How does it look, General?" he asked breathlessly.

Nathanael turned in the saddle to observe the action. "We had them at a snail's pace most of the day. Brought quite a few down. Whether or not they will push forward, I cannot say. But, if I were Cornwallis, I would," he said, facing Henry.

Henry's eyes nervously darted to Nathanael's. "Let's hope Cornwallis does not think like you."

Lord Stirling came from the rear of Nathanael's detachment and guided his horse next to his fellow officers. "We lost a man on the way in, sir," he announced.

"Nay!" Nathanael protested in disbelief. Having gone all day with no casualties, it disturbed him that one fell so close to the safety of the camp.

"You are not going to like this, General—" Lord Stirling began. "Those miserable Hessians. They are nothing but hired murderers, and those sons of Lucifer find pleasure in it—"

"What happened?"

"They overcame the chaplain that was riding with us. Good God, Nat! He was no threat to them. They tortured him before they killed him."

Again, Nathanael turned in his saddle and stared blankly at the skirmish occurring at the bottom of the hill. He took a deep breath. "Where is he?"

"Out there," Lord Stirling said, gesturing to the area beyond the cannons. "We cannot get to him."

"Are you sure he is dead?" Henry asked.

"He is dead. They stripped him of his clothes and left him to rot."

The generals remained silent for a moment.

"We are due at Headquarters," Henry announced, breaking the somber silence. He removed his watch from the pocket inside his jacket. "Your timing is perfect, gentlemen. His Excellency called for a council of war, which is scheduled to assemble in fifteen minutes." He pulled on the reins and turned his horse about. There was nothing they could do for their fallen comrade. Each one of them had become accustomed to such horrors of war.

"Tired?" Henry asked his friends as they moved toward Headquarters.

"No," Nathanael replied.

"Do not ask him, Henry. The man is tireless. I am tired, wet, cold and hungry, too." Lord Stirling exclaimed. "We have not eaten all day. What I would not give for roast mutton, fresh vegetables, sweet cake topped with berries and cream, and a glass of Madeira—"

"But he will settle for salted beef, stale bread and dry cheese," Nathanael added. "Has His Excellency given any indication of his plans?" He directed the question to Henry.

"None, but he has had us on alert all day. We heard the gunfire begin early this morning when you intercepted Cornwallis. His Excellency—actually the entire camp has been on edge wondering if you could hold them back."

"We are not ready to face them, Henry. We have too many skittish militia companies and not enough regulars," Nathanael commented.

"Thank God, General Washington was able to convince the New England troops to extend their service," Lord Stirling remarked. Much of his brigade was made up of many of the New Englanders, and he was certain of their ability to stand and fight.

Their term of enlistment had expired two days previously, but the Commander in Chief had implored them to stay on. "Your country is at stake, your wives, your houses, and all that you hold dear," he told them. After pleading with them to stay on for one more month, the homesick New Englanders yielded to his pathetic appeal.

"Thank God," Nathanael agreed. "But if Cornwallis attacks us here, even with the strength of the New England troops, we will not be able to stand against him."

"I do not see that we have much choice," Henry's words were solemn.

George Washington returned the salute of his subordinate generals and silently received Nathanael's report. He was visibly upset over the chaplain's murder. A plate of food was then ordered from the kitchen for Generals Greene and Lord Stirling, which they hungrily devoured as the other generals began to assemble about them.

Just before the council convened, word came from the artillery detachment along the creek. The British were setting up camp for the night. There would be no imminent attack. In unison, the assembled men breathed a sigh of relief when General Washington relayed the news. He then proceeded to present the plans, which he had been working on throughout the day—plans, which depended on the success of Nathanael's mission.

A secret withdrawal of the Continental Army was to be carried out during the night. Men, artillery, stores, supplies—everything would be moved. It was vital that the withdrawal be orderly and completely silent, for the British pickets were within hearing range of the American camp. If they discovered the plan, an attack would be certain.

A night march would bring them to Princeton, New Jersey, where 2,000 British troops were stationed, along with a fair amount of stores and supplies.

"And from there, God willing, New Brunswick will be our aim." General Washington announced, delighting the officers about him. New Brunswick, located just seventeen miles from Princeton, was the British supply center. Those guarding it, at present, were few. If New Brunswick could be taken, the British might very well be forced to surrender, thus putting an end to the war.

"We may have trouble moving the cannon, your Excellency. Last night's rain and today's milder temperatures have left the roads muddy," Nathanael informed him.

General Washington studied his usually optimistic subordinate for a moment. He then turned to Henry Knox. "It is your problem, General Knox. Find a way to move your guns.

"I want the campfires blazing high. The fires must continue well after we are gone in order to keep the British from suspecting our withdrawal," he continued as he turned his attention from Henry Knox to the other generals assembled.

"The regiments are to be called off one at a time. Orders are to be given in low tones. I want nothing to seem amiss. We are to give the appearance of normal camp activity.

"Lord Stirling, the detachment that was out today will be among the last to leave. This will give the men a chance to rest. The remainder of your regiments can busy themselves with stoking the fires—to assist them in keeping warm," he added as an afterthought. "Have them go to work with the pick and shovel. The enemy will assume we are building fortifications."

"Yes, sir," Lord Stirling nodded.

The troops would be divided as they had been on the march to Trenton. General Sullivan's division would come around Princeton from the rear. General Greene's approach was on the main road, after destroying the bridge, which offered access to the town.

When the council adjourned, each of Washington's generals knew precisely what was expected of him in the long night and early morning hours, which lay ahead.

"The temperature's dropped," General Hugh Mercer observed as the officers stepped outside.

"It certainly has," Henry Knox agreed, and walking ahead of the others, he squatted down to feel the ground. "It is freezing up. By the time we are ready to move out, this ground will be hard enough for the cannon to roll with ease." He stood up, wiping his hands together.

"If it gets too cold we may have a problem with the metal wheels clanking against the frozen ground," John Sullivan commented, pulling up the collar of his great coat against the wind.

"We will wrap them in cloth and muffle the sound if need be," Henry's sure response came. "I am going to tell the General. It is one less concern for him." He walked back to the house.

"I need to have a word with ya, General Greene," General Mercer said as the men approached their waiting horses. The others mounted and quickly rode off.

"What is it?" Nathanael asked.

"It is ready," the fifty-year-old Scotsman said.

"What is ready?"

"The tea for yar asthma."

Nathanael smiled at the former physician. "I forgot about it. It has been months since you told me about that concoction of yours."

"The herbs had to be gathered. Some I had to send home to Virginia for. But it is ready now. Yar bound to have an attack in the cold night air. I will bring a canteen-full before we march."

"You are sure it will work, Doctor?" Nathanael asked with a touch of skepticism as both men mounted their horses.

"Aye, laddie, it'll work like a charm."

Nathanael threw him a suspicious smile as both men wheeled their horses about and headed toward their command.

The campfires were set to blazing and Stirling's men began to tear at the earth with picks and shovels as the regiments were called off, one at a time, to form for the march.

"Here ya go, General," Hugh Mercer said softly as he directed his horse alongside Nathanael's. He held a canteen out to him. "Take a swig right now."

Nathanael opened the canteen and brought it to his lips. "This smells horrid," he quietly protested, lowering the canteen from his mouth.

"And it tastes even worse, I promise ya. But ya'll drink it just the same." the doctor said with a stern eye on his superior.

Nathanael raised it to his lips once more and took a gulp. "It is horrible, Mercer." he exclaimed through a choking cough. "And if it weren't for the fact that General Washington, himself, claims you for his trusted physician, I would dump it out right here."

"Ya will appreciate it as the night wears on, sir," Hugh said, slapping Nathanael between the shoulder blades. "Take a swig every hour or so and ya will do just fine. I will tell ya me fee when we get to Princeton." he chuckled. Turning his horse about, he fell back with his brigade.

The cannons began to roll forward, silenced by the cloth, which was securely fastened to the wheels.

The temperature continued to plummet until the sudden freeze, which had been viewed as a blessing earlier in the evening, became a source of distress as the long night wore on. The mud solidified beneath the men's feet. Jagged heaves of frozen earth and random stumps on the partially constructed road, caused man and beast to stumble in the dark, and artillery wagons to sway and tilt. Sheets of ice formed where puddles had been, causing the weighted horses to slide, often top-pling the heavy guns to the ground.

Frequent halts to right the overturned cannons or examine a fallen horse grated on the men's nerves. The frigid night air penetrated their bones as they stood in the darkness, with no means for warming themselves.

Many of those who had spent the previous day stalling the British advance were too exhausted to stay awake, despite the bitter cold or their upright position. Leaning on their muskets, they often dozed while waiting for the march to resume.

Generals Washington, Sullivan and Greene rode up and down the line, person-ally instructing the men when an obstacle was encountered. An artillery wagon located in front of Hugh Mercer's small brigade came to a halt as the horse slid on the ice and stumbled to its knees. Nathanael galloped to the scene and hastily dis-mounted.

The frightened animal was coaxed to stand by Hugh Mercer and some of his men. Nathanael joined the others in verbally calming the animal.

It is all right, boy," he said, rubbing his hand over the horse's back. Squatting, he lifted a hoof and felt in the darkness for a shoe. "Just as I thought; this horse is not even shod," he said to Hugh, who was running his hands down the horse's legs to feel for fractures.

"Most of them are not, General. The Quartermaster's Department has not pro-vided supplies to shoe the artillery horses," one of the artillery officers explained.

"How much money would it take to supply extra shoes for the artillery?" Nathanael was disgusted.

"Is the animal injured?" General Washington called to Nathanael and Hugh from atop his horse. General Sullivan was at his side.

"Does not seem to be, sir," General Mercer replied.

Nathanael and Hugh Mercer mounted their horses.

"With so many delays, I am concerned that an enemy patrol may catch us unawares," George Washington began. "I am going to position General Mercer's brigade as an advance guard to encounter and deal with any patrols."

Hugh Mercer immediately went forward.

The frequent stops continued, yet by dawn, it was discovered that Princeton lay only three miles to the north. Another halt was called, this time by General Washington. A swallow of rum was ordered for each man in the hopes of bringing some warmth.

The men received their meager ration in profound silence, aware of their imminent danger as they drew closer to the town. They observed the winter scene about them with an unusual sense of awe, many wondering if this might be the last morning they would witness.

The sun's first rays danced on the glistening ice, which covered the lifeless trees. The morning temperature remained frigid. The air was still and crisp.

Soon, the march resumed. When Sullivan's column split to the right, each man suddenly felt the excitement of the impending battle. Generals Washington and Greene fell back to encourage and prepare their men. The pace immediately picked up.

The stillness of the January morning was disrupted when a musket shot rang out ahead. Within seconds, a barrage of musketry was heard, followed by a cannon's roar.

General Washington shared an anxious glance with Nathanael.

"Sullivan or Mercer?" General Washington asked, trying to determine the direction of the gunfire.

"Mercer," Nathanael replied without a doubt.

"General Washington spurred his horse forward, followed close behind by his ever-present staff officers.

Impromptu battle plans were put into motion. General Washington ordered the advance regiment of Pennsylvania militia to push forward and reinforce Mercer's men. Nathanael quickly pulled the rear brigade of New England regulars up along with two cannons to fall in behind the Pennsylvania militia.

"Keep the rest of the division in line," Nathanael ordered Lord Stirling who had come up with the regulars. "I am going forward to determine whether Mercer needs our full force." He hurried off with his aides.

Nathanael came to the hilltop, which had, only minutes before, been the scene of Mercer's encounter with the British. Smoke still lingered as Nathanael peered through his spyglass onto the field below.

"It is more than a patrol, sir," Thomas Paine commented on the number of British on the field.

"At least 300. They must have been called out to reinforce General Cornwallis at Trenton."

"Will you call the remaining regiments forward?" Billy Blodget asked.

"No. We already have them outnumbered."

Through the spyglass, Nathanael watched as the opposing armies assembled face to face. Neatly aligned, shoulder to shoulder, the armies walked toward one another at an equal pace. The warrior-like determination of the New England regulars was a remarkable sight.

"Praise be to God they stayed on." Nathanael exclaimed with pride to his aides. Then his tone suddenly changed. "What is he doing? Get him out of there!"

"What's wrong, sir?" Colonel Paine asked with alarm.

"General Washington is directly between the lines. Where are his aides? Why don't they get him out of there?" Nathanael watched helplessly as both lines came to a halt by Washington's command. He heard George Washington's voice carry across the field, "cock firelock—make ready—take aim—"

Nathanael turned his head, unable to witness the certain death of his beloved Commander, who, sitting tall upon his white steed was an easy target for the British guns. A chill ran through Nathanael's body as the final order was given—"fire!" And with it, a barrage of musketry was sounded. He forced his gaze back to the battlefield, straining to see General Washington's form through the smoke of the guns. Bodies were sprawled here and there on the ground. Still mounted before his brave troops was General Washington, rallying his men on as the British fell back in retreat.

"It is a fine fox chase, my boys!" Nathanael and his aides heard the General's shout. It would have been an exhilarating sight to see George Washington excitedly leading his men in the chase, if Nathanael had not been so concerned for the Commander in Chief's safety.

"Colonel Paine, gather a report of General Mercer's casualties," Nathanael barked then turned his horse about and speedily made his way back down the hill to his waiting troops.

"Move them forward," he ordered as he approached the column. His aide, Billy Blodget, immediately went to the head of the column to relay the order.

Within a few minutes, Thomas Paine came up alongside Nathanael. "—General Mercer's men took a beating, sir. The wounded are being prepared for transport to nearby homes. I have ordered some of the surgeons to attend them."

"Numbers, Colonel. Give me numbers." Nathanael demanded, his attention fixed on the troops marching before him. His exhaustion and anxiety over General Washington had put him on edge.

Thomas hesitated. "—Sir, General Mercer is among the wounded—"

Nathanael's eyes darted to Thomas'. The color instantly drained from his face.

"It does not look good, General. He wants to see you—"

Nathanael dropped his forehead into the palm of his gloved hand. He closed his eyes and took a deep breath. "Tell Lord Stirling to take charge. He has to head for Princeton as planned. We need to get there as quickly as possible to assist Sullivan. I will catch up." He lifted his head. The sunlight glistened on his tear-filled eyes. Then turning his horse about, he headed back up the hill.

Slowly Nathanael approached the bent figures of the surgeon and his assistant as they worked on the mortally wounded Hugh Mercer. As accustomed to death as Nathanael had become, even hardened to the agony about him, he discovered he was not prepared to face the death of such an intimate friend.

The surgeon acknowledged Nathanael's presence with a solemn shake of his head. Hugh lay upon the frozen ground, his eyes closed. There was barely a spot of his clothing that was not soaked with blood. As the surgeon gently pressed upon the gaping wounds left by the British bayonets, Hugh moaned, his torn body jerking in pain.

Nathanael knelt opposite the surgeon. He removed his glove, and placed his hand upon his friend's head. Hugh slowly opened his eyes to look at Nathanael, his face contorted with pain.

An agonizing groan rolled uncontrollably from Hugh's lips as he attempted to speak. "They shot me horse down, General," he finally managed to say just above a whisper. "The doctor here says they stuck me seven times. I am afraid I will not be with you to see the final victory." His body stiffened as the surgeon worked.

Nathanael warmed Hugh's cold, bloody hand within his own.

"I lost some good men. They fought well. You'd have been proud to have witnessed it," Hugh said through his pain. "Tell Henry that Captain Neil stayed by his cannon till the end. And Colonel Haslet," he groaned in response to the surgeon's treatment. "—On the fence—" he said, pointing a trembling hand to a spot behind Nathanael.

Nathanael turned to again witness the gruesome scene he had passed when he came up the hill. Young Captain Neil's lifeless body lay sprawled against the cannon; against the rail fence was Colonel Haslet with half his head blown off.

Hugh's hand dropped in exhaustion. "Haslet was ordered to recruitment duty. He just told me this morning that he wanted to be with us in battle, and would leave when the army went into winter quarters." He squeezed Nathanael's hand in response to his pain.

Nathanael let him grip one hand while he laid the other back on his head in an attempt to comfort his dying friend. "His Excellency has them on the run. Our men are on their way to join with Sullivan's. The day is ours, General Mercer." Nathanael said with a forced smile.

"Aye, laddie, the day is ours. And the final victory will be ours as well, for our cause is just—"

"General Greene, we need to get him out of the cold," the surgeon said as a wagon, which had been brought from a nearby farmhouse, was brought up beside the men.

Nathanael assisted the surgeon in removing Hugh's blood-soaked sash which, when stretched out, was designed to take the fallen general from the field. He then helped lift Hugh onto the back of the wagon, and spread the wool blanket he found there over his friend's trembling body.

"Tell me, General Greene, did the tea work?" Hugh asked after the intense pain of being moved subsided enough to again speak.

Nathanael nodded his head, "Like a charm."

"I never told ya my fee, laddie," he whispered with a weak smile.

"You name it, Doctor."

His hand came out from beneath the blanket and grasped Nathanael's. Tears rolled to the back of his head as he spoke, his voice weakening with every exertion, "Remember me, Nat—remember me—"

Nathanael cupped Hugh's cheek with his hand. "I could never forget thee, Hugh Mercer." His voice cracked as the sudden ache in his throat threatened to hinder his words.

"General." The surgeon's brief reminder came.

"They need to get thee to one of the houses, Hugh. I will be back as soon as I am able," Nathanael promised.

Hugh nodded, weakly squeezing his friend's hand before letting go.

Morristown, New Jersey
January 12, 1777

Dear Jacob,

I am in receipt of your last letter, and apologize for not returning your favor more promptly. There has been much activity here. News of our recent victory at Princeton has certainly reached you by now. The spoil was enough to see us through the winter. Our quarters are comfortable, Morristown being a perfect location, geographically, for a winter rest.

General Washington's desire was to take New Brunswick immediately after Princeton, thus cutting the British from their supply base and forcing surrender. However, our people, having marched all night, were incapable of covering the seventeen miles to New Brunswick. "If we only had 1000 fresh troops!" was the united cry of the general officers! But, alas, it was not to be.

General Cornwallis arrived in Princeton two hours after our attack, making much better time on the main road than we had on the back road. Word is that he was fuming over our secret withdrawal, which was not discovered until daybreak. He had difficulty accepting the fact that our illustrious Commander in Chief had outgeneraled him.

May God's name be praised, for we have practically driven the enemy from New Jersey, and rekindled hope in the people once more.

Our losses were minimal, though we had a number of able officers fall in the initial encounter. My friend and brave compatriot, Brigadier General Hugh Mercer, died of multiple stab wounds. His presence shall be sorely missed both on and off the field.

How goes it in Rhode Island? News from Generals Spencer and Arnold is that the British are securely contained within Newport.

General Washington has been given temporary authority by Congress to oversee recruitment, appoint officers (below rank of brigadier general), and forage for supplies— by force if necessary. We can thank the noble John Adams for bringing Congress to their senses in this regard, if only temporarily. I have been communicating these very sentiments to him, which he has apparently verbalized with convincing logic in the assembly.

You tell me that Caty is becoming increasingly distressed as her time draws near. This news is alarming, for her letters reflect the same. Has the doctor been consulted? Are her fears warranted? Keep me informed on this matter, Jacob. Would that she could come to me, but this is not at all prudent considering her condition. I pray that all my brethren act as her protection, counsel, and support in my absence.

Save you and Kitt, my brethren fail to write. One has a greater need of brotherly affection when so distant from kind and familiar surroundings. Tell my delinquent brothers that I long to be assured of their love and prayers. All family and community news is of enormous interest to me, no matter how trivial it may seem to you who live it day to day.

My love to Sister Peggy, the brethren and their wives, and, of course, Mother. I am always your devoted and affectionate brother,

    Nathanael

The howling northeast wind dashed against the windows of the bedchamber, carrying with it snow so thick that Caty could barely see the darkness of the night sky. Such a February storm put her on edge, bringing back frightful memories of her childhood on nearby Block Island. She had not only feared being forever cut off from the mainland by such storms; but as a child, she envisioned herself being blown into the sea by the violent winds. Caty stared at the mass of white flakes being hurled against the windows. The panes of glass rattled against the wind's fury.

"I hate winter," she muttered with a sigh, placing her hand on her extended abdomen as the baby within kicked. "Do not worry, this storm will pass." Though she intended to comfort her unborn child, she found some comfort herself in hearing the words spoken aloud.

Between the noise of the wind and the discomfort of her advanced pregnancy, Caty knew sleep would not come. She tossed back the blankets, and climbed out of bed with great effort, grabbing hold of the extra quilt that lay draped over the footboard.

The warmth of the hearth was inviting, and the brightness of its flames offered an escape from the disturbing uneasiness she had felt in the darkened corner where her bed lay. Caty threw the quilt about her small shoulders and settled into the winged-backed chair, which sat in front of the fire.

Slowly she rubbed her fingers over the smooth ivory silk fabric on the arms of Nathanael's reading chair. A smile came to her lips as she pictured in her mind the form of her husband sitting by the fire. He loved to read. He had a sizable collection of some two hundred books. Each one was carefully chosen. Most were purchased at a considerable expense. Some were quite rare.

He began purchasing them as a boy, earning extra money by fashioning, in his spare time, miniature anchors and doll furnishings at the forge. The front room downstairs was designated the library, where the treasured collection was carefully stored.

It was his habit to read until midnight, an enjoyable discipline he had maintained for many years. "It relaxes my mind," he frequently told her. Even in the army he continued this habit whenever possible, often requesting that she send him specific books.

Caty considered the books he found relaxing. There was always the Scripture, or commentaries on it. There were the Shakespearean plays, or the Latin classics. Very often, his choice of "relaxing" reading material was one of his many historic accounts of military campaigns, or even a text on geometry.

"How strange," she whispered. For his interest in this material, that proved so useful to him now, was sought out well before he had any military aspirations.

His favorite novel was *Tristram Shandy*. Caty laughed aloud as she recalled how Nathanael would imitate the character Dr. Slop. With dramatic zeal, he would drag his leg across the floor, quoting line after line to the delight of his family and friends.

She missed him terribly. He had promised to petition General Washington for leave to be with her for the baby's birth. Caty sensed the disappointment in his last letter when he informed her that His Excellency denied him leave, though he did not give any reason for his denial. Caty could not help but be upset with General Washington, and determined that she would tell him so when they next met.

Caty looked about the semi-darkened room. When she had first seen the house as Nathanael's future bride, she was disappointed to find his taste to be thoroughly Quaker. The simple furnishings and bare white walls revealed the austere style of decorating to which he was accustomed.

The house presented itself as a challenge, both inside and out. First, she determined to bring some color and warmth to the cold decor. This was easily accomplished.

Outside she would try her hand at gardening—flowers, shrubs, even herbs—she imagined in her excitement. Though the effort was made—with great encouragement from Nathanael, it was to little avail. The sandy soil on this hill along Pawtuxet River would not support such beauty.

"Or is it the soil?" Caty wondered as she often did. The constant noise from the iron works—the deafening hammer; the shuffling of the many water wheels; and the sucking and blowing of the bellows would hinder anything so delicate from growing within range of its maddening din. Even the birds forsook the area, though had they dared remain she would never hear their sweet songs above the clamor.

Nathanael had built the house with Jacob's assistance, dubbing it "Spell Hall." He was proud of it, for it was a labor of love—a home for the family he longed to have.

Nathanael and Caty had dreamed of the peaceful years that they would spend at Spell Hall—years of contentment in one another's company. It was so for a full ten months.

Tears began to pool in her violet eyes as she considered just how short their time together had been. She had now lived in this house—Nathanael's house—without him, longer then she had with him.

"No, not again!" she cried aloud, fighting back the gut wrenching sobs which seized her night after night.

Quickly she opened the drawer of the small oval table, which sat next to Nathanael's chair. In this drawer were stored all the letters Nathanael had written her since his departure almost two years ago. Caty laid the pile in her lap and untied the ribbon, which held them together. She picked up the one on top, his most recent letter, and opened it. The words were so familiar; she had read them countless times. To hold the letter in her hands, to let her eyes pore over his attractive handwriting somehow made her feel closer to him.

He was safe, comfortably quartered for the remainder of the winter in the home of Lord Stirling and his wife. Of course, his military family was with him. His aide-de-camp and close friend, Thomas Paine, would soon be leaving the family to accept a writing position in Philadelphia. The main army was encamped only a few miles north in the village of Morristown.

General Washington himself had been ill—frightfully so. His health was now restored, and his lady in camp with him.

Henry Knox had been sent to Massachusetts to find a proper site to locate an arsenal. Lucy, too, was expecting a baby, and Henry would most likely stay close to home until after the event.

Nathanael told her of Lord Stirling's mansion with its spacious rooms and fancy gardens, and of Lady Stirling and their daughter, Kitty. Both were well educated and highly polished.

All the women and Nathanael's military family as well, sent their regards and urged her to hurry to them as soon after the birth of the baby as possible.

Caty placed the letter on the table and picked up the next one. Here he related a detailed account of the battle of Princeton. The first portion of the letter had so thrilled her when she initially read it. By the time she had finished its contents, she felt Nathanael's pain in grieving the death of the gallant Hugh Mercer.

It was in this letter that he had offered hope of obtaining leave to return to her for a short while. Caty placed this letter with the other.

She opened the third. After reading the first paragraph, she clearly recalled the contents, which followed. Clumsily folding the letter again, her hands shaking, she tossed it onto the table.

Caty stared at the paper; nervously wringing her hands together as the crease partially unfolded and revealed Nathanael's words.

"Oh, God!" she mumbled, turning her face away. She had not realized until tonight, how troubled she was by this particular letter.

In it, Nathanael had related to her the barbarous treatment of the country folk in New Jersey by the British and Hessians. Houses were pillaged for food and supplies, leaving families without the bare necessities. The enemy, often in plain view of their bound husbands and fathers, ravished woman, old and young—even girls.

Caty suddenly broke out in a cold sweat; her body trembled beneath the quilt. "Rhode Island is occupied by the enemy now!" she cried, her words were choppy as the sobs began. "They know I am here—the wife of a major general, barely more than a stone's throw away. And where is my husband? Safely resting in the luxury of Lord Stirling's home. I am here with no one but Quakers to protect me! What protection will Quakers be if the British come for me and my babies—God help us!"

As the winter night continued to threaten the house with its howling winds and thrashing snow, the dancing flames threw eerie shadows upon the wall of the gloomy bedchamber. Caty buried her face in her hands and sobbed uncontrollably.

"My heart mourns the absence of its counterpart."
(Nathanael Greene to Caty Greene)

CHAPTER SIX

"I DROPPED A stitch." Martha Washington muttered, holding up the woolen fabric bunched between her knitting needles.

"I is sorry ta hear it, ma'am, but I knows you can fix it," the young black servant woman who accompanied Lady Washington from Mount Vernon said with a wide smile. She carefully placed the tray she carried on the small serving table located in front of the settee, then turned to her mistress.

"It a fine shade o' blue, ma'am. Any lil boy dressed in dat sweata shuwa ta be a dappa sight."

"It is quite a mess at this point, Sally." Martha was disgusted with the many mistakes she found as she examined the partially knit sweater. Looking up she smiled at Sally. "But by the time little George Washington Greene arrives, it will be a handsome sweater indeed."

"Have you finished da blanket, ma'am?"

Martha grabbed the heap of white fabric, which spilled out of the basket at her feet. She stood up and stretched the small blanket against her flowing skirt. "What do you think?"

"It lovely, ma'am. Jus' lovely." Sally lifted a corner of the blanket and brushed the soft fabric against her cheek.

"Just what I wanted to hear," Martha Washington said with a laugh. "And I cannot wait to wrap that baby in it. See that it is washed, Sally." She handed the blanket to the servant and sat down, picking the sweater up.

"Genal Greene shuwa is proud o dat lil gal o' his," Sally chuckled as she folded the blanket.

"He certainly is," Martha agreed with a smile. She recalled her husband's account of the birth announcement. Poor Nathanael, knowing that the baby's birth must have occurred, anxiously awaited the news from home. It was during an unusually long, dull report of the Quartermaster's Department that General Spencer's courier arrived from Rhode Island.

General Washington thumbed through the sealed dispatches the courier handed him, searching for Spencer or Arnold's correspondence. Paying no heed to the rest, he tossed them on the table.

As he opened Spencer's dispatch, he glanced at Nathanael, who was honored with the seat to the right of the Commander. Nathanael, always attentively taking notes during the dry report of the Quartermaster General, had his eyes fixed on the tossed pile of mail.

General Washington looked down at the table to see what held the younger man's attention. As he did, Nathanael's gaze turned back to the speaker. Within the tossed heap of mail, George Washington spotted a letter addressed *General N. Greene*.

The meeting wore on, but Nathanael's thoughts were elsewhere. The Commander in Chief watched with sympathetic amusement as the young general's eyes were drawn back to the letter repeatedly.

"Any questions or comments, gentlemen?" Quartermaster General Thomas Mifflin asked. He looked from one general to the next, finally settling his expectant gaze on Nathanael.

The focus of every man in the room turned on him, for he always had a list of questions or comments, which were certain to lead to a somewhat, heated discussion.

Nathanael appeared confused by the sudden attention. He shook his head at General Mifflin. The others raised a few questions; a few comments made. In what seemed an eternity to Nathanael Greene, General Washington felt sure, the meeting was finally adjourned.

"There is a letter in Spencer's dispatch addressed to you," General Washington said with a warm smile. He picked up the letter he spoke of, and handed it to the younger man. Then, leaning back in the chair, he waited.

Nathanael eagerly accepted the letter, but hesitated to open it.

"Go on, General. I am almost as anxious as you." George Washington exclaimed.

Nathanael immediately set to scratching the seal. "It is from my brother Kitt," he informed General Washington as he quickly read his brother's greeting. He scanned over the words of the letter, breathing an audible sigh of relief. "Caty's fine—thank God—"

"And the baby?" George Washington's concern came through.

"The baby is healthy—" Nathanael related as he continued to read. He looked up at General Washington; a beaming smile suddenly came to his face. "It is a girl—" he announced in awe. "A daughter—I grew up in a houseful of brothers. I never figured I would have anything but a houseful of sons—A little girl!" He let out a joyous laugh, which was joined in by George Washington and his fellow officers who had gathered about to hear the happy news.

Martha's smile widened as she tried to envision the baby Kitt Greene had described—her little namesake, Martha Washington Greene—with eyes and hair as black as her mama's, and a feisty spirit as well; yet so tiny as to almost fit completely on the palm of Kitt's hand.

"Da tea's hot, Miz Washinton," Sally announced, disrupting Martha's thoughts. "Shell I pour you a cup, ma'm?"

"No, I will wait for General Washington and General Greene."

"Da tea may be cold for dey come outa dat room, ma'm," Sally pointed out, staring across the parlor to the closed door on the opposite side of the hall.

"How long have they been in there?"

"Dey went in right afta dinna. Dat was near two hou's ago."

"Umm—" Martha was thoughtful as she studied the closed door. "A short break for tea should be welcomed by now. Go tell the General that I request their company."

"Yas'm." She walked across the hall and knocked on the door. After relaying the message, Sally returned to the parlor and poured the steaming brew into the three awaiting cups.

The office door promptly opened. Martha placed her knitting in the basket at her feet. The men continued their conversation as they entered the room and sat down. Sally handed each of them a cup and saucer and quietly left the room, the baby blanket draped over her arm.

"Do we have a crisis on our hands, gentlemen?" Martha asked. Slowly she sipped her tea, peering at her husband over the tilted cup.

"The fact that more than half the army is sick as a result of the pox inoculation might be considered a crisis—at least it will be if the British get wind of it." George Washington replied, curious about his wife's question. She was well aware of the threatened smallpox epidemic.

"I thought that particular situation was under control," she replied.

He only grunted.

"I was beginning to wonder if perhaps an attack was imminent the way you two coop yourselves up in that room as often as you do," she commented.

"Have we neglected you, Patsy?" George Washington smiled, then, turning to Nathanael, he added. "We have behaved rudely, General Greene."

"Pay no attention to him, General Greene. I am simply curious as to what you discuss for so long. All day I hear about the problems facing the army, and complaints about Congress. But I suspect these private conversations have little to do with either."

"Our conversations would only prove to bore you, my dear."

"Perhaps you should let me be the judge, your Excellency."

George Washington laughed, but Nathanael only smiled, and a very weak smile at that, Martha noted. She recalled how quiet he had been during dinner.

"General Greene gave me some excellent advice in improving our small forge at Mount Vernon. I will promptly send the information on to my cousin. The improvements should be in effect before you return home.

"Patsy, were you aware that the Greene forge works one hundred men? Would that our friend here could persuade his Quaker brothers to turn out cannon."

"You discussed this for two hours?" Martha asked.

"No. That discussion led to the topic of slave labor, which General Greene holds a strong Quaker position on." George Washington smiled at the younger man who appeared rather sheepish now, though he had spoken quite fervently on the subject earlier. "We also had a lengthy discussion on Freemasonry. Nathanael was raised in a military lodge, and therefore did not have much opportunity for instruction."

"And you are seeing to that yourself?" Martha asked.

He smiled and nodded.

"Good," she said, knowing her husband would take pleasure in taking on that responsibility.

"As I said, Patsy, you would be quite bored."

"Excuse me, your Excellency," Colonel Hamilton stood at the entrance to the parlor. "Dr. Shippen has arrived."

"This will take but a minute, my dear. Entertain our Quaker preacher until I return," he said, patting Nathanael on the shoulder as he passed by.

"Dr. Shippen at this hour?" Martha asked, guessing by Nathanael's nonchalant manner that he knew why the doctor had come.

"A scolding, I am afraid," he said with a weak smile. "Dr. Shippen has not given a frequent update on the condition of those taken ill, as was requested."

"I am certainly glad I was inoculated last year. I sympathize with the men who are suffering through it now. When was it that you were inoculated, General?" she asked, knowing that he must have been or he would now be in his sickbed with the others.

"A number of years ago. I went to New York on family business only to find the town threatened by an epidemic. It didn't require much persuasion to get me to take it."

"Then you came through it with no problems?" Martha asked.

"With relative ease, except for a scar on my eye."

"Really? I have never noticed." Martha strained to see the scar he spoke of from across the room. "Does it bother you?"

"Occasionally."

Martha nodded in reply.

"Are the men still angry with the General for ordering the inoculation?" she asked.

"A few will always stir up dissension. It is the nature of man," Nathanael's casual reply came.

Martha took a sip of tea. Nathanael did the same.

"I thoroughly enjoyed last night's dinner at Lord Stirling's. His lady is a gracious hostess. She said that they're delighted with your company."

"She has taken pity on me as you have, dear lady," was his forlorn response.

Martha smiled at him. "It will not be long before Caty's brilliant smile is enlivening this camp. And little George will bring hours of pleasure. And, of course, I expect to spend many hours rocking that new baby. There's a rocking chair upstairs which I will have brought down and placed right there." She pointed to a spot near the hearth. "Lady Stirling has a cradle and rocker which she intends to make available. Did she tell you?"

Nathanael nodded. He reached out and placed his cup and saucer on the serving tray. Resting his elbows on his knees, his eyes became fixed on the colorful Persian rug beneath his feet.

"What's wrong, General Greene?"

He did not respond right away. Martha waited patiently.

"It has been more than two months since the baby was born. The last I heard from Caty, she was planning to make the trip very soon. That was over a month ago. I have heard nothing since."

"Have your brothers said anything of her plans?"

"I have not heard from my brothers either."

"Then the British must be intercepting the mail that is moving out of Rhode Island."

Nathanael shook his head. "A dispatch came from Rhode Island today. There is no report of any trouble with the mail. They are simply not writing. I have sent letter after letter. I kindly requested a response at first, then I began scolding, then demanding, now I am pleading, and still no one answers."

Martha was at a loss for words. Nathanael looked up and met her concerned gaze. His face was tense.

"I did not want to trouble you before—I know how attached you have become to

Caty."

"Trouble me with what?"

"My family was greatly concerned about Caty's emotional state before the baby was born. She had slipped into a severe depression. It got so bad; she was unable to care for little George. My brother Jacob convinced her to stay with my stepmother in Potowomut."

"Is she still there?"

"Last I heard she was. And she seemed to be doing fine. But now—I am afraid that something is wrong, and the fact that my brothers are not responding to my letters leads me to think that the situation is very bad—he may be depressed again, or perhaps she has taken ill, or something has happened to one of the babies—"

"I do not see why General Spencer cannot send someone to your stepmother's and get a full account of the situation."

At the mention of Spencer's name, Nathanael's countenance changed. His eyes jerked from Martha's as he threw himself back in the chair.

"Spencer—" he contemptuously mumbled the name under his breath.

Martha remained silent, her gaze still on him.

"If only I were where Spencer is—" he said almost in a whisper. "If only I—" He stopped in mid-sentence, his averted eyes returned to hers momentarily, then dropped down once again.

"If only you had command in Rhode Island rather than General Spencer," Martha finished his sentence.

His eyes shot up, revealing his shame. "Forgive me, Lady Washington. I should not question His Excellency's orders."

"You wonder why I am keeping you from that command, General Greene?" George Washington's question came from the entrance of the parlor.

Nathanael straightened up in the chair. He had no idea how much of the conversation General Washington had overheard, but knew that Martha Washington had a clear view of the doorway the entire time.

George Washington walked across the room; and, sitting opposite Nathanael, he positioned his elbows comfortably on the arms of the chair. The palms of his hands were pressed together, his fingers gently resting against his lips. "Well, General?"

"—Yes, sir, I do wonder. And though I have tried to question you on it, I have not received an answer."

Silently George Washington studied his subordinate officer. He moved his hands away from his lips. "Yes, you have attempted to question me on it. And no, I did not respond."

"And will you now, sir?" Nathanael asked respectfully though with a keen sense of determination.

"Yes, General Greene, I will," he began. There was a noticeable glimmer in his gray eyes. "Do you recall when I was sick? The night I summoned all the general officers to my bedside?"

"Yes, sir, I do."

"My condition was guarded. I knew there was concern that I might not recover. I brought you together to offer encouragement should it be so." General Washington turned to his wife, who had not arrived at camp until after this ordeal, and smiled reassuringly. "I realize my perception of what occurred may have been altered by the fever," he continued, looking back at Nathanael. "But as I recall, I was asked who the Command should fall to if I were to die. Is that so?"

"Yes, sir. That question was asked."

"Oh, my!" Martha gasped.

"It was a question that needed to be asked," George Washington said to his wife though his gaze remained on Nathanael. "And I gave my answer, General?"

"I am not sure, sir," Nathanael replied awkwardly.

George Washington smiled at him affectionately.

"What was your answer?" Martha asked, confused by Nathanael's reaction and her husband's smile.

George Washington looked at Martha. "I was unable to speak, my throat being greatly inflamed. So in response to the question I looked from man to man—" he hesitated and turned his gaze back to Nathanael. "—When my eyes fell on General Greene I nodded—"

George Washington shared a quick smile with his wife. Then turning to Nathanael, he said. "There is a fair amount of jealousy among my generals. Some believe you are my favorite, and so you are, but my decision to pass the Command to you, should it be necessary, is based on more than mere affection.

"Your ability as a strategist and tactician, as well as your proven command of the men, has earned you the title of commander in chief should I be killed or taken captive. You are the most able of my generals. I have made this fact known to Congress, requesting you be commissioned Lieutenant-General."

"How wonderful!" Martha exclaimed.

George Washington grunted. "But it is just like Congress to refuse me. They insist that they cannot make a rank higher than major general, other than my own. It does not matter. I know, you know and they know that you are, in fact, second in command.

"If I were to send you anywhere right now, it would be to take command in

Canada. Spencer can handle the situation in Rhode Island. It is no more than a nuisance at this point. I understand your desire to be there, but—I have few I can confide in, Nathanael. Your loyalty is untarnished. Your honesty is greatly appreciated." He turned to Martha and then right back to Nathanael. "I simply need you here with me," he said apologetically.

"—I do not know what to say, your Excellency," Nathanael's mixed emotions had him confused; though honored at being so esteemed in his commander's sight, his sense of dread over Caty's health remained. "I shall endeavor, by the grace of God, to never give cause for your confidence in my ability to wane. Thank you, your Excellency."

"A letter from your family will arrive with General Spencer's next dispatch. I will make certain that Spencer understands it is to be given highest priority."

"Thank you, sir."

"If you are in Philadelphia when it arrives, I will have an express rider deliver it to you immediately."

"Sir?"

"I cannot make the scheduled sessions of Congress with this smallpox crisis on my hands. You'll go in my stead." General Washington turned to Martha. "I am sorry, Patsy, I know you were looking forward to the trip."

Nathanael shifted position in his seat, uncomfortable with General Washington's announcement.

"Is something wrong, General Greene?" the Commander asked with an amused twinkle to his eyes.

"I—Congress—" He stumbled over his words, keenly aware that the Commander had just praised him for his devotion and loyalty. "Sir, General Sullivan would probably do a much better job of presenting our position before Congress. He sat in that distinguished body, as you did—"

"I want you to go," General Washington interrupted, smiling at Nathanael's obvious discomfort. "You will not compromise our situation, General Greene. You are exactly the man I want in my stead."

Days filled with tiresome jabbering and evenings with senseless pomp were driving Nathanael to distraction. He was a man of quick and usually sound decision, and the constant indecisiveness of Congress proved unnerving. In his estimation, the only commendable thing they had done of late was to pass a resolution to set up monuments to the memory of America's three fallen generals: Joseph

Warren, Hugh Mercer, and the hero of the Quebec expedition, Richard Montgomery.

Nathanael Greene was reared in simplicity; and, though he had experienced a sense of enjoyment in lively social settings in the years just prior to the war, he now found himself appalled by such wastefulness in the midst of his country's suffering and despair. He wanted nothing more than to excuse himself from this dinner party, supposedly in his honor, and retire to the solitude of his room. *Perhaps*, he thought, *the only good that will come from this trip is the new uniform presented me.*

"Are you enjoying yourself, General Greene?" the short, plump, round-faced John Adams asked after Nathanael excused himself from one conversation and attempted to avoid another.

"Actually, Mr. Adams, no, I am not."

John Adams laughed. "I appreciate your honesty, sir. What I would give to walk away from all of this and go home to my family in Massachusetts.

"If you want to escape, I will be happy to make your apologies to our host. Mr. Hancock and I go back many, many years. Believe me, neither his wealth nor his title intimidate me. When I look at that man, I see nothing but the bare-legged, dirty-faced lad that I once climbed trees with."

Nathanael's appreciation was in his smile. "No, Mr. Adams, I will endure rather than risk offending our gracious host, though I do thank you from the bottom of my heart."

"Excuse me, General."

Nathanael turned. Before him stood a young captain, smartly saluting. He returned the salute.

"An express from Headquarters, sir. Shall I await your reply?"

Nathanael took the mail—a letter from Caty and one from General Washington. "Yes, Captain." He turned back to John Adams. "Will you excuse me, Mr. Adams?" Without waiting for a reply, he hurried toward the stairs of the Hancock mansion. Closing the door to the guest chamber, Nathanael anxiously tore the seal off Caty's letter.

Potowomut, Rhode Island
May 15, 1777

My Dearest Nathanael,

How can I fully relate to you my great distress upon discovering that no response has ben maid to your frekwent inkwiries in the past munth. Each one of your brothers, it seems, xpected that the other was to take it upon himself to repli. Nun, I fear, did.

I shall make no excuses for them, and I pity their position when your rath is pored out for their neglijence!

My reson for not making a repli will, I trust, free me from your ill-favor. Being in a weakened condision, I managed to develop newmonia. For the past munth, I have ben put threw countless treatments. I begged the doctor to hasten my recovery that I mite be with you. I have discovered that one does not recover from newmonia in hast, much like your xperience with the pewtrid fever, I suspect.

But, at last, my stregth is returning. You said that because of my late arrival at camp I might onle arrive to see you leave. I am willing to risk this. I shall plan to leave here by the first of June, if you will be kind enuf to send an aide to accompane me. Plese tell me it is agreeable to you, for I do not know if I can bear any other response.

The children are well. His little Excellency is not at all sure what to make of his sister competing for Mama's attension. And our little Martha is simply beutiful. Your famile, all but dear Kitt, claim she is an xact replaca of her papa. You may judge for yourself when you meet her. I think there may be some prejudis on their part.

I am forsed to close here, for General Spencer's aide is paciently waiting. My regards to all your military famile and my friends in camp. I shall eagerly await your favorable respons by the hand of your aide. I shall count the hours, and am most affectionately and completely yours,

Caty

"Pneumonia!" He uttered the word though the shock of it was not fully comprehended. "Oh, thank Thee Father for Thy healing touch," he whispered his simple prayer, and then looked at the letter again, smiling affectionately at Caty's atrocious spelling.

His hands visibly trembled as he folded the letter and placed it inside his pocket. The weeks of pent up worry and frustration threatened to explode in a show of joyful tears. Forcing his attention to General Washington's letter, he began to read it as a knock sounded on the chamber door.

"Is everything all right?" John Adams asked as soon as the door was opened. "I was concerned that the express from Morristown might be of military importance."

"News from home, sir."

"Good news, I hope."

"Wonderful news, Mr. Adams. My family is in good health—safe and happy."

"I am glad to hear it, sir," John Adams said, smiling in response to Nathanael's bright countenance. "And General Washington's dispatch?"

"It seems to be only personal instructions," Nathanael said as he scanned the letter. "It does not even require a reply."

"I see. Good news all around then. Come, perhaps you feel like celebrating now."

"Indeed I do, sir."

The constant pounding of the horses' hooves blended rhythmically with the clatter of the heavy wheels upon the hard-packed earth, as the seemingly endless miles continued to pass beneath the coach. Jostled with every bump, the four passengers within endured the final day of their journey in relative silence. The stifling heat had taken its toll. The hot, dusty air, which streamed in through the small windows, offered no relief.

Caty watched the wooded scenery, dotted occasionally by a country farmhouse, whisk by. She wondered how much farther it could possibly be to the village known as Morristown.

Baby Martha stirred in her bassinet, safely positioned on the floor of the coach. The bobbing of her tiny head, covered in a white-laced bonnet followed a soft whimper.

Caty glanced at the indentured servant girl who had accompanied her for the express purpose of helping with the babies. To her dismay, the girl was sound asleep.

"Oh, please go back to sleep." Caty' whispered to the baby. Her own head was beginning to ache and the continuous jarring of the coach only assisted in her discomfort.

With a deep sigh, Caty finally decided she would have to pick up the squirming infant. Just as she leaned forward and reached out for Martha, an air bubble escaped the baby's stomach. Her wobbly head plopped down, and the rocking motion of the coach quickly lulled her back to sleep.

George sat across from his mother, smiling at his little sister's belch. The small boy turned his smiling face upward to his mother. He was the very image of his father with his bright blue eyes and golden curls. Even his mannerisms were the same, a fact that never failed to amaze Caty. That same brilliant smile of Nathanael's that always proved to lift her spirits was now shining from the face of her young son.

George's attention was quickly drawn back to the small wooden horses his Uncle Perry had presented to him just prior to the trip. *That was only four days ago. It seems much longer,* Caty thought as she leaned her head back on the cushioned seat and began fanning herself with the delicate silk fan that lay on her lap.

Nathanael's family had thought it too soon after her recovery to undertake such a trip, especially with two small children in tow. Caty had come to realize they were right.

The discomfort of the rattling coach and suffocating heat was sufficient to bring about exhaustion. Perhaps alone she could have compensated with a good night's sleep and a more relaxed attitude throughout. However, the children slept a good deal during the endless hours in the coach—though never at the same time. When lodging was taken for the night, they were wide-awake. Even with the girl's help, a good night's sleep, crowded as they were in the small stuffy tavern bedchamber, with only one bed to share, was impossible.

The shopping spree just prior to this trip certainly should not have been undertaken, she reluctantly conceded. Nathanael's brother Perry had patiently endured the hours of Caty trying on gowns, deciding on fabrics and colors and picking out accessories. Then she repeated the entire process in the purchase of a complete wardrobe for each child.

Prior to the trip, it seemed important that her attire should be the most fashionable and becoming. After all, she convinced herself, her wardrobe needed to be updated. Her illness had reduced her weight, and her old gowns hung upon her diminished form like tents. "And then there is my competition—" she whispered, slowly rolling her head upon the back of the seat to face the window. Lady Stirling and her lovely daughter Kitty had become a major source of irritation in Caty's life. Nathanael never failed to mention their graceful carriage, polished manners, elegant dress or fine education. Caty felt her blood begin to boil as she remembered the letters. Nathanael had changed. It was a slow, subtle change that somehow had caught Caty off-guard.

His position and title brought with them honor and respect. His lack of formal education, always a disgrace to him, was compensated by a disciplined mind, which forced itself to learn that which was necessary to superbly carry on his responsibilities as a major general of the Continental Army.

He was constantly communicating the needs of the army with Congress, various governors and private citizens of distinguished positions. Such communications not only demanded his reasoning be clearly thought out and intelligently presented; but they also developed in him an even greater admiration for those well educated.

Caty was not.

Though he met and intermingled with men of the world—and their accomplished ladies—she, in her every day existence seemed still to be merely the wife of an absent Quaker ironmaster. Supported by the work of the forge, surrounded by

Quakers, tending to the needs of two babies day in and day out, Caty lived in a world that virtually remained the same as Nathanael's constantly expanded.

Even Lucy Knox's better breeding had been clearly pointed out to her in one of Nathanael's recent letters. Caty fumed within as she recalled his remarks about her poor spelling, and how she must try to correct this bad habit when writing to Lucy. Her spelling had never bothered him before. In fact, he had once told her, as he tenderly embraced her in his arms, that her need for his assistance in this matter endeared her to him even more. "That was before Lady Stirling and her smugness, Lady Kitty, appeared," Caty muttered grudgingly.

At least she would not be forced to face them in her present, untidy condition. Nathanael's aide had informed her that his headquarters had recently been moved to the home of a family named Lott. Now she would have time to rest and prepare herself before meeting the Ladies Stirling.

The ache in Caty's head intensified due to the stressful condition her present thoughts induced. She suddenly became dizzy and closed her eyes in an attempt to relieve it. The new clothing meant little now.

"Covered with dust," Caty whispered, remembering with annoyance last night's discovery of the fine powder, which had worked its way into the trunk. "And Nathanael may grumble when the bill catches up to him," she complained. Suddenly her face brightened. "I will just point out that an accomplished lady must have an elegant wardrobe. The Stirlings are no real threat. Once I am there, he will soon forget this foolish infatuation. It cannot be too difficult to learn to spell correctly—"

Nathanael cocked his head toward the open window of his office. "Do you hear that?" he asked his staff officers.

"Hear what, sir?" his secretary asked.

"There's a coach approaching!" he exclaimed, jumping from his chair and bounding toward the door. The men looked at one another, wondering how he could possibly detect the sound of a coach amongst the traffic and noise outside.

Nathanael stepped hatless into the street, squinting against the sun's glare. The dark-green coach, drawn by a team of four, approached the house, pulling to a gentle halt directly in front of him. Nathanael returned a quick salute to his aide, Billy Blodget, who had safely transported his family from Rhode Island. As he reached to open the coach door, Nathanael was relieved to see that the family crest had been removed as he had instructed. The British would take great pleasure in claiming as their prisoners the family of a "rebel" general; therefore, it was best that their identity not be flaunted.

Caty placed her hand in his and had only time enough to gasp as he gently, though determinedly lifted her from the coach and into his strong arms. He chanced no awkward reunion by fumbling for the first words after a year's separation, but intended to immediately assure her of his love and desire with a long, passionate kiss.

"Nathanael!" she exclaimed breathlessly when he finally loosened his hold. "The entire camp must surely be watching."

He laughed at her embarrassment, having never witnessed it before. "My men are well-disciplined, Angel. See for yourself," he said turning his head from one side to the other. "They have duties to attend and not a free moment to gawk at their general welcoming his beautiful wife to camp."

Nathanael studied Caty's frail appearance while she looked about. She felt like mere skin and bones within his arms. "Has the trip been difficult?" he asked. His concern for her health was reflected in his eyes.

"I will be fine, now that I am here," Caty assured him with an affectionate smile.

"Mama—" Little George stood at the open door.

Nathanael's arms dropped from Caty's waist. He stared at the small boy in disbelief. "—It cannot be—" He was astonished. Though he expected his son to have changed, his last memory of George as a helpless infant somehow hindered his mind from preparing itself for the reality of it all. The small, bright eyes studied the strange man before them. George looked toward his mother for reassurance.

"This is your papa, George," Caty said. Her words did not seem to appease George's apprehension.

"What's that thee have, George?" Nathanael asked his son, longing to whisk him into his arms.

"Horsy," George replied, holding it out to his father. As soon as Nathanael took it, the toddler disappeared and quickly returned with the other one. "Horsy!" he exclaimed with a dimpled grin.

"Two of them? My! Can I see that one, too?" Nathanael asked.

George nodded and held it out to his father. Nathanael handed Caty the first horse and reached for the boy, lifting him into his arms. The boy's small arms went around his father's neck in response to Nathanael's tender embrace.

"Baby," George said, twisting his body to face the coach. He pointed his chubby finger toward the bassinet. "Marfa."

Nathanael gazed affectionately at the sleeping form of his infant daughter, then back at George. "She sure is pretty."

"Ah, ha," the boy agreed.

"Are you hungry?" Nathanael asked his son.

George nodded, staring into his father's eyes. "Ah, ha."

"Papa will take you, Martha and Mama inside and we will get something to eat."

George nodded his approval.

Nathanael shared a smile with Caty as he placed the small boy down next to her. After acknowledging the servant girl's presence, he reached into the coach for the bassinet. Slowly he pulled it across the floor to the door and bent down to kiss the sleeping infant's cheek.

"Nathanael!" Caty's cry was barely audible.

He turned just as Caty's legs buckled, catching her in his arms.

"Billy!" he called. His aide quickly appeared from the backside of the coach. "Caty's ill! Help with the children!"

Nathanael pushed the partially open door with his foot. "Major Burnet!"

The aide appeared in the office doorway, his mouth gaping at the sight of Caty unconscious in the general's arms.

"Send for a physician!" Nathanael headed for the stairs. "Captain Mayhew!"

The secretary appeared and moved to the bottom of the staircase to receive his orders.

"Tell Lady Washington that Mrs. Greene is ill!"

Silently Caty watched from the bed as Martha Washington tied the pale-blue curtains back from the window. *How long have I been sleeping?* Caty wondered. *Apparently not too long, for the sun is still shining.*

Someone had not only changed her into a fresh nightgown and braided her hair, but sponged her down as well, for her skin felt clean against the soft cotton sheets.

"Do I have you to thank for taking such good care of me?" Caty asked.

Martha turned to face her. A bright smile came to her lips. "I insisted that General Greene bring you and the babies here." She walked to the bed and sat on it, facing Caty, and took the younger woman's thin hand into her own.

"Then you have seen the children? Oh, drat! I wanted to see your expression when you saw Martha." Caty was disappointed.

"I have been thoroughly enjoying her. Sally kept her last night. She sleeps sound for such a little one. I made a bed for George in our room—"

"Kept her last night?" Caty echoed. "Have I been here all night?"

"You quite exhausted yourself on this trip. The doctor said that you are to remain in bed for at least three days."

"Three days? I can hardly stay here for three days!" Caty protested though the thought of being mothered by Martha Washington was pleasant. "And whose room have I taken?" Caty knew that many members of the General's staff occupied every room at Headquarters, often.

"Colonel Tilghman and Colonel Hamilton were happy to make their room available to you."

"And where are they sleeping?"

"In with the secretaries."

"On the floor?"

"No. The secretaries are on the floor. The benefit of rank." Martha said with a grin.

"Poor Nathanael. He must be worried sick. Where is he?"

"Off attending to his many duties. He sat with you until late last night. We had to shoo him out to make certain he got some sleep. Then, there he was on the doorstep first thing this morning."

"Poor Nathanael. Perhaps I should rest at his quarters. Do you suppose Mrs. Lott would be willing to help tend the children? Or maybe we could even hire another girl—"

"You are much better off right here for now. The Lott home is quite overcrowded. As far as I know, General Greene is sharing his bedchamber with three of his staff. He tried to find larger quarters in Morristown, but there is simply nothing available," Martha explained.

"Why did he leave the Stirling's?"

"To be closer to Morristown."

"We have to squeeze into a room with his staff officers?" Caty asked.

"The hardships of war, child," Martha said with a comforting smile, patting her hand. "I guess he was willing to sacrifice any romantic notions just to have you close by. But now—" Martha paused, squeezing her hand gently, "—The British are preparing to move and General Greene is under orders to march his division southward."

"When?"

"They are expected to move out in two days."

"Two days?" Caty asked in disbelief. "I do not understand—how long had he known this?"

"Since the arrival of spring we have all expected a move. But he only received definite orders within the week."

"Then he intends to send me back to Rhode Island just like the last time I came?" Tears began to pool in Caty's eyes. "He must think a marriage can survive on such brief interludes once a year—" Caty forgot, in her despair, that Nathanael had warned her of such a possibility, and that it was Martha Washington's husband who gave Nathanael his orders.

"No, child, it is not like that at all." Martha said, wiping a tear from Caty's cheek with her hand. "He has been anticipating your arrival since the baby's birth. There has not been a more miserable or lonely man in the entire camp. And though it is time to resume the fighting, he wants you to remain with the Lotts in the hope that he can see you on occasion."

"I know nothing of the Lott family," Caty protested.

"They're a lovely family."

"Probably Quakers."

"No, child, they are not Quakers." A sympathetic smile accompanied Martha's words. "Roll over and let me rub your back."

Caty turned on her side. Martha's fingers began to firmly massage her aching muscles, sore from the long hours in the coach.

"Will you be leaving Morristown?" Caty asked.

"When General Washington is ready to move out, I will be headed for Philadelphia."

"I would rather go with you—"

Caty had no idea how much Martha longed for her and the children to do just that. However, it was not possible. "I will be heading for Mount Vernon from there. It is a long journey. Anyway, you need to go where your husband wants you. It will be a comfort to him just to know you are close by."

Caty remained silent while Martha finished rubbing her back.

"General Greene wanted me to send word just as soon as you woke up. I had better go see to it. I will get you some breakfast, too. You must be hungry." Martha pulled the sheet up over Caty's shoulder. "You just rest now."

She stood up and walked to the door. With her hand on the doorknob, Martha turned to face Caty's back. "General Washington is eager to visit with you. Shall I send him if he is available?"

"—No—" Caty's voice was trembling. "—Not just yet."

"I understand. I will be back shortly."

The door closed. Caty was alone with her anger, alone with her fear. *No!* she shouted in her mind. *I do not want to see General Washington. Isn't it he who had kept Nathanael from me? Isn't it he who is now sending him out of my reach once more? Yet* despite her anger toward George Washington, she knew she loved him, even as a father she loved him.

She rolled onto her back, fighting her tears. The frustration she felt over Nathanael's imminent departure was overwhelming. Two days and he would be gone. How long would it be until they would meet again? Six months? Another year? Or perhaps they never would meet again. There was always the agonizing reality that he would not return from battle.

"Nathanael." She spoke his name through her sobs. "I need you!" All she wanted was for him to take her back to Coventry—back to the simple life they had envisioned before the war. But that was the one thing he could not do. He could no longer meet her needs she decided. "I will take care of myself," she muttered defiantly through her tears. "I do not need him to be happy!"

"God grant us more wisdom and virtue or else I shall begin to despair our cause."
(Nathanael Greene)

CHAPTER SEVEN

THE HALF-STARVED men threw down their tools and gathered alongside the road, uncertain whether their eyes truly beheld the sight before them. Meals of late had consisted of little more than fire-cake and water. It offered little nutrition, less taste, and failed to relieve the constant gnawing in their bellies. Now, before them was fresh beef on the hoof. All at once, as the reality of the scene hit them, the men shouted in unison their jubilation.

"Atta-boy, General Wayne!" Someone cried out to the officer of the foraging party as he passed.

"Three cheers for General Wayne!" The huzzahs rang out as Anthony Wayne smiled and tipped his hat in response.

Nathanael and Henry Knox stepped out of a small cabin to determine the cause for the celebration. Neither one took time to grab a cape or hat to protect them from the winter air.

"Where in the world did you find them?" Nathanael called to Anthony Wayne who had already dismounted, and was headed in Nathanael's direction to make his report.

"Sixty miles west of here, sir." He said with a smart salute.

Nathanael watched the passing cattle in astonishment. "You purchased them with Continental notes?" As officer in charge of the foraging details, Nathanael was surprised that such a large purchase was made with the inflated currency.

"Not exactly."

"You stole them?" Henry asked.

"No—I compensated for them, so to speak."

Nathanael studied his subordinate for a moment. "From a Tory?"

Anthony reluctantly nodded his head. "I left him a promissory note, and assured him that Congress will be only too happy to make good on it," he said with a grin.

Nathanael looked at Henry. "Congress will not come to the aid of the army. Do you suppose they will help out our poor Tory friend?"

"Nothing would surprise me," Henry replied. Then turning back to Anthony, he slapped him on the back. "Aha! I cannot wait for that steak!"

"I came across the Emlens sisters on the way in." Anthony directed his words to Nathanael.

"Came across them?"

"They were walking down the road to bring bread, or some such thing, to an old widow nearby," he said. "They certainly are a pretty bunch." Anthony waited for a response from Nathanael. There was none. "I pride myself on being rather suave with the ladies, but those Quaker girls totally ignore my advances."

"What would a Quaker girl want with a soldier?" Henry asked with a chuckle.

"Oh, it has nothing to do with my military involvement. To the contrary, they are obviously quite smitten with our Quaker general here, and want only to speak of him."

"What are you talking about?" Nathanael chided.

"Our lovely Quaker neighbors are infatuated with you, General. Is it true you have paid visits to them?"

"I have spoken to their father on many occasions. He even invited me to dine with his family once or twice."

"Twice," Anthony quickly confirmed. "His daughters gave detailed accounts of your visits, even of how you spoke in their tongue. I tried that myself but they didn't seem at all impressed."

"Perhaps it didn't sound natural," Henry offered.

"Oh, it was natural enough; I have spent weeks at a time with Quaker cousins. I could not help but talk like them by the time I left."

"Then it is probably just Nat's New England charm. A Pennsylvania boy can hardly compete with that." Henry offered with a grin.

"You have no business flirting with them anyway," Nathanael said with a smile. "Why don't you direct that energy toward encouraging your wife to join you here instead?"

Anthony's expression became blank. He stared down the road toward the moving cattle. "—It is a lost cause—" he said. Then turning back to Nathanael, he added, "And it seems Mrs. Greene has become of the same mind set as my wife."

Nathanael was obviously taken aback by his statement.

"You'd better get back inside, gentlemen, before you catch your death. I need to go explain my means of purchase to His Excellency." Anthony said with an apologetic smile for Nathanael. After mounting his horse, he turned it about and rode off.

"Let's get this inspection over with." Nathanael muttered to Henry. In silence, they retrieved their winter wraps from the cabin and mounted their horses.

"This contest the General came up with for building the cabins was an ingenious idea," Henry began after riding for a few minutes in awkward silence. "The camp is certainly shaping up, and I am amazed the men are in such good spirits. I would not have thought it possible to lift their spirits coming into winter quarters with such want, especially after what Congress perceives as a disastrous summer campaign." Henry peeked at his optimistic friend out of the corner of his eye, expecting Nathanael to take the bait.

"It was not disastrous, Henry." Nathanael insisted. "True we were forced to retreat at both the Brandywine and Germantown, but we held our own."

"Except for my blunder at Germantown—" Henry interjected, recalling his insistence that the Continentals drive a small force of the British from a stone house they had occupied. The attempt proved unsuccessful—costing precious lives and vital time.

"Let it go, Henry. Let's learn from our mistakes and not repeat them."

Nathanael empathized with Henry's sorrow, remembering its overwhelming effect after his disastrous misjudgment at Fort Washington. "We did put up a good fight in both battles. And do not forget the victory at Fort Mercer!"

"Ah. Fort Mercer. A glorious victory, and, of course, a Greene was in command." Henry chuckled, sharing Nathanael's pride in his cousin, Colonel Christopher Greene's magnificent victory in defense of the fort.

"As for Congress, they want complete and utter victory in every battle, regardless of the odds or our continuous state of short supply," Nathanael began, obviously irritated. "Does it matter that at Germantown we were forced to fight in fog too thick to see thirty feet in front of us? And our reward? The threat of our command being usurped by foreigners proclaiming themselves to be mighty warriors; seducing the naive delegates that make up our Congress."

"Thank you for coming to my defense." Henry said, still deeply touched by the fact that both Nathanael and John Sullivan had submitted their own resignation to Congress, along with his, when the news arrived that a French army engineer named Philippe Tronson du Coudray had been commissioned major general and appointed commander of artillery.

Congress quickly reconsidered the appointment, but scolded the three American generals for questioning their authority with the threat of resignation.

Congress demanded a written apology from each one of them. No apology was ever submitted. Henry was aware that his friend's unyielding position in his defense, as well as the defense of his own seniority, had virtually destroyed the relationship Nathanael had developed, through years of correspondence, with John Adams. Mr. Adams had been the loudest voice in demanding the apologies.

"Henry, you thank me every time the subject comes up," Nathanael said with a smile. "It was an injustice, which I could not give my consent to by remaining passive."

"Spoken like a true Quaker." Henry chuckled. "Tell me the truth; did you think the marquis was a soldier of fortune as well?"

Nathanael looked at Henry and smiled. "Of course I did, and so did you." he said knowingly. "You should have seen the expression on His Excellency's face when the lad showed up at Headquarters with a Congressional commission of major general and the grand title of Marquis de Lafayette!"

"Marie Josph Paul Yves Roche Gilbert du Motier!" Henry recited the marquis' full name and laughed heartily. "Ah, but General Washington accepted him a lot quicker than we did."

"Do not be too sure. Why do you think His Excellency appointed him as a personal aide rather than giving him a command? He watched in silence while we challenged the lad's integrity and loyalty, not to mention his ability."

"I am still amazed that a nineteen-year-old, wealthy, French marquis would leave his country, indeed, sneak out of his country, leaving a wife and infant daughter, and come fight our battle."

"Liberty, my friend. A universal love, which our young marquis appreciates every bit as much as we."

"When did he finally win your confidence?" Henry asked.

Nathanael thought about the question for a moment then smiled. "The eve of the Battle of Brandywine. I had been in the saddle for thirty hours and without sleep for forty. The night before the battle my division was situated, my orders clear, and I finally had the opportunity to rest. As soon as I dropped on the bed, in a state of utter exhaustion, I discovered it was covered with dust."

"It would not have bothered me any being that tired." Henry interjected.

"You do not have asthma," Nathanael responded. "Though I moved as quickly and carefully as I could to get out of the bed and not stir up the dust, it was too late. I suffered one of the worst attacks I have ever had. In the midst of it, the marquis came by to deliver a dispatch from General Washington. Of course, my aides were there, assisting me as they could; but the marquis stayed for almost an hour, offering words of comfort and trying to help. Quite honestly, I did not hear anything the lad said, my aides told me later. All I could think about at the time was breathing." Nathanael paused.

"And then, when the lad took that bullet in his leg the next day and kept on fighting—Who could deny his loyalty or courage?"

"You did not sleep the night before the battle?" Henry asked.

"A couple of hours."

Henry looked at his friend in amazement. "You were brilliant during that battle. I still hear talk among the officers of how you led your men over four miles of rough terrain to come to Sullivan's aid with such speed. Some who marched it said it would be humanly impossible to do again. They do not honestly know how they did it the first time. You saved the army from a premature retreat, and possible disaster."

"By the grace of God, Henry," was Nathanael's humble response.

"I do not understand why His Excellency did not write up a commendation on your achievement that day," Henry said.

"He had his reasons, I suppose," was Nathanael's stiff reply.

They continued in silence for a few minutes.

"Caty and the marquis would get along splendidly, don't you think?" Nathanael suddenly asked. "She has been diligently studying French with Cornelia Lott for the past nine months."

"Yes, I ran into Colonel Cary the other day. He told me she speaks the language fluently."

Nathanael shot his head around at the mention of Cary's name. "What else did he tell you?" His voice was strained; his jaw set.

Henry shrugged. "What do you mean?"

"Did he tell you of the parties and dances he attended with my wife?"

Henry did not need Colonel Cary to inform him of Caty Greene's frolicking. Lucy brought news of it all the way from Boston; for Caty's unseemly behavior had become a topic of conversation.

Henry wanted to avoid the question. "He just mentioned that he saw her. What is wrong, Nat?"

"He came into Headquarters going on about what a wonderful dancing partner my wife is, how charming she is, how pleasant his hours with her were—I do not want to hear about how others are enjoying my wife's company when I have not seen her for nine months. No, I take that back. We had dinner together seven months ago," he said with a short, sarcastic laugh, as he recalled the brief visit he was able to make at the Lott home when he passed through Morristown with General Washington.

"Why isn't she coming to camp?"

"I do not know."

"What do you mean, you do not know?"

"She always seems to have an excuse why she cannot come just yet. The truth is, she does not want to come and I do not know why. I must have done something or wrote something in a letter—Lord knows we have had precious little time together in the past two years. Maybe she does not feel what she once did."

An awkward silence elapsed as Henry searched for words of encouragement.

"Why does not Anthony Wayne's wife come to camp?" Nathanael asked. Henry hesitated. "Come on, Henry. I know your wife well enough to know that she is up on the latest gossip and told you all about it."

"—It seems Wayne took her on a surveying expedition into Indian Territory for their honeymoon. Mrs. Wayne vowed after her return never to leave the safety of her home again."

"Is she aware of his attention to the ladies?"

"Those who are acquainted with her say she is. Word is that she is insanely jealous, but still too traumatized by that ordeal to venture out."

"Do they have children?"

"Two little ones."

"The poor woman," Nathanael said with a sigh.

"Why don't you plan to have dinner with Lucy and me. I do not know what it will be, but Lucy always manages to conjure up something. The marquis will be there."

"Your cabin will be too crowded with me there."

"Nonsense, we will squeeze in. It will make for a cozy evening." Henry offered with a smile for his friend.

Nathanael returned to his own quarters after making the inspection of the newly built cabins with Henry. He attended to some minor needs of his men, and prepared for the foraging party he would take out at dawn.

Then, sitting down with quill pen in hand, he set out to once again request that his wife join him. The letter began cheerfully as Nathanael masked his pain.

He stopped writing and carefully read the words on the paper. Then dipping the quill into the ink he continued, hesitantly at first, then with a sense of determination, telling her of the pretty Quaker girls who lived nearby, and expressing his concern that the extreme loneliness he was experiencing might put him in the way of temptation.

Purposely Nathanael left off his signature. Then dusting the letter he quickly sealed and addressed it, placing it on the pile of mail, which was to be delivered to the courier that evening. It would reach Caty within the week.

He stood up, draped his cape about his shoulders, picked up his hat and headed for the door. Opening it, he turned to look at the letter on the table. "I do not mean any of it," he whispered, his guilt pulling on him to tear the letter up and write another. He pushed the door open. "God forgive me," he said as he stepped through the small frame and walked into the darkness. The letter remained with the outgoing mail.

The coach slowed down as it pulled into the American encampment. As it descended from the higher elevation into the Pennsylvania valley, surrounded by a semicircle of high ridges, Caty had a breathtaking view of the Schuylkill River flowing through its midst. The beauty of nature was quickly forgotten however as scenes of human suffering were forced upon her. Caty noticed that only ragged blankets, as protection against the freezing temperatures, covered some of the soldiers standing guard duty. Their faces were emaciated and their appearance sickly.

The coach passed hundreds of newly erected log cabins, almost identical in size and construction; Caty viewed the men at work. Many had no coats, hats, shirts or even shoes. Their ragged clothes hung loosely upon their skeletal forms. Their feet, dried and cracked from exposure to the frozen ground, left bloody footprints in the snow.

They pulled to a halt before one of the cabins, which was a bit larger than those surrounding it were. Caty quickly pulled away from the coach window, apprehensive about her coming encounter with Nathanael. As the coach door was pulled open, she took a deep breath.

"Welcome to Valley Forge, Caty!" The familiar voice of her cousin, Sam Ward, greeted her. With a warm smile, he extended his hand to his cousin and helped her out.

"Sammy!" Caty exclaimed, throwing her arms around his neck for a more familiar greeting. Nathanael had joyously related Sam's recent release from a prisoner of war camp to Caty. After two years of imprisonment following the Battle of Quebec, Sam now took his place in Nathanael's military family as an aide-de-camp.

"Let me get a look at you, Caty. As beautiful as ever." he exclaimed, his hands resting on her arms. "Where are those babies? Nat is so proud of those babies!"

"I sent them back to Rhode Island. Nathanael painted a rather dismal picture of the camp. I have been torturing myself with feelings of guilt for having done it; but now, seeing that the conditions are worse than he described, I am glad I did— Oh, but Sammy! Look at you, thin and pale!" She cupped her hand against his cheek.

"The British have little regard for their prisoners."

"It must have been horrible!"

"It was. But it is behind me now. Come on; let us get you inside out of the cold."

"Where's Nathanael?" Caty asked apprehensively as they walked toward the cabin.

"Over at Headquarters. As soon as I saw the coach, I sent one of the men to inform him. If he can get away, he will be here momentarily." Sam pulled the cabin door open and motioned for Caty to step inside.

Slowly she scanned her new home. The cabin, little more than fourteen-by-sixteen feet, had a low, sloping roof and a dirt floor. A crudely built bed frame was on one side of the room, barely large enough for a man. A makeshift table and a few wobbly chairs sat on the opposite side. A small window allowed the weak rays of the sun to filter in revealing the smoke and dust emitted by the poorly vented fireplace.

"It is quite dreary," Caty remarked.

"Do not fret, Cousin. These are only temporary quarters. Now that the men are in their own cabins, the general officers will be able to move into more comfortable quarters themselves."

"Certainly His Excellency is not housed in one of these!" Caty exclaimed as she removed her winter wraps and draped them over a chair.

"Actually it was worse. He was quartered in his tent until recently. He refused to dwell in comfort while the men were still exposed to the elements, despite his general officers' disapproval. But now that Lady Washington has arrived he is quartered in a comfortable home not far from here."

A soldier carried Caty's trunk into the cabin and carefully set it on the dirt floor as they spoke.

"Sam, the men I saw coming into camp are hardly dressed for this cold weather! What's being done for them?"

"Everything that can be, which amounts to very little. The Quartermaster General has virtually deserted his post. Congress is in a total upheaval having been run out of Philadelphia by the British." Sam walked to the fireplace and threw a few logs into the flames. "We are only twenty miles from Philadelphia where the enemy rests in comfort, and we are faced with disease, starvation, and the constant threat of frostbite. The men you saw outside are well dressed compared to the ones you didn't see."

Caty looked at him questioningly.

"Those whose clothing are so threadbare as to expose their nakedness stay within the cabins. I understand Lady Washington and some of the other wives have been getting together to sew and knit what they can for the men. You can join them, Caty."

"Sam, you know I cannot sew or knit."

Sam was aware that their aunt put more stock in teaching Caty to be a proper hostess than a seamstress, but he assumed that the needs of her family would have compelled her to learn such domestic tasks. "Then, it seems to me, it is time you learned. The men need clothing. I am sure the ladies would be happy to teach you."

"Really, Sam! You expect me to ask Lady Washington to teach me to sew?" she asked with a forced giggle as she pulled a gown from the trunk. She shook the wrinkles from the fabric, and then searched the cabin for an appropriate place to hang it. "My gowns will reek of smoke in this cabin," she complained.

"I have heard that Lord Stirling's daughter is a fine seamstress. She is about your age. I am sure she'd be delighted to assist you."

"Of course she is a fine seamstress. Is there anything her ladyship cannot do?" Caty muttered sarcastically under her breath.

"What was that?"

"I would be embarrassed to ask Lady Kitty. I barely know the girl."

"Really? I assumed you would be well acquainted by now. I understand Lord Stirling's estate is not far from the Lott's home. Didn't you visit one another?"

"Of course we did. But the girl is rather snobbish. The fact that she is the daughter of an earl, not that it means anything in this case, seems to have gone to her head."

"I do not think it is that, Caty. I think the girl is just shy. And I do not think it matters to her that her father carries the title of an earl; she simply adores him just because he is her father. And there's no doubt that she is the apple of Lord Stirling's eye."

Caty pretended to ignore his remarks.

"Then why don't you ask Mrs. Knox to teach you to sew? She will appreciate your company. Were you aware that the Knox's infant son died a few weeks ago?"

Caty nodded. "I was sorry to hear it. Poor, dear Lucy—what is it, Sam?" she asked, looking from him to the gowns that held his attention.

"—I hope you brought more than fancy party gowns with you. I hate to tell you this, Cousin, but there is no partying in this camp. No dances, no dinner socials, not even any card playing is allowed. When the generals and their wives get together, it is over a simple cup of coffee. The only entertainment provided is if one of them is willing to sing for the rest."

"Things are that bad?" she asked. She had not brought any other dresses.

"Words cannot adequately relate how bad they truly are."

She wished she had stayed in Morristown. If it were not for Nathanael's strange letter, she would have. Now, she thought, her anger building, she would be forced to suffer with the army and return home in the spring to face, no doubt, another long, lonely pregnancy. "Is there an iron forge nearby?" she asked, suddenly curious as to the valley's name.

"Yeah. It is not in operation now though."

Nathanael must feel quite at home here, she thought, her bitterness ruling her heart, *close to a forge and surrounded by Quakers.*

Nathanael rode from Headquarters at a rather leisurely pace. He remembered the joyful reunions of the past when he felt confident of his wife's affection. He could hardly snatch her into his arms now, as he had before when she had come to him of her own free will. She was forced to join him now, and that fact brought with it a deep sense of insecurity and pain.

He searched his memory as he rode, in the hope of discovering what he had done to alienate her. She was understandably disappointed when he had left her at Morristown. However, he had warned her of his possible departure before she set out from Coventry. Moreover, he had spent every available moment with her and the children before he was forced to march his division out. The situation had been completely beyond his control. Certainly, she did not hold that against him!

He had written numerous letters. The eve of the Battle of Brandywine, after forty hours with no sleep, he took time to write her—what did he say? Was it not something to the effect that he longed to hold her again, and that her love sustained him through the hardships of war? Letter after letter poured through his mind. All with relatively the same message. His head began to ache as he pushed himself to determine exactly what offense he had committed. Nevertheless, it was all to no avail. Nathanael was uncertain of how to behave once he saw her, and apprehensive as to how she would respond. He dismounted in front of the cabin, and handed the reins to one of his men; then with a deep sigh, he pulled the door open.

Caty and Sam's lively conversation ceased as their attention was immediately drawn to Nathanael's entrance. He stepped inside, removing his hat. His eyes met those of his wife. Each was conscious of the other's discomfort.

"Thee are looking well, Caty," his awkward greeting came.

"It is good to see you. You seem to have lost weight," she remarked noticing his rather gaunt appearance.

He nodded in response.

"Why don't I leave you two alone," Sam said, assuming his presence was the reason for the restraint in their reunion. "I can catch up on family news tomorrow, Caty. I will talk to you later, Nat." He said as he passed his friend.

"Good-bye, Sam! Thank you for helping me settle in." Caty walked behind him to the door, grateful for an excuse to move away from Nathanael's steady gaze.

"Did you decide to send the children home?"

She turned to face him. He was no longer looking at her, but at the gowns as he removed his cape. "I thought it best."

Nathanael nodded. "They're well?"

"Growing like weeds," she said with a forced smile. "George is speaking in complete sentences now. He is a bright child. Even the Lott's said so. And Patty— the Lott's began calling her Patty rather than Martha, and I have become so accustomed to it I found myself calling her Patty too! Anyway, she should be walking soon! Can you believe it?"

Nathanael stared at her, his expression blank. He slowly shook his head. "No, Caty. I cannot believe it." His children were strangers to him. He longed to be a father to them and witness, with his wife, their every accomplishment. He sat on the edge of the bed, dropping his head down; his arms hung limp upon his knees.

Caty was surprised by his reaction. For a moment, she was at a loss as how to respond. Then, slowly, she walked to the bed and squatted in front of her husband, taking his hands into her own. "I tell them daily of their papa's love—I—" her voice gave out as tears rolled freely down her cheeks. "I could never let a day go by without telling them about you."

As Nathanael looked down at her tear-stained face, he realized that they had become victims of war. Casualties were not only meted out on the battlefield. He wondered, as he stood and took Caty into his arms, if the physical pain of a battle wound could compare to the emotional pain he suffered over the unexplainable loss of his wife's affection or the permanent loss of time from his family.

"What have I done, Angel?" he asked as he held her close to himself. "Give me the opportunity to repent of my sin."

She did not reply.

He placed his finger under her chin and gently forced her to look at him. "Please, Caty," he pleaded.

She laid her cheek against his chest. "Just tell me you love me, Nathanael. Tell me you love as much as you did the day we were wed," she wept.

"Dear, sweet Caty! I love thee more than the day we were wed!"

Within his arms, she dismissed her fears. In response to his kisses, her insecurity was forgotten. The joy of their reunion temporarily eased the pain of the wounds inflicted by war.

Except for the delivery of a meager portion of watered down-broth, accompanied by fire-cake, there was no disturbance. The hours passed in conversation as details of their lives apart were exchanged. Nathanael could not hear enough about the children. His questions about them led Caty from one pleasant account to another.

However, his stories were not so pleasant. She learned that he had purposely held back from telling her of the hardships of Valley Forge; for fear that the enemy might intercept his letters. Were they to discover the utter weakness of the Continental Army, the end would come quickly. Orders were clear from Headquarters—no one was to relate the devastating conditions by letter.

"But you'll be adequately cared for," he assured her. Though they sat across the table from one another, their hands were tightly clasped. "I would never have sent for you if I thought you'd be subject to starvation. I have been given charge of the foraging details, a service I find most disagreeable." He stopped speaking and suddenly became uneasy.

"—I am sorry, Angel, but I have to go out tomorrow. I will be leaving before dawn and I promise I will be back by sunset." He waited for a reaction.

Caty smiled at him. "You need to get some sleep if you are getting up that early." She climbed into the bed while he threw more wood on the fire. When he lay down beside her, she snuggled close against him.

"You be sure to sleep in, in the morning. I will leave orders to have a wagon and driver at your disposal. My aides will see to your needs."

"Why do you find this duty so disagreeable?" Caty asked.

"The farmers do not want to sell to the army, and I can hardly blame them. All we can offer are Continental notes for their livestock or grain, notes that are depreciating more with each passing day. It is their livelihood, Caty; and, though we would never take everything and thus deprive them of food for their own families, we are forced to take what we need to keep from starving. It is a horrible moral dilemma, and I hate it—" His tone revealed his turmoil. "They hide the livestock from us. You cannot imagine how well they hide it."

"Certainly not cattle?" Caty found it hard to believe that something as big as a cow could be hid.

"Chickens, sheep, hogs, cattle and horses."

"Horses?"

"We've lost hundreds of our own to starvation. We do not have enough hay to feed them. The poor creatures gnaw on the fence rails, trying to relieve their hunger—"

"Then you are not eating them." Caty was relieved.

"If the men could get to them quickly enough after they die, they'd eat them—"

"Oh, Nathanael!"

"Many of the farmers secretly transport their livestock and grain to Philadelphia. The British pay gold. When I catch them—God forgive me—I am under orders to make an example of them by way of one hundred lashes. They cry out for mercy, but like Pharaoh I harden my heart."

Caty caressed his cheek with her fingers, in an attempt to offer him comfort.

"Many of the farmers are Quakers. They justify selling to the British, reasoning that since we are in want, and the British in plenty, God's favor must be with them— Mifflin's deserted his post," he informed her, referring to the quartermaster general who was also a former Quaker. "Congress is trying to persuade me to take the position of quartermaster, and His Excellency is anxious for me to accept it as well."

"But you are a major general. What of your rank and command?"

"There'll be no need of major generals, for there will not be an army if we cannot supply it."

"Why you?"

"Partly because of my experience in managing the forge, and partly because I understand the needs of this army—but mainly because I proved myself. Unbeknownst to me I was put to the test, and I passed with flying colors." His somber tone communicated his distress.

"Who made you prove yourself? For what?" Caty was confused.

"General Washington and a committee Congress sent to evaluate the needs of the army. They interviewed me for the position of quartermaster general. I told them plainly that I did not want the position. The next day I was given command of the foraging detail by His Excellency." Nathanael looked down at Caty. Her eyes were already fixed on him. "I didn't give it a second thought. I took my men out for eleven days, all the while sending food and supplies back to camp."

"You accomplished more than was expected?" It was more of a statement than a question, for Caty knew her industrious husband very well.

"It would seem so. The committee was impressed, and have been determined since, that I take the position."

"Just as His Excellency knew they would?" Caty fully expected Nathanael to reply. He only sighed, turning his attention to the reflection of the dancing flames from the fireplace on the ceiling above.

"He knows you, Nathanael. He had no doubt but that you'd be successful."

"It bothers me, Caty. I feel as though I have been betrayed. And at the same time, I am tormented with guilt for feeling it." Nathanael confessed. "His Excellency has the enormous burden of trying to manage the quartermaster's department on top of his other responsibilities. It is too much for a dozen men to deal with."

"What's involved in taking the position?"

"Being responsible to oversee the supply of everything you can imagine an army might need, from cannons to nails. He must keep the roads in proper repair; establish waterways if possible; choose the location of winter quarters; oversee the establishment of the camp; and find suitable private dwellings to house the general officers. Then he must be responsible for the integrity and honesty of every man in the department, for there are millions of dollars involved. Caty, how can any one man be responsible for the honesty of another?"

She, too, found it difficult to imagine one man overseeing such responsibilities. "Perhaps General Mifflin was overwhelmed by the position." She felt Nathanael's body stiffen as the words were spoken.

"General Mifflin took command of the quartermaster's department when there was some semblance of order and motion to it. His inattentive attitude concerning his duties has brought the army to near ruin. Moreover, Mifflin has done more than desert his post. He has become involved in what appears to be a faction bent on removing His Excellency from his command."

"I have heard talk that there are some who are trying to replace the General with Horatio Gates," Caty said.

"It is more than just talk," again Nathanael looked down at his wife momentarily. "And they may even succeed. The Northern army's victory at Saratoga presented General Gates as a competent, successful and ingenious commander. Unfortunately, Congress and the public at large believe it. We have reports from subordinate officers who fought that battle; Gates had little to do with the victory. The general most responsible for what occurred up there was Benedict Arnold. He is perhaps the most outstanding battlefield officer we have in this army, and Congress consistently overlooks his accomplishments. Gates is eager to take the title of commander in chief, and I tremble to think of it."

"How's General Washington holding up under the strain?" Caty asked.

"It bothers him a good deal more than he lets on. Most of the Congressional delegates that elected him at the start of the war are no longer in Congress. Those who remain, and have become part of this scheme, have caused great pain to His Excellency— If they would stop investing so much of their energy in such foolishness and instead work at meeting our desperate needs for food, clothing and medical supplies, then perhaps we would have the ability to turn this army into something to be proud of." Nathanael suspected that Caty was frightened. He rolled on his side and pulled her close.

"His Excellency has taken to retiring to a private spot near his quarters to pray. Heaven will answer his pleas, along with those of so many others. There is no need to fear, Angel. It will work out for the best—"

The late morning sun was inviting. Though Caty intended to take advantage of the wagon Nathanael had at her disposal, she decided that after being cooped up in a coach all the way from Morristown, and then spending half the day in the smoky cabin, a walk in the fresh, crisp air would be invigorating.

It was only about a mile to General Washington's Headquarters, and the road was clear. Caty wrapped herself warmly against the cold air and started on her trek. The greetings of soldiers she met along the way were returned with a brilliant smile and cheery hello. She even stopped to chat a bit every now and then. As she continued, she discovered that little sun fell on the road east of Nathanael's cabin. This prevented the snow from melting. With her skirt hoisted a bit higher, she trudged on.

The sound of a rider approaching from behind prompted Caty to move to the side of the road. As the horse came close, she turned her head to see if she recognized the rider. He was an officer she surmised by his uniform, but his cape partially covered his jacket so that she could not determine his rank. He was young, certainly no more than a major, she thought. Caty politely nodded as he tipped his hat. He seemed in no rush, riding at a slow trot behind her. She therefore moved back onto the road where the snow was more firmly packed.

"Where are you headed?" the rider asked.

Caty glanced at him over her shoulder, but offered no reply to his question.

"I asked you where you were headed?" he repeated, a bit louder this time.

"I am not in the habit of answering the questions of strangers," her pert reply came.

"I am aware that General Greene left orders for a wagon and driver to be available to you. I do not understand why you didn't use the means of transportation your husband provided."

"It is really none of your business!" she shot back, as she trudged forward.

"Let's say I am making it my business."

"Let's say I do not care!" she replied, then momentarily lost her balance as her foot hit a piece of ice.

"Those party shoes are hardly fit for walking, especially in this weather. You will be coming upon a steep decline ahead. If you persist in walking you are bound to slip and end up in a most unladylike position."

Caty ignored his words and walked in silence. She was curious as to whom this overbearing officer might be, but was too annoyed by his behavior to even show the least interest by asking his name. As she walked, she noticed the soldiers stopping to salute him. Even a major came to full attention as he passed. So perhaps he was a colonel, she thought.

She came to the hill of which he spoke. Determined not to let it stop her, Caty continued on. She had not taken three steps before she slipped, but quickly recovered her balance. His laughter annoyed her. "He will be sorry when I report him to Nathanael!" she whispered.

The officer dismounted and walked toward her. "I must insist that you let me escort you to His Excellency's quarters upon my horse."

"Who said I was going to His Excellency's?"

"If you do not want to go to General Washington's quarters, then I will take you back to your husband's quarters. Nevertheless, either way you will ride upon my horse. I am under orders to see to your comfort and safety. Would that your husband assigned you to one of his aides, but no, I accepted thinking I would be doing him a favor. I would have preferred to take out the foraging party. Now get on the horse, for General Greene would probably be upset if you were to fall and break that pretty neck."

Caty was delighted with his boldness. "My neck is completely covered, sir, how could you determine whether or not it is pretty?" Her huge eyes grew larger still as she fixed them on his.

With a definite air of confidence, he met her gaze. "Such a lovely face must grace an equally lovely neck. Let me introduce myself, madam—" he said with a bow.

"Oh, no, there's no need. I have figured it out. I am well aware of to whom I am speaking."

He smiled, obviously amused by her tone. "How would you know?"

"Descriptions of you have been given by many of my correspondents, mostly females, of your auburn curls and piercing brown eyes; your perfect features and tawny coloring even in the dead of winter. Your scrupulous dress," she continued with a flirtatious smile as she ran her eyes up and down his form. "A military man through and through; a swashbuckler in fact, and ever attentive to the ladies. If I had any remaining doubt as to your identity, your Pennsylvania accent removed it, General Wayne. But I am surprised none of my correspondents dared mention your extreme arrogance."

Anthony Wayne laughed. "I get the distinct impression that you view arrogance as a positive character trait, Mrs. Greene. Now, madam, if you will permit me." He took hold of Caty's arm and led her alongside his horse. Placing his hands about her waist, he gently and effortlessly lifted her onto the saddle. "Again I will ask the question. Where are you headed?"

"To visit Lady Washington, of course!"

"And to disrupt the activity of Headquarters, I will wager." Anthony commented as he took hold of the reins and led the horse forward.

"I beg your pardon?"

"I understand there's many a man in this camp that would volunteer for extra fatigue if it meant you would smile in his direction."

"And from where did you hear this?"

"From many a man."

*"All of you will be immortalizing yourselves in
the golden pages of history,
while I am confined to a series of drudgery to
pave the way for it."
(Nathanael Greene)*

CHAPTER EIGHT

GENERAL WASHINGTON'S SUDDEN appearance brought an immediate hush throughout the room. With a flawlessly erect posture, he sauntered across the sitting room. Warmly, the ladies returned his smile. Certain of his officers nodded as he stopped to quietly relate instructions. When he came upon his wife's seated form, with two-year-old Julia Knox asleep on her lap, he stood beside her chair and bent down to speak to her.

"You must forgive me, Patsy, for neglecting my social duties. Are you enjoying yourself?" he asked as he gently pushed a misplaced lock of the baby's hair from her face.

"Is there a difference, George, or is it just my imagination?" she asked her eyes fixed on the vivacious Caty Greene and her small, attentive audience. "Since she arrived, the conversation is livelier; the smiles are quick and genuine. Somehow, that girl has the ability to make them forget their troubles. Even poor Lucy Knox is laughing."

"There certainly is a difference, and I am delighted that she has joined us. The marquis has found a compassionate friend," he said as he observed the marquis' frustration in failing to understand the fast-paced conversation about him. Caty, aware of his confusion, interpreted into French what was said. The Marquis de Lafayette immediately joined in the laughter of the others.

"Caty says she has adopted him as a younger brother. Have you heard her scold him for his poor English?"

"I have. And he her for her poor French." George Washington said with a chuckle.

Martha smiled in response to his remark. "And what shall we do about young General Wayne?"

"Whatever do you mean?" George Washington looked at Anthony Wayne, who sat beside Caty, seemingly amused by her every word.

"He is obviously infatuated with her," Martha informed him.

"Nathanael does not seem to be concerned."

"Nathanael Greene is the most trusting man I have ever met."

"You do not think he should trust his wife?"

"Oh, no. It is General Wayne he should not trust. That man exuberates charm."

"Really? Perhaps it is not General Greene that should keep a watchful eye on his wife, but me!"

Martha turned her head to look at her husband, and laughed at his pretense of jealousy. "You have no reason to worry, old man. Where is General Greene?" she asked, remembering that he had whisked Nathanael into his office the minute he and Caty arrived.

"He is contemplating a matter we discussed."

"Are you still pressing him to accept the position of quartermaster general?"

"Day and night," he said, turning away from her gaze.

"Oh, George. Must you burden him with it? You know if you continue to press him he will accept out of loyalty to you."

George Washington stood erect. "I have no choice, Patsy. I believe he will do justice to that department because of the ability he has shown in such matters, not to mention his honesty and genuine concern for this army. The task before our new quartermaster general is all but impossible to accomplish. If anyone can do it, Nathanael Greene can."

"But he will consider it a demotion, to go from a field commander to a staff officer."

"Indeed he does," George Washington sighed. "But I have pleaded with him to make the sacrifice. Now, my dear, if you will grant me further indulgence, I have a matter to discuss with a few of my men."

As he walked back across the sitting room, the officers he had whispered to earlier stood and followed.

Nathanael was standing by the window when the men entered the office. In silence, he nodded in response to the greetings of his friends. General Washington briefly laid a comforting hand upon the distraught general's shoulder as he passed by.

Nathanael moved to the chair to the right of General Washington and waited with the others.

"Be seated, gentlemen," George Washington instructed as he sat down. "How do I begin?" he muttered. Reaching into his jacket, he pulled out a letter from the inner pocket and opened it, then slowly looked at the faces gathered at the table: John Sullivan, Henry Knox, Lord Stirling, Alexander Hamilton, and Nathanael Greene. Each one, he had no doubt, would prove himself faithful to the point of death.

"My enemies persist, gentlemen. Would that I meant Generals Howe, Cornwallis and Clinton only. I expect their criticism. I welcome their challenge.

"But my brothers have become my enemies—men like Generals Horatio Gates, Thomas Conway, Thomas Mifflin, and Dr. Benjamin Rush. And who knows how many more are involved." He momentarily stared at the letter, and then took a deep breath.

"They are determined to remove me from command, we all know this. But they seemingly have come to the realization that they cannot bring me down unless they bring you down as well. Because you have been my trusted confidants and council; because you are my friends, you are subject to the same libelous criticism as I." He emphasized his words by holding the letter up. "I thought it best to inform each of you of the slander being made against your character because of this letter, before you hear it elsewhere. Dr. Benjamin Rush made the remarks herein.

"Nathanael," he looked directly at him. "You are reported to flatter me for your own self-interest, a subordinate parasite who is timid, speculative, and without enterprise."

He looked at General Sullivan. "John, Dr. Rush says you are weak, vain, without dignity—and in the field a madman."

Alexander Hamilton was next. "Alec, can you take criticism along with my generals?"

"Yes, sir." the colonel replied, prepared for the blow.

"You have reason to be proud, my boy; your criticism is similar to that of General Greene's," Washington said with an affectionate, though forced smile, for both Colonel Hamilton and Nathanael. "You are referred to as a self-seeking flatterer as well, though inferior to the general."

"Lord Stirling," the Commander paused, obviously troubled by the words before him. "You are reported as being proud, vain, lazy, ignorant—and a drunkard."

Lord Stirling chuckled. "Has there ever been an earl who did not enjoy his drink?"

The others smiled in response. It was true that Lord Stirling enjoyed his drink, but none of them had ever seen him intoxicated.

General Washington handed the letter to Nathanael, allowing each of them the opportunity to see the words for themselves.

Henry Knox lifted his hand. "Your Excellency, you failed to report on my character assassination."

"Forgive me, Henry." General Washington said, smiling at Henry's pretense of being upset by the oversight. He turned to Nathanael. "What does it say about General Knox?"

"He is not mentioned, sir."

"I am not?" Henry asked in exaggerated disbelief, laying his hand over his heart. "I am truly insulted, gentlemen, not to be included in your company."

"Indeed, General Knox. I am so accustomed to you being among my most trusted companions, I assumed you were mentioned. But have no fear. I am certain Dr. Rush will realize his blunder and add your name to the list as an afterthought."

Though the men smiled, they remained unusually quiet. Each was as troubled by the cutting remarks made against his friends as by those made against himself.

"I understand there has been talk by some of defending my honor," General Washington began, his tone grave. "I am not sure if such action has been contemplated by any in this room. Let me make one thing clear. I will not tolerate such behavior from my officers. Dueling is not the way to handle such insults, though human nature cries for a means to avenge itself. We shall strive to ignore the verbal attacks and continue in a steadfast manner to lead this army to an honorable victory over our real enemy."

After each man had read the letter, John Sullivan handed it to George Washington. He placed it back into his pocket and stood up. "Gentlemen, you are dismissed."

Both Martha and Caty immediately noted the dismal expressions of the men, as they entered the parlor. Quickly interpreting Martha's glance, Caty excused herself from those about her. As she stood, she threw a reassuring smile in Martha's direction, and then walked toward Nathanael and General Washington.

"Have you two decided to grace us with your presence?" she asked, and moving between them, she turned about and slipped her arms through both of theirs. "I was about to ask Lady Washington if we should move into the office and serve coffee there instead.

"Gentlemen, I must insist you put off your gloomy faces as a favor to me. Sit, sit, sit!" she ordered, guiding them both to seats on the right and left of Martha Washington.

"Sally." she called out to the Washingtons servant. "Generals Washington and Greene have no coffee. And I am certain the other gentlemen are in need of a refill."

Caty sat next to Nathanael and leaned forward prepared to direct a question to General Washington, as Sally poured his coffee. Before she could speak, Nathanael did. His words were not directed toward her or the Washingtons, but to Kitty Stirling.

"You remembered. How thoughtful." he said with a warm smile for Kitty who was walking toward him with a book in her hand.

"I hope you enjoy it, General Greene," she said softly as she handed him the book. Then turning, she walked across the room to where Alexander Hamilton stood.

Caty turned to Nathanael. "What is it?" she asked.

"Poetry," he replied, gently flipping through the pages.

"Poetry?" Caty repeated.

Nathanael grinned. "Perhaps I will be inspired to memorize a romantic verse or two and recite them for you one evening," he said with a wink. A question from Lady Washington distracted his attention as Caty focused hers on Kitty.

A book of poetry? How obvious. Caty thought. *Even Colonel Hamilton is infatuated with her,* her thoughts continued. *Look at her! The pink of perfection—perfect posture, perfect figure, not a blonde hair out of place. But she can hardly be described as beautiful. Cute, in a childish sort of way, but certainly not beautiful.* Her anger intensified. Caty heard Anthony Wayne speak to her, but only responded to his words with a forced smile. Her mind was preoccupied.

The gathering needed to be livened up, Caty decided, looking around the room; and she knew just how to go about it.

"Lord Stirling!" she called out cheerfully, bringing every conversation to a halt. "I have decided that your lovely daughter and Colonel Hamilton make an exquisite couple! Don't you agree your ladyship?" she smiled at Lady Stirling as she stood and walked past her to where the embarrassed Kitty and Colonel Hamilton stood.

"Certainly your Excellency agrees," she said with a glowing smile as she took both of them by the arm and led them to the spinet.

"A handsome couple indeed." George Washington replied with a grin.

"I have had the pleasure of hearing Colonel Hamilton's wonderful baritone. And General Greene tells me Lady Kitty has a sweet, sweet voice. Perhaps we can persuade them to sing a duet. I will be only too happy to play!"

A few of the men began to clap, making humorous remarks to the coquettish Hamilton. Soon everyone in the room joined in the applause, indicating their desire to be entertained. Caty gracefully sat down before the spinet. "Certainly you know *'My Days Have Been So Wondrous Free?'* "

Both of them nodded.

"Wonderful! What a treat!" she exclaimed. As she began to play, Caty glanced around the room, her fingers instinctively moving across the keyboard. She had accomplished what she had set out to do. Every face was aglow—except that of Lady Kitty.

"Nat. Is that you?" Lord Stirling called through the darkness from the cobblestone path, which led to George Washington's Headquarters. He left Henry Knox and John Sullivan behind, intent in their conversation, and walked to the carriage. "Good evening, Mrs. Greene," he said with a slight bow. Then holding out his gloved hand, he reached for Caty's. She removed her right hand from a fox fur muff and took hold of Lord Stirling's, allowing him to help her from the carriage. Nathanael jumped down from the opposite side and secured the horse.

"A social visit with the Washingtons?" Lord Stirling asked Caty as Nathanael approached.

"Lady Washington and I will certainly enjoy our visit." She said, inserting her free hand back into the warmth of the muff.

"I hope you can use that charm of yours to get His Excellency to sit down and relax for an hour or so."

"I haven't found His Excellency to be much in the way of socializing since I arrived in camp. I am beginning to take offense," she pouted beneath the hooded cape.

Lord Stirling looked at Nathanael. "I am worried about him, Nat. You'll find him in a most disagreeable mood tonight, I am afraid."

"Any particular reason?" Nathanael asked.

"Probably the fact that we have an execution scheduled for tomorrow, on top of everything else he has on his mind."

Caty's sigh of disapproval was audible. "I forgot about that."

"You are not expected to attend," Nathanael assured her.

"I know, but it sets the mood in the camp for the entire day. It is so barbaric!"

"The man was caught passing information to the enemy," Nathanael's gentle reminder came. "Such treasonous acts can cost us hundreds of lives."

"I still think it is barbaric."

"It is a necessary detriment to keep others from participating in such treachery," Lord Stirling interjected.

"If there is nothing wrong with killing the man, then why is His Excellency upset over it?" Caty's saucy reply came, her chin held high.

"It is a necessary task, madam, though a disagreeable one," Lord Stirling said.

"My wife is a delicate creature, your Lordship. And I am sure you understand that being forced to live among barbarians such as ourselves is difficult on her," Nathanael said with a playful smile for Caty. "And being as delicate as you are," he added, "you must be extremely cold. Why don't you go inside? I will be just a few minutes."

"He is not so much concerned about my being cold as he is about His Excellency's mood," she said to Lord Stirling. "General Greene is hoping I will be able to cheer him up before he comes in, aren't you, General?"

"I certainly would appreciate it, Angel." he replied with a wink.

"I will see what I can do. Good evening, your Lordship."

"Your servant, Mrs. Greene," Lord Stirling said with a grin, tipping his hat.

Nathanael heard Caty greet Henry and John Sullivan as she made her way to the front door. After she had passed, Henry and John began to walk toward the carriage.

"I need to get back," Lord Stirling suddenly announced. "I will see you in the morning, Nat." Without giving Nathanael a chance to respond, he slipped off into the darkness.

Nathanael was still looking in the direction in which he had disappeared when Henry and John greeted him.

"Good evening," Nathanael returned their greetings.

"—Did His Lordship tell you?"

Nathanael waited for John Sullivan to complete his sentence. He realized that John did not intend to complete it. "All he told me was that His Excellency is in a disagreeable mood. What's going on?" he asked, confused by their peculiar behavior.

Henry and John shared an anxious glance. "—I have been," John began reluctantly, his eyes cast downward.

Nathanael threw a perplexed look at Henry.

"—John has been given command of the Rhode Island forces," Henry informed him, bracing himself for Nathanael's reaction to the announcement.

Nathanael grinned at his friends' discomfort. *No doubt, this was the very reason Lord Stirling slipped away as he did*, Nathanael thought. "Congratulations, General Sullivan." he responded, holding out his hand to John.

"I know how much you wanted that command, Nat," John's rueful reply came as he returned Nathanael's handshake.

Nathanael shrugged. "I gave up any hope of that a long time ago. In fact, I strongly suggested you be given the command. If an attack is made against

Newport, you'll be dealing with large numbers of New England militia companies."
He smiled knowingly, looking briefly in the direction of Headquarters. He continued in lower tones, with the pretense of secrecy. "You both know those militia companies will only submit to the authority of a New England commander," he said with a wink.

Then his eyes suddenly latched onto John's. "I do envy you. And I charge you, General Sullivan, to be victorious in driving the enemy out of my native state."

"I understand, Nat. I will do everything in my power to achieve it. We need to talk about the political atmosphere in Rhode Island. I must know what help I can expect from the governor and congress."

Nathanael nodded. "I will be of assistance in any way I can."

"Many thanks. I knew I could depend on you. Maybe tomorrow we can discuss it. I have to run, gentlemen. I suddenly find myself at a full gallop!" He was obviously delighted with his predicament.

"Good night, John," Nathanael and Henry said in unison.

"Lucy tells me that Caty's been feeling poorly. I hope it is not camp fever coming on."

"I think Caty would prefer camp fever to what diagnosis the doctor gave her."

"What did the doctor say?" Henry's alarm was evident.

"That it appears to be nothing more than a case of morning sickness, and the poor girl is not at all pleased. Keep it to yourself, Henry," Nathanael ordered, knowing that if Lucy heard of Caty's condition the entire camp would soon be informed.

"I understand," Henry replied.

"And to add to Caty's distress, we received word today that our daughter has been diagnosed with a mild case of rickets."

"I am sorry to hear it. And your son Washington?"

"The lad is in good health, thank God."

"Your brothers will do whatever is necessary to restore the baby's health. And, when Caty returns, they will be sure to help her through her ordeal as well," Henry tried to reassure his friend.

"My brothers have problems of their own." Nathanael's concern over his personal problems was suddenly visible in his countenance. "The family business is in trouble. The fact that the British have occupied Newport has severely cut back the work of the forge. The worst of it is that my brothers are bickering among themselves. Some want to dissolve the partnership, the others do not-—" Looking upward at the moonlit sky, Nathanael sighed. "It breaks my heart to see them at odds. One of the greatest joys of my life has been the affection and commitment we have shared— Enough of my sorrows. How is your bookstore doing these days, Henry?"

"My brother seems to be managing things nicely."

"I am glad to hear it."

"Nat, why didn't you get the command in Rhode Island?" Henry suddenly asked, anxious to know the truth. "With the announcement of General Spencer's intention to resign, and the fact that General Arnold was sent to assist in the Northern Campaign, I thought for sure you would be appointed."

Nathanael shrugged.

"Are you telling me you do not know why? I can hardly believe that. You have been in conference with His Excellency day and night."

Still Nathanael made no response.

"The British are building up their forces in Rhode Island. It can no longer be considered a dormant situation, and Sullivan is given charge when the political hierarchy of the state is crying for you to take command?"

"Are you questioning General Washington's decision, General Knox? Nathanael asked with a hint of a smile.

Henry glanced toward Headquarters. "Let's just say I am curious. Somehow I suspect it is not so much the General's decision as it is Congress' disapproval of you taking command."

Nathanael's eyebrows were inquisitively cocked.

"Come on, Nat. We both know Congress has been upset with you since you threatened to resign on my account."

"Sullivan threatened to resign, too."

"Yeah, but Sullivan is easily manipulated. A little flattery goes a long way. The members of Congress are well acquainted with his ego and can easily control him."

Nathanael smiled at Henry's words of truth.

"Well?" Henry persisted.

"Congress has something else in store for me. A proper punishment for what they consider blatant insubordination," Nathanael's smile was waning.

"Are they still pressing you to become quartermaster general?"

"Yes, but to be candid about it, their influence has little effect. His Excellency's persistence disturbs me. He is under immense pressure, Henry. Unless the quartermaster's department begins to function properly, we will not have an army to turn out come spring."

"So you have decided to accept?"

"God knows I loathe the position." Nathanael exclaimed. "And He also knows I care about that man—" He looked toward Headquarters. "I do not remember ever feeling so miserable. The thought of losing my command tears me up inside. The splendor of the field will be yours, General Knox, while I deal with horses, wagons, tents, and latrine shovels—"

"An army cannot exist without a functioning quartermaster's department. You said so yourself."

"Yes, but who ever read of a quartermaster general in the golden pages of history?"

"Who says you have to give up your command, Nat? And who says it has to be a permanent position?" Henry laid his big hand upon Nathanael's shoulder. "You can determine the conditions."

"General Washington has given me the same counsel. But, Henry, no one could serve both positions effectively."

"You could if you personally appointed trustworthy assistants who could run the department while you took command in the field when necessary."

Nathanael was thoughtful. "I do not know, Henry. I am not even sure I can bring any order to the quartermaster's department on a full-time basis. How could I consider any other duty?"

"Do you know what your problem is, General Greene?"

Nathanael shook his head.

"You are too efficient," Henry said with a chuckle. "General Washington is right; you are the best man for the position of quartermaster general. But you are also too valuable to lose in the field. Do not agree to conditions you may regret later."

"You are assuming I am going to accept."

"Of course you are. Like you said, you care about that man." Henry tilted his head toward Headquarters. "And you care about the men that serve in this ragtag army. In fact, I would wager that you planned to inform His Excellency tonight of your acceptance."

Though Henry's words had a definite effect on his friend, Nathanael still felt torn. His will had not yet yielded.

"—I better get inside. The General will think I have deserted."

"Naw. Caty is in there. He knows you would never leave without her." Henry chuckled. "I will see you in the morning, General."

"Good night, Henry. Thanks for listening."

"Do not mention it." Henry patted his friend on the back. They both moved in separate directions.

The warm air, which greeted Nathanael as he entered Headquarters, was inviting. He removed his gloves, hat and cape, laying them across a chair in the foyer. Though the door to the General's office was closed, Nathanael could hear the voices of the men within as they continued in their endless toil of war correspondence. To the right of the foyer was the sitting room. Only Caty and Mrs. Washington could be heard conversing.

"Good evening, Lady Washington," Nathanael said as he entered the room, interrupting the women's conversation.

"Good evening, General Greene. Has General Washington already finished with you? I am afraid your wife and I have not visited long enough. You will just have to sit down and join us. Sally. Get General Greene a cup of coffee—" Martha called to her servant.

"Thank you, madam, but I cannot stay. I have been outside with General Knox. I have not even reported to your husband yet. I was hoping I would find him in here." Nathanael directed his gaze toward Caty.

"He has not even come out of that office to greet me! No one admires His Excellency more than I," Caty said looking from Nathanael to Martha. "But he is greatly lacking in social graces since I arrived. I shall scold him for it the first chance I get!"

"You be sure to do just that." Martha's laughing encouragement came. "He may listen to you. Lord knows I have not had any success."

"I understand he is not feeling well tonight?" Nathanael asked, trying to determine just how disagreeable the General's mood was.

Martha smiled at him. "General Knox warned you, hey?" Suddenly her expression became grave. She turned her eyes downward. "He's quite exhausted. He sleeps very little, and what sleep he does get is restless. I do not know how much longer he can hold up under the strain. He is carrying a burden too heavy for one man."

"I intend to take a bit of that weight from him."

Martha's eyes shot up to meet Nathanael's. "I did not mean to imply anything personal, General Greene. Please forgive me if it sounded so."

"You have no reason to ask my forgiveness. But perhaps I have reason to seek yours, Lady Washington. I intend to take the position as quartermaster general." He looked briefly toward Caty who knowing his struggle encouraged him in his decision with a weak, affectionate smile.

"I am sorry that the General had to carry the burden in overseeing the department while awaiting my decision. Now, if you will excuse me, ladies, I will go see if I cannot make His Excellency smile."

The atmosphere in the office changed when Nathanael entered. Though the aides and secretaries continued to write, Nathanael sensed that each one leaned an attentive ear toward him.

General Washington completed his dictation to one of the secretaries before acknowledging Nathanael's presence with a blank stare.

"I have made my decision, sir." Nathanael announced after offering his salute.

Every pen stopped. Every head turned.

"May we speak in private?" He added.

Without a word, George Washington rose to his feet and led the way up the stairs to his private chamber. Here Nathanael presented his conditions of acceptance as quartermaster general: he would retain his rank and command in time of battle; he, not Congress, would appoint his assistants; he would commit himself for only a year, expecting no compensation beyond that of his current monthly pay as a major general.

"Why not take the commission due you?" General Washington asked in response to his desire to serve in a voluntary capacity.

"I refuse to give Congress the opportunity to discredit me. If I serve on a voluntary basis, all they can do, if not satisfied with my work, is thank me for the effort and replace me with someone who they think can do a better job.

"If, on the other hand, I receive a commission and disappoint them, I will be accused of concerning myself only with lining my pockets. There is a great deal of money to be made in this position: enough to cause jealousy and suspicion. I would rather forego the riches and avoid any public attack against my character."

"Perhaps you are right, but I hate to see you take on the burden and not be compensated," George Washington replied.

"I will take on the burden in order to keep this army in the field. My conviction is yours: that we stand and fight. If this can be done then my compensation will come in knowing I was used in this manner."

George Washington reached across the table and placed his hands on Nathanael's arms. Nathanael had become well acquainted with his Commander's mannerisms in the four years they had been together—when his emotions were deeply stirred, it was often expressed through physical touch.

A smile came to George Washington's face—a smile that reflected his appreciation. And, for the first time in their two months' stay in the desolate camp in Valley Forge, Nathanael saw a glimmer of hope in his beloved Commander's eyes.

"Put your terms of acceptance in writing," George Washington said, pushing an ink well, quill pen and paper before him. "I will have it delivered to the committee immediately."

Nathanael could not help but smile at his Commander's eagerness to make the appointment official.

"This arrived today," General Washington said when Nathanael had finished writing out his terms. He pulled a letter from his jacket and exchanged it for Nathanael's paper. While Nathanael busied himself with reading, General Washington wrote a short cover letter to the Congressional Committee, powdered it, then folded it together with Nathanael's terms of acceptance and carefully applied his seal.

"Praise be to Heaven. Have you replied to this, sir?"

George Washington laughed at Nathanael's jubilant reaction to the letter. "I certainly did. A Prussian general volunteering to join our cause without rank. A general of none other than Frederick the Great. You can be sure I answered it immediately."

"Do you have a position in mind for him, sir?"

"Inspector-general," the Commander said matter-of-factly.

"I had not heard. Has the present inspector general resigned, sir?" Nathanael was hopeful. General Thomas Conway did little to fulfill his duty to the post. His interest, instead, lay in devising ways to bring into question the Commander in Chief's integrity and ability, as well as the integrity and ability of his closest officers.

"No. But if Baron von Steuben proves to be half the military expert our foreign ministers claim he is— I have been praying for a man with the ability to properly drill and train this army. Steuben may be that man. If he is the answer to my prayers, God, Himself, will take care of Conway.

"And word is that the alliance with France is fairly certain. Would to God we receive news from Europe soon. If the alliance is official, we will have a naval fleet to fight.

"The dawn is fast approaching, Nathanael. I believe the frightful darkness we have experienced is behind us. We have passed the test, my friend, and it is time to lead this army back into the light."

Caty snuggled close to Nathanael in an attempt to gain some warmth from him during the short ride back to their cabin. Unusually quiet, Nathanael assumed she was tired. He kissed her hood-covered head, which rested against his shoulder.

After pulling to a smooth halt in front of the cabin, he was surprised when she immediately perked up, gratefully accepting the hand of an eager soldier who offered to help her out of the carriage.

"See to the horses, Morris," Nathanael said to another soldier as he opened the cabin door and waited for Caty to enter.

The return to the dreary atmosphere of their rustic cabin after being at Headquarters always triggered a slight depression in Caty. Her sigh upon entering the cabin was usually met with a positive response from her husband. Tonight, however, he spoke before she even had the opportunity to sigh.

"His Excellency informed me that you will be required to make a sacrifice because of my appointment as quartermaster general," he said as he lit the candles on the table then threw a few logs in the hearth.

"What sacrifice?" Caty seemed a bit taken aback as she removed her cape.

"I am sorry, Angel. I do not exactly know how to break this to you—"

Caty saw the twinkle in his eyes that always appeared when he was teasing. "Break what to me?" she asked with a grin.

"We will have to give up our cozy little cabin and move into Moore Hall. There's just not enough room here to carry on the business."

"Moore Hall!" she exclaimed with delight, familiar with the stately home owned by an elderly couple only a few miles from camp. "No more of this smoke filled cabin?" she cried, throwing her arms out for emphasis.

"No more," he laughed, taking off his cape.

"No more of this damp, dirt floor?"

"No more."

"No more of being squashed against the wall on that small bed?"

"Squashed against the wall? Caty, I practically fall out of bed every night dangling on the edge as I do to give you enough room," he protested with a grin.

"One arm hanging off that horrid mattress hardly defines dangling on the edge, Nathanael." she replied pertly.

"One arm?" He pretended to be angry as he pulled her close. "I have gladly suffered without a good night's sleep since you arrived."

"If you have suffered without sleep it is because you have had so much on your mind, not because you were not comfortably sprawled out on the bed! Anyway, you do not require any sleep."

"Whatever do you mean?" he asked with a chuckle.

"I have never known you to be in bed before midnight; and you are always up before dawn—I have never known you to eat three full meals a day. Nathanael, you were born for military life!" she exclaimed as though the realization had just hit her. "And when you do sleep, it is so sound the British could attack this camp and you would not hear a thing—" Caty stopped abruptly, obviously troubled.

"What's wrong, Angel?"

She lowered her gaze as though ashamed. "Here I am joking about you sleeping through an attack, but for some of General Wayne's men it was a gruesome reality. Anthony told me, just this afternoon, about how the British snuck up on his men during the night at Paoli. It must have been horrible."

Nathanael pulled away from her and walked a few steps to the crudely fashioned table. "Ninety men massacred; many of them were killed in their sleep. It is a miracle General Wayne escaped."

"He is determined to avenge them. In fact, he says he is obsessed with the thought. Nathanael, he was practically in tears when he told me. Do you realize how devastated he is over it?"

"He is not said much to me, though I have suspected it. I am happy he has found such a compassionate friend to talk to." Nathanael pulled a chair out from the table and sat down. After picking up a quill pen, he remained motionless, staring at the blank paper before him. He took a deep breath. "Where do I begin to feed, clothe and equip an army of 5000?"

He began to write, only to stop after a few minutes, crumple the paper and toss it aside.

"Who are you writing to?" Caty asked, sitting across from him with the intention of answering a letter from home.

"The men I would like to appoint as my assistants."

"Who are they?"

"I would like to keep Colonel Biddle on as foragemaster general." Caty was well acquainted with the young Quaker colonel and his wife. "John Cox and Charles Pettit would be trustworthy and dependable assistants. They are both successful merchants with the wherewithal to purchase in the volumes we will be dealing in. And then there's the position of commissary general; Jeremiah Wadesworth of Connecticut would be ideal for the post—"

Caty did not recognize any of the names. "Civilians?" she asked, surprised that the appointments would not automatically fall to military officers.

"Do not let my uniform fool you, or the rank of colonel they will all receive if they accept. This will prove to be more of a civilian post than a military one." He returned to his writing.

Caty left the table and quietly washed up and slipped into a nightgown. After pulling the blankets down on the bed, she sat on the edge and removed her shoes and stockings. Comfortably positioning herself, her legs crossed Indian fashion under the blankets; she removed the pins from her hair, allowing the dark curls to fall loosely about her shoulders. Then picking up the brush that was tucked under her pillow, she slowly ran it through her thick hair.

"Lord, God, where do I begin?" Caty heard him whisper.

"Is there anything I can do to help?" she asked.

"No you need to get some sleep, Angel. I think I will go walk for awhile."

She nodded, recognizing his need to be alone and think.

"It is simply not the same army I witnessed two months ago," Commissary General Jeremiah Wadesworth remarked. The wealthy, elegant, rather astute Connecticutian did much of his work in supplying the army with food from his home state. "It is remarkable. They are well fed, decently clothed, properly equipped and seem to have a true sense of military pride. You are to be commended, Nat."

"Your help has proved invaluable, gentlemen," Nathanael said with a warm smile for Colonel Wadesworth, as well as for his assistants Colonels Pettit and Cox. "We will share in the credit as we do in the commission." His request to serve the position voluntarily had been rejected by Congress, and the fractional percentage he earned in relation to purchases made was quickly adding up to a sizable fee. This was the main reason Jeremiah Wadesworth had arrived in camp—to discuss the investment of Nathanael's earnings in a joint business venture.

"Let us be on our way, Colonel Hamilton," Nathanael said to General Washington's aide as he picked up a pile of papers from his desk and walked to the closed office door.

Nathanael immediately responded to Caty's knock from the opposite side of the door. "My, my! Aren't we on top of things this morning!" she exclaimed, surprised by his promptness.

He laughed at her obvious surprise.

"General Wayne is in dire need of a new saddle and bridle," she said looking at Anthony Wayne who stood by her side. "I insisted he make it known to you in person."

Nathanael nodded in response to Anthony's casual salute. "Colonel Pettit, General Wayne has a request. Please see to it right away."

Anthony stepped into the office.

"Where have you been all morning?" Nathanael whispered to his wife as Anthony engaged the other men in conversation.

"Out riding with General Wayne," she returned in a similar tone. "The entire encampment is taking advantage of this lovely May morning. They're airing their cabins—even cutting windows in them."

"Is it wise to be out riding?"

"I would prefer to ride with you, but you never have the time anymore. General Wayne was kind enough—"

"That's not what I mean. Is it wise to ride in your condition?"

Her hand instinctively went to her abdomen. She had masterfully concealed her advancing pregnancy from all but Nathanael. Soon her snug-fitting clothing would reveal her secret, and he refused to send for her maternity clothes stating that by the time they arrived the army would probably be ready to take to the field. Already he was making plans for her exile back to Rhode Island, pointing out that not only was she in need of her maternity wardrobe, but the children were in need of her after their lengthy separation.

All the other wives will stay until the last possible moment, Caty thought as she met Nathanael's concerned gaze with a look of defiance. She realized that all his arguments were sound, but she was hurt and angry just the same.

"It is a beautiful morning, Nathanael. You should go out and enjoy it, if only for a few short minutes." She replied, totally ignoring his question.

"Caty!" He was obviously exasperated, though still whispering. "We will talk about this later."

She smiled. "Are you headed outside now?" She asked sweetly, and in a normal tone, noticing the papers in his hand. "Where are you going?"

"To Headquarters."

"Why?" she asked, knowing that his frustration with her would prevent him from freely offering the information.

"Hamilton brought word that General Washington wants a full account of the planned festivities."

"I do not trust men making plans for such a gala event as the French Alliance. His Excellency should assign the task to the womenfolk. Lucy and I would do a fine job—"

The others joined Nathanael's snicker. "Our budget could not meet the expenses you and Lucy Knox would incur."

"It would be an event no one in this camp would ever forget!" Caty said dreamily.

"No doubt."

"I think General Lee is of the opinion that this celebration is to welcome him back to camp." Colonel Hamilton said with a grin.

"Do you jest, Alec?" Caty asked. "Charles Lee is so arrogant I would tend to believe he is of that opinion."

"Caty." Nathanael's softly spoken, though firm warning came. "General Lee's safe return from captivity was indeed a happy event. But the private dinner party we had in his honor is all that he will be receiving I am afraid."

Charles Lee had few friends in camp before his being taken prisoner, and fewer still, it seemed, since his release. News of his rather luxurious life style and frequent social involvement with British General Howe brought a sense of mistrust throughout the camp.

"General Greene, I am sure you have already attended to it; but, in case you haven't not, may I suggest you look into purchasing a pair of spectacles for Mr. Duponceau." Alexander Hamilton said, obviously expecting a response.

"What has he done now, Colonel?" Nathanael asked with an expectant grin.

"Who is Mr. Duponceau?" Colonel Wadesworth asked eager to get in on the jest.

"A mindless fool," Anthony muttered.

"He is General Steuben's aide," Nathanael replied, ignoring Anthony's comment.

"He follows the Baron around like a puppy. If you meet the Baron von Steuben, you will meet Duponceau," Anthony interjected.

"Duponceau is the Baron's interpreter. General Steuben has not yet mastered English. He did not know a word of it when he arrived," Nathanael added.

"That is not so, General," Caty corrected him with a grin. She went on to recite for Colonel Wadesworth, in the deepest voice she could manage, General Steuben's English expletives, which he resorted to when frustrated with the performance of the soldiers he was drilling.

Caty's ability to mimic his accent altered the words so that they were not actually the English-sounding version of the cusses implied. But Nathanael had previously warned her that the implication was bad enough, and her mimicking it was quite unladylike. Though she sensed his disapproval, she ignored it, finding encouragement in the laughter of Colonel Wadesworth and the others.

"Von Steuben—general of Frederick the Great." Colonel Wadesworth continued laughing as he spoke. "How long did he have you all fooled?"

Nathanael chuckled. "Long enough to prove to us that he was able to effectively train men in the art of war. Why would we suspect it was a fabrication? He was recommended by Benjamin Franklin himself."

"Fabrication? Nat, it was an out-and-out lie." Colonel Wadesworth corrected. "What was he? A captain?"

"Yes, a captain—but serving as an aide-de-camp to Frederick." Colonel Hamilton quickly offered.

"Well, Dr. Franklin was in on the lie. And though I do not approve of lying, let us just say that Dr. Franklin's letter of recommendation, listing the Baron's slightly exaggerated credentials—" Nathanael's choice of words sent Colonel Wadesworth to laughing again, infectiously setting off the others.

"His letter assured von Steuben the position of inspector general. And thank God we have him." Nathanael shouted above the laughter.

"And what of this Duponceau?" Colonel Wadesworth asked.

"The poor lad—he is merely a boy, no more than seventeen," Nathanael began, looking toward Alexander Hamilton for verification. The colonel nodded.

"The boy is nearsighted. About two weeks ago General Washington ordered a sham battle between two divisions to test the men's training."

Everyone but Nathanael, Colonel Wadesworth and General Wayne burst out laughing knowing what was to come. Nathanael hesitated, on the verge of joining them.

"I will never finish the story if you keep it up," he warned them. They struggled to contain themselves.

"Duponceau was sent out by General Steuben to reconnoiter and return immediately if he spotted any troops from the other division. He returned in a state of near hysteria to tell General Steuben that the enemy was marching upon us. Scarlet coats were what he reported the troops to be wearing. None of our men had scarlet coats.

"A general alarm was sounded throughout the camp as General Steuben led the men forward, prepared to meet the British—"

Anthony Wayne's audible sigh of disgust drew everyone's attention. Hilarity once again filled the room.

Nathanael was unable to continue through his own laughter.

"What happened?" Colonel Wadesworth shouted.

"I will tell you what happened, Colonel." Anthony replied straight-faced. "I did not find it a bit amusing." His words only proved to intensify the hysteria.

"The absentminded, blind fool had us all ready to defend the camp. Do you have any idea of the excited tension in the air thinking we were moments away from a surprise attack? A quarter mile outside the camp General Steuben encountered the enemy—a fence lined with red petticoats! Freshly washed petticoats drying in the sun! If I could have laid my hands on the lad, I would have thrashed him soundly. I lived through one surprise attack; and, by God, I will not be surprised again!"

The laughter immediately ceased—each one keenly aware of General Wayne's nightmarish experience when ninety of his men were massacred during the night. There was an awkward silence.

"It proved to be a harmless mistake, General. And the lad suffered enough from the humiliation," Nathanael reminded Anthony, and then directed his attention to Colonel Wadesworth. "His Excellency was delighted by the immediate response to the threat, though he considered placing a ban on red petticoats being laundered within a ten mile radius of the camp."

"He did not." Caty protested with a grin.

"Petticoats!" Anthony exclaimed, finally smiling. "Von Steuben is a genius, and what does he have as his personal aide but a court jester! Can't we somehow persuade the enemy to take him?"

"Ah, my friend, without the likes of Pierre Duponceau camp life would grow very dull." Nathanael commented.

"Duponceau is not nearsighted when it comes to women." Alexander Hamilton suddenly exclaimed. The others looked at him questioningly.

"He can spot a woman and identify her long before I can. The more beautiful the woman, the quicker he recognizes her. Mrs. Greene, you and Lady Kitty seem to be tied in his estimation of beauty. He has pointed you both out to me from such a distance that I wagered money he was wrong—I do not do that anymore."

Caty's smile waned at the mention of Lady Kitty.

"How much money did you lose?" Colonel Wadesworth asked.

"I am too embarrassed to say."

"I must meet this Duponceau."

"Speaking of Lady Kitty—when are you going to propose marriage, Hamilton?" Anthony asked bluntly.

"Propose marriage, sir? I am not ready for that; and anyway, begging your pardon, sir, and yours too, General Greene, I would never marry a general's daughter."

Nathanael and Anthony exchanged a glance. "And why not, Colonel?" Anthony asked.

"I intend to be master of my home. If I marry a general's daughter, my wife would always be considered just that; and my children would be referred to as the general's grandchildren. And as for Lord Stirling—he dotes so on that girl. I am not sure he will ever let her go."

"Were you aware that he has an older daughter?" Nathanael asked.

"Kitty mentioned her a few times—never said much though. Married, isn't she, sir?" Colonel Hamilton asked.

"Yes, to a militant Tory. His Lordship has not quite accepted it, or forgiven her. He will let Kitty go when the time comes, though reluctantly perhaps."

"The dear girl believes everything her father tells her," Anthony stated, looking straight at Nathanael. "She recently related to me how a Tory barber, posing as a patriot, cut off your queue, and was overpowered before he could do any physical harm to you with his scissors. I burst out laughing and asked the poor, gullible creature who had told her such a tale. When she told me, I laughed even more. I am sure His Lordship never considered that she actually believed the story."

"What happened to your hair?" Colonel Wadesworth asked, suddenly noticing his stubby queue.

"Mrs. Greene decided she did not want to return to Rhode Island alone," Colonel Cox began with a straight face. "Inspired by the story of Samson and Delilah, she cut his hair while he slept, hoping he'd grow weak and lose his ability to command.

"It worked. He woke up in a feeble state. But His Excellency, as wise as he is, realized it was simply a matter of time before his hair would grow back. So he transferred him from field command to the Quartermaster's Department."

Colonel Wadesworth looked around the room at the smiling faces, fixing his gaze on Caty's.

"You certainly do not believe it, do you, Colonel?" she asked.

"Among this bunch I do not know what to believe."

"I will tell you the truth, Colonel," she promised. "General Greene and his aide, Major Blodget, were in the midst of the Battle of the Brandywine. Bullets were whizzing by their heads as the general directed his troops from the saddle.

"Now you must understand the personality of our dear Billy Blodget. He is a Rhode Islander through and through—a long-time friend who is forever pulling a prank or telling a joke. He's a big man," Caty said in a deep voice, puffing out her cheeks and throwing out her abdomen.

Nathanael rolled his eyes, but quickly joined in the laughter.

"Billy watched a bullet fly behind Nathanael's head. 'General Greene,' " she said, mimicking the major. " 'You had better check your head, sir. Your queue is gone.'

"Even as he spoke a bullet went over his own head. 'And you had better jump down and fetch your wig, Major.' " Caty said, imitating her husband's voice.

"Of course neither one believed the other, but just to be sure they casually looked down to find the queue and wig on the ground. Billy quickly jumped down and fetched them—the two of them laughing like school boys as the bullets continued to fly."

"Come now, Mrs. Greene. I would believe the Samson and Delilah story before I would believe that!" Colonel Wadesworth exclaimed with a smile.

"Oh, it is true, Colonel," Anthony Wayne assured him. "In fact I have spoken to a few officers who witnessed the entire scene. They claim the men were inspired to fight harder after seeing the carefree attitude of their general and his aide to the danger."

"One of those officers will have to relate that story to General Mifflin and prove his accusation is false, sir," Colonel Hamilton said to Nathanael.

"What accusation?" Nathanael asked.

"About the bullets, sir."

"I do not know what you are talking about, Colonel."

"His Excellency did not tell you, General?" Colonel Hamilton was visibly uneasy.

"Not that I recall. Refresh my memory, Colonel Hamilton." The anger in response to an accusation by the former quartermaster general was already showing in Nathanael's face.

"Well done, Hamilton," Anthony muttered.

"Go on, Colonel," Nathanael ordered.

"—General Mifflin claims that you took the desk assignment of quartermaster general to get out of the way of bullets."

Nathanael's anger visibly intensified as the blood rushed to his face. "The man does not have a clue! I am demoted to clean up his mess, and he has the gall to say such a thing! Lord, help me! He actually said I took the assignment to get out of the way of bullets?" he roared.

"—Yes, sir."

Nathanael studied Alexander Hamilton's anxious expression for a moment, as the others in the room remained apprehensively silent. To everyone's surprise, his face broke out into a smile as he shook his head.

"It is amazing what the human heart will resort to in order to justify its own shortcomings. Come on, Colonel. His Excellency is waiting."

"I am headed that way myself. May I ride with you, sir?" Anthony asked.

"Certainly."

"Hamilton," Anthony began, walking toward the door with the colonel. "I heard some of the men talking about His Excellency playing ball yesterday. Is it true?"

"Yes," the colonel laughed. "He played wicket with a few of them—what a powerful arm on that man!"

Nathanael motioned for General Wayne and Colonel Hamilton to wait for him outside. Then turning to Caty he whispered. "You be sure to rest this afternoon. And we will discuss this morning's frolic."

"But of course, sir." she replied pertly, standing on her toes to kiss his cheek.

"Woman, you are more difficult to handle than an entire division," he complained with a hint of a smile.

"Think how dull camp life will be without me." She took hold of his arm and walked with him to the door. After saying good-bye, she watched from the window as the three men rode away.

The joyous celebration of France's alliance with the United States of America opened with the firing of cannon. The assembled brigades stood at attention as the formal announcement of the alliance was read. The chaplains were called upon to offer prayers of thanksgiving for this important event.

Nathanael took his place next to the Commander in Chief on the platform, which had been erected for the general officers to review the troops. General Steuben proudly paraded the troops before the platform, stopping to salute his superior officers.

The sight of this skillful army, which had entered the Pennsylvania valley only seven months prior, with little hope of holding together let alone fighting again, was charged with emotion. The brilliance of their arms; the remarkable liveliness with which they performed; their uniform and tidy dress; and their healthy, proud appearance deeply affected each man on the reviewing stand.

Valley Forge, Nathanael considered the name as he thoughtfully gazed at the scene before him—a place of testing, a place of purging. Here, in this crucible of freedom, the iron of the weakened army was forged into steel. The tempering process was difficult—almost unbearable at times, but the finished product—the army that came through it was hard-core steel.

The parade followed, with a formal dinner for the officers in which General Washington toasted Nathanael and General Steuben for their role in bringing the army out of the throes of certain death. After the meal, Nathanael led Caty out for the first dance, along with the Washingtons, Stirlings, and Knoxes. Shortly after the dance ended, he was begging leave of General Washington.

"Certainly you can stay longer, General Greene," George Washington commented loud enough to be heard above the excitement about them.

"I wish I could, sir, but with the army preparing to take to the field, and General Sullivan's troops in need of supply as well, I simply cannot neglect my post a moment longer. I will be bold enough to ask a favor of you, sir."

"What is it, General?"

"Would you see to it that Mrs. Greene enjoys herself in my absence." He looked at Caty who had hold of his arm, and smiled tenderly. "She is been looking forward to this event and is quite wroth at me for leaving as I am."

George Washington grinned at Caty. "Ah, but I have found Catharine to be a brave soldier. She will cheerfully make the sacrifice for the cause. Consider your favor granted, General Greene. Catharine, you are under direct orders to enjoy yourself."

"Yes, your Excellency," she replied with amusement as she bent in a graceful curtsey. Then taking hold of the Commander's extended arm, she joined him in the next dance as Nathanael made his way back to his headquarters at Moore Hall.

A soft knock on the office door drew Nathanael's attention from the endless pile of correspondence and paper work before him. He welcomed the distraction.

"Please, come in!" he called. To his surprise, Caty entered. "Back already? My aides returned after the festivities and reported that you were invited to the Stirlings to continue the celebration!"

"It is almost midnight," she laughed.

"Is it really?" he pulled out his pocket watch and gazed at it in astonishment as he reached his other hand to the back of his neck.

"Is your neck sore?"

"Umm—" he moaned.

She walked behind him and began to massage it.

"That feels good," he said, closing his eyes.

Caty felt his tense muscles relax under her touch. "How is your eye?" she asked referring to the scar that often gave him trouble.

"Stinging."

"And your hand?"

"Cramped."

She moved to his side, and bending down softly kissed his right eye then reached for his right hand and began to rub it. "I should think it would be cramped after so many hours of writing." She glanced at the pile of outgoing correspondence.

"I have barely made a dent," he replied.

"Nathanael, you drive yourself too hard. Where are Colonels Cox and Pettit?"

"Out tending to the never-ending needs of the army," he said, massaging his eyes with his free hand.

"And why were Colonels Wadesworth and Biddle at the festivities while you and the others were forced to work?"

He smiled at her, touched by her concern. "Because our positions are more demanding, especially with the army making ready to break camp— Tell me you enjoyed yourself, Angel!" he said, grabbing her hand and squeezing it.

"I did," she assured him. "I could have danced well into the morning." She let go of his hand, and moving away from the desk began to twirl gracefully about the room, her hoop skirt slowing her spin.

Nathanael was delighted with her performance. "Caty, there is not a man in this camp that could keep up with you on the dance floor."

"Oh yes there is. His Excellency enjoys dancing every bit as much as I."

"But he certainly does not share your stamina. Who, besides His Excellency, should I thank tomorrow for accommodating you in my absence?"

She stopped dancing and thought for a moment. "There were so many of them." she exclaimed laughing. "They were all quite gracious—General Steuben and the Marquis, His Lordship; Generals DeKalb and St. Clair; dear old Put; Anthony; Alec; Billy; Rob; Colonels Tilghman, Wadesworth, and Biddle; and, of course our, dear Harry," she referred to Henry Knox, using Lucy's pet name. "Even Charles Lee—and the list goes on and on. All of them were perfect gentlemen."

Nathanael smiled in response, then turned around in his seat, and again picked up the quill.

"Oh, Nathanael—" she moaned.

"What is it?" he asked without looking up.

"Please stop."

"Do you still want to talk?" he asked, quickly finishing the last line of the correspondence before him.

"No, I want you to dance with Me." she blurted.

"Caty."

"I do. I truly do!" she exclaimed, tugging on his arm. "I will be leaving in just a few days and—I need you to dance with me, Nathanael, like you did when we were courting."

"In your uncle's parlor?" he asked with a smile as he yielded to her tug and rose to his feet.

"Yes," she replied, positioning her hands. "Just like you did in my uncle's parlor when we would try to make our infrequent visits last as long as possible."

Caty began to softly hum a tune then followed Nathanael's lead. The two of them moved rhythmically across the floor.

"Time has always been against us, hasn't it Caty?" he said mournfully.

She stopped humming and looked up at him, meeting his sorrowful gaze.

"During our courtship overseeing the forge and the political fervor were ever present, demanding my attention. And the distance from Coventry to your uncle's house did not help. Then the war—"

She laid her head against his chest and closed her eyes in an attempt to capture the moment. His strong body felt good against her petite form. The sound of his heartbeat was reassuring.

"I will make it up to you. Someday, my dear Caty, I will make it all up to you and the children—"

Nathanael Greene, painting by Charles Willson Peale
Courtesy, Independence National Historical Park

Freedom's Cost

George Washington, painting by Charles Willson Peale
Courtesy, Independence National Historical Park

Martha Washington, painting by Michael Deas
Copyright Michael J. Deas

Henry Knox, painting by Charles Willson Peale
Courtesy, Independence National Historical Park

William Alexander, The Lord of Stirling, painting by Bass Otis
Courtesy, Independence National Historical Park

Anthony Wayne, painting by James Sharples, Sr.
Courtesy, Independence National Historical Park

Marie-Josph Paul Yves Rach Gilbert Du Motier, Marquis de Lafayette,
painting by Charles Willson Peale
Courtesy, Independence National Historical Park

Baron Frederick Wilhelm von Steuben, painting by Ralph Earl
National Archives and Records Administration

Hugh Mercer

Alexander Hamilton, painting by Charles Willson Peale
Courtesy, Independence National Historical Park

Thomas Paine, engraving from painting by Romney
National Archives and Records Administration

GENERAL GEORGE WASHINGTON DANCING WITH CATY GREENE
AT AN OFFICER'S BALL.

General George Washington Dancing with Caty Greene, painting by Ferris

Masonic Medallion given to Nathanael Greene by the Marquis de Lafayette
Courtesy of the Grand Lodge of Rhode Island and Providence Plantations
(Photo by Rick Lynch)

Freedom's Cost

Horatio Gates, Mezzotint published by John Morris
National Archives and Records Administration

Charles Lee, engraving by G.R. Hall
National Archives and Records Administration

Benedict Arnold, engraving by H.B. Hall
National Archives and Records Administration

Mrs. Benedict Arnold (Peggy Shippen) and child, painting
by Sir Thomas Lawrence
National Archives and Records Administration

"I say we fight...I say we fight...I say we fight..."
(Anthony Wayne at Council of War)

CHAPTER NINE

CIRCULATING RUMORS OF British commander General William Howe's replacement were quickly verified at American Headquarters. The realization that two British commanders had been replaced in only three years' time was encouraging. Great Britain's boast of quickly squashing the colonial rebellion haunted them now, as their highly trained military generals, Thomas Gage and Sir William Howe, had proved inadequate for the task.

The American Commander in Chief, with his train of general officers, waited for the newly appointed British commander to make his move. Sir Henry Clinton with 12,000 troops had spent a restful winter in Philadelphia; but he would be forced, so it seemed, to march northward to New York and take command of the main army.

On the eighteenth of June 1778, Sir Henry Clinton evacuated his troops from Philadelphia. Within twenty-four hours, George Washington once again had possession of the pillaged town, placing the injured General Benedict Arnold in the position of military governor.

The troops at Valley Forge waited while their Commander patiently watched the enemy's direction of march. Numerous councils of war brought various opinions. But once the enemy's destination was unquestionably established, George Washington was ready to move. Though a discrepancy of opinions continued among Washington's general officers, delaying any offensive move, the early summer rains and unusual intensity of the heat slowed Clinton's march to a snail's pace.

"Colonel Hamilton, do you have the paperwork I requested?" Nathanael asked as the general officers filed out of the stuffy room.

Alexander Hamilton appeared confused by the question. "Paperwork, sir? — Oh, yes, right here." He thumbed through the papers spread before him on the table and pulled out the sought-after pages. After handing the papers to Nathanael, he anxiously sought the gaze of his superior officer.

"Is something wrong, Colonel?" Nathanael asked in response to his expression.

"—I—." Hamilton nervously looked about the room to be sure all had departed.

"—I—" he awkwardly repeated, then directed his full attention to straightening the papers on the table, muttering to himself, "Forget it, Alec. You have no business commenting
at all——"

"Is there something I can help you with, Colonel?"

"—It is in regard to the council of war—an observation, sir," he said hesitantly.

Nathanael nodded, indicating his permission for the colonel to speak.

"Sir, I believe the discussion here would have done honor to a group of midwives and to them only!" he fervently blurted.

Nathanael smiled in response.

"May I speak candidly, sir?"

"It seems you have, but by all means, Colonel, continue."

"I am concerned about General Lee's influence over the general officers," he hesitated, fixing his eyes on Nathanael's. "—Especially over His Excellency. It is frightening, sir. Though I have tried, I cannot account for it. It appears to me that Charles Lee has gone mad."

Hamilton misinterpreted Nathanael's thoughtful expression to the statement as one of doubt.

"I am quite serious, sir. The filth he lives in—even letting his dogs eat off his own plate!" The colonel's contorted expression emphasized his disgust. "One of his aides recently told me that the man has been known to check with his staff officers during an engagement with the enemy to ask if his conduct is proper.

"General Greene, we had twelve generals attend this council. You alone boldly opposed General Lee's plan—and you are entirely right, sir. Our strength demands a confrontation. The people of America do expect some sort of offensive action from us."

"Wayne, Lafayette, and Cadwalader were opposed to Lee's plan," Nathanael reminded him, pointing to the papers on the table where the minutes of the council were recorded in Colonel Hamilton's own hand.

"General Wayne is always in favor of confrontation, despite the odds, although today I feared for his health, his face as crimson as it was—wringing his hands and muttering to himself."

Nathanael could not help but smile at the colonel's descriptive account. Poor Anthony Wayne, the junior of Washington's generals, sat in a corner muttering throughout; "I say we fight! —I say we fight! —I say we fight!"

"As for Generals Lafayette and Cadwalader, they only dared to voice their timid opposition because you had already taken a stand. Had they been more forceful— Had you—begging the General's pardon—" Hamilton hesitated.

"Go on, Colonel. Had I what?"

"Had you been persistent, sir, I think you could have broken Lee's spell, or whatever it was, on His Excellency!"

"I clearly stated my position, Colonel Hamilton. You seem to have forgotten, I have not been given a command for this engagement; and, therefore, am only present at the council of war as a staff officer," Nathanael pointed out, trying to mask his disappointment at this fact with a forced smile.

"Just the same, sir, General Washington listens to you. Your opinion is highly regarded by His Excellency. You and perhaps you alone, can counter General Lee's negative influence!"

Nathanael laid his hand on the colonel's shoulder. "Thank you for your confidence, Alec; and, believe me, I am sensible to the danger of Lee's stand. I intend to immediately put my opposition in writing for His Excellency's review."

Hamilton breathed an audible sigh of relief as Nathanael, papers in hand, headed for the closed door.

Nathanael's respectful letter of logical strategy resulted in a more offensive stand by General Washington. As the Quartermaster General laid out the direction of march and attempted to plan for the army's needs, a dispatch arrived from Headquarters.

"The man has gone mad!" Nathanael exclaimed as he read General Washington's words.

"His Excellency?" Colonel Cox asked in disbelief.

Nathanael's eyes immediately darted from the paper to Colonels Cox and Pettit. "Certainly not! Charles Lee! The man was offered command of the sizable detachment ordered out to harass Clinton's rear guard. Lee promptly turned down the command stating that he was happy to be free of all responsibility from a plan that was sure to fail. So the command was given to General Lafayette—the lad's been itching for such a command since he came to us, and His Excellency has been eager to give him the opportunity." Nathanael hesitated, his eyebrows cocked.

"It seems General Lee became jealous over the 4,000 men in the marquis' command. Lee changed his mind, requesting the command for himself, which General Washington gave him— And that is not the end of it," Nathanael added, having his assistants' full attention.

"Lee again refused the command; and, after Lafayette was well under way, he whined once more, and has been given the command for the third time." Nathanael took a deep breath, obviously troubled by George Washington's decision. "And the poor marquis is left without as much as a regiment under him—" As Nathanael contemplated the plight of his young friend, he continued to read the dispatch.

"Praise be!" he suddenly shouted, jumping to his feet. "You are on your own, boys, and God bless you! The right wing is mine!" His words came in response to the astonished looks of his assistants as he waved the dispatch in the air. "A-ha-ha! I will gladly trade my pen for my sword!"

Charles Pettit and John Cox realized, under the conditions of their acceptance to the post as assistants to the quartermaster general that in time of battle the burden of the department would fall on them. But, because of Nathanael Greene's diligence, the present burden was relatively light. The troops were well equipped for the pending battle. Various routes of march had been laid out. Fully stocked depots had been established along the routes. The roads were repaired in advance for easy passage of baggage, artillery and troops. All was in readiness, and Quartermaster General Nathanael Greene put off the concerns of his department in exchange for the position he loved—that of battlefield commander.

The strategy was sound. General Lee was to harass the British rear guard coaxing them, if possible, into a general action. General Greene's right wing of 4,000 men, and General Lord Stirling's left wing of equal number, was to come to Lee's assistance should the enemy be successfully drawn out. The opposing armies were of equal strength with approximately 12,000 each. The well-trained, well-equipped, and eager Continentals balanced even the discipline of the king's troops.

The blistering sun beat down upon Nathanael's division as he marched them to position. Their progress was slow but steady. Though the distant sound of brief musketry and cannon fire earlier had hastened the men's pace, Nathanael ordered them to slow down. The men needed to be as fresh as possible for the impending battle—a difficult task with the temperature nearing 100 degrees. The horses, too, showed the effect of the heat by plodding along under their burdens, their responses to the tug of the reins noticeably delayed.

Years of labor before the blazing inferno of the forge had increased Nathanael's endurance of such heat—but in the forge, he could shed the layers of cumbersome clothing. Now his shirt and waistcoat, topped by the wool coat of continental blue, soon became drenched as his body compensated for the arid temperature. Henry Knox rode silently by his side; drops of sweat continuously poured down the artillery commander's face, dripping from his chin and the tip of his nose.

Nathanael ignored his own discomfort as he observed Henry's obvious distress and considered the plight of his men on foot, with backpacks full of provisions and muskets in hand. And, despite the seeming handicap of his burdened men, Nathanael was aware that the British and Hessian soldiers were worse off. Unlike his enlisted men, many dressed in no more than breeches and a linen shirt, each of the enemy would be dressed in full uniform with layers of clothing and wool coats every bit as cumbersome as his now felt. They would not be allowed to strip down for battle, regardless of the suffocating heat—another requirement of professional European warfare, which might prove devastating as the day progressed.

"General Greene." Billy Blodget came from behind at a full gallop.

Nathanael pulled back on the reins as Billy reined his mare in at the general's side.

"Sir, our advance corps is in retreat." Billy reported breathlessly.

"Retreat? You must be mistaken, Major!"

"No, sir. They are definitely in retreat. I spoke with both Generals Lafayette and Wayne."

Nathanael shared an anxious glance with Henry. "Bring the troops to a halt!" He shouted to his aide, Rob Burnet, who immediately spurred his horse forward to the front of the columns.

"By whose order has this retreat been called?" Nathanael roared, aware from the earlier sound of gunfire that little more than a skirmish had occurred.

"General Lee's, sir."

"Why?"

"I do not know, sir. A state of confusion prevails on the front line. Generals Lafayette and Wayne have no idea why the retreat was ordered. General Wayne is in a rage."

"And my orders?"

"I could not locate His Excellency. I was told that he verbally reprimanded General Lee and has taken direct command of Lee's division. I searched for him, but he is reported to be everywhere at once trying to regroup."

"For an attack?" Nathanael demanded just as the sound of artillery and musketry began in the distance.

"It would appear so, sir. I suspect that's General Wayne's brigade taking the fire. At the sight of our retreat, he feared the enemy might pursue. He was making ready to turn his brigade about and attempt to hold them back for as long as possible."

"Good Lord. He may face Clinton's entire force alone." Nathanael exclaimed.

"He will too. Wayne and his Pennsylvanians will stand and fight regardless of the odds." Henry remarked as the brigadier generals arrived, gathering about their commander.

Nathanael began to rub his upper lip with his left hand as he turned his head in the direction of the gunfire, then back in the direction they had come. "No new orders," he muttered to himself, momentarily uncertain of how to proceed.

"Why not go forward as planned?" Henry asked.

"Because I have no idea how far the British have advanced. We may be marching right into the midst of their line." Nathanael paused and called for the map from Sam Ward. He scanned it carefully then thoughtfully gazed up and down the road once again. "We are heading back, gentlemen," he said to his brigadier generals. "Turn them about." his decisive order was given to the aides. A chorus of affirmative replies was followed by the clopping of hooves as the aides set out to deliver the order to the various brigades.

"What are your plans, sir?" General Cadwalader asked, confidant of Nathanael's strategic ability.

"We will come in behind General Washington's division where I can determine the situation, and flank their right, assured of the enemy's position. If we continue as ordered, I am no better off than a blind man—what is the status of His Excellency? Is Lord Stirling in position? I may very well find myself in a worse situation than our friend Wayne is in now."

The men, eager to prove their ability, retraced their three-mile march with a sense of determination. They trusted their commander and were confident in their training.

Coming behind General Washington's troops, Nathanael flanked their right, strategically placing Henry's eight cannon upon a hill overlooking General Wayne's hard-fighting brigade. The British soon acknowledged Nathanael's presence by forming an attack against his division. Nathanael waited for the enemy to advance, and then ordered the cannons to roar, sending deadly grapeshot into the marching lines. The continuous firing of the cannon forced the British to the ground-- crawling on their bellies to continue their pathetic attack.

Nathanael kept a close eye on the enemy during the first vital minutes of the engagement, as he continuously received reports from the various regiments in his command—reports, which aided him in strategically maneuvering his men in response to the enemy's movements. He observed Anthony Wayne's men below, savagely fighting as one would expect Wayne's men to do. Reports from Washington and Stirling were nonexistent, forcing him to act, as they too were acting in regard to him, with a sense of intuition and trust for their decisions and ability. All the while, with his attention constantly in demand, and bullets flying about him, he kept a keen eye on the battery of cannon, surprised to see the presence of a woman among the artillery detachment.

"General Knox, there's a woman on the field!" Nathanael shouted above the thunderous clamor of the battle, pointing toward the cannon.

Even as he spoke, an artilleryman was shot down. In amazement, the two generals watched as the woman took the fallen soldier's place at the cannon without a moment's hesitation. Henry spurred his horse forward, galloping toward his men.

The battle raged on under the relentless sun. Men began to drop on both sides from heat exhaustion and sunstroke with little more than spindly pines to offer meager shade. Nathanael made his way about the battlefield, personally observing his strengths and weaknesses. With a parched throat, his dry, swollen tongue cleaving to the roof of his mouth, he continued to relay his orders.

As darkness approached, the sound of musketry faded, though the cannons continued to duel as the British made a slow retreat from the field. No attempt was made to follow. Four hours of fighting left the men in no condition to immediately pursue the enemy. After quenching their tormenting thirst, the battle-worn soldiers fell to the ground in exhausted slumber as the medical detachments moved onto the battlefield to begin the frustrating task of determining in the darkness who was dead, who was wounded, and who was simply sleeping among the casualties.

Nathanael, with his brigadier generals, sought out the Commander in Chief. The present situation was evaluated; casualties were estimated; and plans for a possible morning attack discussed. Generals Greene, Lafayette and Lord Stirling were ordered to remain as the others were dismissed.

Nathanael and Lord Stirling, too weary to stand erect leaned upon the wheels of a silenced cannon. The Commander, himself, was forced to sit on a nearby tree stump, his long legs uncomfortably bent in this position so close to the ground. Only Lafayette, who was in command of the rear guard throughout the day and saw little action, was strong enough to stand.

"They may attempt to escape during the night," George Washington commented; his arms lay limp upon his knees; his head hung wearily.

"I do not think they could manage it," Lord Stirling responded.

George Washington looked up at him. "It is amazing what a sense of desperation can inspire." His remark was obviously in reference to their own night maneuvers—the escape from Long Island and the marches on Trenton and Princeton.

"Will we pursue should they retreat further?" the Marquis de Lafayette queried, still eager for battle.

"—No. We are in no condition to pursue—unless, gentlemen, you care to express a different opinion," he said, looking from Nathanael to Lord Stirling.

Both replied with a weary, "No, sir," much to the marquis' disappointment.

"How will Congress view today's engagement, gentlemen?" the Commander in Chief asked.

"As a draw," Lord Stirling quickly replied. "From the regimental reports and my observations of the battle, our casualties were about equal."

George Washington looked at Nathanael. By the campfire's light, he detected a gleam in the younger man's eyes. "General Greene, your opinion, please." he said with an expectant smile.

"A victory, your Excellency! True our casualties are equal, but we occupy the ground!" Nathanael exclaimed, laying a hand on Lord Stirling's shoulder. "And word is that hundreds of British and Hessian soldiers are deserting."

"A glorious victory, General Greene?" George Washington asked with a grin to match Nathanael's.

"Congress may not view it as glorious, but we can be proud of the results. The men stood and fought despite our initial weakness. They regrouped and worked as a unit for the very first time. Their endurance was incredible."

"A glorious victory, Lord Stirling?" General Washington asked the earl's opinion again, certain that Nathanael's enthusiasm had its effect.

"Indeed, sir." he replied with a chuckle, his own hand now placed on Nathanael's shoulder. "To us a glorious victory, but to Congress—who knows?"

"And who cares?" General Washington muttered in his exhaustion. His uncharacteristic words of insubordination brought an instant smile to the lips of his three generals.

"Get some rest, gentlemen; we will bivouac here. With the morning light, hopefully we will have the opportunity to entertain Sir Henry again."

As Nathanael turned to walk the few feet to his waiting aide, he heard the Commander speak again.

"General Greene, I was concerned about your health today. Were you plagued by the asthma?"

Nathanael turned to face him. "Though the sandy soil is considered a curse by most, I considered it a Godsend today—less dust being stirred up."

"Sleep well, Nathanael," George Washington said with an affectionate smile; then turning to the Marquis de Lafayette, he spoke again.

"General Lafayette, have you no cape?"

"I seem to have lost it, sir."

"Then come and share mine."

As Nathanael untied his own rolled-up cape from his saddle, he watched General Washington and the young marquis remove their swords then lay side by side on the bare ground, the General carefully draping his cape across them both. Choosing a nearby spot under a spindly pine tree, Nathanael removed his own sword and jacket and lay down close to his aide, pulling his cape over his weary body.

The American sentries tirelessly stood guard over their sleeping comrades while the chaplains, medical detachments, and burial details made their morbid search of the battlefield. Nathanael listened to the muffled words of those busy with the aftermath of the day. He heard the moans of the wounded, and the creak of the wagons—wagons he, himself, had made provision for as quartermaster general—as they transported the dead and injured. And amidst this scene, draped in the darkness of the still, summer night, he began to doze, his last thoughts lingering on the success of this battle fought near a courthouse called Monmouth—success for the command of Washington, Stirling, and himself—but what of Charles Lee?

With the morning light, the discovery was made of General Clinton's withdrawal. George Washington did not pursue.

"I will decide on Lee's guilt or innocence after I have heard all the evidence at the court-martial. Thank God I am not appointed to sit in judgment; for, between you two and Colonel Hamilton's free account of General Lee's conduct on the battlefield, I might have to disqualify myself due to prejudice before the court-martial convenes." Nathanael exclaimed, momentarily silencing Anthony Wayne and the Marquis de Lafayette. "I trust you have not spoken so freely with those who will sit in judgment."

"No. Lord Stirling's given clear warning," Anthony replied rather sheepishly.

"Good. I certainly do not envy His Lordship the responsibility of this court-martial. It seems, despite your obvious views, gentlemen, that other than the charge of disrespect shown to the Command-in-Chief following the battle, the charges are questionable."

"Questionable?" Anthony Wayne bellowed, joined by the marquis' objection spoken in French.

"Yes, gentlemen, questionable. Failure to follow orders is the first charge—the orders, of which I have read a copy, were ambiguous. 'Attack if possible.' The response to such an order is highly subjective. What I view as possible may not be what you view as possible," Nathanael paused looking straight at the Marquis de Lafayette, "—I have been there, gentlemen. I have received ambiguous orders and interpreted them wrongly—and I am grateful that a court-martial was not called in regard to my blunder."

Nathanael was suddenly aware of the intense frustration expressed on the young marquis' face. Though barely nineteen years old, under calmer circumstances he already had the appearance of one much older. His youthful body, tall and slender with large, powerful shoulders, was adorned with the head of an aging man. His auburn hair was receding prematurely; his sharp facial features combined to make him unattractive. But now, with the added pressure at hand, the boy general, as his comrades affectionately referred to him, appeared older still.

Nathanael noted Anthony Wayne's expression revealed the same intensity as young Lafayette. For the young marquis it was the frustration of being robbed of his command—a command that very well may have led the American Army to a far greater victory. For the Pennsylvanian swashbuckler, it was the frustration of having needlessly faced the brunt of the attack for four grueling hours—losing men that might not have been killed had the detachment not been ordered to retreat.

"General Lee was in a position to attack." Anthony protested.

"Yes, to attack the British rear guard, but that's not what he claims to have found when he finally came into contact with the enemy. Lee claims it was Clinton's entire force—the odds were then three to one—too steep, in his estimation. Again, ambiguous orders."

"He never intended to fight," the marquis declared.

"What do you mean?"

"The eve of the battle there were no plans for an attack. Tell him, General Wayne!" the marquis implored Anthony, then turned back to Nathanael and continued in his excitement. "He had no orders to give us. At the onset of the battle, I was with General Lee. I urged him to outflank the British. Lee replied that I did not know how the British fought, and that we could not stand against them and must be cautious. I proceeded to tell General Lee that British soldiers had been beaten before and could be beaten again!"

"Are you prepared to state this under oath?" Nathanael asked, appalled by the account, yet wondering if the marquis might be jealous of losing his command to Lee—or could it be even deeper than this? It was known among the young marquis' intimate friends the contempt that he held toward the British. Not only had Great Britain been the long time nemesis of France, but also, it was by the hand of a British officer that the young general's father had been killed. Lafayette was but a babe at the time, with no memory of his honored parent, only emptiness—an endless sense of loss and grief. Charles Lee, being a former British officer may have stirred a passion for revenge within the French nobleman.

"But most certainly I will state this under oath! Lafayette exclaimed. "I sincerely question the man's patriotism."

Nathanael held the boy general under a steady gaze, fairly certain now that pent up anger over his father's death was inciting the rash statements. "His loyalty to the cause?" He pointedly asked.

"Treason?" Anthony queried further, equally concerned by the remark.

"Treason? No, no, I do not mean that," Lafayette quickly protested. "I perceive that he has been abused by the British Parliament and has reason for personal animosity. He is determined to bring embarrassment upon them. It's an old grudge, perhaps going back to when he served as a British officer."

The statement was spoken with tenderness, and revealed a depth of insight, which seemed to counter Nathanael's previous thoughts.

The marquis paused as though uncertain of how to continue. "—He is not fighting as we are for the independence of the colonies. He has nothing but contempt for the soldiers of this army and usually speaks of them with a sneer."

He stopped speaking, as tears pooled in his brown eyes. With great solemnity, he looked from Anthony to Nathanael and continued, "Do you not feel it, my friends? Do you not know it for yourselves? Charles Lee is not an American at heart."

Anthony glanced at Nathanael, a slow, affectionate smile forming on both their faces.

"Would that all Americans had the love for this land that our dear Fayette does." Anthony exclaimed.

In July of 1778, a committee of twelve general officers with Major General William Alexander, the Lord of Stirling, serving as president, heard the evidence in the court-martial of Major General Charles Lee. Their verdict of guilt on all charges and sentence of suspension from command for one year was reviewed and upheld by the Continental Congress of the United States of America.

The sound of approaching footsteps distracted Nathanael from his work. Surprised that one of his aides would be awake at such a late hour, he turned to the open doorway, fully expecting one of them to appear. To his utter astonishment, the Marquis de Lafayette came into view.

"What are you doing here at this hour?" Nathanael asked, his voice lowered out of consideration for those sleeping within the small house.

"Your pardon, General Greene!" Lafayette exclaimed softly. "I was passing by and saw the light. I did not intend to disturb you."

"You are not disturbing me; it is just that I am surprised to see you. It must be nearing 2:00."

Lafayette nodded.

"Sit down, Fayette," Nathanael said pointing to a chair as he rose to his feet and closed the door behind him.

"Too excited to sleep?" Nathanael asked knowingly.

"I am— My countrymen are finally arriving in force. How can I sleep with the prospect of the glory ahead?"

"And you shall be draped in laurels, my dear Marquis." Nathanael said with an affectionate smile for the sentimental Frenchman. "Whether His Excellency combines the strength of both forces against Clinton in New York, or forms for an attack in Rhode Island, you are guaranteed a command."

"—I understand you have been assigned the task of relocating the army," Lafayette began hesitantly.

"The very reason I am burning the oil tonight—hoping to get things in order before I go."

"How long shall you be gone?"

"About a week."

"Ah. Enough time to get a taste of civilian life," the marquis said with a teasing smile.

"Hardly. Oh, I will escape the sound of reveille and tattoo, but they have little bearing on my day anyway. I am usually awake long before the former and always awake long after the latter," he said with a chuckle. "You may be on your way to Rhode Island before I return," Nathanael stated matter-of-factly, noting an instant change in the young man's countenance.

"Then you believe there is a good possibility New York will not be our aim?"

"The British fleet is tucked within Sandy Hook. I question whether the weightier French vessels can safely maneuver close enough to do damage to the British fleet. And I seriously doubt they will draw them out under the circumstances— What is it, Fayette?" he asked, aware of the marquis' sudden uneasiness.

Lafayette stared at him for a moment. "—As excited as I am about this command, I would gladly share with you the laurels certain to be obtained."

Nathanael, touched by the marquis' words, was unable to respond immediately.

"—Thank you, my friend. I know how much this command means to you, and, how sincere your offer is. What a grand opportunity is before you—to command a division in the first battle with the aid of the French. And what a child of fortune John Sullivan is—to have command of the combined army. Your influence, my dear Marquis, played a great part in making it all possible. And your presence will prove invaluable."

"As would yours," Lafayette replied.

Nathanael smiled. "I have resigned myself to the fact that Rhode Island shall be delivered without me, though in my own way I have assisted by seeing that your men will be adequately supplied, and the march is as easy as possible." Nathanael laid his hand upon a formidable stack of papers, some of which recorded the many purchases for the impending battle, and the others mapped out each day's march to both New York and Rhode Island.

"You have my blessings, General Lafayette—and my charge to be victorious."

"How can we fail?" the marquis asked with a brilliant smile. "As your Congress said, the French shall be America's deliverer!"

Hearing the statement somehow disturbed Nathanael just as it did when he read it previously.

"How long has it been since you were last home?" Lafayette asked.

"Three years."

"You mentioned that I may be only a few miles from your family—how do you say the name of the town—Covetry?"

"Coventry," Nathanael corrected.

"If I have time, I should feel it my duty and privilege, to visit them."

"I expected that you would show your kindness to both Caty and me by paying her a visit if at all possible. She will be delighted to see you. And kiss my sweet, fatherless children for me, Fayette. How I long to hear my little ones prattle about."

Lafayette's sympathetic gaze clearly communicated his response to Nathanael's request. Separated from his own wife and daughter, he understood the heartache of his friend. "That I will do and return with a full report of their every move," he said, and then turned his attention to a medallion fastened to the vest beneath his jacket. After unfastening the object, he held it out to Nathanael. "I wish to present this to you."

Nathanael took hold of the medallion, which was about four inches in diameter. The center of the object depicted a Masonic scene encased beneath delicate glass. The scene was surrounded by a gold perimeter depicting the rays of the sun.

"There is little opportunity for attention to presenting jewels in military lodges," the marquis said with a sad smile. "I want you to have this—a symbol of my affection for you, my brother."

"This map is full of inaccuracies. I reconnoitered this piece of land myself, and this does not give a precise accounting!" Nathanael roared grabbing the map from the table and shoving it into Major Rob Burnet's hands. "If this cartographer cannot produce an accurate drawing of this area by tomorrow morning, then find me one that can!"

"Yes, sir." Rob said and headed for the door. Nathanael, still fuming, watched him leave the room.

Just outside the tavern, Rob encountered a young captain who immediately saluted his superior. "Sir, could you please tell me where I might find General Greene?"

"Inside the tavern. He's in the bedchamber to the right at the top of the stairs."

"Thank you, sir."

"Do you have a message for him?" Rob asked, mounting his horse.

"I do, sir."

"You'd better pray it is good news, Captain, for he is already in as foul a mood as I have ever seen him."

The captain appeared dumbfounded, looking down at the sealed letter in his hand, then upward to the lighted window on the second floor.

Rob threw a sympathetic smile at the young man and then set his spurs to the horse.

Major Billy Blodget quickly answered a hesitant knock on the chamber door. "A message from Headquarters for General Greene, sir."

Billy stepped aside providing the nervous captain with a clear view of the general seated at a small table.

"Good news I trust," Nathanael barked, ignoring the captain's salute. His hand was extended to receive the dispatch.

He nervously walked to the table and handed Nathanael the letter, waiting at full attention.

Impatiently tearing apart the seal, Nathanael began reading, expecting an update on the pending battle in Rhode Island. The tone of General Washington's harsh words was hardly anticipated. In a state of disbelief, Nathanael read the unexpected reprimand. His countenance fully revealed his shock.

"Is everything all right, General?" Billy asked with concern.

"—It is a personal matter," he replied softly without looking up. Then turning to the captain he added, "Did His Excellency seem upset when he gave you this?"

"I didn't see His Excellency. It was given to me by Colonel Tilghman, sir."

"I see— Major Blodget, be sure that the captain is comfortably bedded down for the night. And no doubt, you are tired after riding with me all day. Get some sleep yourself."

Billy was still concerned about Nathanael's reaction to the dispatch. "Are you certain that I cannot be of further assistance to you tonight, sir?"

"No. Until I have that map— Get your rest while you can, Billy. I promise to have you at a gallop tomorrow," he said with a forced smile.

"Good night, sir," Billy said, echoed by the young captain.

"Good night, gentlemen."

When the door closed behind them, Nathanael slowly read the dispatch again.

"I do not understand," he muttered to himself, laying it down on the table only to quickly pick it up and pore over the words once more.

When the initial shock subsided, anger took its place. "Neglect?" he angrily muttered. "I was ordered to come here. How can I be in two places at one time? How can I possibly meet the demands and not destroy my health in the process?"

Nathanael rose to his feet and restlessly paced the floor. "Lord! Can I be charged with being inattentive or negligent to my duties as quartermaster general? Nay! I have been ever attentive, neglecting my own ease and interests to put this department in order—this blasted department!"

His eye caught a glimpse of Caty's recent letter lying on the dresser, which he picked up. "My wife laments the fact that I will not return home and fight for my own state—nay, she blames me! It is beyond my control, yet somehow, I am the fiend! Though I submit to that which I cannot change and pour myself into the job before me, it is not enough! I cannot please either of them!"

He scanned Caty's words, words that pricked his very heart. "Surely she knows how I long to return home to be with her—to see my children—"

He looked over at George Washington's letter on the table. "And certainly he knows that no other man on earth could have influenced me to take on this miserable, thankless job!"

A soft knock on the door disrupted the venting of his frustration.

"Come in."

Rob Burnet opened the door and stepped into the room. "Sir, the cartographer has assured me of an accurate map by morning. He will deliver it at first light."

Nathanael nodded. "Get some sleep, Major."

The major turned to leave.

"Rob."

"The aide quickly turned about. "Sir?"

"Thank you."

"Your welcome, sir."

Nathanael stood alone in the room once more—the anger had dissipated—yet the anger was easier to deal with than the lingering pain that remained. He laid

Caty's letter down on the dresser, a letter he had painstakingly responded to already.

He walked to the table and sat down. Taking pen in hand, he dipped it in the ink well as he reached for a fresh sheet of paper. The letter was addressed to George Washington, and in a respectful manner, Nathanael expressed his anguish in having received the Commander's written rebuke.

A summons to Headquarters upon Nathanael's return to camp was immediately heeded. George Washington received Nathanael's salute and in silence led him to the privacy of his own chamber.

"I have a report of the possible sites along the Croton River per your order, sir," Nathanael said stiffly, handing General Washington the paperwork as soon as the chamber door was closed.

"You'll find the area just west of what's known as Cooper's Ford is suitable to our needs—though I am of the opinion, after reconnoitering the area, that our present site is more advantageous. My reasons are carefully documented." Nathanael lifted his arm and gestured to the detailed accounts in the Commander's hand.

"We will go over this later. I have another matter to discuss presently. Please, Nathanael, sit down," George Washington said with a warm, though uneasy, smile. He moved to the chair opposite Nathanael's at the small chamber table and sat. "I trust you received my reply to your letter."

"I did, sir." The stiffness in Nathanael's tone remained; the former ease he had displayed in the Commander's presence was gone.

"It was written in haste, for I had many demands on me at the time," George Washington began, his attention seemingly fixed on the papers lying before him. Slowly he lifted his eyes to meet Nathanael's. "Though it was brief, all else waited until it was written; and had I been able to take the time to write more this awkward moment would, I should hope, be behind us."

George Washington reached into his jacket and pulled Nathanael's lengthy response to the charge of neglect out of his inner pocket laying it on top of the papers before him.

"You are right, General Greene; I do expect more from you than is humanly possible because I am accustomed to receiving that from you. It's easy to fall prey to taking advantage of one as industrious as yourself—"

He paused for a moment as if searching for the right words. "I am ever aware of your devotion to the public good, to this army, and most especially to me. You accepted the responsibilities of quartermaster general at a most desperate moment. We came out of Valley Forge victorious in battle. And perhaps—should we be ultimately victorious—General Steuben shall go down in history as being responsible for our success. But I know differently—all of America should know. Von Steuben would not have had an army to train had it not been for the selfless attitude and tireless effort of Quartermaster General Nathanael Greene. That is how history should read." the General exclaimed with a proud gleam in his eyes.

"I was pressed by the French fleet for instructions as where to attack, New York or Rhode Island. I longed for your counsel, not only as a superb battlefield commander, but as quartermaster general as well. There was much to consider in making the decision. I am sorry, Nathanael. My guilt is in not telling those closest to me how very much I appreciate them."

"I fully understand the pressure you were under, sir, and only wish I could have been here to offer counsel," Nathanael replied with all sincerity.

"There is more to discuss," George Washington said.

"Sir?"

"The Battle of Brandywine. You mentioned in your letter the hurt you experienced when I failed to commend to Congress your men and your command on that day."

"It was foolish of me to make mention of it, sir. That battle was fought nearly a year ago," Nathanael said, visibly embarrassed.

"The battle was fought a year ago, yes. But your pain remains. I can see now that my failure to commend your extraordinary action that day was wrong. As you know, I have always made it my practice to make mention to Congress the general officer most distinguished in each battle. Anthony Wayne's praise was sung for Monmouth—the praise due you at the Brandywine, though as deserved, was not given. At the time I thought my reasons made perfect sense."

George Washington reached over and grasped Nathanael's forearm. "I feared Congress might accuse me of showing partiality to you. Your brigades consisted mainly of Virginians—my own statesmen. And you—it is well known in Congress that I favor you.

"There was no general on the field that day who out performed you. My sincere apologies, sir." He said without loosening his hold.

Nathanael responded with a silent nod and warm smile.

George Washington let go of his arm. "No doubt you have much to attend to in your department."

"Indeed I do, sir."

"Then I will not keep you. I will review your report and discuss it with you this evening over dinner."

"Yes, sir." Nathanael stood and left the room.

In silence, George Washington stared at the closed door, contemplating his next act. Carefully pushing aside the pile of papers on the table, he reached for a fresh sheet of paper. After dipping his quill, he began to write, addressing his letter to the president of the Continental Congress, stating that he judged it advisable to send General Nathanael Greene to Rhode Island. He reminded them that the services of the native Rhode Islander would be invaluable in the upcoming conflict with the enemy.

He stopped and considered the other reason for sending the Rhode-Island warrior home—a reason he could not list to Congress.

"Because I owe him as much—" he said aloud.

"Would to God it was in my power to give peace to your bosom, which I fear is like the troubled ocean."
(Nathanael Greene to Caty Greene)

CHAPTER TEN

DARKNESS CREPT QUICKLY upon the Rhode-Island countryside. The soft summer breezes joined by the serenade of the hidden night creatures brought back to Nathanael's mind pleasant memories of home as he quickened his pace the closer he came to Coventry.

"We will be there soon." he assured the only remaining aide, Rob Burnet. Both Billy Blodget and Sam Ward were spending the night with their own families, having already taken leave of their commander, turning off the road toward their homes.

Familiar with the landmarks around him, even in the darkness, Nathanael realized that the house was but a few minutes away. "It's around the bend sitting atop the hill." he suddenly exclaimed to the weary aide, setting his spurs to an equally weary horse in an attempt to hasten his arrival. The horse, after a grueling four-day trip of two hundred miles, loyally submitted to its master's prodding.

Eagerly, Nathanael reined the horse in before the front door, then leaping from the saddle, bounded inside. "Caty! Caty!" he cried, straining to get a glimpse of her in the rooms adjoining the downstairs hallway as he tore the gloves from his hands.

"Nat! Peggy, it is Nat!" Jacob exclaimed from the entrance to the library. Peggy stepped out of the kitchen just as the brothers fell into one another's arms.

His sister-in-law patiently waited her turn.

"It is good to have thee home, Brother." Peggy managed through her tears as Nathanael held her in a warm embrace.

"And wonderful to be here, Sister."

"We did not expect thee until the morrow. Mother Greene and the brethren are all eagerly awaiting!" Jacob exclaimed, firmly taking hold of his younger brother's arm.

"We made excellent time— Caty!" he gasped, his eyes suddenly diverted to the stairway at the end of the hall.

She remained transfixed at the bend in the staircase. Her soft black curls flowed freely about her shoulders; her loose-fitting night clothing failed to hide her advanced pregnancy.

"Did I awaken thee?" Nathanael asked with a grin, assuming by her slowness to react that she had been stirred from a sound sleep.

"—No—" she replied just above a whisper. "I was reading—Nathanael, I cannot believe you are here." She remained on the staircase as if afraid the sight of him was a dream that might end abruptly.

"I am here, Angel." He walked to the bottom of the staircase and extended his hand to her. Slowly she made her descent, sobbing as he took her into his arms.

"I have come home, Caty— I have come home at last," he whispered, holding her tight.

Rob Burnet came through the open doorway with a brown paper package in his hand. After smiling at his preoccupied commander, he turned to Jacob and Peggy and introduced himself.

"Brother Nathanael said in his letter that thee would be accompanying him. We prepared the guest chamber," Peggy informed him with a welcoming smile.

"I only received your letter three days ago!" Caty exclaimed as if in response to Peggy's statement. "Have you seen General Sullivan?" she quickly added.

"I spoke with him briefly."

"Then you know that the French war ships have already begun the attack."

Nathanael smiled tenderly, cupping her cheek in his hand. "Not quite yet. They are shelling Newport, it is true; but the attack will not come for a few more days, and I will speak no more of it tonight. Tomorrow afternoon I will return to my duties; but until then the hours I have in Coventry will be free from the concerns of the war."

A child's giggle echoed down the staircase. Nathanael's eyes were suddenly drawn to the upper level. "Are the children still awake?"

"They should not be, but it appears that they are." Caty replied with a smile.

"Shall I get them?" Peggy offered, noting his excitement.

"Please!"

Peggy soon appeared at the top of the staircase with little Patty upon her hip. The baby's dark eyes peered at the strange man below.

Nathanael watched in utter amazement as two-year-old George made his way down the stairs with one hand holding tightly onto his aunt's, and the other carefully lifting his nightshirt to avoid being tripped. His bright blue eyes were intent on the staircase as his exposed, chubby legs descended each step with great care. When he reached the bottom, his proud smile greeted everyone alike.

Peggy stood one-year-old Patty alongside her brother. The timid baby, her dark short curls poking from beneath her bonnet, immediately scooted behind her aunt's skirt as Nathanael squatted before the children.

"Sir, the gifts you brought," Rob reminded him in a soft tone, handing the brown package to his commander.

Nathanael opened the package and took from it a wooden whistle. "This is for thee, George. Listen to what thee can do with it." he said, putting it to his lips and blowing. The shrill sound delighted the boy, who immediately reached up to accept it from his father and try it for himself.

Little Patty, frightened by the sound, retreated further behind Peggy's skirt.

"See what Papa has for thee, Patty," he said softly, picking up a small rag doll from the wrappings. The child could not be enticed by the toy, and began crying, holding her arms out to her aunt in a pathetic attempt to be rescued.

"Patty. Come see the pretty dolly Papa brought for you." Caty coaxed, reaching for the little girl's hand.

"Do not force her, Caty," Nathanael said softly, continuing to smile at the baby.

"She is tired," Peggy explained. "I will see if I can get her to sleep." She picked the crying baby up. "Shall I take George with me?"

"Nay." Nathanael's quiet, but immediate response came. "Perhaps she will take this from thee." Nathanael handed the doll to his sister-in-law.

"I know the whistle came from the army's supply, but where did you get the doll?" Caty asked.

"Colonel Cox purchased it for me. He is quite sensible to the wants of girls, having a house full of daughters. If the doll was supposed to win her affection, it appears I have failed miserably." he lamented, watching Peggy ascend the stairs with his clinging daughter.

"Thee are a total stranger to her, Nat. She will warm up to thee in the morning," Jacob offered, laying his strong hand on his brother's shoulder. "Come, thee both must be famished."

Nathanael reached down and picked George up; then grabbing Caty's hand with his free hand, he followed Jacob to the kitchen with Rob Burnet close behind.

George played contentedly about the kitchen as the adults conversed. Before long, the little boy was tugging on his father's arm in an attempt to climb upon his lap. Nathanael effortlessly lifted the two-year-old, who snuggled into a comfortable position and was soon fast asleep.

Rob, soon excused himself from the conversation, unable to stay awake any longer. Peggy was quick to follow, offering to put the sleeping child in bed. His father still refused.

Nathanael, eager to hear every bit of family and community news, fought his own exhaustion. But, as Caty and Jacob's yawns became more frequent, he was forced to yield to his own body's desperate need for sleep.

"I will see thee in the morning, Nat," Jacob said as his brother laid his sleeping son in the bed next to Patty.

"Thee should sleep in, though I suspect the sound of the forge will have thee up at first light."

"No doubt," Nathanael agreed. "Good night, Jacob."

He lingered in the room for a few minutes, lovingly admiring his sleeping children. Patty was clinging to her new doll, and George continued to grasp the whistle. Securely tucking the linen sheet about them, he bent down, kissing them both on the forehead, then joined Caty in their bedchamber.

George and Patty tagged behind their father as he stepped out into the morning sunshine. From the granite step at the rear entrance, he gazed off through the woods in the direction of the ironworks.

George clumsily made his way past Nathanael, knocking his unsteady sister. The baby groped at her father's leg in a desperate attempt to regain her balance. Quickly Nathanael reached down and took hold of the small girl, whisking her into his arms.

"Do you want to walk with Papa?" he asked, kissing her on the cheek. She smiled at him, her constant companion still in her arms.

"Me come too?" George asked.

"Of course you may come."

Slowly he made his way to the backyard where three of his brothers stood conversing with Rob Burnet.

"We wondered how long it would be before the women drove thee out of the kitchen!" Bill Greene exclaimed.

"They do not look much like officers to me." Perry commented, noting that Nathanael was casually dressed in his civilian clothing and Rob Burnet in a borrowed outfit.

"Sister Peggy was kind enough to wash our uniforms," Nathanael informed him.

"Bill just told me an outrageous story. What time did thee say brother Nat got out of bed?" Kitt Greene asked Bill in disbelief.

"Sister Caty said it was 8:00." Bill replied.

"Nat. I have never known thee to be so slothful. Army life has corrupted thee." Kitt said with a teasing grin for his older brother.

"Army life has exhausted me, brother."

"Uncle John and cousin Griffin came by this morning to say hello, only to find him still in bed." Bill told Kitt. "Uncle John claims that considering his slothful habits, he would expect no more from him in the forge, should he return, than the labor of a coal runner."

Nathanael laughed at hearing the story again. He turned his head toward the ironworks. Though not seen, it noisily made its presence known. "Uncle John's enticement for me to prove myself will simply not work." Nathanael assured his brothers.

He then turned to face the house, visually inspecting it.

"Jacob has done well in keeping it up," Kitt commented.

"He certainly has," Nathanael agreed. "My! This land is so hopelessly barren!" he exclaimed looking about the yard, then turning his gaze toward the ironworks once more. "Where are Jacob and Elihue?" he asked, aware that the two missing brothers were not in the house.

"They are down at the forge," Kitt answered.

"Would thee like to inspect the ironworks, Nat?" Bill asked.

"—I should repay Uncle John and Griffin's kindness—"

"Oh, do not worry about that. They will be up for dinner," Perry offered.

"I would like to say hello to the men—" He quickly added.

The brothers smiled at one another knowingly.

"Have you ever visited an ironworks, Rob?" Nathanael asked his aide.

"No sir, I have not."

"Caty!" he suddenly cried out, walking back toward the open door.

Caty soon appeared.

"I am heading down to the forge. I am afraid these little darlings might try to follow," he said, Patty still within his arms and George at his heels. "I will only be a few minutes," he added, kissing her quickly on the lips as he handed her the baby.

The thud of the massive hammer intensified as the men moved closer to the ironworks on the well-worn path leading through the woods. By the time the building, which housed the ironworks, came in sight, Rob had all he could do not to block his ears against the deafening sound. The Greene brothers, who had gradually intensified the volume of their own conversation as they neared the building, were now shouting to one another to be heard. Rob suddenly realized how his commander could effortlessly make known his orders amidst the clamor and confusion of the battlefield.

The scene of the forest about him and the waterfall tumbling into the crystal river below were robbed of their beauty amidst the violent clamor. The large, rustic, frame structure, which housed the ironworks, dominated the scene. Its sloping roof came almost to the ground on the side away from the river.

As the men stepped inside the building, they were greeted by the smell of burning charcoal and semi-molten iron, coupled with the heat of the many blazing fires used to make pliable the metal.

A wide grin on John Greene's face was exactly the response Nathanael had anticipated from his uncle. As the older man walked toward his nephew, he patted his son Griffin on the back and pointed toward Nathanael. Within a moment, the deafening sound of the massive hammer ceased as the signal was given to stop the waterwheel.

"Ah, lad! It is good to see thee!" The old Quaker shouted, taking Nathanael into his bear-like arms.

"David! Thee have come to drive the Philistines from us!" Griffin exclaimed, enveloping his cousin in his own strong arms as soon as his father released his hold.

Eagerly, the men working at the forge gathered to greet their former master as Kitt introduced Rob to his uncle and cousin.

"We came to the house to see thee earlier," Uncle John began with the pretense of being annoyed. "I found thee behaving in a most sluggardly fashion."

"The very reason I am here, sir, to repay the kindness."

Uncle John laughed. "Thee are here because thee could not stay away! Iron is in your blood, boy. But I will be honest, lad, I do not think thee have what it takes." He reached out and grabbed Nathanael's upper arm. "Jelly. Not enough strength in that arm to forge a horseshoe, never mind an anchor."

Nathanael met his teasing smile but offered no response.

"What is the boy's record for bar iron, Elihue?" Uncle John called out without shifting his gaze.

"Eighteen minutes, Uncle," Elihue Greene's immediate reply came. Nathanael's skill had been unmatched by any in the forge—except that of Nathanael, Sr.

"A bar in twenty minutes. I will graciously give thee two extra minutes. Can thee do it boy? I have my doubts."

Still Nathanael did not verbally reply though the sparkle in his eyes and the widening smile on his lips communicated to John Greene that his nephew's will was weakening. Nathanael was never one to turn down a challenge; the older man was very aware of this fact.

"My goodness! Bar iron is hardly a test of strength; why I have been teaching little George how to make one!" he said causing the men gathered about to break out in laughter.

"I will make thee a bar in twenty minutes," Nathanael said coolly.

"So thee do not have the ability to do it in eighteen?" Uncle John asked with a laugh.

"Elihue! What's Uncle John's time on bar iron?" Nathanael asked with a firm, smiling gaze on his uncle.

"Twenty- two minutes."

"I have been away from the forge for three years, sir, yet I will still beat that time." Nathanael teased as he began to remove his waistcoat and shirt, revealing, so it seemed to Rob, a physical strength every bit as powerful as that of his kin.

"Throw me an apron, Kitt!" he yelled to his brother as the men moved away giving him plenty of room to work.

Griffin pulled out a pocket watch and checked the time just as Nathanael finished tying the leather apron around his waist, and took hold of a pair of massive iron tongs. Rob watched as his commander, with seeming effortlessness, grabbed a large piece of iron from the chafery fire with the gigantic tongs.

"That is called an ancony." Kitt Greene informed the observant aide, pointing to the iron clutched within the tongs. "It has gone through two stages already from what is called a loop, which is basically a mass of semi-molten iron; the slag was pounded out forming a rather crude, bulky bar."

Jacob Greene released the flow of water onto the powerful wheel outside, which set the five-hundred-pound hammer in motion. The incessant pounding began.

"The crude bar was transformed to this stage," Kitt shouted, again pointing to the
odd shaped bar as Nathanael pulled it across the dirt floor atop a line of metal plates.

The bar, Rob noted, had bulbous projections, rectangular in shape on both ends, the
center having been hammered to a cross section of about two inches square.

"And what shall the finished product look like?" Rob asked his voice barely audible above the surrounding clamor.

"If properly done it will be approximately two inches wide, one half inch thick and fourteen feet long."

"And how much does that piece of iron weigh?"

"About fifty pounds."

Rob shot his head around to look at Kitt. "Fifty pounds?" Came the incredulous response. "How can he possibly do this in twenty minutes?"

Kitt grinned. "If I were a betting man I would wager he will do it in less—"

Nathanael watched the massive hammer, carefully timing his next move by its rhythm. After crashing onto the bare anvil, the hammer began its slow, cumbersome ascent. Quickly, Nathanael lifted the weighty tongs, with a firm grip on the ancony, and placed it on top of the anvil, bracing his body for the hammer's plunge.

The massive weight crashed against the iron, sending streams of hot metal flying. Though some of the sparks hit Nathanael's bare arms and shoulders, he barely flinched, maneuvering the ancony just so with the tongs, so that the hammer's next blow would be most effective.

After a few minutes of manipulating the iron under the hammer's weight, Nathanael pulled it off the anvil and tossed it in the nearby chafery fire, softening once more the cooling metal. Slowly the men returned to their various tasks, keeping a keen eye on the progress of the former iron master.

Rob watched in amazement as the ancony began to take on the shape of a long, thin bar. The process appeared simple enough, periods of pounding interrupted by momentary plunges into the intense heat of the chafery fire. But the aide realized that only an experienced man would know where the blows would be most effective, or when the feel of the iron warranted more heat. Only a man accustomed to years of such backbreaking labor could possibly maneuver the weight of the tongs and iron, endure the flying sparks, and the maddening crash of the hammer with such ability and concentration.

Perspiration now covered Nathanael's body, emphasizing his muscular form. The veins of his arms and neck bulged under the constant strain of the weight. Suddenly yanking the tongs away from the hammer, Nathanael tossed a smooth, straight bar onto the ground and then dropped the tongs next to it.

"Time!" he called out breathlessly, which brought all work to a halt.

"Nineteen minutes!" Griffin cried.

John Greene's laughter filled the building as the roar of the water wheel ceased.

"Iron is in your blood, boy—forever in your blood! Your father would be proud!"

"Pull yourself away from that map, Nat, and join us in a toast." General John Sullivan called out from across the dining room where General James Mitchell Varnum was handed a choice bottle of wine by his servant, and proceeded to pour a generous portion for the five officers present.

"The council of war has ended, General Greene; it is time to relax and celebrate our forthcoming victory."

Freedom's Cost

"Relax? It is upon the adjournment of a council of war that I begin to worry," Nathanael said with a smile, taking the goblet his friend Jim Varnum held out to him. "Your celebration is a bit premature, isn't it, John?"

"How can we fail? Even as we speak, Admiral d'Estaing is harassing the British with his twelve ships of the line, and will soon disembark 1,500 French troops on the shores of Rhode Island. One thousand five hundred seasoned regulars will arrive in the next day or two," he said smiling at the young marquis who had arrived along with Jim Varnum ahead of the marching Continentals, which included General Varnum's all black battalion. Varnum had petitioned General Washington to recruit black troops from Rhode Island, offering any man who was a slave his freedom in exchange. This battalion quickly numbered 130 men.

"And General John Hancock will soon follow with an estimated 7,000 militia. Combine this with the superb command ability in this very room, and I shall ask you again—how can we fail? To our victory, gentlemen." Sullivan said holding his goblet up. "A victory that will prove to forever bind us to our French deliverers."

Nathanael reluctantly took a sip of the wine.

"General Hancock's influence as former president of the Continental Congress has certainly proved invaluable in recruiting militia," Colonel Christopher Greene commented.

Colonel Greene looked at Generals Sullivan, Lafayette, and Varnum as he spoke, then rested his eyes upon his cousin. "Don't you agree, Nat?" he asked, confused by his cousin's whimsical expression.

"But of course, Cousin Chris; tribute to whom tribute is due, and honor to whom honor is due." he replied; then, directing his attention to John Sullivan, he added, "We should always treat those of Congress, who join our ranks, with great care. For we may see them return again to that august body, and hopefully they will not forget their needy brothers in arms."

John Sullivan laughed, his dark eyes gleaming. "You will not persuade me to return to Congress. I prefer the fight on the battlefield to the fight on the senate floor." As he finished speaking the dining room door opened. Caty entered the room accompanied by the wives of Jim Varnum and Chris Greene, and followed by bustling servants who quickly went to work preparing the table for dinner.

"You had a nice, long chat, gentlemen. Was anything accomplished?" Caty asked cheerfully, slipping her arm through Nathanael's.

"That is the purpose of calling a council of war, madam." John Sullivan replied with a chuckle.

"According to General Greene, the best way to accomplish nothing is to call a council of war.," she pertly replied, smiling up at Nathanael.

John looked from her to Nathanael and back again, his eyebrows cocked. "You had best not repeat your husband's words in the presence of His Excellency."

"Oh, but I have. And His Excellency told me that he is forming the same opinion."

"Your secrets are not safe with your wife, General Greene," Lafayette said with a chuckle.

"My wife does not know my secrets," Nathanael replied winking at Caty.

"Nat's made no secret of the fact that he prefers a written proposal from field commanders in lieu of a council of war," Jim Varnum interjected.

"Why?" Chris Greene asked.

"You bypass the endless debate. When you have ten or twelve field commanders present, you often have many varying opinions. To write out the proposal provides the Commander with clear and precise strategies and tactics without the emotional input which often brings confusion," Nathanael explained.

"But have no fear ladies, we are of like mind and are confident of our success in driving the enemy from your home state," John Sullivan remarked, his face aglow.

As the others continued to converse, Nathanael's attention drifted to the view outside the dining room window.

"What are you thinking about, Nat?" Jim asked, noting his friend's distraction.

Nathanael turned to him and smiled, then directed his full attention to John Sullivan. "John, being an attorney you must appreciate the location of this fine house," he said.

John glanced out the window and immediately noticed the clear view of the courthouse below. Beyond it laid the seascape of Greenwich Bay.

"General Varnum was the most prominent attorney in the area prior to the war. He carefully chose this location and then hovered over the builders day in and day out as they worked," Nathanael informed him.

"I was not that bad!" Jim protested.

Nathanael laughed. "You should hear the stories the carpenters tell. Isn't it so, Cousin Chris?"

"It is."

"It's a magnificent house, General Varnum. And from one attorney to another, the location is perfect." John offered.

"Thank you, sir."

"So, you have known each other for quite some time?" Lafayette asked.

"We go back a number of years," Jim began. "I handled a few minor cases pertaining to the Greene ironworks and mills, and I represented Nat in the *Gaspee*

Affair—"

"The *Gaspee*!" John's eyes darted between Nathanael and Jim. "Wasn't that the British revenue schooner that illegally seized local merchant ships charging the owners with smuggling?"

"It was," Jim replied.

"That incident caused almost as much excitement throughout the colonies as the Boston Tea Party! What was your involvement?" he asked Nathanael.

"I am innocent of all charges." Nathanael timidly replied, laying his right hand upon his heart. There was a definite twinkle in his blue eyes.

"Charges! What charges?" John asked in astonishment.

When he saw that Nathanael intended only to answer his question with a sheepish grin, John turned to Jim Varnum. "Counselor, what were the charges?"

"Nat was accused of leading the mob in setting fire to the beached schooner."

John cast a thoughtful gaze on Nathanael. "You declare your innocence—who was your accuser, and why would you be singled out?"

"My accuser was a British officer aboard the schooner. A reward was being offered for information leading to the arrest of those responsible for the torching. The fact that I was determined to be vindicated in court for the seizure of a merchant ship belonging to the family business was reason enough, it seems, to name me, and thus end my court appeal. Yet, I had an alibi—three witnesses were with me at my home, some ten miles from the beached schooner, at the time of the torching."

"A highly questionable alibi," Caty interjected.

Nathanael smiled at her. "My wife thought the entire incident was a great feat of daring; and, though we were only casually acquainted at the time, she would like to believe I was the ringleader."

John looked at Caty. "Why do you doubt his alibi?" he asked, seemingly ignoring Nathanael's words.

"The three witnesses were General Greene's brother, Kitt; his cousin, Griffin; and Mrs. Utter, an elderly housekeeper who treated him like a son. All three were devoted to him. Not one of them would hesitate to lie to protect his life."

"As I recall, those involved were being threatened with deportation to Great Britain for trial and possible execution— Did they lie for you?" John asked bluntly.

Again, Nathanael smiled. "You must keep in mind, John, that I was a peaceful Quaker at the time."

Nathanael's reply caused Christopher Greene, Jim Varnum and Caty to burst into laughter.

"And your letter to Sam Ward at the time, in regard to the accusation truly reflected your pacifist beliefs! Did you ever see that particular letter, cousin Caty?" Chris asked.

"The one in which our peaceful Quaker threatened to blow a hole in his accuser, big enough to let the sun shine through?" she asked, her teasing smile fixed on her husband.

"It was written in a moment of frustration," he explained with a smirk, which quickly disappeared. "The entire affair was a bit unnerving, occurring about the same time the Coventry ironworks had burnt to the ground—"

"General Varnum, dinner is ready, sir," a servant announced.

"Please be seated," Jim Varnum said to his guests, gesturing toward the table with his arm.

"The *Gaspee* affair forced us to consider how far we were willing to go to regain our liberty," Jim began as everyone took his or her seats. "The Boston Tea Party followed shortly thereafter, then the British occupation of Boston. Nat, Chris and I became involved in forming a local militia company, which we named the Kentish Guards. We began to drill, rather awkwardly at first; then Nat managed to smuggle a British deserter out of Boston to help us. It was about that time the Society of Friends confronted you both about your interest in the military, wasn't it?"

Nathanael and Chris nodded.

"I suppose you could hardly deny your interest at that point, having the commission of militia officers." John said with a chuckle.

Nathanael's blank stare greeted him from across the table—a short grunt was his only response.

John became aware of a sudden uneasiness in the room. He looked from face to face, expecting an explanation. There was none. He shared a bewildered glance with the marquis, and both of them turned to Nathanael once more.

"I did not receive a commission. I served as a private," Nathanael offered in response to their unspoken question.

"A private! You helped found the company and then served only as a private! Why?" Lafayette exclaimed.

"—My limp was considered a blemish to some. It was thought unbefitting of an officer in their estimation—"

"I cannot believe it! Are you serious, Nat?" John asked.

"Quite," was his soft reply.

"Chris and I were so incensed by the insult that we planned to resign our own commissions," Jim explained. "But Nat dissuaded us for fear that the company would disband in short order."

"You simply fell into line as a private after forming the company, obtaining a drill instructor, and being chastised by your congregation?" John asked in disbelief.

"—Not quite—" Nathanael began hesitantly. "I was a bit upset at first—"

"A bit upset!" Caty laughed. "He was mortified and moped around for days!"

"As I recall, mortified is the word you used to express how you felt, sir," Jim agreed with a grin.

Nathanael smiled at them. "All right, I was mortified and did mope for days. I even threatened to quit the company altogether! But I realized that my defense of liberty did not rest on whether or not I fought in the ranks or as an officer. When the general alarm was given upon hearing of the battle in Lexington, I marched with the Kentish Guard as a private, prepared to assist our Massachusetts brothers."

"—How can that be? Nat, I met you only a few weeks after Lexington, and you bore the commission of brigadier general over the Rhode Island militia companies. Are you telling me that you went from private to brigadier general in just a few short weeks?"

"No, it was not a few weeks. I went from private to brigadier general in one day!" Nathanael corrected him with a smile.

John flung himself back in his seat, obviously astonished by the entire conversation. "How?"

Nathanael shrugged. "I am not really sure, but I suppose that my input on the committee to revise the military law of the province had an effect on the Rhode Island Assembly."

"Nat had the keenest mind in the colony in regard to military matters," Jim offered. "I, too, was a member of that committee. The fact that a private was assigned to it shows the confidence many had in him. His ability to quickly discern a matter, his effortless analysis, and the logic of his reasoning made a great impression on those in the assembly," Jim stated.

"General Knox's statement makes sense now," the marquis said thoughtfully. "He was sharing with me accounts of the army's early struggles during the siege of Boston. He told me that General Greene came as the rawest, most untutored of the general officers; but in less than twelve months, he was equal in military knowledge to any general officer in the army, and superior to most."

"It was his destiny from birth—" Chris Greene stated just above a whisper. When Nathanael turned to look at Chris, his cousin met his gaze with a sense of wonder.

"—Nat! Old Doc Spencer's prophecy! I had forgotten until now about that prophecy!"

"What is this about a prophecy?" the marquis asked.

"Nat's father often spoke of the prophecy given upon his birth of how he would one day become a mighty man in Israel."

"I can assure you that my father anticipated a very different fulfillment," Nathanael said with a smile. "But if, in fact, it was a prophecy from Heaven, I do not consider it fulfilled yet."

"What do you mean?" Chris asked.

"If we lose this war, none of us will be remembered except as a reproach for our rebellion against the might of Great Britain and her sovereign, King George III. If Israel denotes the United States in this prophecy, I can assure you that none within this army, or in Congress, will be viewed as mighty men unless we gain the final victory—not a Washington, Hancock, Sullivan, Lafayette, Varnum or a Greene! Our graves will be trampled on and our names despised. Few remember the noble and just reasons for an uprising if it ends in defeat—"

Silence filled the room as Nathanael's eyes locked onto the map of Rhode Island displayed behind John Sullivan's seated form. He appeared disturbed.

John glanced over his shoulder at the map that held his friend's attention, and then turned back to Nathanael. "We have the victory, General Greene; a victory that has the potential of driving the British from America for good. The prophecy shall soon be fulfilled! What could go wrong?"

"If we could form for the attack tomorrow, I would share your confidence, sir. But the fact that we must wait ten days to proceed—much can happen in ten days—much too much!"

Coventry, Rhode Island
September 1, 1778

Dear Henry,

By now, news of the battle in Rhode Island has reached you. Details of our situation have been sent to His Excellency who can fill you in. Suffice it to say that the devil has gotten into the French fleet. Poor General Sullivan, so certain of ultimate success and disappointed that that which was in his grasp was whisked away, has displayed his Irish temper in such a way as to possibly threaten our future alliance with France.

The situation remains in a state of turmoil—and our dearly bought victory has left a bitter taste. We should have been successful in driving the British from Rhode Island; and,

though we drove them back on the battlefield, alas, they remain in Newport, now rein-
forced in their position. Though you can be sure, I took great pleasure in watching the
enemy flee from the field before us, the results were hardly what we had hoped. I have
confused you no doubt. But such is the situation—confusion prevails. Let me backtrack
and see if I cannot briefly explain the chain of events.

The joint attack was set for the tenth of August. But, when General Sullivan discov-
ered that the British abandoned their works to the extreme north of Newport, he ordered
the army to at once occupy the abandoned posts. When Admiral d'Estaing learned of our
move, he was very annoyed, believing, so it seemed, that General Sullivan was eager to
reap glory by being the first on enemy ground.

D'Estaing quickly landed his 4,000 marines that were to form a combined French-
American division under Lafayette. Our total force numbered 12,000, plus twelve ships of
the line to back our advance. This gave us a fair advantage for an offensive attack against
the estimated 6,000 British.

Before all was in readiness, however, d'Estaing learned that the British had sent rein-
forcements by sea. Rather than leave his marines with us and sail out to meet the enemy
fleet, he insisted on reboarding the men—who were in truth of no value to him, but of
immense value to us!

We were uncertain of how to proceed. Though 7,000 militia appear substantial, we
know very well that they cannot be depended on under fire. Our strength was in the
French troops and fleet combined with our small number of regulars.

For two days, the opposing fleets sailed upon the high sea; then on the third day a vio-
lent storm, of hurricane proportion blew in. Our concern for the fleet was all but forgotten
in the wake of our own immediate danger. Tents were carried away by the wind and
whipped into threads, leaving our men exposed. A few of our people were killed, as were
many horses. Our powder was virtually destroyed.

When the storm finally ended, the battered French ships made their way back to the
Rhode Island's harbor. Admiral d'Estaing immediately notified us of his intention to pro-
ceed to Boston to refit—with his 4,000 marines!

We were stunned! General Sullivan, already in a rage, ordered me to sail out to the
French flagship and try to persuade d'Estaing to change his mind, with Lafayette at my
side serving as interpreter.

I pointed out to the admiral that the fleet could refit just as well in one of the Rhode
Island ports. He would not listen. I tried to reason with him in regard to leaving the
marines with us but to no avail. (The evening may not have been a total loss had I been
able to indulge in the fine meal set before us—the first good meal I had seen in days; but,
overcome with seasickness, I was forced to avoid the table and present my appeal between
spells of vomiting)

General Sullivan, infuriated even more by Admiral d'Estaing's refusal to listen to rea-
son, published in his general orders a stinging insult against the Admiral—indeed,
against the French alliance! This, in turn, set our entire camp to murmuring against the
French—which they fell into naturally considering our long, bitter enmity with France in
our former position as the subjects of the English throne.

Lafayette declared that he felt as welcome in the American camp as he would in the
British camp. He and General Sullivan, as you can well imagine, went at it in heated
rage. The poor marquis! Torn between loyalty to his countrymen and his deep affection
for his American comrades in arms.

Sullivan, coming to his senses, sent the marquis to Boston to present his apologies for
his insulting remark, and attempt to persuade the Admiral to return as soon as possible—
or to march the troops back with Lafayette.

As the days passed, our shaky militia units began to dwindle. It was quickly decided
upon to attempt against the enemy before our numbers were too weakened to consider any
move. And so, on the twenty-ninth of August we faced the British on the field in a heat-
ed and well -fought battle. Casualties on both sides were high considering the numbers
involved. Three times, we drove them back, finally taking the field.

Concerned that we might find ourselves trapped should the British fleet return with
their reinforcements, we made our escape under the cover of darkness with General
Glover's able Massachusetts regiment of fishermen transporting us across the water as
they had at both Long Island and Trenton. Our timing was Providential, for with the
morning light the British fleet appeared upon the horizon!

And here we are—d'Estaing still in Boston (the marquis having missed the battle
entirely); General Hancock unable to hold the militia together longer than the time agreed
upon in the terms of their enlistment; and poor John Sullivan, with troops too few to face
the strengthened British force. The enemy will continue to occupy Rhode Island and at
present, we are unable to do anything about it.

My plans are to head back to camp within the week. I will welcome your words of
encouragement upon my return. I am, dear sir, your obedient and humble servant,

Nathanael

As Nathanael completed his signature, the library door slowly creaked open. He
turned to see Caty's head peek through.

"Well, here they are!" she exclaimed looking at George and Patty playing on the
floor beside their father's desk. "Peggy! Nathanael brought the children into the
library!" she called out, and then stepped into the room. "We thought they were
upstairs all this time. Nathanael! They are not normally allowed in this room. We

shall have a time of keeping them out once you have gone back to camp!" she scolded with a smile as Peggy entered behind her.

"They did not disturb a thing. They have played contentedly the whole while," he assured her.

"Of course they played contentedly, for they already know that if they do not disturb you, you will stop to toss them in the air or wrestle with them on the floor every now and again! You already have them spoiled!"

"Do not waste your breath, sister Caty!" Peggy said with a teasing smile for her brother-in-law. "Look at him, just as smug as he can be! Here we are searching frantically about the house for the missing babies, and he takes his scolding with the grin of a Cheshire cat! I suppose we will not even get an apology for the scare!"

"I should think, ladies, that when you discovered the children were not in their chamber that the first place you would look was in here!"

"What did I tell thee, sister Caty—no apology?" Peggy said with a laugh as she coaxed the children to stand.

"Would you mind if we put them to bed, General, as it is well past their bedtime?" Caty asked.

Immediately little George began to protest. "I no wanna go to bed!"

"Where is your whistle, George?" Nathanael asked, holding out his hand. The small boy picked up the whistle from the floor and handed it to his father. Nathanael put the wooden piece to his own lips and blew one of the tunes he had been teaching his son. "Tattoo has sounded—now it is time for all good little soldiers to go to sleep!" Lifting both children upon his knees, he kissed them goodnight and sent them upstairs with their aunt.

"And when does tattoo sound for the general?" Caty asked, stepping behind his chair and gently massaging his tired shoulders.

"When my arm is too weary to write another stroke."

"Are you writing to His Excellency?" she asked, noting the letter he had just finished.

"No. It is to Henry. Shall I extend your greetings?"

"—Of course."

Nathanael picked up the quill pen and added a few more lines.

"Have you written to His Excellency yet?' she asked, peering at the stack of outgoing correspondence.

"Not today."

"Will you be tonight?"

"I have no reason to— Why?"

Immediately she removed her hands from his shoulders and walked toward the open door.

"What is wrong, Angel?" Nathanael asked, turning to face her.

"You promised last night that you would write to General Washington and request a leave of absence!" she exclaimed, her back still toward him.

"I made no such promise," he softly replied.

"You did! It was the last thing you told me."

Nathanael laughed. "Now that you mention it, I vaguely remember you questioning me. Caty, if I made such a promise it was in a state of semi-consciousness."

His laughter infuriated her. "It's not fair, Nathanael!" she yelled, turning to face him. "Henry Knox stayed with Lucy when she had her last baby! And both Colonel Cox and Colonel Biddle were given leave by you to attend their wives! Are they somehow more important than me?"

"Caty," he began softly, all trace of his prior laughter gone. "The families of both Biddle and Cox live close by the camp. And as for the Knoxes—Henry was sent to Massachusetts to locate a site for the arsenal—you know that."

"But his stay was extended because of Lucy's condition!" she pointed out defiantly.

"It was; but, if you will recall, Henry was not with Lucy when their first baby was born. I was with you at George's birth."

"But you were not with me the last time, and you will not be here this time if you get your way!" she sobbed.

Nathanael stood and walked to her, taking her into his arms.

"Why won't you ask for leave? Why?"

"Because you have a number of weeks to go yet, and I cannot neglect my department that long."

She forcefully pushed against him with her arms, freeing herself from his embrace. "What about me, Nathanael?" she shouted. "You've neglected me for three years now! I hate your blasted quartermaster's department, and I hate your army! I hate this house and I hate being alone!"

"Angel, certainly you know I would rather stay here with you and the children," Nathanael offered tenderly.

"No! I do not know that at all! It is so easy for you, isn't it? You go back to your precious army with all the pomp and honor due your rank— You can spend the next few weeks being entertained by the Ladies Stirling with little thought of me or this child!"

"What are you talking about?" Nathanael was both shocked and confused by her outburst. "There are no family members presently in camp—my thoughts will constantly be with you and the baby—"

"Go ahead and leave, Nathanael!" she screamed. "Go back to your army! But be certain of this, when you say good-bye this time, it will be our last good-bye!"

"Caty! What are thee saying?" his dumbfounded response came.

"You determine the meaning, General!" Sobbing, she quickly exited through the open doorway.

Nathanael immediately went after her, only to be stopped at the threshold by Jacob, who guided his brother back into the library, closing the door behind them.

"I have to go to her, Brother!" Nathanael protested, trying to get past Jacob.

"Nay! Peggy is with her. Your presence right now would only prove to disturb her all the more."

"I had no idea she was so wrought about her delivery—I knew she was overly fearful for my safety during the battle, but—"

"It was not just the battle. It was the storm and the fact that the British remain in Rhode Island. Do thee have any idea how terrified she is of having the British and Hessians nearby?"

Nathanael shook his head.

"Brother, for all of her outward show of gaiety and her appearance of maturity, within she is just a frightened child—afraid of life in general. Under normal circumstances she may be able to cope, but her circumstances are far from normal."

"She is threatening to leave me, Jacob!" Distraught, Nathanael threw his hands out before him in a display of helplessness.

"Nay."

"Thee heard what she said, Brother, that this will be our last good-bye!"

"Nathanael, your wife believes that she will die birthing this child—and so she may—"

"Jacob! Do not even speak such a thing!"

"Take heed, Nathanael. She is not strong, and she is pleading for thee to uphold her through this ordeal. She almost did not make it after Patty was born. I do not expect she will this time if thee leave. Can thee live with that, Brother?"

Nathanael turned from his brother, putting distance between them. Then, swinging around, he glared at Jacob. "Am I a fiend in your eyes, Jacob? Do thee question my love for my wife and child?"

"Nay, Brother. Thee will do what is right," Jacob, said walking to Nathanael and laying a comforting hand on his shoulder.

Nathanael met his brother's compassionate gaze. Then turning away, he walked to his desk, thoughtfully staring at the papers before him.

"—I will do what I can to supply the army from here. I fear it will not be a very efficient attempt—the pressure of finding winter quarters for the army will soon be upon me. Pettit and Cox will do their part from the camp—" Turning to Jacob he added, "Will thee assist me here, Jacob?"

"Both Griffin and I are already agents in the department. We will do whatever needs to be done in assisting thee."

Nathanael's weak smile showed his appreciation. "I may have to spend some time in Boston. A fair amount of the army's supplies can be furnished from that town if they are willing to negotiate a fair price. Do thee think Caty will be all right if I go to Boston for a few days?" he asked timidly, obviously disturbed by the fact that his brother was more sensitive to his wife's emotional state.

"I think she will be fine."

Nathanael pulled his chair out from the desk and sat down. After selecting a fresh sheet of paper, he took the pen and dipped it into the ink well. Jacob quietly made his way to the door as Nathanael began to write out his request for a leave of absence.

"I would say your remaining in the area has been Providential, General Greene. Had you left when initially proposed, any hope of future joint maneuvers with our French allies would have been dismal at best," Governor John Hancock stated, then took a drag from the pipe in his hand.

Despite the fact that John Hancock had invested much of his money in the war, he remained one of the wealthiest men in America, and it was apparent. Nathanael could not help but admire his host's amber, satin coat, trimmed in gold braid, though his thin frame, slight stoop and nervous mannerisms failed to enhance the finely tailored suit. Nor could he help but admire the fine furnishing, lavish wallpaper and rich, heavy draperies. And the portrait above the intricately carved mantle drew his attention.

"Your services as a diplomat have proved invaluable. Admiral d'Estaing sings your praise—he trusts you exceedingly." The governor stopped speaking as a servant came in and poured tea for himself, his wife Dolly, Nathanael and his two aides.

"The Admiral claims you are a French brother. Whatever does he mean?" Dolly Hancock asked, her own burgundy silk gown was as rich in appearance as her husband's clothing.

"My grandmother was French, madam," Nathanael informed her with a friendly smile.

"I see. And General Lafayette feels this fraternal bond as well, it seems. He, too, is grateful for your taking on the role as peacemaker," she added with a most attentive, sweet smile for the major general. Blond curls hung gracefully from a neat bun atop her head. Her vivacious personality was reflected in her youthful and attractive appearance.

"I cannot sit here and take all the credit." Nathanael gladly turned his attention back to John Hancock. "Your Excellency worked tirelessly in removing the wedge placed between our forces over this late battle."

"To be candid, General, there were moments when I felt our attempts would prove fruitless," John Hancock confessed, the smoke curling up from his pipe. "I still shudder when I think of that French naval officer—a nobleman nonetheless—being killed by one of my townsmen in a foolish scuffle."

"There still may be repercussions for that," Nathanael pointed out, for it would be weeks before news of the young aristocrat's death reached France.

"The admiral has accepted it in stride, so I hope his will be the prevailing attitude. My greatest fear right now is that General Sullivan may once again let his temper get the better of him and make another inappropriate remark, which would undo all that we've managed to accomplish." Taking another drag from his pipe, Governor Hancock failed to see the knowing glance shared by Nathanael and his aides.

"What is it, General?" the observant Dolly Hancock inquired.

"Madam?"

"My husband's words seem to have triggered a response between you and your officers. We are well acquainted with John Sullivan and his Irish temper. My husband's fear stems from an intimate knowledge of General Sullivan's disposition."

"Has he endangered our position, General?" John Hancock asked.

"General Sullivan has been given direct orders from both the Commander in Chief as well as the Continental Congress to reserve all negative comments in regard to the French alliance."

"What further incident occurred to bring that on?" John Hancock coaxed.

"General Sullivan sent a censured account of the Battle of Rhode Island to the state's congress."

Governor Hancock shook his head and sighed. "And was it read aloud to the members?"

"No, thank God. I received word that it had been sent, and with all haste went to the state house, disturbing the congressional session, I am afraid, with my unannounced entrance."

John Hancock smiled, imagining the congress's reaction to the bold, and no doubt, dramatic entrance of this physically powerful man. "And then what happened, General?"

"I went straight to the table of the speaker, who was preparing to read the report, pounded my fist on the table, and in the name of God pleaded with him not to make public the report until he reviewed it. He had the good sense to immediately call a recess, review the report, and extract that which was harmful."

"And hopefully you gave a sound verbal lashing to our dear General Sullivan." John Hancock said with a warm smile.

Nathanael returned the smile. "In truth, sir, I understand his frustration. But, we are not in a position to make public our disappointment. I tried to warn him of the possibility of a turn of events."

"I suspect that General Washington is disappointed that you were not given the command in Rhode Island." John Hancock remarked.

"My duties as quartermaster general are too pressing to take full command of such an engagement."

"I fully understand, sir, yet cannot help but lament the fact. Had you been in command, I have little doubt but that the outcome would have been vastly different," John Hancock said matter-of-factly, then took a long drag on his pipe.

"Thank you for your confidence, sir; but I must say in John Sullivan's defense that he is a fine general, and my superior in rank."

"He may be a fine general, and your superior in rank; but you are his superior in ability. Would that your attention was not needed in the quartermaster's department."

"I will gladly turn the department over to another when my year is up." Nathanael assured him with a smile.

"You have made remarkable progress with the department."

"Thank you, sir. My assistants, agents, and aides have worked diligently to get it back in order."

"I hear talk that some of your Southern agents may be defrauding the government. How might I respond to such gossip? Or is it gossip, General?" John Hancock asked with a curious smile.

"I have nearly 300 agents working under me throughout the United States. Most of them were in the department before I was appointed. I cannot sit here and tell you that none is, in fact, defrauding the government. But I can tell you this, that though my agents as a whole are not as good as they probably should be—they are by no means as bad as they are thought to be."

John and Dolly Hancock laughed at his reply.

"The expenses in my department are enormous, and rising with each passing day. This is not due to the fact that my agents are dishonest, as many would like to think, but because of the rapid inflation of our currency. If the economic situation in this country continues as is, soon there will not be enough funds in the universe to keep the army in the field."

"Are you still of the opinion that the Continental Congress should levy a federal tax for keeping the army?" John Hancock asked, familiar with Nathanael's proposals to Congress.

"I am, sir."

"A free people will not readily submit to federal taxation," the former president of the Continental Congress pointed out.

"Begging your pardon, your Excellency, but we are still fighting for our freedom. And until we drive the British from our shores and obtain Great Britain's acknowledgment of this nation being free and independent, we can tell ourselves we are free, but we have not yet truly obtained that state. I cannot keep an army in the field on the illusion of freedom. And if the citizens of this new nation will not submit to being taxed for this purpose, our struggle will be drug out, sir, and the outcome is highly questionable. Many will die who need not die."

As John Hancock prepared to rebut Nathanael's argument, Dolly interrupted. "General Greene, you could not imagine how many discussions on taxation have been held in this very room through the years. The names and faces are all coming back to me now: Samuel and John Adams, James Otis, Josiah Quincy, and, of course, Joseph Warren," she turned to look at the portrait of Dr. Warren above the mantle, which had drawn Nathanael's attention earlier. "And now your name is added to these and so many others."

John Hancock noted Nathanael's lingering stare at the portrait. "If I had to name one individual who was most responsible for educating and preparing the people for our stand against Great Britain, it would be Joseph Warren. He was a remarkable man."

"I quite agree, sir," Nathanael said, still gazing at the portrait.

"While presiding over Congress, I often found myself discouraged over the great responsibilities and decisions before me. I sometimes let my thoughts wander to conversations I had with him, or experiences we shared. In these memories I have found strength to go on."

"I knew him only briefly, but can fully appreciate what you are saying," Nathanael said turning from the portrait. He rose to his feet; his aides followed his lead. "We must beg leave, your Excellency, for we have a long ride ahead of us tomorrow."

"I wish we could persuade you to stay a few days longer, General Greene. There are more contacts to be made—"

"I will have to trust my local agent with making them, sir. I promised my wife I would be back within the week."

"And of course you must go to her. I am sure she is anxiously awaiting your return," Dolly agreed.

"She has another month to go, but yes she is anxious to have me close by. We will be leaving at first light, sir, so we will take this opportunity to extend to you both our thanks for your generous hospitality."

"It has been our great pleasure, General Greene," John Hancock said with a firm handshake for each of them.

The hours passed in conversation as the three men made their way back to Rhode Island. Rob Burnet, his cheeks aching from continuous laughter, listened to one humorous tale after another as his riding companions competed in telling amusing anecdotes of their youth. Nathanael Greene and Billy Blodget, with their country witticism, produced story after story.

"With all due respect, General Greene, certainly you do not expect us to believe that outrageous story?" Rob exclaimed through his laughter.

"And why not, Major? It is true."

Rob turned questioningly to Billy. "Speak for yourself, boy. I have heard the story told elsewhere. I know the Greene brothers. It is true." Billy assured him with a shrug of his shoulders.

Rob turned his attention back to Nathanael. "You expect me to believe that you moved a boulder, sir?"

"Not me alone. My brothers helped."

"Even still—a boulder? How large was this boulder?"

"Large enough that it required the lot of us." Nathanael said with a chuckle. "You have to understand the desperation, lad. Our father rarely gave permission for us to attend such a worldly function as a dance. We could attend the dance if we plowed the field out as far as the boulder."

"Why didn't you just plow the field out to the boulder?"

"It was a mighty big field, boy!"

"So you moved the boulder?" Rob repeated.

"We would have moved a mountain if it would have gotten us passage to that dance."

"What is the problem, Rob? You have seen the Greene brothers—they are pure muscle. Ingenious, that is what it was, absolutely ingenious. And how did your father react to it?" Billy asked.

"We moved the boulder more than half way across the field and plowed out as far as the boulder. We were only told to plow to the boulder; nothing was said about its location. We all attended the dance."

Billy was doubled over on his horse with laughter. Rob soon joined in.

"Looks like it is going to rain." Nathanael commented as large drops began to fall from the overcast sky.

A cold, steady rain plummeted from the sky, hastening the fall of the brilliant leaves adorning the well-traveled New England road. Before long, the three travelers were soaked. The energy previously lent to their story telling now was directed toward quickening their pace to the nearest tavern to wait out the storm. They proceeded at a canter until brought to a dead halt by an approaching rider.

"General Greene!"

Nathanael immediately recognized the rider as a boy who worked at the forge. "What is it, lad?"

"A message from Mr. Jacob, sir!" The boy pulled a letter from his coat pocket and handed it to Nathanael.

"When did you leave Coventry?" Nathanael asked, the paper drooping around his hand as it quickly became saturated with water.

"About four hours ago, sir."

"What is it, Nat?" Billy asked.

"Caty has gone into labor."

Billy peered through the raindrops for a landmark. "We can make it back in less than three hours," he said pointing to a farmhouse down the road that he knew would be familiar to Nathanael.

"Let's go!" Nathanael agreed, setting his spurs to his horse. Both aides followed close behind leaving the young messenger to return home at his own pace.

Jacob heard the horses approach the house and quickly opened the door to Nathanael and his aides.

"How is she?" Nathanael's frantic question came. Jacob immediately noted his brother's labored breathing.

"As well as can be expected. She fell into a depression shortly after thee left, and has been threatening to give birth for the past two days."

"Why did thee not send for me sooner, Jacob?" Nathanael exclaimed.

"The doctor thought that confining her to bed would halt it. I sent for thee as soon as it was apparent that it could not be stopped. The doctor is with her. Mother and Peggy are up there too."

Nathanael headed for the stairs. Jacob grabbed hold of his arm as he passed. "Thee are soaked to the skin, and on the verge of being ill. Change into some of my clothes; then come and have a cup of coffee; and some nourishment."

"I will change my clothes; bring me up some coffee, I cannot eat right now—"

"Nathanael," Jacob locked his eyes onto his brother's. "—The doctor does not offer much hope for the baby—I am sorry."

Caty's moans echoed through the house as Nathanael hurriedly pulled the wet clothing from his shivering body and clumsily put on Jacob's dry clothes. Quickly he went from Jacob's bedchamber, meeting his brother in the hall with a steaming cup of coffee. After taking a gulp of the hot brew, he handed the mug back to his brother and walked to the closed door of his own bedchamber, offering a silent prayer before entering.

"You are just in time, General—not a minute too soon I should say." the doctor greeted him as he walked to the side of the bed.

His stepmother moved from the chair at the bedside where she had busied herself with dampening Caty's forehead, cheeks and neck with a cool wet cloth. Nathanael sat down. Caty rested on her side facing him. He immediately took her tense hand into his own. Her dark eyes locked onto his, reflecting her agony and fear.

"I came as quickly as I could—"

"It is too soon, Nathanael!" Once again, the relentless pain gripped her. Caty's body tensed as she moaned in protest.

"Do not fight it, Caty. Take short, quick breaths." Peggy instructed as she went to work vigorously massaging Caty's lower back.

Caty loosened her grip on Nathanael's hand as she followed Peggy's instructions. When the contraction ceased, she looked at him with tear-filled eyes. "I want it to stop, Nathanael! I cannot stand it anymore!"

Anxiously, Nathanael turned to the doctor.

"It will be over very soon, General," the doctor assured him.

"It will not be long, Caty," Mother Greene called out.

As another contraction came, Peggy immediately busied herself with the massage. "It is a normal reaction toward the end for a woman to feel that she can no longer cope with the pain," she explained to her brother-in-law. "She has endured it well."

When the next contraction ceased, Nathanael dampened the cloth in a bowlful of water and gently dabbed his wife's flushed cheeks and forehead.

With the next contraction, Caty immediately perked up. "It is time!" she shouted, and to Nathanael's astonishment, she positioned herself on the bed and with all the energy she could muster, she bore down. Within a few minutes, her efforts were rewarded with the weak squall of an infant.

Exhausted, Caty dropped back on the pillows; perspiration beaded on her forehead. There was no excited announcement. The doctor handed the frail newborn to Mother Greene, who quickly wrapped the baby in a warm blanket.

"Perhaps there is a slim chance after all," the doctor said, turning his attention back to Nathanael and Caty. "You have a daughter. I do not know why, but such small, sickly ones tend to do better when they are female."

No sigh of relief followed—no joyous laughter or proud examination of their newborn child. When the pathetic squall of the infant was quieted in her grandmother's warm embrace, the room was filled with a mournful silence. Nathanael looked at his wife; tears rolled from her closed eyes as her lower lip quivered. He took her hand into his own and squeezed it gently.

Caty's recovery was slow, as though her own health would return only with the baby's increased strength. Day passed into day—each one offering renewed hope for the tiny infant.

The hopelessness faded as little Cornelia Lott Greene began to thrive. Smiles once again appeared, and the gloom of pending death was replaced with newness of life.

"Be honest with me, Nathanael," Caty said as he took the sleeping infant from her arms and gently placed her in the cradle beside the hearth. "Are you disappointed at not having another son?"

"No," he said, carefully tucking a blanket around the baby. "She is everything I could have hoped for."

"What were the odds at camp?" Caty asked knowingly.

Nathanael chuckled. "Last I heard it was ten to one that you would have a boy. The prevailing attitude is that any child conceived at Valley Forge had to be a male."

"Ten to one! Well, didn't we show them, Cornelia and me!"

Nathanael lingered at the cradle for a moment, silently contemplating Corneilla's initial struggle to survive. It somehow seemed fitting that this child, who had spent the earliest weeks of her life with the suffering army at Valley Forge, should, like them, struggle for her very existence. Now, like them, she should grow strong and excel, he prayed, leaning over to kiss her tiny cheek.

"I heard Billy make mention that a letter arrived from Headquarters today," Caty said as Nathanael grabbed a book from the nightstand and climbed into the bed next to his wife. "What are your orders?"

Nathanael saw the apprehension on her face. "—I am to head back as soon as possible."

"When will that be?" she asked, directing her attention to the ceiling.

"I should have things tied up here by the week's end."

Caty wiped her eyes in an attempt to hide her tears. "When were you going to tell me?"

"I planned to break the news to you tonight—"

Nathanael placed the book back on the nightstand and turned on his side taking her into his arms. "General Washington sends his greetings and his congratulations—"

Caty turned her head away from him.

"He is anxious to go into winter quarters."

"It is too early," Caty argued, still looking away.

"The British are showing no sign of venturing out of New York. His Excellency does not feel we will face them again until spring and therefore sees no reason to remain in the field. The sooner I return, the sooner I can send for you."

Slowly, Caty turned her head to face him.

"I am seriously considering setting up camp in Middlebrook, New Jersey again. The Lott family would be close by. Wouldn't it be nice to introduce your dear friend Cornelia to her little namesake?" he asked, hoping to cheer her.

"Middlebrook?" she asked, a faint glimmer appeared in her eyes.

"Middlebrook is a beautiful valley, and perfectly situated for the army," Nathanael said. "I will find us a handsome home where you can entertain to your heart's delight. And we will probably spend some time in Philadelphia, for I have business to attend to there."

"How long before you send for me?" she asked, her eyes now alive with anticipation.

"If we go to Middlebrook, I would say about a month."

"Only a month? Oh, my. I will need some new dresses! I will have to make a trip to Boston—I will have to—"

"Wait just a minute, woman!" he laughed, leaning over and kissing her on the lips. "You must regain your strength before you go off on a shopping spree! Remember the last time you did that?"

"I do," she meekly replied.

"As soon as you are well enough, you go and buy yourself a new wardrobe. I will leave plenty of money to cover the expenses—in fact, buy a new wardrobe for each of the children as well," he instructed.

"Do we really have the money to pay for it up front?" she asked with a beaming smile.

"We may not be wealthy, but my commission affords us to live in comfort. And, if I cannot find a suitable investment the moment I receive it, I would just as soon spend it. The blasted currency loses its value each day, nay, each moment it sits in my pocket."

"An entire wardrobe with no argument?" Caty felt the need to double-check.

"An entire wardrobe with my blessing," he said kissing her once again.

"We had a little dance at my quarters a few evenings past. His Excellency and Mrs. Greene danced upwards of three hours without once sitting down."

(Nathanael Greene)

CHAPTER ELEVEN

"YOU WILL FIND it futile to avoid it, gentlemen," General Benedict Arnold began, his dark eyes bulging unattractively from a moon shaped face that turned from General Washington to General Greene. "The people of Philadelphia all but worship the officers of the Continental Army. Should you fail to socialize with the distinguished citizens and guests of this fair city, you are certain to offend them."

"Have you heard the distinguished citizens or guests of Philadelphia complain that our behavior is socially unacceptable, General Arnold?" George Washington asked, his brow cocked.

"Some have noted of late that you, sir, and General Greene, barely partake of the feasting. You have formed the habit of passing the evening in a corner of the room, as you are even now, discussing matters between yourselves while the others enjoy the social gaieties about you."

"It was spoken as a complaint, General?" George Washington queried further.

"Not exactly, sir. It is assumed that your discussions are of military importance and as for the lack of appetite—"

"It is not so much a lack of appetite as it is revulsion to gluttony!" Nathanael interrupted. "I counted 160 dishes at last night's affair. Each night the tables are similarly laden with food. I must have put on ten pounds in the past month and struggle to fit into my breeches."

When General Arnold's laughter was not joined by that of Washington or Greene, he appeared momentarily confused.

"—Gentlemen, the concerns of the army are ever present and overwhelming. A few hours of leisure in the evening can only prove beneficial to you both. See how your wives glow in the social setting about them!"

The three men looked toward the women. Martha Washington seemed absorbed in the constant flow of conversation, representing her illustrious husband with a sense of royalty.

Caty stood with another group. Alongside her was Alec Hamilton. With one hand clenching his arm for support, Caty leaned forward consumed in her laughter.

"She actually named it Hamilton?" Caty's question was easily heard by the men in the corner.

"I do not find it so amusing!" Alec replied, obviously embarrassed by the sudden attention.

"It is absolutely hilarious! Where is she?" Caty searched the faces about her. Spotting Martha Washington close by, she grinned, already holding the older woman's attention.

"Is it so, Lady Washington, that you named your tom cat for our prowling colonel?"

"Hamilton seemed a fitting name for this particular tom!" Martha replied with a smile for the humiliated colonel. Once again, Caty was consumed with laughter.

"Your wife thrives in this setting, Nat!" Benedict Arnold said with a chuckle.

"We are delighted that our wives are enjoying themselves," George Washington began. "But our concerns are with the army and our desire is to return to camp speedily. We would gladly occupy our evenings with the business at hand rather than in such frolicking."

"Indeed! I believe the business I have with Congress might have been completed in a few hours rather than the weeks I have spent here, had they the ability, or is it simply the desire, to come to a decision and forsake the continuous yearning for entertainment. Such extravagance—" Nathanael complained.

"Such extravagance seems in line with your station, Nat." Benedict Arnold finished the sentence for him with a coy smile.

"I beg your pardon?"

"Word is that your department expects to spend some forty million dollars this year alone. Is it true?"

Nathanael looked him straight in the eye. Having already come under the scrutiny of Congress for the department's expenditures, he was well prepared to defend himself against any innuendoes from Benedict Arnold. "No, Ben. I can tell you without hesitation that it is not true. With the economy at present, and our currency depreciating as rapidly as it is, I expect to spend no less than fifty million. Feel free, my friend, to correct those who are speculating with such error about my department."

Benedict Arnold was awe struck as much by the exorbitant price as by both Nathanael and George Washington's nonchalant manner in regard to it.

"Now, you were saying something about my station, Ben?" Nathanael reminded him.

"You receive a commission of that total sum—one percent, isn't it?"

"My commission is split evenly with my assistants. I therefore receive one-third of a percent," Nathanael corrected him.

"Still a staggering sum, sir! Many would consider you a wealthy man, and this life-style to be in line with your wealth."

"Would they now?" Nathanael said with a chuckle. He had always been impressed with Benedict Arnold's boldness on the battlefield, and was not the least bit offended with it now. He could handle, with great patience and civility, direct questions. It was the rumors and murmuring that quickly brought his blood to a boil.

"One would have to possess some wealth to get by in Philadelphia. One of our soldiers would be forced to spend a half-year's pay to live here but a week! You must remember, Ben, my commission is paid in the same worthless notes with which I am forced to purchase supplies. I can account for all the money entrusted to me; and, as for my commission, I never wanted it in the first place. So, if some have a complaint in regard to it, let them take it to our Congress which set the percentage," Nathanael said, casually glancing around the room. "The truth is that I grew up in simplicity, sir, and much prefer it to this—"

"Ah! New England pietism—I, myself, have come to detest it!" Benedict Arnold's contemptuous reply came. "Only in New England were we taught that to have less somehow meant one was holier—and to drive oneself from sunup to sundown was a sign of righteousness. Puritan mumbo jumbo—"

"Is that what you call it in Connecticut?" George Washington asked with a glimmer in his eyes. "In Virginia we refer to it as the Puritan work ethic. And though my mother is an Episcopalian, she lives by it and taught me to do the same."

"I—I did not mean to imply—" Benedict Arnold stumbled over his words.

"The situation in Philadelphia is alarming, General Arnold," George Washington began as he grimly scanned the scene about them. "Neither General Greene nor I are opposed to social gatherings. We partake of them often in camp, as you well know. But this obsession with it has proved detrimental, certainly to the needs of the army and to the needs of the nation as well." He fixed his eyes on General Arnold's.

"You say that the people of Philadelphia all but worship the officers of the army? I tremble to think of it. Our struggle is not over, and the end not yet determined, though one might think otherwise by the constant celebration about us. Let this people not anger the Almighty with their idolatry and pride—for we on the battle-field will be the first to witness His chastisement."

"I think it is no more than a release of tension, your Excellency—a passing fancy for those who have so long endured the strain of the monumental task before them in Congress," Benedict Arnold offered in their defense.

"A fancy which has likewise, spread to Boston," Nathanael commented having witnessed a similar state of affairs on his recent trip. "Such extravagance—such an insatiable desire for wealth amid a declining currency are poor materials to build our independence upon."

"Some would accuse you of elaborate spending with a fifty million dollar budg-et, sir!" Benedict Arnold snickered.

"I buy what is necessary to keep the men in the field; well fed; decently clothed; healthy and properly equipped—no more, no less," Nathanael returned.

"Do our men not deserve as much, General Arnold?" the Commander in Chief's question came as he gazed out over the ballroom.

"Excuse me, gentlemen." Caty suddenly interrupted the conversation placing her arm around Nathanael's, "I wonder if I could steal my husband away for a few moments. He has neglected to lead me in a single dance this evening! What do you think of that, your Excellency?" She asked pretending to be annoyed.

George Washington smiled rather sheepishly.

"No response? Just as I expected? I could always depend on you for at least one dance—but of late you too have neglected me!"

"I am sorry, Catharine."

"Indeed, you ought to be!" she scolded playfully. "And after General Greene pacifies me with one dance will you attempt to redeem yourself as well?"

"Most certainly, madam," he said with a slight bow.

"And might I extend my thanks to you, General Arnold, for playing the part of the gentleman tonight in being attentive to the ladies. It is reassuring to know that not all the general officers present have forgotten their social graces! Now, gentle-men, will you excuse us?"

George Washington nodded. Benedict Arnold bowed. Nathanael shook his head in amused disbelief as his wife led him away.

"I am sorry, Angel," Nathanael said placing one hand in hers and laying the other gently about her waist as the dance began.

"No you are not," she smiled.

"I am sorry that I neglected you. You are looking exceptionally beautiful tonight."

When she looked up, he was staring at her. "Have you only now noticed?" Her huge eyes locked onto his, enchanting him all the more.

"No. The truth is I have been admiring you all evening. It is hard to believe you had a baby only a few weeks ago. No doubt you are the envy of every woman here."

"Of course I am, but not because I quickly recovered my figure, but because I have General Greene's attention."

Nathanael laughed. "Thank you for forcing me to dance. The time I spend with you is the only pleasure I find in this insatiable frolicking."

"Then why don't you simply dance with me more often?"

"Because this leg cannot tolerate more than one dance anymore. I am sorry, Angel, but it seems I am growing old on you."

"Never. You have the stamina of a twenty-year-old. You just need a bit more sleep and much less stress."

"And I am not going to get either as long as we remain in Philadelphia. But praise be to God, it looks like we will be able to return to camp within the week. Night after night of partying, I will be glad for you to get a bit of rest yourself."

"Rest? Have you forgotten the grand ball the Knoxes have planned to celebrate the anniversary of the French Alliance?"

"I would like to forget it—" Nathanael muttered bringing an instant smile to Caty's lips. "French dignitaries, Congressmen, three hundred guests, military protocol, political pomp—I just want to go home, climb into bed and sleep for a long, long time-—"

"Right through the ball?"

"Through the ball and beyond!"

"If you sleep too long you will miss our own dinner party."

"What dinner party?"

"The one I am giving a week after Lucy's gala event!"

"Aw, Caty." Nathanael complained. "Why so soon?"

"A week is more than enough time to recuperate."

"Aw, Caty."

"You promised me I could entertain to my heart's delight, General. Are you going back on your promise?" she pouted.

"But a week?"

"You promised!"

"Caty, I am more worried about your health than my own. Despite your appearance, the fact is you did just give birth and you need to take care of yourself."

"I am fine, Nathanael."

"I worry about you—"

"I am fine, Nathanael."

"I must put my foot down! I—"

Caty laid her finger over his lips as the dance ended.

"You promised, and it will make me very sad indeed to discover that General Greene does not keep his promises."

He took her hand into his own moving it as he softly groaned, "Aw, Caty! Please!"

"What do you think of him, Nat? I want your honest opinion. He has asked for her hand in marriage and I must give my response soon." Lord Stirling gazed past the dancing couples filling the Greene's parlor, straight at his daughter, Kitty, and the debonair, young Congressman, William Duer.

"My opinion is unimportant, your Lordship." Nathanael replied, taking a sip from the goblet in his hand.

"Stop being evasive, Nat. It is as difficult a decision as I have ever made. I can command on the battlefield, in the hottest encounter, against fantastic odds, with relative ease compared to this. Help me out, General Greene, please!"

Nathanael laughed at his obvious desperation. "How many opinions do you intend to solicit in the matter?"

"One from every man I trust in this room."

"It sounds like a council of war to me."

"Exactly."

"Kitty may be upset to discover that every general officer in camp was consulted as to her marriage partner."

"Kitty is aware that every general officer in this camp is concerned for her well-being, and will be flattered by their concern."

Nathanael watched the dancing couple in silence for a moment. "We have many fine officers that desire her hand. Why must she choose to return the affection of a congressman?"

Now it was Lord Stirling's turn to laugh. "Forget the fact that he is a member of that distinguished body if you would, Quartermaster General, and give me your opinion of the man."

"I have few friends in Congress, and unfortunately William Duer is not among them."

"Then perhaps the marriage would prove advantageous in this regard—Kitty is very fond of you."

"And I of her," Nathanael replied with a warm smile in Kitty's direction. "But, I could never use our friendship in such a manner. Does Kitty love him? Is she happy?" Nathanael asked, his full attention now fixed on Lord Stirling.

"She tells me as much."

"She is a wise girl. If she feels the man is worthy of her love and devotion then that is enough for me."

The cessation of music scattered the dancers from the center floor.

"She has about worn me out and every other man in the room, General Greene!" Anthony Wayne exclaimed with Caty at his side. "I should think you are rested enough to lead her in the next dance."

"General Greene has allotted me his one dance. That is all I can expect anymore," Caty pouted taking the goblet from her husband's hand and slowly sipping its contents.

"It might be a good idea to take a rest," Nathanael suggested to his wife.

"Fiddle sticks!" her instant reply came with a radiant smile. "The night is young, General Greene, and I have many more dances in me yet. But—" she said looking about the room, "until I find a partner I suppose I have no choice but to rest— Tell me, Lord Stirling, how serious is Mr. Duer in regard to dear Kitty?" she asked focusing her full attention on Lord Stirling.

"He has requested her hand."

"Indeed? How exciting! And, of course, you agreed."

"—No. Not yet."

"And why ever not? They simply make a darling couple!" Nathanael cleared his throat, and Anthony Wayne burst into laughter. Lord Stirling held Caty's attention with an incredulous smile.

"A darling couple?" Anthony echoed sarcastically.

"They certainly do! Don't you agree, your Lordship?"

"My concern as her father goes well beyond whether they make a darling couple," he said with a chuckle.

"Well of course it does, but certainly that counts for something!"

The men shared an amused glance. "Was that the prerequisite for marrying your husband, Mrs. Greene?" Lord Stirling asked.

Caty turned a playful stare on Nathanael looking him up and down. Then turning back to Lord Stirling, she said with a smile, "You can be certain I took it under consideration. Wouldn't you describe us as a darling couple, your Lordship?"

Nathanael rolled his eyes as his friends began to laugh. "Most assuredly, Mrs. Greene! Most assuredly. And I shall take your observation under careful consideration."

"Do not delay in your decision, sir, for poor Kitty isn't getting any younger. How old is the dear girl, twenty-three? My goodness, there are some who fear the fate of spinsterhood awaits her!"

"She has had her share of suitors, Mrs. Greene."

"That she has, your Lordship, but none have proposed marriage!"

"It is not as much lack of love for the girl as it is overwhelming fear of her father." Anthony began with a wide grin. "Former suitors have been soldiers—subordinate to His Lordship's rank. Duer is a congressman; and our dear General Lord Stirling is, in fact, subordinate to him." Then turning to Caty he insightfully added, "Is your sense of urgency in seeing Miss Kitty married off truly in response to her age, or is there more to it?"

"I do not have the foggiest notion what you are talking about!" Caty's saucy reply came.

Anthony, his brows cocked, looked briefly at Nathanael before directing a question to Lord Stirling.

Caty gazed out over the dancing couples focusing on Kitty and her beau. Grace and charm radiated from the earl's daughter—a grace and charm resulting from her better breeding, which Caty deeply coveted. Given over to the belief that she could never attain the grandness of Lady Kitty's feminine qualities, Caty lamented her lot, convinced that her husband would never be satisfied with her lack of such qualities in comparison.

Nathanael's stare drew her attention. He smiled as the others continued to converse about him, never realizing she felt such insecurity, and therefore never suspecting the need she had to be reassured in the matter.

Lord Stirling's greeting of General Washington drew their attention.

"Are you having a grand time, your Excellency?" Caty, ever the proper hostess asked.

"Indeed I am, Catharine. General Stirling, your wife, as always, is most graceful on the dance floor. My sincere thanks, Lady Stirling, for accompanying me." George Washington bowed as he gently transferred Lady Stirling's arm from his own to Lord Stirling's. "It was my privilege," Lady Stirling replied with a perfect curtsy. Adorned in a wide-hooped gown of pearl gray satin with delicate embroidery along the hemline, she radiated regality. Though nearing her fiftieth year, Lady Stirling's slender figure and soft features lent to her a most youthful and handsome appearance.

"Have you run out of dancing partners, your Excellency?" Caty asked.

"It would appear so."

"So have I," she said with a playful glare for the men around her. Anthony and Lord Stirling lowered their heads in response; Nathanael only smiled, slowly shaking his head. "I could simply dance forever!" she exclaimed.

George Washington grinned. "Forever is a long time, Catharine."

"I could out last you!" she stated, her chin held high.

The eyes of all present focused on the Commander in Chief.

"Indeed?"

"Most certainly!"

Looking about the room George Washington searched for his wife. He quickly located her sitting among a group but a few feet away, and called out, "Lady Washington, Mrs. Greene claims she can outlast me on the dance floor. What do you think?"

"I think, old man," Martha said with an amused smile, "that you do not have enough sense in this matter to ignore her challenge. And I also think that we shall have a long night ahead!"

George Washington laughed at his wife's reaction. "She knows me too well I fear! Mrs. Greene," he said extending his arm to her. "With your husband's permission, I will accept your challenge." As Caty placed her arm on his, George Washington received Nathanael's permission in the form of a playful salute. A loud applause arose from all present quickly followed by murmuring throughout the room as to who would be the first to quit.

When the music began, Nathanael pulled his pocket watch out checking the time against those of General Stirling and Wayne's. Putting it back in place, he walked over to where Martha sat. Those about her cleared away seeing him approach.

"What do you think, General Greene?" She asked, watching the two on the dance floor.

"Sometimes I almost believe she could dance forever. With all due respect to the General, madam, he does not have her youth and vigor."

"That she certainly has," Martha agreed, turning a playful smile on Nathanael. "But, with all due respect to your lady, sir, she does not have the General's stubborn endurance."

"Neither one will concede, I am afraid."

"I believe you are right—and both shall be miserable come morning."

"And you and I with them," Nathanael chuckled.

"Please sit down, General." Martha gestured to the empty chair beside her. "You have become somewhat of a stranger on the dance floor. You once seemed to enjoy it almost as much as they." There was a question in her statement.

Nathanael smiled. "I have been attributing it to aging, but how can I when your old man," he said with a wink, "Puts me to such shame. For some reason my leg has been troubling me whenever I indulge. Leading Caty out in the first dance seems to be my limit anymore."

"I am sorry to hear it, as no doubt will be the women who've had the pleasure of being your partner."

Nathanael laughed. "The pleasure of being my partner? It is kind of you to say so, Lady Washington, but it is clear you have never experienced my lead!"

Martha, who herself only participated in the lead dance with her husband, was surprised by his reaction.

"It is my leg," he said in response to her expression. "A few of my partners have complained over the years though it never dissuaded me. I remember the first time I danced with Caty—'You dance clumsily,' she informed me. 'Ah, but I dance strong,' I quickly pointed out!" Staring at his wife, he chuckled as he recalled the scene. "She has a much more graceful partner tonight!" he added.

"What happened to your leg?" Martha asked, her full attention fixed on him.

Nathanael shot his head around to face her, surprised by the boldness of her question, and the expectation of an answer.

"An accident in the forge?" she prodded. "Most think that's what happened."

"I know," he said, leaning forward and looking down at the floor.

"But it is not," she said knowingly. "Yet you do not bother to tell them so."

"Few ever ask."

"I suppose they feel uncomfortable prying."

"But you do not," he said with a soft smile.

"It would appear that we have much time to converse, General Greene. And I am curious. I also think that we are comfortable enough in our friendship to know you'll simply tell me it is none of my business if you do not wish to discuss it—I sense it has caused you some distress."

"Only on the dance floor really," he gestured to the graceful couples before them moving rhythmically to the music. "And once, prior to the war, when my militia company refused me rank because they considered it a blemish to the unit."

Martha had heard the unbelievable story from General James Varnum.

He turned again to face her. "I was a rebellious lad, Lady Washington. My father was a strict and pious man, extraordinarily hard working—tireless, so it seemed. He had a farm, a number of mills, and two forges to man—and sired seven sons to help him do just that.

"We began working almost from infancy with house or farm chores then worked our way to the mills and finally the forges.

"My father had little tolerance for idleness, not for any extended period of time anyway. Do not get me wrong," Nathanael said, wanting to be certain she understood him. "He was a good man—a compassionate man for the most part, but he was a disciplined man—the truth is he would have been a fine military officer!" Nathanael chuckled.

"My older brothers pretty much followed suit, whether by inner drive or fear of punishment, I do not really know. Then I came along—a rambunctious, foolish youth that came to discover the bright social nightlife, which existed beyond our little world. I guess you would call me a prodigal son, for once I tasted of the festivity and became enchanted on the dance floor by the pretty girls—oh, not our plain, shamefaced Quaker girls, mind you, but the worldly Baptists, Congregationalists and Episcopalians," he chuckled. "It would take more than the threat of a thrashing to keep me away."

Nathanael paused as a servant approached with a tray full of refreshments.

"Go on, General," Martha prompted, having taken a cup of tea.

"I would wait until the house was quiet in the evening and sneak out of my second story chamber window jumping onto the roof of a shed below and then climbing to the ground. It worked quite well time after time.

"Then, once, I slipped on the shed roof crashing to the ground and twisting my knee. Had I the sense to go back into the house, perhaps it would have healed properly. Instead I went to town putting weight on it all evening, and suffering permanent damage."

Nathanael paused smiling shamefully. "By the time I got home I was in agony. I knew I could not climb back in, and I also knew that if my father heard me come through the front door and up the stairs I would be in for a sound thrashing, but I had no choice. I stopped by the shed and discreetly filled my breeches with shingles—they worked quite well!"

"Then he did hear you come in?"

"He did."

"How old were you?"

"Twenty."

Martha was visibly taken aback by his response, fully expecting him to have been a mere lad of sixteen or seventeen years. "A thrashing for a full-grown son?"

"I still lived in my father's home and was fully expected to abide by the rules. I came to appreciate that more as the years passed, but most especially since I entered the military."

"Any more sneaking out at night?"

Nathanael laughed. "No, I was cured, though I did manage to attend my share of social functions—I suppose there was a change in both of us. I suspect my father saw a bit of himself in me—his own youth replayed! He was a good man, and I miss him a great deal."

Martha considered his story, realizing how profoundly the elder Greene had molded his son for the position he was destined. Nathanael's devoted submission to her husband's authority; his confidence and tireless ability; his loyalty, honesty and piety were deeply ingrained by his father's persevering love.

A dark, foreboding cloud of discouragement hung above the quartermaster's office, threatening to unleash its paralyzing fury on the two men therein. Assistant Quartermaster General Charles Pettit presented the factual accounts regarding the most recent developments in Philadelphia. Little had changed since Nathanael's second trip to Congress. The report ended and there was only silence between the men as the unseen enemy attempted to make willing captives of its victims.

"I do not understand, Nat," Charles broke the silence in a mournful tone. "You have presented our needs out with such detail—they have appointed their special committee to investigate the department's records, Congress knows you have two separate units ready to take the field and are therefore in immediate need of supply, yet they refuse to heed our cry for the money! Our agents are begging to be paid—more than five million dollars has been due to Mr. Otis in Boston for over a month. How can we put them off any longer and still hope that our suppliers will be willing to continue to work with us at the risk of not being paid?"

"I do not know—" came the Quartermaster General's solemn reply as he dropped his weary head in his hands.

Charles sighed as he rose from the seat facing Nathanael's desk, and walked toward his own. He picked up an earthen pitcher from upon the desk, and poured water into two awaiting mugs.

"We cannot make bricks without straw, Nat! Despite the fact that you have this department running as efficiently as any could hope—more efficient than any thought possible – there will be no end to this hand to mouth existence!" He remained standing after setting one of the mugs on Nathanael's desk.

Nathanael did not move from his forlorn position.

"Rumors prevail in Philadelphia that you are fully satisfied with your commission. Though the department has been thoroughly investigated, the implication remains that the department's exorbitant spending is unnecessary except to bring great financial gain to the Quartermaster General and his assistants. Talk is that the commission be abolished." Charles paused, but still there was no response.

"Your latest letter of resignation was received by Congress just before I left—" Finally, there was a spark of interest as Nathanael looked up. Charles detected a faint glimmer of hope in his blue eyes, and took a deep breath before relaying the words he knew would snuff it out.

"It was immediately denied—"

Nathanael slumped back in the chair staring at the mountain of papers before him. The temptation was great—overwhelming in fact—to sweep his arm across the desk and send the mountain of figures and correspondence onto the floor; leaving it there for the members of Congress to reorganize. An act of open defiance and anger that would not accomplish a thing, he quickly realized. And if he were to walk away from this loathsome, thankless task in such a manner, Congress would no doubt demand a court-martial, or worse, a dishonorable discharge from the army— and the one forced to pick up the pieces, for a time anyway, would be George Washington. Nathanael forced his almost spell bound attention away from the desktop audibly sighing as he fought the temptation.

"I agreed to take the position on for a year. My year is up, but they refuse to free me from this bondage. They want to abolish our commissions? Nay!" he shouted, splattering the cup of water as he brought his fist down hard on the desk. "There was a time when I would have forsaken the commission, but I will no longer enter-tain the thought of doing this drudgery without reward. I did not want this job nor do I want it now, and they are at liberty to replace me if they are not pleased with my abilities, but I will not, nor will my assistants, take on such a burden with the treat-ment of a slave!"

"There is a growing move that a dictator be appointed to pull the country through this crisis," Charles informed him.

Nathanael shook his head in silent disgust. "I am aware of it—we are barely out of Egypt and already begging to return. Congress has many crises to deal with, I will concede to that, but their major concern at present must be in keeping this army in the field. With no army, there is no hope for independence. With no inde-pendence, there is no need to worry about squabbles between the states, and no need for a Congress.

"A national tax to support the army during this struggle, derived by a unified Constitution is the only sane and workable means to accomplish this—but such appeals from General Washington and me fall on deaf ears. Therefore we must find a way to make bricks without straw, Charles."

The dark cloud immediately vanished.

"What do I do about Mr. Otis?" Charles asked holding up the most recent pleas for payment, which sat unanswered upon his desk.

"—Perhaps if I write to him myself," Nathanael reached out for the papers and quickly set to respond to the first request for payment. Charles returned to his own desk.

The sound of a dull moan called Charles' attention back to his friend. The moan was accompanied by Nathanael's left hand rising to the right side of his chest and deeply massaging the muscle therein as he continued to write.

"What is wrong, Nat?"

Unaware of his actions, Nathanael turned to him questioningly.

"You seem to be in pain, General."

"Oh, that," he said looking down at his hand and quickly removing it from his chest. "It seems to be related to writing. Have you ever heard of such a thing? Last night I was forced to turn in because of the discomfort." Nathanael turned back to his letter, fighting the pain as long as possible. Then, unable to hold out any longer he again began to rub the offending muscle.

"Have you consulted a physician to be certain it is related to writing?"

"I am quite certain."

"Perhaps you should seriously consider taking a day or two's leave to rest your arm."

"Impossible, Colonel," was his emotionless reply as he continued scratching words on the paper before him.

Charles' concerned gaze was drawn to Jeremiah Wadesworth as he entered the office.

"What's this?" the Commissary General exclaimed. "I usually have to fight my way in here through the throng of officers waiting to be granted a sitting with the army's financial wizard. Not a soul to be seen today?"

"They are supplied for the moment—the cupboard is now bare, and they have enough good sense to know it," Nathanael replied without looking up.

"Is that arm still bothering you, Nat? You really should do something about it." Jeremiah stated.

There was no response.

"When did you get back?" Jeremiah directed his question to Charles.

"About an hour ago."

"Is the night life in Philadelphia as lively as ever?"

"Livelier, I am afraid."

"And is the assistant quartermaster still a welcome figure in the social scene?"

"No. Not really."

"I did not think so. Well, Charles, here you have only arrived back in camp and I am on my way to Connecticut. This army is ready to move, and I do not intend to move with it."

"When are you heading out?"

"Just as soon as I discuss some business with the general."

"Well, I will leave you both alone. I have a few matters to attend to myself." Grabbing a pile of papers, Charles stood up. "God's speed to you, Jeremiah. My compliments to Mrs. Wadesworth." Charles patted his back as he moved past.

"Your wife will be relieved to have you home, and none too soon I should think!" Nathanael commented pushing the completed letter to one side of the desk.

Jeremiah sat down facing him. "Childbirth is women's work—a man appears little more than a nuisance. He's of no value or use in the whole drawn out process, except, it seems to me, to be ridiculed and nagged by the women that congregate for the event!"

"You will survive it, I am sure," Nathanael grinned.

"A son is what I am expecting—I would not know what to do with a daughter—"

"Do not worry about it, Jeremiah. Son or daughter, the child will capture your heart with no effort."

"I do not know—I am not overly fond of children—little rug rats is what they amount to."

"You have taken to my son," Nathanael pointed out.

"George! Everyone has taken to his little Excellency. He's a sweet, well-mannered lad!"

"I have two daughters at home every bit as sweet. When you set your eyes on your own child—hold him or her in your arms, you will surrender your heart."

Jeremiah shrugged, not at all convinced. "Tell me," he began. "Have you made your mind up? What is your decision in this business venture that we discussed? If we are going to invest I would like to do it as soon as I arrive in Connecticut."

"You can call it shipping, but in truth it is privateering—and privateering leaves an unpleasant taste in my mouth," Nathanael replied returning his attention to the paperwork before him.

"It's a cargo sloop!"

"With ten mounted cannon?"

"For defense."

Nathanael shot his head around in amused disbelief.

"And a bit of pirating if the opportunity should present itself," Jeremiah said with a grin. "Come on, Nat, you have invested in such ships before—if I am not mistaken, a firm known as Greene and Company once owned a privateering vessel before the war. You and your brothers, General?"

Nathanael smiled.

"Come now, General. Certainly you do not object to pirating English vessels on the high sea!"

"English vessels with caution. French and Spanish vessels, never!" Nathanael's stern reply came.

"Any American vessel that attacks the French or Spanish has a fool for a captain."

Nathanael's blank stare moved Jeremiah to say more. "I will see that our captain receives my personal orders in regard to it. There! Now will you agree to the investment?"

"I would rather put the money in a piece of land, or a sound business venture."

"As would I, but we need to unload this near worthless currency as soon as possible. We might as well throw it to the wind as leave it in our pockets awaiting the perfect opportunity—let us paper a wall or use it for kindling; it will not be worth much more than that soon."

"I know—I know— Go ahead and make the investment." Nathanael said pulling a wad full of Continental notes from his pocket. "But I do not want Congress to get wind of this. There's bound to be a fair amount of correspondence between us over it."

"Nat, it is not illegal. We are at war with Great Britain, remember? It is our duty to cripple their shipping industry if we can! There are members of Congress with shares in privateering vessels —George Washington, himself, is considering a similar investment."

"I do not mean that—" he latched hold of Jeremiah's eyes with his own. "Certain members of Congress are determined to bring my character into question." There was a sense of agony in that fact, which Nathanael could not verbally relate, though his eyes indicated his pain. "They are welcome to investigate the dealings of my department or my military conduct—I have absolutely nothing to hide. But I will not have them prying into my private dealings. What I do with my commission—the blasted commission they compelled me to take—that's my business!"

"What do you propose? A code of some sort?" Jeremiah asked.

Nathanael nodded in reply.

Jeremiah considered it for a moment. A slow smile came to his lips. "That could work quite nicely. You have enough to do here. I will work on it on the ride home and send you the cipher by an indirect means. Now, General, by your leave, I will be on my way. I need to pay a visit to His Excellency and say my good-byes."

"I have a gift here for your lady," Nathanael said, laying down his pen and searching his desk for the item. Locating a small box, he handed it to the Commissary General.

"It's only a small trinket really—a little something to show my appreciation for her willingness to be parted from you for the past few weeks."

"Hardly a trinket," Jeremiah commented, opening the box and admiring the brooch inside.

"Caty picked it out. I hope it is to Mrs. Wadesworth's liking."

"Your wife has exquisite taste, General. Speaking of Caty, where is the girl? I certainly cannot leave without bidding her a fond farewell, now can I?"

"You should find her at Headquarters. She is visiting with Lady Washington—their last tea frolic for a few months."

"And when will the ladies break camp?"

"All within the next few days."

"How very sad! And what a dull, lifeless camp it will be."

Nathanael smiled at his nonmilitary commissary general. "The winter months are thought by most to be the dormant, restful period for an army. Facing the enemy again can be rather stimulating. You should return, Colonel Wadesworth, and experience it for yourself!"

"No, thank you, General. I am only too happy to feed your army from a distance!" Jeremiah said, extending his hand to receive Nathanael's.

"Dear child, what's on your mind?" Martha Washington asked in the motherly tone, which Caty found such a comfort. "Ever since you arrived your mind has seemed preoccupied."

"It is always so hard to say good-bye."

"But of course it is, so let us enjoy our last moments together!"

Martha's kind face prompted a weak smile from Caty, and an attempt to change the conversation. "I regret not having seen the Marquis this winter."

"Yes. All have genuinely missed his company, though I am happy that he was allowed such a lengthy stay in France. He needed to be with his family—with his young bride. Before long he will be back in camp, sitting around the campfire's light sharing his own treasured memories of home with the other officers. They do treasure their few months of domestic life during the winter months. Often it is these very memories that get them through the difficult time of separation. How often I have listened to such stories from lonely officers." The smile, which accompanied the last statement, indicated to Caty that Nathanael was among the officers she spoke.

"And someday George Washington Greene shall meet George Washington Lafayette!" Martha joyously proclaimed. "Would that the Marquise could come to America to be closer to her husband; and that General Washington could sit both of his namesakes upon his knees!" Martha laughed recalling her husband's pride when General Lafayette's letter arrived announcing the birth of his son.

"Tears began to stream down Caty's cheeks.

"Child, what have I said?" Martha asked, holding her hand out for Caty to come and sit at her side on the settee.

Caty moved from her seat and took hold of Martha's hand. Weeping, she sat down beside the older woman.

"What is it, Caty?"

"His Excellency shall not see either of his namesakes next winter, for I shall not be returning to camp."

"Whatever would keep you away, child?"

"I will be confined to my bed, forced to suffer once more the horrors of childbirth." Her weeping turned to deep sobs.

Martha placed her arms around the younger woman, comforting her in silence for a few minutes. Then, pulling away, she took hold of Caty's hand and began to speak. "It is difficult for you, I know. Your time with your husband is so brief—the separation so frightening, and so very lonely. Do you cry yourself to sleep as often as I do? I am sure you do."

Martha tenderly wiped a tear from Caty's cheek. "No doubt you feel burdened having to face these pregnancies alone—having to go through your travail sometimes without your husband's comfort and support. And I know it is difficult for you to understand, but I do envy you."

Caty watched in amazement as tears began to pool in Martha's soft gray eyes.

"You leave this camp taking a part of your husband. Even now, he lives within you—his child growing stronger with each passing day. A child conceived in love, so very close to your heart. Try to enjoy this time, Caty. Treasure it. Be strong and courageous. How often I longed to bear a child for my husband, but the good Lord did not see fit to answer that prayer— How I do envy you!"

"But how I shall miss seeing you!" Caty cried, laying her head on Martha's shoulder. The older woman lifted her hand and placed it on Caty's head, holding her close.

"No, dear child! If God does not bless us with an ultimate victory during this campaign, then I fully expect to see you at camp come winter. It would take more than the imminent birth of a baby to keep you away!" Martha said with a laugh.

"I have desired Congress to give me leave to resign, as I apprehended a loss of reputation if I continued in the Quartermaster business."
(Nathanael Greene)

CHAPTER TWELVE

A SUDDEN CLAP of thunder startled the horses just as the men prepared to dismount. Through the open windows, the sound of casual conversation was heard from Lord Stirling and his guests.

"I hope for a quick storm or ve vill be soaked on de vay back," Baron von Steuben remarked.

A bolt of lightning shot across the blackened sky. Nathanael searched the foreboding clouds. "You and the others will be soaked—I am staying the night!" he said lifting the saddlebag from the horse.

The Baron laughed heartily. "Ven vill you move out of dat leaky tent into proper quarters?"

The Baron's therapeutic laughter brought a grin to Nathanael's lips. The ornamental gilded star, which adorned the Prussian general's uniform, reflected the candlelight from inside, momentarily drawing Nathanael's attention to it. The stout, balding Baron awaited a verbal response from his friend.

"When the British stop playing this cat and mouse game—enticing us to send detachments here, there and everywhere, then I will be able to settle in. Let's get inside," Nathanael said, handing the horse's reins to a waiting soldier and quickly heading for the door as large raindrops began to splatter onto the ground.

"Welcome, gentlemen, welcome!" Lord Stirling greeted them from the smoke filled drawing room with a warm smile. "My dear Baron, what tactic did you use to entice General Greene to part from his quill?"

"I was beginning to think it had permanently attached itself to his hand," Anthony Wayne called out from an overstuffed wing backed chair. Except for a bandage wrapped about his head the swashbuckler appeared quite relaxed; his feet resting softly on an ottoman; a glass of grog in one hand and a clay pipe in the other.

"We considered sending a dispatch to General Greene's marquee ordering him to report, only to discover no one present outranked him!" Henry Knox called from the opposite side of the room with a chuckle.

Nathanael glanced at the faces about him—Stirling, St. Clair, Wayne, and Knox. All general officers, yet, as Henry stated all his subordinates.

"I simply told him it vas going to rain tonight. He quickly packed a few things and joined me!" the Baron announced with his thunderous laughter.

"Then you are staying the night?" Lord Stirling asked.

"With your permission, your Lordship," Nathanael said with a slight bow, his eyes smiling in response to the Earl's grin.

"I and my staff shall be honored, General Greene—James!" Lord Stirling called to a servant standing ready to tend his master's guests. "See that the bedchamber opposite mine is made ready for General Greene."

"Yez, sa!" The servant quickly dashed out of the room prepared to not only change the bedding in the designated bedchamber, but also assist the dislodged aides into the chamber occupied by the secretaries, and arrange for the ousted secretaries a bed on the floor.

"Come, make yourselves at home, gentlemen," Lord Stirling said gesturing for another servant to offer refreshment to the new arrivals.

Nathanael moved into the room accepting the mug offered, but declining the pipe.

"How is your head?" Nathanael directed his attention to Anthony Wayne as he sat down opposite him.

"The bandage comes off tomorrow."

"No pain?"

"None."

Nathanael sat back in the chair staring intently at his injured comrade. "I remain in awe of your victory—your troops were perfectly disciplined: speed, surprise, coordination, and aggressiveness! A bayonet assault with unloaded muskets. I am in awe! Have you anything to say about it General Steuben?" he asked looking away from Anthony.

"I ave already told im time and again dat no European general could ave done better!"

"It may prove to be the greatest stroke of the war!" Henry Knox added.

"Indeed!" Nathanael agreed.

"Your revenge, General Wayne?" General Arthur St. Clair asked dryly. It was common knowledge by every man in the room that Wayne and St. Clair had their own personal war in progress. "Was it an act of desperation to save face?"

"I do not know what you are talking about General St. Clair. His Excellency assigned me the command—I did not request it. Need I point out, sir, that I was on leave visiting my family when summoned back to make the attack on Stony Point."

"It is well known that you have spouted your obsessive desire to avenge your men massacred at Paoli, Mad Anthony!" St. Clair added, using the nickname the troops had given their commander after his daring attack. "Is that why you were chosen? Because you would blindly lead your men forward in what appeared, according to most, to be a suicidal attempt to take that fort?"

"My orders were to take the fort," Anthony's icy response came. "As to why I was chosen, ask General Greene. He sat in counsel with His Excellency." All eyes turned toward Nathanael.

"Many believed the task to be impossible," Nathanael began knowingly. "General Wayne's desire to avenge his fallen men; his inborn aversion to danger; and the command of 2,000 disciplined, hand-picked soldiers proved to be the precise combination to prove to the enemy that we are able.

"The British have evaded us in the field, instead choosing to plunder and burn coastal towns. General Wayne's attack on Stony Point gave us the upper hand. So to answer the question directly, yes, General Wayne was specially chosen by His Excellency after much careful deliberation. A wise choice considering the outcome, don't you agree, General St. Clair?"

St. Clair failed to respond.

"How goes it with General Sullivan? I have heard talk that he is in poor health these days," Anthony remarked anxious to change the subject.

"I fear he may resign his commission once this Indian uprising is quashed. His letters indicate that his health is declining." Henry said.

"I do not envy him that command. I saw enough of the gruesome savagery in the French and Indian War." a visible shiver went through Lord Stirling's body as he remembered the nightmarish scenes of the decapitated and mutilated bodies of comrades taken captive by Indian warriors, often encouraged by the French.

"Any man dat can go in and murder defenseless voomen and children as long ago lost iz soul to da devil!" Von Steuben exclaimed.

Nathanael recalled the letters received from General Sullivan since his attack on the Iroquois tribes began. It was a time of soul searching for Sullivan as he came face to face with the horror around him. His orders were specific—given verbally and in writing by General Washington with a strong exhortation and clear advice. No commander in the Continental Army had yet to face the extreme situation John Sullivan was up against—his mission was the total destruction and devastation of the Iroquois villages, taking captive their inhabitants.

"Sullivan's letters are getting a bit preachy of late, aren't they?" Anthony asked with a snicker then taking a drag on the pipe, he looked toward Henry and Nathanael for a reply.

"Preachy?" Nathanael asked.

"I read a letter he sent to Henry. Certainly he is sent you similar material."

"Mad Anthony here does not understand John Sullivan's sudden interest in the souls of his men." Henry said in response to Nathanael's apparent confusion.

"Oh that— No, Anthony, I do not suppose you do understand," Nathanael said smiling at him as though dealing with a small child.

"We have chaplains to tend to the men's souls," Anthony interjected.

"Yes, we do. But I suppose John has opportunities to speak of it—like the night before a planned attack, in the security of the camp's fire after all the plans are laid out and all is in readiness. Each of us have been there," Nathanael, said looking around the room. "You cannot sleep—you know you should but you just cannot. The blood pulsates through your veins—the heart pounds in anticipation of the dawn. And what is John Sullivan doing? Writing one last letter to his wife? Contemplating the comforts of home? No! He is seeing that his men are truly prepared for battle in the event that they are transported from this world to the next. Preachy, General Wayne? Would that we could all tend to our men so thoroughly."

"We cannot afford to lose Sullivan's service," General St. Clair stated changing the subject. "Lafayette's mission to France will remove him from command for at least a year. I do not believe Israel Putnam will be able to stay on come winter." Each man was aware of "Old Put's" enfeebled condition. "Even now His Excellency is hard pressed to assign commanders to the threatened coastal towns while having to stand in readiness to defend West Point. What is your status, Nat? Your name was not on the list. Why?"

"What list? What are you talking about?"

"Congress published an updated list of field commanders—your name does not appear."

Confused, Nathanael searched the faces in the room. The eyes of all but Henry and the Baron von Steuben averted his.

"I did not receive any list. Henry, what do you know about this?"

Henry sighed looking around the room for assistance. There was an awkward silence—and a show of cowardice as far as Henry was concerned.

"—I received it yesterday. It is my understanding that it was sent to all commanders."

"I did not receive it. Did you receive it?" Nathanael asked Von Steuben.

"I did."

Slowly Nathanael's gaze drew out each man. They all nodded in response to his unspoken question.

He rubbed his upper lip with the forefinger of his left hand contemplating the apparent oversight. "I do not know why my name is not on that list, General St. Clair, but I thank you for bringing it to my attention. I intend to find out. A mistake, I am sure." But he was not sure at all.

"I do not think so, Nat," Lord Stirling interjected.

Nathanael looked at his friend, who in turn avoided his gaze. "Why do you say that, your Lordship?"

"It is unheard of that the quartermaster general—a staff officer, would take field command—and for very practical reasons."

"The terms in which I took on the quartermaster's department included the fact that I would be given field command at His Excellency's discretion in time of battle."

"For one year," Lord Stirling pointed out. "The original agreement was that you would hold the right to command for one year—the year is up and still you are heading up the quartermaster's department."

"Not by choice!" Nathanael bellowed, rising to his feet. For a moment, he glared at Lord Stirling, and then turning away, he took a few steps in the opposite direction. There was an uneasy silence as he fought to regain his composure. With a deep sigh, he turned back around.

"Do you question my right to command?" the controlled, though strained words came. Lord Stirling finally met his gaze.

"Your ability—never. Our need for you on the field—certainly not. But, under the circumstances, I do question your right to take command."

Though the words hit him hard, Nathanael fought the temptation to react.

"To be quite honest, Nat, if you were to be given command of my division on the eve of battle I would be humiliated and ashamed to ever command that division again. For a year, it was tolerable; your previous command was easily remembered—you were still in touch with the routine of the troops. As it stands now we mold and shape them, gain their confidence, and then you can step in just before they are to be tested and reap the reward of their performance. How is that right or fair?"

Nathanael searched the faces once more. Strengthened by Lord Stirling's words no one looked away now.

"And you, General Wayne. How do you feel?"

"I am inclined to agree with General Stirling, sir."

"General St. Clair?"

"I agree, sir."

General Knox?"

"As commander of artillery it does not affect me, Nat!"

"Your opinion, Henry."

Henry looked around the room. "—I do not know what it is worth, not being in a position to be threatened, but—" He turned his gaze on Nathanael. "You are like a brother to me—I cannot imagine objecting to an older brother by my side."

Nathanael had a weak smile for his devoted friend then directed his attention to the Baron.

"General Steuben?"

"I should sink, my dear General Greene, zat I vould be subordinate to your command. But I am in a different position zan our friends here. Zis iz your army and your var. I am only a foreigner who vishes to help. It iz not my place to question your right to command. It iz a difficult question—a difficult position for your comrades," Von Steuben said smiling at the anxious faces in the room. "My advice to you iz to seek out His Excellency's opinion—after all, it iz he who will decide in zee end, iz it not?"

A soft summer breeze crept over the river's surface brushing the tall grass along its bank. Its warm caress went unnoticed as Nathanael hypnotically watched the rapid passage of the Hudson River. His thoughts were not on the scenery, but the letter in his hand. The message was no easier to accept now then it was upon its arrival hours ago. The handwriting seemed familiar enough—the signature immediately recognized as that of his dear friend—but the message was cold and strange. George Washington, himself, felt that Nathanael no longer held the right of command and advised instead that he focus his full attention on the consuming needs of the quartermaster's department.

It was a crushing blow—intensified by the fact that only because of George Washington's persistence did Nathanael take on the detested position. Now, one by one, the conditions he accepted to serve under were being changed without his consent.

"Getting a bit of fresh air for yourself? Well, well for you!" Henry exclaimed breathlessly as he descended the river's bank. "Dinner will soon be served."

Nathanael nodded, but appeared distant.

"Ah! West Point is a lovely post!" Henry commented sharing the view with Nathanael. "And aren't we blessed to be posted here together. I bet you are delighted to finally be out of that leaky tent. When are you going to send for your wife and children to join us? We are safely tucked in here. Lucy would love the company."

"Caty's in no condition to make such a trip. I could not ask it of her," Nathanael's hesitant response came.

"Why?"

"Didn't I tell you? I am sure I mentioned that she is expecting another baby."

"You did, but I cannot imagine that that would keep your wife away—especially so early on. Is she ill?"

"Yes," Nathanael's abrupt reply came.

"—She will get over that soon enough."

Though Caty implied that her illness was directly related to her pregnancy, Nathanael had his doubts. The stomach pain she hesitantly wrote him of accompanied with vomiting of blood seemed an odd symptom of mere morning sickness. His suspicions were that she had overexerted with the continuous partying in Philadelphia, and frequent entertaining at camp. He feared for her health, blaming himself.

"I do not think she will be coming," he said with a weak, forced smile. Though his lips made a pretense of ease regarding the situation, his eyes gave him away. "I have assured her that I will make an attempt to return home for a few weeks."

"Now?" Henry asked incredulously.

Nathanael shrugged and nodded.

"You will never be given permission to leave while the army remains in the field. You know that!"

Nathanael knew he was right, even as he wrote the words in his last letter to Caty he knew he would never be given leave. Yet, at the same time, he could not bring himself to invite her to join him, fearing the journey would put her at greater risk.

Henry noted the anguish in his friend's eyes. "Is that a letter from home?" he asked.

"No. Here, read it for yourself." Nathanael held the letter out to Henry. A few minutes elapsed as Henry read the words on the page.

Finishing, Henry gazed down at the river, uncertain of how to respond. "—I am sorry. I am sure this came as a shock."

"I never imagined General Washington would relinquish my command. I do not believe I would have taken on this position had I known my right to command would be jeopardized. Henry, I am confused. I believe, with every fiber of my being, that the cause we fight for is just. I am willing to stand and defend the rights given us by the Almighty. I am willing to die, if need be, that posterity might enjoy this liberty. But, Henry," he said, searching his friend's eyes. "I feel more enslaved by my own countrymen than I ever did by the British."

"What are you going to do?"

"What can I do? They have successfully stripped me of my command; they have publicly brought my character into question; my commission is soon to be relinquished in favor of a salary. I can either serve according to their every whim, or resign from the army altogether."

"You would not do that!" Henry's alarm was great.

"If I continue to oppose their changes in the department, and defend myself against their tyrannical attempts, I will be discharged."

"Never!"

"You can count on it."

The sound of an approaching rider drew their immediate attention.

"Excuse me, General Greene, General Knox," An aide said with a formal salute. "General Greene, a man has just arrived in camp urgently requesting to see you. He claims to be your brother, sir."

"My brother?"

"Yes, sir. He bears a striking resemblance—a Quaker gentleman. Christopher was the name he gave. It was suggested that he wait at headquarters while I summoned you, sir, but he refuses to wait and is on his way even as we speak."

"Kitt? What would bring Kitt here?" Nathanael asked Henry, his face blanched. With long strides, he began to ascend the riverbank.

"Did Mr. Greene say what was wrong, Major?" Henry asked his aide.

"No, sir. He was adamant about speaking only to General Greene."

With a burst of energy, Nathanael took off down the road leading to Henry's quarters. Seeing Kitt's approach, he quickened his pace even more.

Nathanael was terrifyingly aware of Kitt's grave expression. No joy was shared in this odd reunion. The brother's came before one another with no embrace to follow—just Kitt's penetrating eyes.

"What has happened, brother? What brings thee here? Is it Caty?" Nathanael exclaimed wheezing.

"Tell me it is not true, Nathanael! Tell me thee have not disgraced the family! Your word, brother, will be enough for the brethren and me."

An immediate sense of joy rose up in Nathanael upon hearing Kitt's strange greeting. *Caty is safe!* His heart leaped. *It is only a rumor that has brought him here,* he rejoiced, then suddenly the relief he felt was replaced with sorrow as he looked upon Kitt's face—sorrow for his brothers in having to stand against such lies, wanting not to believe them, but finding themselves wondering just the same.

"I swear to thee, Kitt," Nathanael began laying his right hand upon his heart. "I swear to thee that whatever has been said of me to cause thee such alarm, it is not true. An honest and good man gave me the name Greene. I shall ever endeavor to pass it on untarnished to my own children."

Kitt hesitated for a moment, and then moved closer to his brother, falling into his arms.

"Thee must tell me what vicious rumor has found its way to my kinsmen, but first—tell me, Kitt, how is my family?"

Kitt stepped back from his brother's embrace wiping his eyes with his hand. "Tolerable," he began, meeting Nathanael's concerned gaze. "—Sister Caty says very little about her health yet she does not look well."

"Has the doctor seen her?"

Kitt nodded. "He assures us that she is fine."

"Is her stomach still bothering her?"

Kitt nodded.

"How can she be fine with stomach pain and bleeding?"

"He claims it is associated with her condition," Kitt tried to assure him though he appeared skeptical.

"I never heard of such a thing. She needs her rest— Is she troubled by the rumors?" Nathanael asked.

"Only by the fact that anyone would dare spread them!" Kitt said with a smile. "I believe if that feisty, frail, little wife of yours were to come upon someone talking about thee she would prove to be more than they could handle."

Nathanael did not find it amusing. "Do whatever thee must to keep her from it, Kitt! Protect her from the rumors, and especially from my enemies. I had none prior to joining the army; now, especially since my appointment to the quartermaster's department, I have acquired many. There are those who would think nothing of offending or mistreating Caty in order to get to me. If that were to happen—" A sudden fear gripped his soul at the thought of it. He knew he could stand up to personal criticism, though he might wince. He could bear their insults and rebukes, though he might become depressed. Even their character assassination would not break him, though his anger would certainly be kindled. But what if his enemies were to discover that Caty was his Achilles heel?

"Would that Caty was able to make the trip—she and the children—"

Kitt heard the desperation in his brother's voice. He placed his hand on Nathanael's shoulder. "We will watch out for her, Nat. Thee can depend on us to protect her."

Nathanael searched his eyes. "But the doctor says she is well—maybe she would be all right if she took the journey slowly."

"Though the doctor may say she is healthy enough to make the journey—in my opinion she is not, and Mother, Sister Peggy and my own Debbie agree. But as soon as she is strong enough, if thee are able to safely accommodate her and the children here, I will personally see to her journey. Thee know there'll be no holding her back once her health is restored!"

"She will tell thee that she is well before she truly is," Nathanael warned knowing his wife's impetuosity.

"I am aware of that," Kitt laughed.

"And do not let her come if she is too close to her time. She will try, Kitt, and as much as I want her here I could not live with myself if my pleasure brought harm to her or the baby—"

"I will do what I can, brother," Kitt offered laying his hand on Nathanael's shoulder as they continued to walk.

"What of my children? Are they well?"

"They are healthy and happy." Kitt said with a comforting smile.

"Mother? The brethren?" his mind quickly went through the faces of family members—sisters-in-law, nieces, nephews, cousin Griffin, Uncle John, and on and on. "The family—how is the family?"

"All are presently blessed with fine health. Their prayers and thoughts are with thee."

"Ah, but save for Jacob, Griffin and you, no one writes. Please tell them for me how much I would appreciate receiving their thoughts on paper!" Nathanael said with a weak smile. "Come now, dinner is waiting. Thee must be hungry."

As they began walking toward headquarters Nathanael said, "Let me hear the charge against my character that I might answer it and put your mind at ease."

"There is no need to answer the charge. Your oath shall always be enough for me, Nat."

"Other family members may not be as easily satisfied."

"Of course they will."

"Tell me, Kitt," Nathanael ordered.

"—I am ashamed to even say it—to even let thee know of our doubts."

Nathanael put his arm around Kitt's shoulders as they walked. "The devil can play tricks on one's mind. We all fall prey to his deceitfulness at one time or another."

"Then thee can forgive us?"

Nathanael smiled and squeezed his shoulder. "I love thee; of course I forgive thee."

"—It is difficult to say it. Talk is that thee have taken your commission and secretly invested it in companies, which in turn sell to the army at exorbitant prices—thus increasing your own commission." Kitt could not bring himself to look at his brother.

"That particular lie has been circulating in these parts for some time. I am surprised it took so long to reach New England."

Turning to face his brother, Kitt could see the pain through the forced smile. Nathanael removed his arm from Kitt's shoulder.

"I do not know who started it. It could have been a member of Congress or a disgruntled fellow officer. Maybe it was a merchant whose wares I turned down, or a member of my department who was rebuked or let go for unethical behavior.

"There are a few soldiers who have come to hate me for disciplinary action I was forced to take, and a few citizens who resent me because of the foraging details I sent out." Nathanael shrugged.

"I have not made any such investment. The only thing that comes close is an investment I made in a furnace over in New Jersey. I thought it a wise move at the time. I know iron, and this particular furnace has the capability of turning out a large volume of cannon. We desperately need cannon and this company desperately needed investors. Production has not yet begun so I can hardly be accused of lining my pockets with profits." He became silent for a moment.

"There is more talk circulating that thee should know of," Nathanael continued. "Congress questions my ethical conduct in assigning positions to family members."

Kitt immediately knew he was speaking of Jacob and Griffin, who were Rhode Island agents for the quartermaster's department.

"I did not even stop to consider it at the time—we'd been in partnership for years. I needed good, honest men as buying agents, and they were willing to take on the job. Was it so wrong of me?" Confusion covered his face.

Now it was Kitt's arm that went about Nathanael's shoulders. "Nay, Brother. As thee said, Jacob and Griffin had been your partners for years. Both are well qualified for such a task, and two more honest men one will not find. Should thee instead entrust the positions to strangers?"

"It seems my every move is scrutinized, and my every motive questioned—I am tired, Kitt, and I would like nothing more than to go home." He took a deep breath. "But, because I am a Greene, I cannot turn my back on my responsibilities, no matter how tempting it might be. Come inside—eat, rest and tell me details of the family and every day occurrences in dear Rhode Island."

"We not only must cease the preparations for the campaign, but shall in all probability, be obliged to disperse, if not disband the army for want of subsistence."

(George Washington to Congress)

CHAPTER THIRTEEN

MORRISTOWN, NEW JERSEY had been the site of a restful repose for the Continental Army during the winter of 1777. This area, protected by large swamps to the eastward and farther east the great natural earthwork of the Watchung Mountains was again chosen by Quartermaster General Greene as a suitable location for the army during the quiet winter months of 1779-1780.

Here the soldiers began the task of building their small city of log huts as laid out by the quartermaster general. With a keen awareness of the weather's premature frigidity Nathanael directed the construction, praying all would be properly sheltered, and, by some great miracle, that the individual states would make whatever sacrifices necessary to supply food for the men before the snow began to fall. Snow enough, he feared, to paralyze the countryside, shut down transportation, and threaten to starve the army.

Though the men wasted no time in constructing their huts, the cruel, unyielding weather lashed out against them bringing their work to a dead halt. Those whose huts were completed hid themselves within, inviting as many as they could fit to share the already cramped space. Those who could not fit sought shelter in their tattered tents. As the weather intensified with its fierce gales and blinding snow, the tents were torn to pieces forcing the destitute inhabitants to seek shelter wherever and however they could, or perish.

For two days, the wind howled. For two days, the men dared not venture beyond the huts for fear of becoming lost in the storm and thus falling victim to the elements. Helplessly Nathanael waited for the storm to end, ever conscious of the fact that the food supply was dangerously low, and all attempts to bring any in would be delayed until the roads were cleared. And if this concern were not enough, he knew that Caty and George were on their way. Did they get to shelter before the storm hit? There was no way of knowing, and absolutely nothing he could do. Thus, he remained trapped in his own quarters—wondering, pleading with Heaven, and waiting for God to extend His mercy.

"I cannot see the road! Where on earth is the road?" Rob Burnet exclaimed standing thigh deep in the newly fallen snow.

The others remained silent, taking in the unbelievable scenery about them. All was still, as the dawn brilliantly broke forth. The intensity of the sun's rays reflecting off the virgin snow was blinding.

Huts surrounding the quartermaster's headquarters were partially covered with drifts more than six feet high. Barren trees poked up from under their blanket of white, great lengths of trunk hidden beneath.

"Billy, I want ten team of horses made ready immediately to clear the road," Nathanael said to Billy Blodget as they gazed across the vast whiteness. Then turning to Sam Ward he said, "Order some boys from the northernmost country to drive the teams—men from upper New York and the Maine and Vermont territories. They are used to clearing snow like this. Rob, you'll assist him."

The aides remained in place.

"Have I not made myself clear, gentlemen?" Nathanael asked with a frown. "This road must be made passable. The longer we delay, the longer the men go without food."

"Yes, sir." they replied almost in unison. Slowly, ever so slowly they set off plodding through the deep snow.

"Major Burnet, notify me when the teams are ready to begin—I will oversee the task myself," he yelled tramping back toward the house. "And I want the walkways to General Washington's Headquarters and my own cleared. Order two details to it immediately."

"Yes, sir."

Hour after hour, the work of clearing the main road continued until day turned into day. The task was prolonged not only by the massive volume of snow to be cleared across miles of the countryside, but by the freezing temperatures as well. Man and beast tired under the strenuous conditions, yet continued as best they could. Their survival was at stake.

Nathanael directed the work from his saddle—exposed to the cold, without adequate sleep or ample sustenance for days. The very existence of the army depended on his ability to dig them out—to make the road passable for the wagons that would deliver forage for the animals and scant provisions for the men. Scant provisions—barely enough to live on, for few, if any merchants were willing to risk the sale of provisions to an army which did not have money to pay.

An exhausted Nathanael watched the men. "They deserve better than this— These brave souls deserve better than this. Lord, help us." he whispered. Billy heard his commander's quiet prayer and nodded in silent agreement.

"General Greene." Colonel Tench Tilghman brought his horse up alongside Nathanael's and saluted. "It's quite a feat you have accomplished, sir. Quite a feat indeed." the colonel said observing the men at work.

"Not me, Colonel—the men. The men alone are to be—" Abruptly his words stopped as a deep, choking cough consumed him.

Colonel Tilghman shared an anxious glance with Billy. "General Washington requests a report in person, sir," he informed Nathanael when the coughing ceased.

Nathanael's blank stare and momentary silence confused the colonel. "—Very well," he finally said in acknowledgment of the order. "Major Blodget, carry on."

"Of course, sir."

Except for occasional bouts of coughing, the men rode in silence. And, except for the occasional bouts of coughing, Tench Tilghman suspected his superior officer and friend was asleep.

"We've arrived, sir," Tench said reaching over and gently shaking Nathanael's slumped form.

Slowly Nathanael dismounted and staggered up the stairs. The impact of the warm air upon entering the house made his surroundings seem to whirl about him. He closed his eyes and took a deep breath, waiting for the momentary state of dizziness to pass. Then removing his hat, and fumbling with his gloves and cape, he handed them to Tench just as Anthony Wayne came from General Washington's office, closing the door behind him.

"General Greene," Anthony said with a nod. "I never would have thought it could get worse than what we experienced at Valley Forge—never would have believed it was possible—" He glanced over his shoulder at the door he just closed then back at Nathanael.

"Is there any way to salvage the army this time, Nat? At Valley Forge, all we needed was a competent quartermaster—we have that. But now it is well beyond that, isn't it?"

"I am sorry," Nathanael replied.

Anthony reached over and briefly touched his arm. "You are not to blame—it is the blasted money, or should I say the lack of it." He looked Nathanael in the eye.

"My men haven't been paid in three months—not that their meager pay could ever provide even the bare necessities for their families. The story is the same throughout the camp. My men are threatening to disband, and between you and me, I do not blame them. No pay, no food, inadequate clothing—" He paused and frowned. "Congress does not seem to think a hat is a necessary part of a soldier's uniform, as they leave our soldiers bareheaded—as well as barefooted. And if they find that we can bare it in the two extremities no doubt they will attempt it in the center as well."

With a sigh, Nathanael slowly nodded in agreement.

"You do not look good, Nat. You need to get some rest."

"There's no time for rest. The men need food."

Anthony sighed, and momentarily diverted his eyes from Nathanael, obviously concerned for his friend's health yet aware that he was right. "When can we expect it to arrive?"

"I do not even know if any is on the way—"

"Foraging parties?"

"They will be out as soon as the road is passable. We will take from the countryside what we can."

Again, Anthony reached out and touched him. "We will hang on until then—there's always black birch bark or roasted leather—I have even seen a few scraggly dogs running about." Though he wore a weak smile, Nathanael knew he was serious. "His Excellency's waiting—I will not keep you, General Greene. Good day to you, sir."

"Good day, General Wayne."

Slowly Nathanael moved toward the dining room, which now served as the General's office. Tench had already announced his arrival and held the door open.

"Come in, General Greene. Please have a seat," the Commander said receiving Nathanael's salute.

The room was bursting with activity, as the seventeen members of the General's staff busied themselves with transcribing letters, pouring over maps, and reading reports as they crowded around the dining room table and at the numerous desks lining the walls. Yet with all the energy exerted in the room, all was orderly and remarkably quiet. General Washington motioned for Nathanael to occupy an empty chair to the right of his at the head of the table.

"I am receiving alarming reports from throughout the camp. What is the progress of the construction?"

"The men are back to felling timber for the huts. But, with the lack of proper winter clothing in this severe weather, I do not have the manpower I need. It will be a number of weeks yet before all are adequately housed. Until then they will be forced into cramped quarters. Major Burnet is overseeing the construction at present." A violent chill went through Nathanael's body followed by a coughing spell.

"Are you ill, General?"

"It would appear so, sir."

"Has a physician tended you?"

"No, sir."

"Colonel Hamilton!" the Commander called. "Summon a physician. Tell him General Greene is ill—and have someone bring coffee in."

"Yes, sir."

"You need some rest, Nathanael."

"There is no time for rest, sir. We must clear the road in order to get the wagons out. Foraging details will be sent out as soon as possible. I am working the teams to the limit, but even grain and hay supplies are low. I cannot overwork them without adequate feed especially in these cold temperatures."

"How low is our food supply?"

Nathanael's eyes locked onto George Washington's. "Frighteningly low. The men were rationed the last of the meat and bread just prior to the blizzard—two pounds of each per man."

George Washington listened in silent disbelief.

"I suspect the entire northern part of the country is buried in snow and to the coast as well. I have no way of knowing the extent of this storm to the southward, but the nearest town that can adequately supply us is Philadelphia. It will take at least two days, once the roads are cleared, to receive supplies, should the merchants even find it within themselves to send any on a promissory note."

"But you will make the attempt just the same."

"I already have, sir. I have a man heading toward both Philadelphia and Newark even as we speak. I have no doubt that my agents in both towns are doing whatever they can to aid us. And I trust that General Arnold is working on clearing the road from Philadelphia to help dig us out—but beyond that—" Nathanael's expression was grim as he gratefully accepted the cup of steaming coffee from the Commander's servant Billy Lee. Draped across Billy's arm was a blanket, which, after giving the generals their coffee, he carefully placed around Nathanael's shoulders.

Nathanael took a sip of the hot liquid and continued. "I have authority from Congress to take what I must from the neighboring countryside to save the army from starvation. But I have no authority or influence over the citizens of Philadelphia, Boston, Hartford, Annapolis or Williamsburg. I presently have no money to offer in exchange for supplies. We managed to make bricks without straw for a time, but even Pharaoh did not expect that the Hebrew slaves could make bricks without mud!"

"I had no idea the situation was so desperate—" George Washington muttered as he rose to his feet.

A visible shiver ran through Nathanael's body. "Please remain seated, Nathanael," the Commander said as the younger man attempted to stand. "You will stay here and await the doctor."

"Sir, except the doctor tells me I am plagued with pneumonia, I must see to my duties."

George Washington nodded, his eyes appeared vacant, and his hands trembled slightly. He motioned to Billy for his hat and cape, which sat neatly on a nearby chair.

"Begging the General's pardon, but where are you going, sir?" Nathanael asked.

Slowly he turned about. "To see to the men, General Greene. To see to our brave men."

Riding through the encampment Nathanael spotted General Washington ahead, plodding through the snow toward one of the crudely built cabins. He knocked on the door and waited until it was opened to him, then disappeared within.

Tench Tilghman waited on the side of the road motionless upon his steed; the Commander's horse at his side. Nathanael quietly approached him, both men keeping a silent vigil over the hut.

No more than fifteen minutes passed when George Washington reappeared preparing, so it seemed, to go straight to the next hut. Upon spotting Nathanael, he moved toward him instead. Dismounting, Nathanael went to meet him.

"—The doctor's diagnosis?" The Commander asked hesitantly as though afraid to hear the reply.

"It's no more than a cold, sir."

"Only a cold? I feared it was more," he said, weakly smiling and reaching out to touch his shoulder with a gloved hand. "May Heaven be praised, Nathanael, for I cannot afford to be without your assistance now—this may prove to be the greatest crisis we have yet faced. We cannot lose hope no matter how dark it seems. We cannot let the men lose hope."

"By the grace of God, sir, we will come through this," Nathanael assured him, reaching up to clasp the hand upon his shoulder.

George Washington squeezed his shoulder and nodded.

The men turned to go their separate ways; the one to bring sustenance to the weary souls—the other to seek sustenance for the weakened bodies.

When the road was finally cleared, the countryside was immediately scoured for food. Never more than a few days meager provisions could be found, and each time the foraging details went out they were forced to go further and further from camp.

With the road made passable to Philadelphia Nathanael received, with a sense of enormous relief, a letter from Caty informing him of her safety, and of her imminent arrival at the camp.

"Well look here, General. It would appear my little cousin has finally arrived!" Sam Ward exclaimed as the men approached headquarters on horseback. With a beaming smile, he pointed to the familiar coach.

"And it would appear all the ladies have congregated to welcome her! You'll have to wait in line to say hello, General!" Billy Blodget added with a teasing grin, noting the empty carriages that lined the roadside.

"Leave it to Cousin Caty to throw a party as soon as she arrives!" Sam quickly added.

"Our headquarters will be overrun with women again!" Billy muttered pretending to be annoyed though his gleaming eyes gave him away. Nathanael grinning offered no reply.

The men reined their horses in alongside the coach and dismounted.

"What is it you call their little gatherings, sir? Tea frolics, isn't it?" Billy asked with a grin.

"That's right, Billy, and I promise you Mrs. Greene brought a trunk full of goods to properly entertain the ladies," he said glancing at the weighted down coach. His face was aglow. "And she will fully expect us to join them. I have no doubt that poor Cox, Pettit, and Burnet are being forced to prove their social graces even now."

"We will be up all night trying to make up for the time we wasted attending tea frolics!" Sam complained.

"Surely the fact that she is about ready to have a baby will slow her down some, won't it?" Billy asked.

Both Nathanael and Sam looked at him dumfoundedly. "Not a chance." they said almost in unison. The three began to laugh.

"Well, gentlemen, we can say good-bye to our quiet routine." Nathanael said patting them both on the shoulders as he gazed at the house.

"Our dull, quiet routine," Sam added.

"Thank God she is here!" Billy exclaimed bringing an immediate grin to each face.

"Please see to my horse, Billy, I must get in line to welcome Mrs. Greene to camp!" Nathanael said handing him the reins and hurriedly heading toward the house.

"There's absolutely no time to waste in preparing for this baby's birth!" Lucy Knox was heard exclaiming as Nathanael quietly entered the foyer, and began to remove his gloves, hat and cape.

"I never doubted you would be with us this winter, dear." Martha Washington said. Her delight came through in her tone. "We must notify a physician—or do you prefer a midwife?"

"I am quite certain that General Greene has made the necessary arrangements," Caty replied. The sound of her voice quickened Nathanael's heartbeat.

"Indeed I have. Dr. Eustis, a young physician from Boston, will attend her," Nathanael announced, suddenly appearing in the doorway.

Caty's face lit up.

"Do not try to stand," he laughed, walking toward her as she struggled to move her bulky form from the settee. "Caty! I cannot believe thee risked this trip in your condition! What ever shall I do with thee? I had hoped, Lady Washington, that your influence would have had its effect by now." He bent down and gently kissed his wife on the cheek, taking hold of her hand.

"Your wife, General Greene, has a mind of her own." Martha stated with a smile. She was delighted with his obvious joy, easily detected in the relapse of his speech.

"Indeed she does, and as strong a will as I have ever seen." Nathanael agreed still holding her hand.

"General Greene, I am beginning to think you would rather I were still in Rhode Island," Caty pretended to pout, her eyes flirtatiously locked on his.

"Never. But woman, I will readily admit that you cause me great concern at times."

"There is not a dull moment with Cousin Caty around!" Sam Ward exclaimed from the doorway. "Good day Mrs. Washington. Ladies!" he said looking around the room, then turning his attention back to Caty he added, "Welcome to camp, Cousin!"

Her joyous smile reflected the affection she held for Sam.

"We should be on our way," Martha announced with a smile, placing her teacup down on the table.

"No, please do not let us disturb your party. Mrs. Greene is extremely fond of these tea frolics," Nathanael said.

"We will have many such occasions in the weeks to come," Martha stated, amused by his term for their social gatherings. "You stay seated, dear," she said as Caty again attempted to stand. "We will let Major Ward see us to the door."

"It will be an honor, ladies," Sam said with a chivalrous bow.

After the women exited the room, Sam reached for the doorknob, winking at Nathanael and Caty as he pulled it shut.

"Same old Sammy!" Caty giggled still staring at the closed door as Nathanael sat down beside her, still holding on to her hand.

A sudden awkwardness came over them with the realization that they were alone.

"Where's George?" Nathanael asked.

"Colonel Cox invited him to ride over to General Washington's Headquarters. I think he was hoping to find you there."

"His Excellency will certainly enjoy his visit." Nathanael smiled.

"And how are you doing, Nathanael?" she asked.

"I am fine," he replied, staring at her hand in his.

"That's not what Lady Washington tells me! You've been sick—"

"It is only a cold, and it is passing." He said no more, nor did he lift his gaze from her hand.

With an amused smile, which he failed to see, Caty leaned toward him, kissing him softly upon the cheek. As was anticipated, Nathanael turned his head to face her. Quickly her lips found his. As she suspected, he offered no resistance.

All hands ceased from writing as the eyes of each man drifted toward the doorway upon hearing Caty's cry of anguish from the upstairs bedchamber. When her cries ended, Nathanael turned to look at little George playing at the table next to him. The four-year-old was visibly tired.

"Let's go read some more of our story, son," Nathanael said with a comforting smile, standing and extending his hand.

"*Gulliver's Travels!*" the boy exclaimed.

"*Gulliver's Travels?*" Billy Blodget echoed, winking at George. "I would not mind listening in myself, sir!"

"Can Uncle Billy come too, Papa?"

Nathanael patted the small boy on the head. "Uncle Billy has work to do," he said, smiling at his aide. "But we will be sure to lend him the book when we are done."

Billy's jovial response was interrupted when the foyer door burst open unleashing a cold draft through the office.

"Shut the door!" Rob Burnet called to Sam Ward from the office threshold.

"I am working on it!" Sam called back struggling to push the weight of the large oak door against the force of the wind's gust. "It's freezing out there!" he exclaimed stomping the snow from his boots. "Has the baby arrived yet?"

A dull moan from upstairs quickly answered his question.

"The entire camp is awaiting the announcement. Did you know there are men keeping a vigil outside, General?" he asked walking toward the office.

"What are you talking about?"

"Come and see!" Sam exclaimed.

Nathanael walked into the foyer and moved to the window where Sam stood. To his amazement, he saw a number of campfires in the front yard ablaze against the frigid temperatures. Men huddled against the fire's warmth—conversing as they busied themselves by whittling small pieces of wood.

Sam laid a hand on his commander's back sensing his astonishment. "They feel a great deal of affection for you, Nat. There's a strong sense of commitment—you have taken care of them—"

"Taken care of them? They're half starved!" he protested, gazing out the window through tear-filled eyes.

"They know you have done everything in your power to supply them. You have shown your concern for them time and again. Now they're showing their concern for you and your family."

An infant's cry pulled Nathanael's attention from the window. Walking to the bottom of the staircase he waited, his military family promptly gathered about. Finally Dr. Eustis appeared, confidently descending the stairs with a pleasant smile.

"You have a son, General. He is a strong, healthy boy. Congratulations."

"And my wife?"

"She came through it just fine."

"A son," Nathanael echoed with an affectionate gaze in little George's direction. A barrage of congratulatory remarks came from those gathered.

"Can I go up, Doctor?" he asked.

Dr. Eustis nodded. "Mrs. Greene is expecting you, sir."

Nathanael extended his hand to George. "Would you like to meet your brother?" He asked the boy. George nodded prompting Nathanael to whisk him into his arms and bound up the staircase.

Before long, he appeared at the top of the staircase holding a small white bundle. Slowly he descended; his eyes hypnotically fixed on the small face peeking out between the blanket and woolen cap. The men met him at the landing, each one beaming with pride as though he was viewing his own son for the first time.

"How I envy you." Colonel John Cox exclaimed, admiring the sleeping infant.

"You'll have one of your own by and by," Nathanael offered the father of five daughters.

"I have given up all hope—ah, girls are not so bad. I would not trade one of them for all the riches of the Indies," he said with a chuckle. "What are you going to name the lad, General?"

"Mrs. Greene has her heart set on naming him Nathanael Ray."

"Ray?" Charles Pettit asked.

"Her mother's maiden name," Sam said knowingly. "And it is a fine name for my little cousin!" He gently caressed the baby's tiny hand, which had worked its way out of the blankets.

"General, the womenfolk will be screaming for the return of that baby to his mother. He has had a good deal of excitement today," Dr. Eustis said.

"Mrs. Greene requested that I make one more announcement, Doctor."

The doctor appeared confused, for every member of Nathanael's military family was present.

Without waiting for a response, Nathanael walked toward the foyer door. "Sam, step outside and call to the men. Tell them we have a son, and that Mrs. Greene is well. Extend to them our compliments."

Sam smiled and nodded. As he stepped outside Nathanael positioned himself in front of the window, holding the baby up. Sam's words were clearly heard inside.

"Gentlemen, General Greene and his lady wish to extend to you their compliments, and announce to you the birth of their son." He paused and gestured to the window with his arm. "Let me present to you our newest recruit—Nathanael Ray Greene!"

Young George Washington Greene's presence at Headquarters was common, and thoroughly enjoyed. As the youngster followed his father into the bustling office, every eye latched onto him. When the four-year-old imitated his father in sharply saluting the Commander in Chief, grins broke out throughout the room.

"Well, Master Greene, will you be dining with us this evening?" George Washington asked receiving the small boy's impressive salute.

"Mama says if I mind my manners I may stay, General Washington!" He beamed.

George Washington gestured for the boy to stand before him. "And where is your mama?" he asked as little George stepped forward.

"She is in there wif Lady Washington," he said twisting his body around and pointing toward the parlor.

"And what about your brother?"

"Natty could not come cause he is not big like me. Natty does not know how to mind his manners. He had to stay wif the nurse, sir."

"I see." George Washington momentarily shifted his affectionate gaze from his namesake to Nathanael. "Then you intend to mind your manners, George?"

"Yes, sir."

"Good! I am delighted to have you sup with me. I will see that you are seated right at my side."

The boy turned and looked up at his father's towering form. He wore a proud smile, for even at such a tender age, little George understood the honor in being seated at the side of the Commander.

George Washington patted the youngster's head. "Go now, and find Lady Washington and your mother. I have some matters to discuss with your father."

"Yes, sir," he said, and again offered his father a smile.

The Commander watched little George leave the room then turned to Nathanael. "Let's go to my chamber." Standing he led the way to the stairs stopping briefly to greet Caty as they passed the open parlor door.

"It seems to me that Catharine is pushing her recovery. Three weeks of confinement hardly seems enough."

"You are entirely right, sir. But my wife has convinced Lady Washington that another day's confinement would drive her to distraction, and your kind wife was gracious enough to offer this invitation."

"I understand she has had numerous visitors," George Washington commented as he pushed open the chamber room door.

"Indeed she has! Your kindness has been shown more than once. Many of the men have crafted small gifts for her and the baby, and have stopped by to present them. The officers' wives come frequently—even the officers themselves stop in every now and then for a quick chat. She is certainly not wanting for company, just activity, which she does not need quite yet. She has heard rumors of a dancing assembly being formed supposedly by you and a number of officers!" Nathanael's laughter was met with a sure smile.

"Then it is true?" he asked incredulously.

"I is a diversionary activity that your wife will not be allowed to participate in for some time yet, and I shall tell her so myself!" The Commander stated authoritatively.

"I truly would appreciate it, your Excellency!"

George Washington smiled and nodded. "Have a seat, Nathanael," he said gesturing to the chair opposite the one he chose at the small table. "The fanfare at dinner will be very modest I am afraid. My staff has forfeited their meat allowance."

"As have most of the officers, but the reality of it is that there's not enough meat even for the officers. I am making certain that the women and children are adequately fed, then the hospitals are supplied, there's never much left—"

"I have good news—" George Washington began, though his countenance did not reflect his words. He became silent for a minute, slowly letting his guard down in the company of this trusted officer and friend. Before Nathanael's eyes he transformed, as he so often did when they met like this, from the unshakable pillar of strength; unable to show fear, confusion or weakness—to the man that he was. A man stronger than most, but still only a man. Nathanael noted in the momentary silence, how much this dear friend had aged in the four years since they met.

"Your words have rung true," George Washington began, lifting up a letter from the table, and instantly letting go of it, almost tossing it aside. "Congress cannot aid us at this time. They will not meet our desperate need for food and clothing. As we discussed I made an appeal on behalf of the army through the magistrates to the citizens of New Jersey for assistance. We have received encouraging responses this afternoon. I trust we will have some relief from our deplorable state forthcoming. The Continental Army shall be ever indebted to the good people of this state for their kindness—" George Washington's eyes drifted away as a simultaneous sigh left Nathanael's lips.

Neither man needed to say a word, for they had spoken so often of their struggle to supply the men in the weeks of their encampment in Morristown. The sense of grief at the abandonment of the Continental Army by Congress was agonizing. The cold fact was that though the men of this army were willing to risk all for the cause of liberty, the very people they fought for had in truth distanced themselves from their suffering. The people had shut the army out of their minds during this, its time of greatest need.

New Jersey would finally come to their aid—God bless the men and women of New Jersey, Nathanael thought. *What of Pennsylvania? Massachusetts? Rhode Island? Virginia? What of the other states? What of the abundance and comfort they enjoyed this unusually fierce winter while these brave souls lacked basic necessities?*

"With news of our relief, my thoughts are now focused southward." George Washington stated, disrupting Nathanael's tormenting thoughts. "If the British are not brought into check in South Carolina I fear a stronghold will quickly be established which will not be easily broken. Much of the deep South is loyal to the British Crown. Tory regiments will prove a great strength to the British forces. We can readily call on the militia companies here, but in the South the local citizenry may choose to fight against us rather than with us." General Washington paused and sighed.

"I cannot risk sending any more troops southward. The British have the numbers to divide into two separate forces. The fact that they pulled troops from Rhode Island only proves that they plan to entrench in the South—and we barely have an army. If New Jersey does not come through with supplies we will be forced to disband altogether."

"Any hope of aid from the French fleet?" Nathanael asked

"Rumors continue to circulate about the movements of the French fleet, but I am aware of no substantial aid forthcoming."

Neither George Washington nor Nathanael Greene had the confidence and blind hope, which most of their countrymen did, that the French would deliver them from their present oppression. The Rhode Island fiasco was still too recent to ignore.

Slowly Nathanael lowered his head as George Washington's eyes drifted to the letter from Congress. There was an uneasy silence as their thoughts came to an abrupt halt. Neither one could think beyond this point—beyond disbanding—what then? The consequences were too difficult to contemplate, and there were some things the mind simply refused to consider. Death was certain for men in their position. This they knew. But what of their families? What of their country? What of the future?

Then suddenly George Washington spoke surprising even himself, so it seemed.

"If we are forced to disband, those officers and their families who are willing to risk it can attempt to cross the Allegheny Mountain Range. We can establish ourselves in the vast wilderness to the west. It will be a struggle at first, but didn't our ancestors face a similar struggle when they settled in this land?"

Nathanael turned to face him and nodded his head.

"Would Catharine be willing to live in the wild?"

Again, Nathanael nodded.

"As would my Patsy," George Washington said softly. "It is only a passing thought. No more than a passing thought. We must believe that the Lord will hold us together. Is there still talk of mutiny?"

"Murmuring—most of the men will remain loyal to the end. Their endurance is incredible."

George Washington studied Nathanael. "If you were free of the position of Quartermaster General I would have recommended to Congress that you had been given command of the Southern Department rather than General Lincoln, and I would be resting a bit easier now."

"General Lincoln will do all in his power. He's a man of action." Nathanael offered.

"Yes, but he is also ailing physically. And very often ill health affects one's ability to think clearly. I would rather you were there."

"I thank you for your confidence, sir. And though I will continue to do all I can to free myself from my present position, I must admit that the thought of commanding the Southern Department is a bit distressing."

George Washington nodded. "You are entirely shut off from the main army, it is true. Any communication I get from South Carolina takes at least six weeks to arrive."

"It's not so much that, sir, as it is—" Nathanael hesitated.

"What is it, General Greene?"

"Forgive me, sir, I am embarrassed to even speak it knowing the sacrifices you have made to home and family these past four years—"

George Washington waited.

"—The distance is so great. I would have no hope of seeing my wife and children should I be sent south. All news from home would be at least six weeks in arriving, and my reply would be that long in returning. It is difficult enough to feel the part of husband and especially father under the present circumstances—but how foolish of me to worry over something that is not so and very likely will never come to pass." He said with a forced smile, trying, but unable, to shake the ominous feeling concerning his fears.

"Begging the General's pardon, but, even if Congress were to miraculously accept my resignation it would not be likely that they'd agree with any recommendation you might give to assign me command of the Southern Department. If General Lincoln should resign due to poor health I suspect General Gates will be Congress' choice for the position."

"And if the position should be offered to you?" There was firmness in George Washington's expression.

"Sir, if you feel that the situation in the South warrants my personal attention—if Congress would agree, then I would consider it a task assigned me by the Throne of Heaven, and set my hand to the plow not looking back."

George Washington's countenance remained firm as he continued to stare at him in silence.

"What is he thinking? Nathanael wondered as he felt the foreboding silence engulf him. *Lord, God, let this cup pass from me!"*

"Billy is back!" Sam Ward exclaimed from across the room. "Life just is not the same without ya, Billy! Welcome home!"

Billy Blodget stepped into the office, smiling, though somehow lacking his usual mirth. "It is terribly stuffy in here. Open some windows, boys! Spring is in full bloom!" With a salute for Nathanael, he offered him a handful of mail. "Correspondence from Philadelphia, sir, and there's even a letter for Mrs. Greene from Mrs. Arnold. Both General Arnold and his lady requested that I personally extend to you their compliments. They desired that I also express how much they enjoyed having you and your lady as house guests during your recent stay in Philadelphia."

Nathanael nodded as he took the mail from Billy and quickly thumbed through it. After tossing the letters on his desk, he stood.

"You are right, it is stuffy in here, and your arrival is a good excuse to go outside and get some fresh air. Let's go for a walk."

Billy followed Nathanael toward the front door. "Your hat, sir?" he asked grabbing his own tricorne off the foyer table. As he expected, Nathanael shook his head. If at all possible, the former iron master always refused to wear a hat on a warm, sunny day. Complete military attire was hardly needed to take a casual walk with an old friend.

The pleasant warmth of the May afternoon invigorated Nathanael as they walked away from the house. The bright sunshine, lively sounds, fragrant odors, and vibrant colors of spring worked together to stir him back to life after being cooped in the office with its constant drudgery. Yet, despite the pleasantness of the day, he was unable to yield to the joy it offered.

"Did you get the transfer?" he finally asked staring straight ahead as though dreading the answer.

"I did, sir."

"Where to?"

"You are not going to believe it, General. Of all places—the Navy! And of all posts—chaplain!"

"The Navy?"

"Yes, sir."

"Chaplain?"

"I told you that you would not believe it. I guess they figure any man who served as aide-de-camp to a Quaker general is highly qualified for the work of a chaplain." Billy chuckled uneasily.

"Your theological studies had nothing to do with it, hey?" Nathanael asked with a weak smile.

Billy shrugged.

"When do you leave?"

"Day after tomorrow. I have been granted a two week leave to return home and tend to personal matters before taking my post."

Nathanael signed, visibly upset at the answer. "I am not ready to lose thee, Billy. Thee have been a trusted friend and faithful companion for so long. Your service to me has been invaluable. Why can't the blasted Congress find a way to keep thee on my staff—or at least with the main army that we might enjoy fellowship—"

He paused, regaining his composure, and then added, "I shall miss you exceedingly."

"And I you, Nat."

An awkward few moments of silence followed as they continued to walk.

"What's this I hear about Mrs. Greene's being given the position of personal bodyguard to His Excellency?"

Nathanael did not respond, pretending not to hear.

"Word is that the General was physically assaulted and only Mrs. Greene had the courage needed to come to his aid. Word is you and a number of other officers cowered in fear." Billy grinned.

Nathanael smiled sheepishly. "You heard this all the way in Philadelphia?"

"Colonel Petitt informed me."

"Ah, dear Charles can always be counted on to pass on all vital information!" Nathanael chuckled.

"So what happened?"

"I thought Charles told you?"

"No details, only that there was a brawl of some sort, and that, begging the general's pardon, that the men proved themselves cowards. He assured me that you would be eager to fill me in on the necessary details."

Nathanael grunted. "Actually it is quite embarrassing— We were invited to spend the evening with the Biddles," Nathanael hesitated.

Billy waited, finding nothing unusual in the fact that he and Caty visited the young foragemaster general and his wife.

"The Washingtons were there when we arrived. Our house guests, George Olney and his wife, came with us."

Again, he hesitated and again Billy found nothing unusual in the account thus far. George Olney was one of Nathanael's Rhode Island agents, a distant cousin. It would be expected that their guests would accompany them.

"—As such gatherings tend to go, the women congregated in the sitting room to have their usual tea frolic while the men gathered about the dining room table. I do not honestly remember what we were discussing," Nathanael said with a shrug. "All I remember is what we did not talk about; no talk of war or shortages or even politics. It was a very lighthearted conversation for His Excellency, Colonel Biddle and I. It was wonderfully refreshing. However, George Olney, it seems, found the conversation to be too light hearted. He quickly became bored with us, and, in my opinion, without properly excusing himself from His Excellency's presence, wandered across the hall to where the ladies had gathered.

"After a few moments we heard the women making a fuss over Olney's attention—loud enough to be heard by us, and obviously desiring a response. General Washington jokingly commented that one of our own had proved a traitor by deserting, and that we must retrieve him quickly before we, too, were expected to partake of the ladies' tea frolic."

Nathanael paused. Looking at Billy his face suddenly distorted with embarrassment, he continued. "Well, being dutiful soldiers we followed our Commander in Chief into the next room where he immediately announced our purpose and took hold of George Olney's arm. Before anyone knew what was happening Mrs. Olney broke out in hysterics and was all over him."

"All over who? Her husband?"

"No! General Washington! She was screaming at him to get his hands off her husband, and 'Just because you are a general it does not give you the right to order my husband about.'" Nathanael mimicked. "She was pulling at his coat and grabbing his arms. Then to make matters worse, before any of us had the opportunity to respond, being utterly astonished at the entire scene, my wife grabbed hold of Mrs. Olney, twirled her around, and knocked her to the floor ready to pounce on top of her!"

Billy burst into laughter.

"It was not funny." Nathanael muttered to no avail.

"A cat fight?" Billy exclaimed through his laugher.

"Almost. By that time I was able to respond, thank God. Speedily I moved behind Caty and grabbed hold of her by the waist, carrying her off to a corner of the room. She was fit to be tied. It took me a few minutes to calm her all the while hearing Mrs. Olney in a rage behind me as her husband spoke to her."

"And what of General Washington?" Billy asked, still laughing.

"He was apologizing the entire time, for what, he had no idea. To this day I do not know what triggered such an outburst in Olney's wife, but you can be sure I gave him a piece of my mind afterward in regard to both her rude behavior and his in taking leave of His Excellency's presence with no due respect shown."

"As for Caty," Nathanael said with a smile and a shrug. "What can I say? She felt His Excellency was in danger and acted upon it. What am I to do with her, Billy? She is graced with great beauty and charm, yet she can be provoked so quickly to act impulsively."

"The truth is, Nat, that you have a most attractively wrapped package with a little tomboy inside! No doubt, it comes of having lost her mother at such a tender age. I understand she spent a good many of her early years in the company of male kin folk."

"I guess you are right." Nathanael agreed.

"Of course I am right. And why not be honest about it, it was not her beauty and charm alone that caught your attention, you were attracted to her high spirits as well. Let us face it, coming as you do from an all male family, any women married to one of the Greene brothers has to have a bit of spunk to survive."

Billy chuckled. "The good Lord in his omniscience gave you exactly the wife you needed. It would take such a woman to fearlessly risk journeying the distance necessary to be with you regardless of the weather or the fact that she was so great with child," he said, rolling his eyes and shaking his head.

"And let us not overlook her ability to fit right in with your military family. The atmosphere of most generals' headquarters changes drastically when the general's lady arrives in camp—like a mother arriving with all the do's and don'ts for her wayward boys—but not ours. Caty brings brightness with her. There is more enjoyment, more liveliness when she arrives. She joins in the jokes, games and pranks. She makes the men feel at home, and lessens their loneliness."

"Some consider her to be flirtatious with the men," Nathanael commented matter-of-factly.

Billy laughed. "Now do not get me wrong, General. She certainly has a strong feminine charm; and she can be most persuasive with those big eyes and dimpled smile. But most of the gossips are nothing but jealous females who do not understand that Caty simply is herself. While most women will put on airs in the company of men, Caty does not change. She has been a true blessing to all of us—a true blessing.

"As for Mrs. Olney—I am sorry for the embarrassment it caused you, sir, but she probably deserved Mrs. Greene's, ah, shall we say, gentle persuasion." Billy said with a grin, clearing his throat. "I understand there was near mutiny this past week. Maybe you should have sent Caty to negotiate with them," he added, the smile quickly fading as a somber expression took its place.

They came upon a fenced pasture and stopped, resting their arms across the railing and gazing out over the field.

"I heard it was some of the Connecticut boys," Billy added.

Nathanael looked at him then immediately turned his attention back to the pasture.

"Yeah, and the truth of it is that I genuinely felt sorry for them. And quite honestly, between you and me, if I were in the ranks I may have been tempted to join them," Nathanael confessed shamefully.

"Temptation is not a sin, Nat. You never would have joined them."

"I am not so sure, Billy. All winter long, they have faced starvation, with hardly enough clothing to modestly cover their bodies. Now spring is here and we are faring no better. Let's not even consider the plight of their families—a major general cannot adequately support his family on the meager wages received, never mind our boys in the ranks."

"I understand it was quickly brought under control."

"Yes—" Nathanael appeared distant. "This time it was, but there will be another attempt—maybe the Pennsylvania boys next time, they've been stirring for a while. Or maybe it will be Connecticut again or our Rhode Island brothers may even surprise us. Where it will start next time I do not really know—but it will come. And I pray, Billy, that no blood is shed."

Nathanael sighed. "It is not us they are mad at—not His Excellency; not the officers; not even the quartermaster's department. It is Congress—it is the recruiting agents. It is all the rhetoric and broken promises—all the bold-faced lies; and an ungrateful people who care only for their security, heedless of the basic needs of these brave souls, which keep the enemy away.

"Congress—" Nathanael muttered the word with contempt, and then sighed as he shook his head. "I have become bitter, my friend, and I do not like the man I now am. Charles Pettit recently told me that he feared my growing resentment of Congress would one day interfere with my usefulness as Quartermaster General. That day has come. I cannot go along with their plan for reorganizing the department. When I consider it logically, I feel my arguments are sound and just. Yet, I must confess, Billy, sometimes I fear that I might be simply refusing to see that anything good could come of the plans of Congress. Perhaps I am so caught up in the gall of bitterness that I simply cannot see."

"Your arguments are sound, General. Their plans for reorganizing the department will not help our plight."

"Oh, Billy," Nathanael began mournfully, shaking his head. "What can I say? I am exceedingly unhappy with your forced transfer, yet, as in so many areas directly pertaining to me, I have no say in the matter. I have tried every way I know to keep you here with me—Caty will be very upset to learn of it. When I finally take field command again what shall I do without you at my side, Major Blodget?"

Staring down at the ground Billy kicked a rock about for a moment. Then, looking up, Nathanael detected a tear in his eye.

"General, sir—Nat, my old friend—there is something more disturbing than my transfer, and I must tell you, but I do not know how to go about it—" The pain reflected in his eyes intensified.

"Tell me what?"

"Your most recent request to be relieved the post of quartermaster general was brought before Congress yesterday."

"And as usual they rejected it," Nathanael's icy words came.

Billy failed to respond leaving Nathanael to believe what he anticipated was so.

Slowly Billy turned to look at him. "Your letter, it seems, evoked a heated debate—an enraged debate. Congress was adjourned because of the emotional stir. It was to reconvene today and continue deliberation on it, but—" He turned away again. "But, the prevailing attitude—the very reason for the outrage on the part of your friends in Congress, is that you not only be removed as quartermaster general, but—but that you also be relieved of all military command—"

An uncomfortable silence elapsed as the shock of Billy's announcement sank in.

"—Who—who told thee this?" Nathanael finally uttered softly.

"General Schuyler, sir."

Nathanael nodded, knowing that the former commander of the Canadian expeditions, turned Congressman, would give an accurate account of the situation.

"Why?" He asked.

"The prevailing attitude is that your letter was presumptuous and rude, and that your insubordinate attitude should be punished with a complete discharge."

There was no response as Nathanael turned his head away from Billy.

"General Schuyler wants you to know that he and those who support you in Congress will continue to fight in your defense, though they are badly outnumbered.

He took the liberty of drafting a letter to General Washington relating the urgency of the situation, and beseeching him to intercede on your behalf."

"Where's this letter?"

"I was instructed by General Schuyler to personally deliver it to His Excellency before reporting to you, sir— I did as I was instructed, and beg your forgiveness if my actions were amiss."

He turned back to Billy finding comfort in his concerned gaze.

"Your actions were not amiss, Major."

Dropping his head down he added, "I cannot believe that they are determined to go to such lengths— What is it they want from me? I do not know what it is they want from me.

"Am I an evil man, Major Blodget, high-minded and proud that I so grieve the thought of losing my command?"

"You are one of the finest general officers in this army, sir—raised up by Jehovah, Himself, if you ask my opinion! No, General Greene, it is not wickedness in you that results in such a malicious act. You are a man of conviction, a man who must serve in the station God has called him to from birth. Congress may threaten, but they cannot thwart the Almighty's calling on your life."

Nathanael noticed none of the usual activity outside of Headquarters as he made his approach—except for Colonel Tench Tilghman's presence in the front yard. Nathanael watched from his saddle, as General Washington's most trusted aide-de-camp approached the post rider, horse at his side, and handed him a single letter. With great haste, the seasoned messenger mounted his horse, wheeled it about, and rode off.

"General Greene," Tench greeted him with a formal salute, drawing Nathanael's attention away from the departing messenger. "General Washington is expecting you, sir. He is in his chamber."

"Thank you, Colonel." Nathanael dismounted and handed the reins to a waiting soldier. "What is the mood at the moment, Colonel?" Nathanael asked his friend as they walked into the house.

"Somewhat tense, sir."

"Aye, I figured as much—"

As Nathanael ascended the staircase, he considered how many times he had been summoned to the General's private chamber in his five years of service—a service that might very well be coming to an abrupt end.

His knock on the door was quickly heeded with a verbal response to enter.

"General Greene," George Washington received Nathanael's prompt salute. "Sit down, please," the Commander said, pointing to the chair opposite his at the small table. Nathanael closed the door, and moved toward the chair, carefully placing his tricorne on the floor beside him. George Washington momentarily focused his attention on the open papers lying on the table. Slowly pushing them aside, he turned his gaze on Nathanael.

"My response to Congress is on its way," he finally stated.

The post rider, Nathanael thought. He had suspected as much, but the haste in it—the utter sense of urgency!

"I do not believe Congress will go through with this foolhardy plan—but one never knows." George Washington took a deep breath, his unyielding gaze still fixed. "I could not argue your service as quartermaster general—they are keenly aware of that. Instead, I pointed them to the fact that if they were to arbitrarily dismiss such a high ranking officer without a hearing then the security of position each and every officer now holds will be felt to be at the whim of Congress. Such an action would meet with the outcry of all the officers in this army."

"Your letter to Congress was reported by General Schuyler to be border line insubordinate in content."

"I do not believe so, sir."

"I am not interested in your opinion at the moment, General!" George Washington exclaimed bringing the palms of his hands down hard on the table. "Certainly General Schuyler would not tell me such a thing if it weren't so—he is for you, Nathanael!" He stopped speaking, leaned forward, and momentarily laid his head in his hand taking a deep breath. "I wonder if your anger has barred your ability to reason," he said looking up. Though Nathanael sat in silence, his expression virtually emotionless, George Washington could see the flame in his eyes.

Nathanael realized he was now being given the opportunity to speak. *General Washington, you are wrong!* he screamed within as he considered the Commander's last statement. *I am angry! I am so very angry! But my reasoning is clear—I think it is clear! I pray it is clear!* He shifted position as he tried to calm the inner rage.

"—I have served this position to the best of my ability—with honesty and integrity." Nathanael began his tone strained. "But they are determined to name me as the scapegoat for a business that has no hope of succeeding because of their incompetence, and because of the lack of compassion in the people of these united states to support this army."

"The only thing that unites the states is the army!" George Washington protested.

"Not any longer, sir. The people have lost their conviction. They desire to be free and independent, but they have grown weary of this war. Save the state we are forced to inhabit, the rest of the country wishes to forget we exist. They want to know we are here to protect their borders, but they do not want to be burdened with sustaining us. And Congress refuses to exert their power to see that the states be responsible for our support."

"Is it true you refused to serve your post?" George Washington asked pointedly.

"Under the new plan, yes, sir, I did."

"You would desert your post and leave this army without a quartermaster general?"

"No, sir. Congress is leaving the army without a quartermaster general."

"I do not appreciate the semantics, General Greene!" George Washington exclaimed.

"Sir, under the new plan much of the present responsibility of my position shall be placed on your shoulders. I am required to do much less, and you much more. Many of my agents are being dismissed as well as one of my assistants. This new plan was even put down by the committee Congress formed to investigate my department. But, because Congress refuses to see that they could be mistaken they've rejected the committee's report and have insisted, no matter how fatal their plan, to have it implemented."

"Your action was irresponsible." George Washington stated.

"My action was necessary, sir. They have refused to accept my resignation in the past. With the forced implementation of their plan I saw a way out."

"Have you forgotten that Congress does have authority over you, General Greene?"

"No, sir. I have not. But when that same Congress violates every term I agreed to serve under—even dismissing assistant Quartermaster General Cox, then I feel the agreement we had is null and void."

George Washington hesitated before replying. The usual calm was once again in his tone. "You may lose your rank. Reacting in anger seldom accomplishes any good purpose, Nathanael. Was it worth such a risk?"

"I was losing my dignity, General Washington. That means far more to me than my rank—"

"Do you blame me, General Greene?" George Washington asked.

"Certainly not, sir."

He was not being completely honest, George Washington knew Nathanael well enough to realize this. "But?" the Commander asked, patiently waiting, all the while holding the younger man under an unyielding gaze.

"—But if it were not for your influence I never would have accepted this post, sir."

"Do you question what I think of your service, Quartermaster General?"

"I have come to question many things these past few months, General Washington—" His tone was firm, but the flame in his eyes had been extinguished. Instead, in its place, George Washington detected agony. Unable to withstand the reflected pain George Washington dropped his eyes downward, and then quickly stood up walking toward the window nearest his chair. Peering out over the front yard he thought—he prayed. *It is a time of preparation—Preparation for what?* He glanced at Nathanael, whose head hung down upon slumped shoulders. *Preparation for what?* The words echoed as an inner peace came that the answer would come in time.

"You have proven yourself remarkably competent in your post, Nathanael," he began, stopping to clear the lump in his throat. "I believe if it weren't for the Hand of Providence in bringing you into this post the army would have ceased to exist. What you accomplished in a few short weeks during our stay at Valley Forge was nothing less than miraculous. I have told you so before, my opinion has not changed. Were it not for your selfless determination to keep the men from starvation and exposure we would have been forced to disband."

Nathanael remained quiet, his head still down.

"—The entire country is waiting for the arrival of the French force that we might annihilate the enemy with the military strength of France. You and I know better. I have been expecting their arrival for weeks. I now know they will not arrive in time to assist us."

Nathanael looked up. George Washington turned to him, their eyes immediately locking.

"I just received word that a force of some 12,000 British and Hessian troops under the command of General Knyphausen are marching toward us. And General Clinton's force has been steadily marching northward since the capture of our troops in South Carolina. They're but a five days march from here."

Nathanael cleared his throat and quickly squared his shoulders, "What do we have, roughly 7,000 men?"

"Yes and only half that number are fit to take the field. I have sent word to the New Jersey militia companies to turn out—" He turned back to the window. "According to General Schuyler you'll be relieved of the duty of quartermaster general. Thomas Pickering will most likely be given the post. But, even if Pickering were to arrive in camp tomorrow, eager to undertake the task, he would not have the time or knowledge of the department and connections needed to adequately supply us for this encounter."

George Washington walked to the table, standing behind his chair; he rested his hands on the back of it. "As I said, you are no longer quartermaster general, and until I receive word that you are officially relieved of all command, and because I do not believe such word will be given, Major General Greene, I am assigning you field command for this battle. But, I must ask a favor of you—for the life of this army, and the sake of your country—"

The pain—the excruciating pain was again pouring from Nathanael's eyes, forcing George Washington to once more turn his own away.

"Please—would you please assist the new quartermaster general in this task? I need you, my friend—"

There was a frightening silence. It lasted but a moment, though it seemed an eternity.

Nathanael stood. George Washington looked at him.

"—I will gather what supplies I can. Where shall I have them transported?"

"Springfield. It appears that Springfield, New Jersey will be a strong place to position ourselves. Do you agree?"

"I do, sir. It is a fine spot"

"And will you map out our march?"

"I will get to it immediately, General." Nathanael picked up his hat. "Will there be a Council of War called, sir?"

"Yes. Seven o'clock this evening."

"May I beg the General's leave? I have much to attend to, including arranging for my family to be escorted home."

"I understand Major Blodget is heading back to Rhode Island," George Washington said.

"He is, sir."

"Might he escort your family?"

"Yes, sir, I have no doubt that he will."

"I am sorry that you are losing the assistance of this friend."

"Thank you, sir. It's difficult."

"One more thing, General Greene."

"Sir?"

"General Schuyler mentioned in his letter that Horatio Gates has been chosen by Congress to take command of the Southern Department."

"I am not surprised, sir."

"Nor am I. I just wish you had been freed from your post prior to this decision—"

"Do you think Congress would have enjoyed banishing me to the South?" Nathanael asked with a weak smile.

"I think Congress enjoys assigning you impossible tasks; for, in truth, they know you are the most capable of my general officers to handle them—you are dismissed, General Greene."

The morning sun peeked out from behind the Watchung Mountains, only to find the headquarters of the quartermaster general already bustling with activity. Men had come and gone all through the night as papers were signed, instructions given, and orders passed on.

"General, I need your signature on this release, sir," Major Rob Burnet said, paper in hand.

Nathanael took the paper and scribbled his signature upon it. As he handed it back, he saw Billy Blodget leaning against the wall in an-out-of-the way spot near the door. They had already said their good-byes long before breakfast, long before the sun broke through the night sky. And, as hard as it was for Nathanael to accept the fact that Billy was leaving momentarily, it was harder still to know that the reason he now lingered was to wait on Caty, little Nathanael, and George.

Nathanael glanced toward the staircase in the foyer. There was no sign of them. *Good!* He thought pathetically, holding onto every second they were still in the house, still in his care. They had to leave, he realized this; but he longed to avoid that tormenting moment he knew all too well, when they would move from his embrace and then fade from sight.

He turned his attention to a waiting wagoneer, only to hear Billy's voice from behind.

"Are you ready, Caty? Here let me take that bag."

Nathanael turned, finding Caty standing in the doorway with Natty in her arms and George by her side.

"Are you sure you have everything?" he asked, secretly hoping the answer would be no, thus postponing the inevitable.

"I think so," came her soft reply.

Nathanael's aides and assistants offered a sad smile. Though their formal good-byes, along with a warm embrace, were spoken at breakfast, they could not restrain themselves now.

"God's speed, Mrs. Greene."

"We will help the General count the days until you return, ma'am."

"It's sure going to be lonely here without you, Mrs. Greene."

"Hey, Cousin," Sam Ward joined in. "Give everyone my love— I sure will miss you, Caty."

Caty smiled in response, fighting back her tears.

"I will carry the baby," Nathanael offered, taking Natty and cradling him in one arm; then grasping hold of her hand with his, they headed for the door.

Stopping at the coach, he gazed at his infant son. At six-months little Natty was full of wonder and joy. "I will not recognize him when I see him next. I cannot tell you how much that disturbs me—." He softly kissed the baby's forehead.

Caty watched in silence as Nathanael placed Natty in the bassinet on the floor of the coach, kissing him once again before pushing it safely away from the open door.

"Come here, George, and climb in the coach with your brother!" Nathanael called.

"But, Papa, Uncle Billy says maybe I can ride up there!" He pointed to the driver's seat towering above him.

"Are you sure about this, Billy? He will not give you a moment's rest!" Nathanael informed him.

"I will enjoy the company, sir."

"If Uncle Billy says it is all right, then it is fine with me. Come here and give me a big hug then I will put you up there."

George jumped into his father's arms, tightly embracing him around the neck.

"I love thee, son," Nathanael whispered, and then kissed the small boy's cheek. "Now you get on up there, and keep Uncle Billy company."

"Yes, sir." the small boy exclaimed as he was lifted into Billy's waiting arms.

"I think I will just put my feet up, lean back, and let his little Excellency drive the team home!" Billy said with a chuckle, reclining into the position.

"I am sure he fully expects to drive that team, and he needs absolutely no encouragement from you, Major Blodget." Nathanael said forcing his smile into a fatherly glare.

"Yes, sir, General Greene!" Billy saluted.

Laughing, Nathanael extended his hand to his aide. "God bless thee my friend. We shall catch up to one another at home in the not too distant future, I pray. Let us gather around your kitchen hearth, and share our new war stories, hey?"

"I will look forward to that day, Nat. I cannot tell you how much I will look forward to that day."

As he turned to face his wife, Nathanael realized the moment he dreaded most had come. Laying his hands on her shoulders, he gazed into her troubled eyes.

"The winter ahead will be different for us—much more relaxing than we have known for awhile. I will have a great deal of time to spend with you, being free of the quartermaster's post. How I pray that the season's campaign ends early so that you might come before the cold weather sets in, and all four children can come with you. Caty! To have all of our children with us—to have them all in my presence at the same time! It's a glorious dream that I pray will soon come true!"

"If it is at all possible, I will be sure to bring them," she promised.

He pulled her close, enfolding her in his strong arms. She immediately buried her face against his chest.

"A few short months, that's all, and we will be together again! " He felt her sobs, and kissed her head. "It will be a wonderful reunion! Hope with me, Angel. Pray with me. Dream with me—"

She nodded, her face still hidden. Slowly she lifted her head to meet his loving gaze.

"—I know I have to be strong—" she wept. "I know I must be courageous, but I do not feel very strong or courageous."

Nathanael offered a tender smile. "Nor do I, my love."

"I keep hoping this is just a nightmare—a horribly wicked dream; and, if you hold me long enough it will pass—" she whispered.

"It is not a nightmare, it is far worse. But I promise you it will pass just the same. And in the meantime, be sure of this: you shall always hold a vital place in my heart, which none other shares."

Caty nodded, tears streaming down her cheeks.

"Did you hear what young Major Morris said to you?" Nathanael asked, referring to his new aide.

"He said he would help you count the days until my return," she replied softly.

"And he will. He is smitten with you. Nathanael grinned, prompting a smile from his wife. "So you see, you will have plenty of prayers in regard to your safe passage and return. Now you be sure that, when you write, you ask about young Morris; so I can tell him you asked, and brighten his week."

Caty nodded, the smile still upon her lips. Nathanael brought his head down, his lips meeting hers in a soft kiss, a kiss full of all the love Nathanael felt for his departing wife.

When he lifted his head, she again buried her face against his chest, holding onto him with all her might.

268

"There has been unfolded at this place a scene of the blackest treason. Arnold has fled to the enemy."
(Alexander Hamilton to Nathanael Greene)

CHAPTER FOURTEEN

TENCH TILGHMAN CAREFULLY made his way down the semi-darkened hall. A formidable stack of papers was securely tucked under his arm, while he balanced a steaming cup of diluted coffee upon a saucer with one hand and a single lit candle with the other. As he slowly turned at the base of the staircase, preparing to make his treacherous ascent, the foyer door burst open, immediately snuffing out the candle's flame.

"Give me one good reason why I should believe you, Wayne." Lord Stirling exclaimed, stepping from the blackness into the partially lit foyer.

"It is of no concern to me whether or not you believe me, your Lordship. Feel free to discover the matter for yourself." Anthony Wayne returned with a wide grin. "Ask Tench. He will confirm my report."

Seemingly undaunted by the intrusion, Tench twisted his head to view the scene, his body remaining fixed in position.

Lord Stirling looked up at Tench. "Tell me, Colonel, General Wayne is spreading a tall tale about His Excellency having turned the command over to—" he hesitated. "Never mind. What am I doing? You are every bit as much of a prankster as General Wayne. He has probably cued you in on the jest already. Is the General in there?" He asked tilting his head toward the closed dining room door.

"Yes, sir. Welcome back to camp, General Stirling." Tench called after him as he determinedly moved toward the door.

"Thank you, Colonel. It is good to be back."

"What is going on?" Tench asked the grinning Anthony Wayne.

"Try as I may to keep the good general abreast of the goings on in camp and this is the thanks I get: my character brought into question!" He replied loudly, his attention focused on Lord Stirling's back.

His Lordship stopped and turned. "Are you coming with me?"

"But, of course, sir!" Anthony pranced down the hallway stopping at Lord Stirling's side.

Taking hold of the doorknob, His Lordship opened the door and stepped into the room, scanning the scene about him. As usual, aides and secretaries busied themselves in their endless tasks.

"Well, bless my soul, it is true!" Lord Stirling exclaimed, fixing his eyes on Nathanael Greene's seated form at the head of the table. "A few months back he was denied any command, and now he has command of the whole blasted army!"

Nathanael met Lord Stirling's odd greeting with a warm smile. "That is exactly right, your Lordship; and, therefore, I should think a proper greeting is in order."

Lord Stirling and Anthony came to full attention with the most formal salute Nathanael had witnessed from either one. He nodded in response as he placed a quill pen in its holder, and then stood, beckoning them to follow him into the parlor.

"I understand Lady Kitty has adapted nicely to married life," Nathanael stated as they walked.

"Indeed, she has."

"I expect she will still pay us a visit in camp on occasion."

"I expect she will."

"And Lady Stirling is well?" Nathanael inquired further.

"Much better now that I am gone—I am not a very good patient."

Nathanael smiled in response as the three seated themselves in the parlor.

"How fortunate to be this close to home in order to recuperate from your rheumatism. Your appearance is much better than when I saw you last."

"I feel much better. Blasted rheumatism. I never had a problem with it before that march on Trenton. What a cold, miserable night that was."

"Cold? You've not experienced cold until you've marched on Montreal in the dead of winter." Anthony piped in.

"It was cold!" Lord Stirling insisted. "We had men freeze to death. Tell him, Nat."

Scenes of that night flooded Nathanael's mind—it seemed so long ago. Many of the faces were different then: Hugh Mercer, gone to his reward; John Sullivan, retired from command; Thomas Paine, a successful publisher; Billy Blodget—how he still missed Billy.

Suddenly realizing a response was expected, he muttered, "It was a miserable night—"

"Ah—" Anthony protested. "The earl, here, is simply determined to find something to blame his rheumatism on. He cannot admit the real reason for it—age."

Lord Stirling smiled, holding him under a steady gaze. "How old are you, lad?"

"Twenty-nine, sir!" he gloated.

"I do not believe any man should be given the commission of a general under the age of thirty-five. Don't you agree, General Greene?"

"Since I recently passed that milestone, I have no problem agreeing with that." Nathanael said with a grin. "But we might cause a bit of strife with our French allies. Remember our boy general is a mere twenty," he added.

Lord Stirling smiled. "Well, we cannot cause strife with the French now, can we. You are right, General Wayne, the years are catching up with me; and, if this war does not end soon, army life will kill me." He turned his attention to Nathanael. "Speaking of the French, Anthony tells me that His Excellency is in Connecticut conferring with the French Naval command."

"He *was* in Connecticut," Nathanael corrected him. "The General should be well on his way back by now. In fact, he is scheduled to inspect West Point tomorrow, and expected back in camp within the next two or three days."

"Then he has been gone for some time?"

"About two weeks." Nathanael leaned back, comfortably folding his arms behind his head, and placing his feet on the ottoman before him. "This makes an important man of me for the time being." He said with a playful grin.

Lord Stirling smiled. "I am away for a few short weeks and entirely uninformed. Who accompanied His Excellency?"

"The marquis, of course, also the Baron von Steuben, Henry Knox and Alec Hamilton."

"Then General Washington already met with the French? Any word of a planned joint attack?" Lord Stirling asked.

"I have heard nothing yet."

"What is your opinion in the matter?" Lord Stirling appeared hopeful.

Nathanael looked from him to Anthony and back again. He could feel their excitement and hesitated to disappoint them with his reply.

"—If a carefully planned attack can be carried out against New York, this war could be near its end."

"Ah-ha!" Anthony exclaimed slapping his thigh with his hand. "I fully agree!"

Lord Stirling did not yet share his jubilation. He studied Nathanael in a silence for a moment. "If?" He echoed Nathanael's first word.

Nathanael offered a weak smile. "Somewhere—someday we will successfully combine our forces. I feel Providence has destined it to be so. But here and now—" he slowly shook his head.

"What is the morale of the troops?" Lord Stirling asked.

"Excellent considering the circumstances," Anthony replied. "Half starved; virtually serving without pay; the Southern Campaign in a disastrous state—"

A somber silence fell on the room. Then Nathanael spoke, "They survive on hope—hope that maybe tomorrow the French will offer an alliance of power. Hope that tomorrow the citizenry of this country will come to their aid with food and supplies. Hope that Heaven will smile on us as it did in our recent battle at Springfield."

"And how is our new quartermaster general faring?" Lord Stirling asked Nathanael.

"He has not even arrived at camp yet. He is still in Philadelphia vainly attempting to get cash in hand—may God bless his efforts."

"Guess who has been placed in charge of the foraging details?" Anthony asked Lord Stirling, his expression was suddenly distorted as though overcome with pity. His Lordship watched as Anthony's eyes slowly came to rest on Nathanael.

Lord Stirling looked at Nathanael. "Not you!" His dumbfounded response came.

Nathanael shrugged. "At least we have been able to keep from starving these past few weeks."

"Such a disagreeable task to be forced to take from civilians. And you have certainly had your fill of the post. Has there been much opposition?" His Lordship asked.

"No, not anything of a serious nature, not from the civilians—but at first our men—" Nathanael's words drifted off as though he were troubled. Rather than complete the sentence, he called for an aide to bring some coffee.

"What about the men, sir?" Lord Stirling asked.

Nathanael looked at Anthony. It was Anthony who spoke. "There were individuals assigned to the first foraging detail, who greatly abused the people of the countryside. General Greene reported the crimes to His Excellency requesting that the men responsible be executed by way of example for fear the countryside be pillaged by our men."

"And did he grant permission?" Lord Stirling asked softly, sensing Nathanael's grief in having to make such a hideous request.

Nathanael nodded, his words were spoken softly, "—Immediately. We cannot tolerate such acts of barbarism from our men—even half-starved they are to act with decency. The scenes I witnessed were no less offensive than what has been reported of the Hessians' treatment of the civilians."

"I agree with your request, General Greene," Lord Stirling said as he accepted a steaming mug of watered-down coffee from an aide. "Though distasteful to carry out, quite necessary to keep discipline in the ranks—let it go, Nat."

Nathanael offered a weak smile, and slowly nodded his head.

"What of these reports I am hearing from the South? Certainly, Horatio Gates could not be as incompetent as is being rumored. What's the official word?"

"General Gates will be facing a congressionally ordered court-martial in regard to his defeat at Camden. The reports are still somewhat sketchy, but witnesses claim it was a poorly executed battle from the start. Some have gone so far as to refer to it as military absurdity contrary to the maxims of war and common sense."

"What of our casualties?"

"One thousand men killed or wounded. The number of those missing hasn't been determined."

Lord Stirling sighed. "But the rumors of his fleeing—leaving his own men

behind—whatever we may think personally of the man, certainly the record of his command in Canada stares in the face of such nonsense. A military man of his caliber is not capable of such an act of cowardice."

"Consider Charles Lee's military record prior to the Battle of Monmouth." Anthony interjected excitedly, still bitter over the fiasco two years prior that cost the lives of many in his brigade. "Both Lee and Gates are English born—once officers in the King's service let us not forget."

"Are you implying that Gates and Lee acted treasonously?" Lord Stirling asked, his brow cocked.

"I am not implying any such thing. I am simply pointing out that both were trained by what is considered the greatest military force on the face of the earth. I have served under both of them, as well as both of you. Though the Britons and all of Europe scoff at our amateur command, I have found your generalships superior to theirs. And, as far as personal integrity, there is no comparison."

There was a stunned silence. Anthony looked at Lord Stirling—there was fire in his eyes. "Horatio Gates fled from the enemy leaving his own men behind in his shameful retreat; thoroughly destroying his military career."

"If Gates is found unfit for command, who is being considered to take the position?" His Lordship asked.

Nathanael hesitated. "—Congress has not taken it under consideration."

"Officially," Anthony interjected, "my understanding is that General Greene is being considered."

"I do not want the post," Nathanael said quietly.

"If it does not fall to you, then who might be appointed?" Lord Stirling asked.

"Why not you?" Anthony shot back.

"My present health would not permit me to accept such a task."

"Nonsense. The Southern climate would probably do you a world of good, your Lordship." Anthony grinned.

"The Southern climate is deadly. Putrid fever is rampant. Quinine is a necessary part of one's daily diet for survival in the summer. Nat, your asthma would surely become a constant plague in the warm months." Lord Stirling pointed out.

"It certainly would," Nathanael stated. He pointed at Anthony Wayne and added, "I am all for 'Mad Anthony' here being promoted to major general, and sending him southward."

"I am ready!" Anthony exclaimed causing his friends to laugh.

"Perhaps Congress will lure our dear John Sullivan back into active duty with such an appointment," Lord Stirling suggested.

"I do not think so. It seems John is planning to take a seat in that august body himself very soon. Heaven knows we can use empathic friends among the members of Congress," Nathanael chided. "Anyway, I am not sure John could handle what may very well transpire in the South—I am not sure any of us can—" Nathanael's words drifted off as though he never intended to speak them.

"What do you mean?" Anthony asked.

"I do not know—a premonition perhaps, or just a fear." Both men were staring at him, anticipating his answer. "—I believe that the war is going to shift to the South. From a strategic point-of-view, it would be a wise move for the British. We are extremely weak in the South. If they build their forces there and maintain a sizable army here as well—" Nathanael hesitated and sighed deeply. "—We would not be able to risk transferring the main army southward—it would leave the North wide open to attack. And it will take a good while to build a force in the South, not to mention how quickly or by what means we could supply it—"

"Well, then, let's send Ben Arnold down. Now there's a qualified commander who will welcome the challenge." Anthony said.

"He is a cripple." Lord Stirling pointed out.

Anthony scoffed, "He is about as crippled as I am modest. He plays up his old battle wounds to obtain the plush posts to which he is assigned: military governorship of Philadelphia and now commander of West Point. How much more comfort can one endure? The man has a limp. Nat, here, commands superbly on the battlefield with a limp. I bet deep down Ben is just itching to get out on the field to once again make a name for himself."

"He is a military genius," Lord Stirling agreed.

"Wonderful. It is unanimous. General Benedict Arnold should be appointed commander in chief of the Southern army!" Nathanael exclaimed. "Now do you suppose Congress will heed our counsel? I would not mind taking command of West Point—"

Like stage curtains dropping, Nathanael's eyelids hung heavily as he fought to read the final paragraph of the page before him. The words became a blur, the meaning completely muddled in his weary mind.

The sound of an approaching rider outside roused him. He listened for a moment, his attention coming to focus on the dancing flames of the hearth. Their warmth was relaxing as they chased away the crispness of the late autumn night.

Quickly his thoughts turned to Caty and the children as they so often did in the evening's solitude. And, as often occurred, what began as pleasant memories and daydreams of domestic tranquility quickly transformed into a tormenting longing for his family's presence, and homesickness, which pierced his very soul.

"Lord, watch over and protect them," he whispered. A more lengthy prayer was too much to dwell on at present. That was somehow better accomplished, and routinely done, in the fullness of day.

Standing, Nathanael walked over to the bedside and gently laid the book on the nightstand. Then turning to the window, he lifted his hand to pull the curtain shut against the night sky. There was no sign of activity below, as a soft rain was beginning to fall from a blackened sky. He surmised the rider he heard must have been an aide returning to Headquarters—or perhaps it was General Stirling's aide; for His Lordship had failed to take the book he had requested to borrow earlier that evening.

A light tap on the bedchamber door prompted a soft reply.

"Enter."

Partially opening the door, Lewis Morris popped his head in to view his commander at the window comfortably attired in only his shirt and breeches. "May I be of any further assistance to you, sir?" the aide asked, eager to please.

"No, Lewis, I am ready to call it a night," Nathanael said, pulling the curtain shut.

"That is a fine idea, sir." He immediately went to the plump feather mattress and pulled back the bedding. "If I cannot be of further assistance, then I, too, shall retire."

"Goodnight, Lewis. Sleep well."

"You, too, sir," the aide replied. Moving toward the threshold, he came face to face with Tench Tilghman.

"Excuse me, General." Tench exclaimed, stepping past Lewis. "A message from Colonel Hamilton. It's labeled urgent, sir—" His tone was apprehensive.

"Hamilton?" Nathanael echoed, reaching out to take the folded letter in Tench's hand. He quickly broke the seal, and opened it. He did not readily recognize Hamilton's handwriting. Instead of the graceful form to which he was accustomed, he viewed scrawling letters as though written by a trembling hand.

His eyes dashed across the page. "Dear God, no." He whispered. Then, in shocked disbelief, he read the message again.

"General, has something happened to His Excellency?" Tench asked, his eyes searched Nathanael's pale face.

Nathanael handed Tench the paper, and turned back to the window.

"— It—it cannot be true—" Tench managed to utter.

There was a dead silence. Lewis' eyes nervously darted from Nathanael to Tench and back again. Nathanael, gazing into the darkness, began to rub his upper lip, as was his habit when faced with a monumental, immediate decision.

The inexperienced aide looked at Tench—uncertain of what to do or how to feel at the moment. The only thing he was certain of was that to speak now would disrupt the commander's concentration.

Tench, sensing the younger man's apprehension, held Hamilton's note out with a trembling hand. Lewis took it and read the shocking words for himself: *There has just been unfolded at this place a scene of the blackest treason. Arnold has fled to the enemy. André, the British adjutant general, is in our possession as a spy. His capture unraveled the mystery. West Point was to have been the sacrifice. All the dispositions have been made for the purpose; and 'tis possible, though not probable, tonight may see the execution.*

"Colonel Tilghman," Nathanael's steady voice suddenly broke the silence. "See that all general officers are put on the alert for a possible attack. General St. Clair's division is to prepare immediately to march on King's Ferry. General Wayne is to prepare to march his brigade to West Point. What time is it?" he asked Lewis Morris.

The aide pulled a pocket watch from his coat. "It's midnight, sir."

"Tell Generals St. Clair and Wayne that I expect them to begin their march within three hours. All general officers are to report to me as soon as these orders are put into effect."

"Yes, sir," Tench replied, preparing to leave.

"Colonel."

"Sir?"

"Give the orders, but no more. I will inform the generals myself."

"Of course, sir."

"Major Morris."

"Sir?"

"Summon two post riders. I will have an account ready for Congress and a response to Colonel Hamilton's message within the half hour."

"Yes, sir," Lewis said, and handing Alexander Hamilton's message back, he turned and left.

Nathanael sat down at the table, and laid the message before him, painfully studying the words thereon as he contemplated his report to Congress: *Blackest treason—Arnold fled to the enemy—West Point was to have been the sacrifice—*

Rain began to fall hard upon the rooftop as the wind blew and thunder sounded in the distance. It went unnoticed. For even if a whirlwind was to tear the very roof from above his head, it would prove less startling than the shocking news Nathanael Greene received just moments before.

Headquarters became instantly hushed with George Washington's appearance. Walking toward Nathanael, he passed a throng of saluting aides, secretaries and couriers lining the foyer and dining room, nodding his head in acknowledgement of their respectful greeting.

His shoulders slumped forward a bit, Nathanael observed, but only slightly; and only one familiar with his perfect posture would ever notice. His face was weary. His eyes—what was it? Whatever Nathanael saw reflected in the gray eyes was unfamiliar and disturbing.

"Welcome back, your Excellency. I wish it were under better circumstances, sir," Nathanael said with a formal salute.

"As do I, General Greene," George Washington replied, returning the salute. "Has the prisoner arrived?"

"Yes, sir, late this morning. I placed him under heavy guard at the Mabie Tavern, as per your written order."

"Very well. Please join me upstairs, General Greene." Turning around he walked out of the room, stopping to speak softly to Henry Knox who stood in the foyer. In response, Henry followed behind Nathanael.

"I trust your stay here was comfortable," General Washington said after the men were seated in his bedchamber.

"It was, sir."

"Good."

"I imagine the information you have received over the past week has been rather piecemeal," George Washington said softly.

"It has been, sir. I have been anxious to know details."

"You know General Arnold has made his escape?"

"Onto a British warship—I know that much. How long, sir? How long has he been betraying us?" Nathanael asked, his face full of anguish.

George Washington sighed deeply. He leaned his head back and closed his eyes. "I do not know, Nathanael," he moaned. Lifting his head upright, he immediately cast his eyes downward, avoiding the gaze of his generals.

"All I know is that I trusted him—I held him in esteem for his courageous example on the battlefield. I felt for him when Congress continued to overlook him for promotion, coming to his defense each time. I anguished over his battle wounds, granting him the most honorable positions available during his convalescence. I rejoiced at his wedding and delighted in the news of the birth of his son.

"Never—never did I doubt him. Never did I question his character or distrust him. How long has he been betraying us?" George Washington echoed the words. "Long enough to play each of us for a fool, and most especially myself."

A tear slowly ran down the Commander's cheek. Nathanael and Henry exchanged a quick glance, equally distraught.

"It is a most disconcerting feeling to be so completely betrayed," he continued. "Word is he was to receive 20,000 pounds in payment for West Point, and a general's commission in the British army."

Fury flashed through Nathanael's eyes. "And what of André? I understand there is question as to whether or not his actions were protected under a flag of truce."

"André, it seems, was summoned to meet Arnold under the cover of darkness. He claims they met on neutral ground, and he wore his uniform during this meeting," George Washington began.

"In his uniform—by summons of Arnold? Then he did come under a sanction of truce," Nathanael stated.

"The situation was altered," Henry began. He looked at George Washington who motioned for him to continue. "The meeting lasted too long, and the sun was beginning to rise before they realized it. Rather than send André back, Arnold provided accommodations for him, keeping him out of view for the day. He also issued passes to get him through our lines and back to the British, identifying him by the name of 'John Anderson'."

"Is it true that there were papers found on his person?" Nathanael asked Henry.

"Yes. Arnold gave him plans of the West Point garrison. The papers were found hidden in his boot. And somewhere along the way he changed into civilian clothing."

"How was he discovered?" Nathanael asked.

"We can bless God alone for the discovery. André successfully passed through two of our posts. Then, coming upon three civilians, he mistook them for Tories and declared his identity."

Nathanael looked at George Washington, and said, "Sir, regardless of whether Major André took part in this parley with Arnold under a sanction of truce, it is evident that he became knowingly involved in a blatant act of espionage. Under the Articles of War and by virtue of your commission from Congress—for that matter by the law of nations—you can forego a trial, charge him as a spy and be done with it."

"I am aware of that, but Major André is not only adjutant general to Sir Henry Clinton; he is the intelligence chief as well. Our actions in this matter will be carefully scrutinized. I intend to exercise great caution. Therefore, a court of inquiry will hear the evidence and decide the matter. If André is found guilty of espionage, he will suffer the consequences the British have dealt in the past to our operatives. If he is found guilty, the only thing that will keep him from the gallows is if Arnold is returned to us."

"The British would never agree to such a trade, sir. It would squelch any future hope of luring our officers into passing information over to them," Henry remarked.

"I would tend to agree, but it has been reported that young Major André is favored among General Clinton's officers—treated like a son. General Clinton feels a great deal of affection for the lad, and none for Arnold." George Washington turned his gaze to Nathanael, "Henry tells me that André is an unusual man. Did you speak to him?"

"No, sir. I observed his arrival from a distance. Surrounded by at least a hundred of our dragoons I barely caught a glimpse of the man."

"Nor have I spoken with him and feel it prudent to avoid any contact. The task ahead, I fear, will be difficult enough—allowing any personal feelings to develop would not be wise."

Nathanael was a bit confused by his fear of personal attachment. Not knowing what to make of it or how to respond, he changed the subject. "What of Arnold's wife and child?"

"Not only has Arnold deserted his country," George Washington began, "but his heart is so hardened that he fled from his wife and infant son as well, pushing the poor woman into a state of near lunacy."

"Where is the poor girl now?" Nathanael asked, imagining Caty's alarm in learning of her friend's grief. Caty enjoyed Peggy Arnold's company, both being very close in age and sharing many similar interests.

"She and the child were escorted to Philadelphia to be with her family," Henry replied.

A thought flashed through Nathanael's mind as though an alarm had sounded. Her family—Peggy Arnold was the daughter of Edward Shippen, a well-known Tory. The Shippen family was said to have frequently entertained British officers during the British occupation of Philadelphia. Could she be in on the deception?

"—You say Mrs. Arnold was noticeably disturbed by the news?" Nathanael asked hesitantly.

"The woman was absolutely frantic—terrified that we were going to kill her and the baby because of her husband's act. A physician had to be called in to sedate her."

Nathanael nodded, ashamed for the fleeting thought about her possible guilt.

"André's hearing will begin tomorrow," George Washington said. "A board of fourteen generals will be called to examine the evidence and cross examine Major André. Both of you will be assigned to this board. I am sorry, Henry."

Henry nodded in response.

"And, Nathanael, you will preside over it—"

Normally lost in lively conversation, especially after a period of separation, Nathanael and Henry left Headquarters with a somber silence between them.

"Have you had contact with this man André?" Nathanael finally asked, puzzled by the Commander's apology in assigning Henry to the board of inquiry.

"I have," Henry replied as they came upon their tethered horses. Loosening the reins in silence, both men mounted their steeds and wheeled them about.

"I am certain I must have told you about him when we were in Massachusetts."

"Massachusetts?"

"I met John André when I was sent to Fort Ticonderoga to transport the artillery down. There was a fierce storm, which forced many to take shelter in a local inn for the night. John André was serving in the Quartermaster's Department at the time, and free to act in that capacity even after we captured the fort. As Providence would have it, we shared a room that night. The young British officer and the young Continental officer—enemies and bedfellows, hey." Henry's laugh was forced.

"We became fast friends, talking the night away of our common interests—he is a fascinating, talented fellow; a gentleman in every sense of the word. It will be a difficult thing to face him again like this—"

"I vaguely remember you telling me the story. You could request not to serve on the board," Nathanael suggested, feeling his friend's anguish.

"No. His Excellency must have his reasons for appointing me. It does not matter anyway. By the time the hearing has concluded, you and every member of that board will feel an attachment to André. His character is such that it cannot be helped; and I fully agree the General should, and must, deny himself all personal contact with the man."

On the morning of September 29, 1780, the court of inquiry convened at the old Dutch church in Tappen, New York. Major General Nathanael Greene called the board of general officers to order and signaled for the guards to bring the prisoner in.

The adjutant general to the British army stepped into the room donned in full military attire—delivered to him earlier that morning by a personal servant. Major John André appeared much younger than his thirty years. His round face and soft features lent to him a child-like quality. He was flawlessly groomed; his powdered queue done up in a stylish ribbon. There was a confidence in his gait, not arrogance, but an assurance that he had nothing to fear. He stood before the rows of pews where the generals had assembled, and bowed respectfully.

Nathanael proceeded to introduce himself, and then to identify each officer on the board. Major André smiled affectionately and nodded his head in the form of a greeting when Henry's name was called.

The advocate general then began by advising the major to feel no pressure in answering the questions put to him; and not to hesitate to speak up if any question were to seem unclear. He continued by stating the known facts of the case, and invited the board of general officers to begin their cross-examination.

The questions were continuous, though not overbearing. Had he crossed the American lines under the cover of darkness? Did he conceal secret papers on his person? Did he disguise himself in an attempt to pass back through the American lines? Did he carry a pass made out to 'John Anderson'? Did he confer with Major general Benedict Arnold concerning the West Point garrison?

André answered in the affirmative to the questions, but he explained that he initially met with Arnold on neutral ground in full uniform. Much to his dismay, the meeting ran longer than planned; and Arnold strongly suggested that he stay out of sight until that evening.

"Was it your understanding, Major André, that your meeting with General Benedict Arnold was to be carried out under a flag of truce?" Nathanael asked forthrightly.

"No, General Greene. It is impossible for me to suppose I came under a flag of truce; for, if I did, then I should have been returned under it as well."

The murmuring of the general officers revealed their surprise at Andrés bold and honest reply.

"May I speak, General Greene?"

"Yes, Major, you may."

"It was never my intention to cross enemy lines, and I was not aware I had done so until General Arnold was challenged by a sentry on our way to the house I was kept in for the day. I was then asked to change into civilian attire in order to pass more freely back to my lines. I was mortified, and did so under protest. Nor was it my desire to carry any papers on my person, but was pressured into it by General Arnold."

"Major André, did you come to this parley with Arnold as a private citizen or as a British officer?" Nathanael asked, giving him every opportunity to vindicate himself.

"I wore my uniform, sir, and undoubtedly esteemed myself to be what indeed I was—a British officer."

"Major André," General Steuben began, understanding what Nathanael's question was attempting to determine. "Vere you avare of Arnold's intentions to defect prior to dis parley, or did you come by a summons of Arnold unavare of his intentions?"

"I came as the deputy of General Clinton, not as a spy."

"But vere you avare of Arnold's intentions?" Von Steuben persisted.

"Yes, sir. We were aware of his intent; and it was my duty as British chief of intelligence to pursue his defection, as would your intelligence chief were one of our generals to defect."

The questioning ceased.

"Gentlemen, do you have any more questions for the major?" Nathanael asked his comrades.

"No, sir," each one replied softly.

"Very well. Major André, is there anything else you would care to add?"

"Yes, General Greene. I would extend to the Board my gratitude in having been shown such respect. I flatter myself that I have held no personal animosity to any Americans; but, if there was any hidden prejudice in my mind, your treatment of me has obliterated it."

He was dismissed, and walked out of the church with the American intelligence deputy, Major Benjamin Tallmadge, at his side.

Freedom's Cost

The fourteen generals remained speechless for a minute: stunned by the dignity and composure of the British officer and equally perplexed by his candor in admitting to the charges.

"Gentlemen," the advocate general broke the silence. "I have the plans of the West Point garrison which were found in Major Andrés boot, and the pass signed by General Arnold, which was issued to 'John Anderson'. I also have letters sent to His Excellency, General Washington, from British Headquarters this morning. They are from General Clinton, Colonel Robinson, deputy of British intelligence, and—" He paused, his eyes painfully scanning the faces of his comrades. They settled on Nathanael. "—And Benedict Arnold." He handed the papers to Nathanael. He read each one and passed them on.

The letters all stressed that André acted under a flag of truce, thus being under Arnold's orders while in the American lines. This being so, he could not be considered a spy. Yet, André, by his own admission stated that there had been no flag; and, to the Board's extreme sorrow, the charge of espionage stood.

Having reached their verdict, every member of the board signed the unanimous opinion: Major André, Adjutant General to the British Army was guilty of espionage and condemned to suffer death.

Upon Nathanael's delivery of the Board's opinion, General Washington was noticeably shaken. "From all I have heard of this man, André, I consider that he is a victim of misfortune more so than he is a criminal," was his response.

After requesting one of the secretaries to officially document the charge, verdict and sentence, Nathanael watched the hand of the commander in chief of the Continental Army shake uncontrollably as he signed the paper. "I want Arnold," George Washington said just above a whisper. Placing the quill pen in its holder, he looked up at Nathanael and added, "I could spare this man's life if they were to give me Arnold!"

The aides bickered back and forth, as they rode. Nathanael could not help but smile as he listened. He never forbade minor squabbles between those in his military family, anymore than a father could, in fact, keep his sons from such minor disagreements. He enjoyed their differing personalities; each offered a special quality to his headquarters.

"Please, General, set him straight in the matter." Rob Burnet finally pleaded.

Nathanael looked from Rob to young Lewis Morris, and back again, his own face somewhat contorted.

"The truth is I find myself agreeing with him, Rob." Nathanael said with a smile, bringing an end to the squabble and a wide grin to Lewis' face.

Though his attention was fixed ahead, Rob felt the amused gaze of his companions, and could not help but break into a grin himself. "There's a rider approaching, sir. I believe it is Major Tallmadge," he informed his distracted commander.

Nathanael looked ahead. "So it is," he replied, surprised to run into the intelligence officer. Since André's capture, Tallmadge had been with his prisoner both day and night.

The major approached, reined in his horse and offered Nathanael a salute. "On your way to Headquarters, General? I just left there; General Washington said he was expecting you, sir."

"That is where I am headed—how are things going, Major?"

"As well as can be expected, sir—well, I mean Major André has come to terms with his imminent death. At least he says he has. The only concern he has voiced is that his mother and sisters be compensated for by the British government, and that he face a firing squad rather than the gallows."

"The fate of a spy is the gallows," Nathanael pointed out.

"I know that, sir. And His Excellency feels obligated to carry the sentence out thusly. Colonel Hamilton even took it upon himself to present Major André's wish to him, but to no avail. We had hoped he could be persuaded. I am afraid the General's position on the matter may cause a rift between Hamilton and himself."

"I would hate to see their relationship suffer because of this," Nathanael said.

"As would I, sir."

"Do you understand the General's position, Major? If André is not executed in this manner, it would leave doubt in the minds of many as to his true status. The practice and usage of war demand the gallows."

"I do understand it, sir—it is just that I find it difficult at times to sort it all out." Major Tallmadge glanced at the aides then cast his eyes downward.

Nathanael sensed the major's need to verbalize his conflicting emotions, and his hesitancy to do so with so many listening. Thus, he instructed his aides to go forward to Headquarters.

"It is difficult to sort it out, Major Tallmadge. At times, it is extremely difficult. You have spent many hours in Major André's company. He is a very personable fellow. No doubt you have become attached to him."

"I have become attached to him, sir," Major Tallmadge confessed. "He does not deserve this fate. He is guilty of espionage, I know that; but in pursuing Arnold's defection, he did what any intelligence officer must do. And Arnold remains free."

What he did was unthinkable. He was willing to sacrifice the 2,000 men in his command—men who were dependent on him. And he was willing to offer up General Washington as well. The General has shown him nothing but respect and honor. He was willing to do all of this for what? Personal gain and glory! Arnold is an evil man."

"I agree with you that Arnold is an evil man, but I do not believe he is free."

Major Tallmadge was obviously confused by Nathanael's words.

"Arnold has created his own prison, and the torture therein will be worse than you or I could imagine. One thing this war has taught me, Major, is that only a virtuous man is truly content. Arnold has no virtue; therefore Arnold has no contentment; therefore Arnold shall live his life out in utter misery." Nathanael heard himself speak the words, and honestly believed them to be true; yet he felt his own emotional struggle well up within. The utter humiliation and shame that a fellow officer, a fellow New Englander and trusted friend, could in fact be so treacherous. Arnold in the end would suffer the fullness of his actions, but the pain many now faced because of his treachery was agonizing.

"Was André shocked by the board's verdict?" Nathanael asked, thinking back on his seeming confidence during the hearing.

"No. He hoped for the best, but I attempted to prepare him days before the hearing of what his fate would most likely be—Nathan Hale—" Major Tallmadge spoke the name and stopped.

The name was familiar to Nathanael—well known to every soldier of the Continental Army.

"Nathan was a friend of mine—a dear friend. We attended Yale together, serving as schoolmasters upon graduation. The war began just as we took our teaching positions. We spoke frequently of our duty. Nathan enlisted—I did not. It took a year of Nathan's imploring letters from camp before I yielded.

"You know how the story goes, sir. He was captured within enemy lines in civilian clothing with secret papers on his person. And he was hanged without the benefit of clergy or access to a Bible, without the decency of a last letter to his loved ones. He was not an evil man by any stretch of the imagination—he was a good man; doomed to die because he dared to take on a dangerous mission— John André's death will force me to relive Nathan's. Some say I should feel vindicated for my friend's death—a life for a life. I do not." His eyes were fixed on Nathanael's, his jaw set. "General Greene, I hate this war!"

Upon arriving at Headquarters, Nathanael was taken into private chambers with the Commander to discuss a turn in events. When British commander in chief, Sir

Henry Clinton received notification from General Washington about John Andrés scheduled execution, he requested a meeting with three of his officers that they might give a "true state of facts" in support of Andrés role.

George Washington, eager to attempt to trade the unfortunate spy for Benedict Arnold, agreed to the parley. He chose Nathanael Greene to serve as his representative, instructing him to meet under a flag of truce, and to strongly urge the exchange.

Nathanael set out for the appointed location along the bank of the Hudson River with Alexander Hamilton at his side. Hamilton was quiet, Nathanael noted. He remembered Major Tallmadge had mentioned there was a possible rift developing between Hamilton and the General. The strain of the situation was weighing heavily on all concerned.

Upon meeting the British delegation, Nathanael began by introducing himself and Hamilton. He then made it quite clear that he would speak privately with the ranking officer. British General James Robertson took offense.

"And what, sir, shall my men do while we talk?" He demanded.

"Let them take a walk, General. Colonel Hamilton will be happy to accompany them."

General Robertson hesitated.

"I will consent to speak only to you, sir. If this is disagreeable to you then so be it."

"I agree to your terms, General Greene," he said begrudgingly as he motioned for his aides to depart. Alexander Hamilton led them away down the path along the river's bank.

The parley began with General Robertson insisting that André acted under a flag of truce. Nathanael countered his every statement with Major Andrés own testimony.

"Whether a flag was flying or not is of no account." Robertson finally blurted. "Major André landed and acted under General Arnold's direction."

"That is not so. André was as much involved as Arnold," Nathanael replied coolly.

"His Excellency General Clinton requests that another inquiry be called, and that Hessian General Knyphausen and French Admiral Rochambeau hear the testimony. Both are distinguished gentlemen with knowledge of war and nations; and, since they are neither British nor American, they will undoubtedly be more objective."

Nathanael only looked at him, offering no reply to the preposterous request, which would deem the Continental tribunal as incompetent to determine the case.

Robertson, obviously disconcerted by Nathanael's silence, pulled a letter from his jacket and handed it to him. "A letter from General Arnold."

In a struggle to contain his rage, Nathanael read Arnold's letter. In it Arnold acknowledged being fully responsible for Andrés apparent misconduct. *How easy to take the blame when you are safely tucked behind enemy lines, you scoundrel!* Nathanael screamed within. He dropped the letter to the ground and laid his heel upon it, grinding it into the dirt.

Then, without the slightest hint of emotion, he said, "Major André freely admitted to the charges put before him. Arnold is a rascal and André a man of honor whom I believe. We will consent to no further inquiry or parley for evidence."

Nathanael fixed a stern gaze on Robertson. "Give us Arnold and Andréwill be surrendered!"

"I have the authority to offer you any American prisoners in our possession. State your terms, General Greene!"

"No other will satisfy our thirst. Give us Arnold!"

Robertson's scornful glare was the response Nathanael received.

"I should think, General Robertson that we have come to an impasse. It is time for me to return."

"You will please report my words fairly to your Commander."

"To the best of my memory, sir, I promise you I will."

"Thank you, General, I can ask no more."

It was a summer-like day. Golden foliage adorned the hardwood trees surrounding the field at the top of the hill. In the clearing stood the gallows, patiently awaiting its victim. To one side was a cart carrying a black coffin, to the other an open grave.

Nathanael sat on horseback with the Board of General Officers mounted to his right. They, along with the assembled ranks of Continental troops, watched in silence as Major John André made his approach under heavy guard. The fife and drum corps dutifully played the *Dead March*.

When they reached the gallows, the guards moved away from their prisoner forming three circles around the beams, their backs to it with bayonets fixed.

Major André passed before the line of fourteen generals, bowing respectfully to each. There was a pleasant smile upon his lips though his face was as pale as death. Coming to Nathanael, he saluted. Nathanael returned the salute.

The major turned about, and walked toward the gallows, meeting Benjamin Tallmadge on the way. André stopped, holding his hand out to his friend and speaking softly to him for a brief moment.

André stepped near the wagon. The death sentence was read aloud as the accused nervously pushed a stone about with his foot in an attempt to avoid the sight of the noose. Then, being summoned upon the wagon, his hands were bound, the noose put in place and a blindfold tied across his eyes.

"Major André," the officer of the day called out. "If you have anything more you would wish to say, you now have the opportunity."

"I have nothing more than this—that I would have you gentlemen bear me witness that I die like a brave man."

Nathanael saw the signal given to the hangman. He heard the crack of the whip. His own heart pounded violently within; his body trembled. As he turned his eyes away, his gaze fell on Benjamin Tallmadge whose large shoulders jerked in uncontrollable sobs.

"I am at this moment setting off for the southward, having kept expresses flying all night to see if I could hear anything of you.....God grace you patience and fortitude to bear the disappointment. My apprehension for your safety distresses me exceedingly. If heaven preserves us until we meet, our felicity will repay all the painful moments of a long separation. I am forever and forever yours, most sincerely and affectionately."
(Nathanael to Caty)

CHAPTER FIFTEEN

THE MEN WALKED away in silence from the house, which served as Nathanael's headquarters, stopping at the precipice high above the Hudson River. From here, the view was unobstructed, and Lord Stirling's audible sigh was expected.

"It is beautiful," he said, gazing up and down the river below. The powerful Hudson peacefully continued on, easing gracefully around the majestic mountains rising on either side.

The West Point garrison could be seen in the distance. Nathanael rose his arm pointing as he described the vulnerable areas purposed by Benedict Arnold's treachery. Lord Stirling nodded then directed specific questions back concerning its repair.

"With the repairs complete, the post will prove a great stronghold. The very reason the British were so eager to get it from Arnold." Lord Stirling looked from the scenic view to Nathanael. "I will be honest. I envy you this post, but I cannot think of any who deserves it more. Will you be sending for your family?"

Nathanael chuckled. "Between me and you, my first act upon taking command was to send Sam Ward home to gather up my family and bring them to me just as quickly as possible. I expect their arrival daily."

Lord Stirling smiled gazing back toward the house. "Are all the children coming?"

"All four?"

The earl looked at him; and, with a glimmer in his eyes, he said, "Are you sure you can handle it, General? A woman making social demands, and four noisy, whining children. My goodness, two of them must still be in diapers. Consider the solitude you now have—within a few days your headquarters will be in a constant state of turmoil."

"I know, and it sounds wonderful, doesn't it?" Nathanael shot back with a grin.

"That it does—it most certainly does." His Lordship agreed with a chuckle. "Perhaps I will be fortunate enough to witness their arrival tonight and share in some of that domestic upheaval."

Nathanael escorted Lord Stirling through the garrison, giving him a personal tour and the opportunity to reacquaint himself with a few officers who once served under his command. The evening hours, intermingled with occasional duties of command and pleasant conversation with His Lordship, were interrupted by Alexander Hamilton's unexpected arrival.

"Welcome, Colonel." Nathanael warmly greeted the saluting aide. "Come and sit down. I will have a room prepared for you," he offered, assuming that the aide was on his way to or from an official run that, by chance, brought him to West Point.

"What brings you out this way, Hamilton?" Lord Stirling asked.

Alec remained standing, and turning from Lord Stirling to Nathanael he said, "I have a letter for you, General Greene."

"Me?" he said, momentarily confused by the announcement. Then he recalled that General Washington was hoping to set up Headquarters near West Point. No doubt, the letter was in reference to this—but an aide-de-camp sent to deliver it? It seemed rather odd. The thought lingered as he reached out to take the letter from Alec.

"Is everything all right, Hamilton?" Lord Stirling asked as Nathanael opened the letter.

"Yes, your Lordship. In my opinion the situation is exactly as it should be," was his odd reply.

"Whatever do you mean?" Lord Stirling looked from Alexander to Nathanael. Nathanael's hands were steadily holding the letter before him and his face was void of emotion, yet all color had visibly drained from his cheeks.

"What is it, General?" Lord Stirling asked.

A brief silence followed. Nathanael cleared his throat, swallowed, and took a deep breath. "Congress has given His Excellency the choice of the Southern command. My orders are to take the post immediately—"

Lord Stirling offered no response.

"I am instructed that you have verbal orders for me, Colonel."

"Yes, sir. Temporary command of this garrison is to be given to Brigadier General Stark until a major general is appointed. You are expected to report at Headquarters on Thursday instant. Congress expects your arrival in Philadelphia within the week."

"Thursday? That only gives me two days. My family is en route even as we speak. I must beg leave of His Excellency that I might escort my family home, and further request two weeks in Rhode Island to get my personal affairs in order." Nathanael paused looking down at George Washington's words. His hand was now trembling slightly. "Thee will return to Headquarters on the morrow and make my request known, Colonel, for my time of service to the South may be lengthy, and I must see to the financial needs and stability of my family before I can go."

Alec looked uneasy. After taking a deep breath, he said, "Your request was anticipated by His Excellency, sir. The General extends his regrets that it will not be possible to grant any leave due to the desperate situation southward. Your prompt departure and the transfer of command cannot be delayed any longer."

Nathanael was visibly taken aback by the reply. "The man that does not provide for his family is worse than an infidel," he uttered the Scripture teaching in response to the overwhelming guilt surging within. "She is on her way—Caty is on her way—" he muttered looking from Alec to Lord Stirling.

"If your family is close enough, a rider may be able to reach them and speed up the pace. Perhaps they can make it by Thursday," Lord Stirling offered.

Nathanael's eyes were fixed on his. Though the earl stopped speaking, Nathanael's steady gaze remained. His mind did not comprehend the earl's seated form. As if in a trance, he continued to focus while thought after thought worked its way through his troubled mind.

Command of the South! I do not want it! I can turn it down—my health—who would question an asthmatic not wanting to risk such a climate? I can turn it down—Caty and the children! To be so far from them for so long—no one would question it—my service record is true. I have gone beyond the call of duty—no one would question it!

Then suddenly a memory was illuminated from a darkened corner of his mind. It was real—too real as it replayed in his thoughts. He longed to whisk it once again into the darkness, but was helpless to do so. The more he fought it, the stronger it came forward: he was at Headquarters in private conference with George Washington. Nothing unusual in that—it was the conversation; his own words that he wanted to escape. For the first time General Washington verbalized his desire for Nathanael to take command of the South. It was spoken long before General Gates' retreat, even before General Lincoln's capture. It occurred months ago, when his position as quartermaster general still rendered it impossible to comply with the Commander's desire.

"And if the position should be offered to you?" General Washington asked pointedly after making clear his desire and patiently listening to Nathanael's polite, though negative response.

George Washington's expression was firm as he awaited a reply; and now, even in this replay of the moment, the Commander waited as Nathanael fought to hold back the memory of his reply. It could not be done. "Sir, if you feel that the situation in the South warrants my personal attention—if Congress would agree—then I should consider it a task assigned me from Heaven itself, and set my hand to the plow not looking back!"

In a brisk canter, Lewis Morris entered the garrison, reined the horse in before a hitching post, and quickly dismounted. "Captain!" he called out to a nearby officer.

"Sir?"

"Have you seen General Greene?"

"Yes, sir. He and General Stark were conferring with the artillery commander. They were heading in the direction of the west wall last I saw them—probably going to inspect the guns that were mounted yesterday."

"Thank you." Lewis said dashing off in the direction indicated.

"Don't mention it, sir. Glad to be of assistance." the captain called after him, shrugging his shoulders.

"General Greene!" Lewis excitedly called out climbing atop the platform where the three officers stood. Visibly out of breath, he acknowledged General Stark and the artillery commander with a quick salute.

"Pardon me, sir, but word has arrived that Mrs. Greene's coach was spotted five miles north of Fishkill. Sir, they are very close indeed. They should be here within two hours."

"What do you mean the coach was spotted? Did the messenger speak to Mrs. Greene or Major Ward?" Nathanael asked, eagerly anticipating a positive reply.

"No, sir. He viewed the coach through a spyglass and raced here to tell you."

"It could be a false alarm, Nat," General Stark warned.

"It could be, but it is the only word of her whereabouts I have had thus far. I think I will ride toward Fishkill," he announced, pulling the leather gloves from his belt and slipping them over his hands.

"Shall I ride with you, sir?" Lewis asked as Nathanael made his way to the ladder.

He turned to Lewis and smiled remembering the aide's infatuation with his vivacious and beautiful wife. "No, Lewis, you are of greater service here at present. General Stark, I should return within a few hours."

"Take your time, sir, and I pray the report is accurate; and you have a most delightful ride back with an adoring wife at your side and four babies fighting over who'll be next to bounce upon your knees."

The road to Fishkill, New York was familiar to Nathanael who had made frequent trips through the quaint village while serving as quartermaster general. The excited anticipation, which had his heart pounding when he set out, began to wane as he came closer and closer to the village. *I should have intercepted the coach by now,* he thought. Growing more discouraged with each passing mile, he continued just the same, refusing to allow himself to consciously consider that the reported coach was not Caty's.

As he entered Fishkill, Nathanael failed to see the curious stares of passersby taking note of the seemingly distracted, lone Continental officer gracing their streets. He rode to the opposite end of the village and stopped. *Surely, they would have arrived at least this far by now, he thought.* With a sigh, he guided the horse back into the village. There was still hope—perhaps they were forced to stop. A visit to the livery, physician's surgery and the local tavern proved fruitless. The messenger was mistaken; no one by the name of Samuel Ward or Catharine Greene had stopped in Fishkill, nor had the coach Nathanael described been seen passing through—though there was one similar to that description an hour or so back headed for Peekskill the tavern keeper informed him. The passengers were an elderly couple by the name of Reeves.

After thanking the tavern keeper for his help, Nathanael headed back toward West Point. Sullen and depressed, he considered his plight: tomorrow he would leave for Headquarters—then he was to report to Congress in Philadelphia, and from there the long, arduous journey south to take his command.

If she does not arrive by morning, she will not be able to catch up to me, he lamented. As he came to the edge of the village, he wheeled the horse about, mournfully scanning the deserted road one last time. Wheeling the horse about, he headed toward West Point.

"General Greene, welcome," George Washington stood and received Nathanael's sharp salute. "Good afternoon, gentlemen," he added, acknowledging Rob Burnet and Lewis Morris.

"Good afternoon, sir," they replied, standing at attention.

"We have much to discuss, General." George Washington stepped over and laid a large hand on Nathanael's shoulder as he spoke. "Let's retire to my chamber."

Nathanael followed him up the stairs leaving his aides with the Commander's to catch up on the news of Headquarters.

"Colonel Hamilton informed me that you were momentarily expecting Catharine's arrival. Did she make it?" George Washington asked as he closed the door behind them.

"No, sir. I had riders out all night trying to locate her, but to no avail. Even as we left this morning, I found myself frequently looking over my shoulder in the hope that by some miracle her coach might still appear."

"I am sorry, Nathanael. If it were at all possible—I am truly sorry," the Commander said sitting at the small table, and gesturing for Nathanael to do the same.

"I know, sir—I understand."

"Your family's comfort will be seen to when they arrive. I imagine Catharine will be deeply upset upon discovering your orders," he looked at Nathanael expecting a response. Nathanael slowly nodded, his expression full of concern.

"Did you mention to her the possibility of your being appointed to the Southern command?"

"Just that it was your desire, though highly improbable."

"The poor girl," George Washington muttered, obviously distressed. "Might you want her to stay in camp for the winter? The officers' wives will be arriving soon; then she will at least have the gaiety of their social gatherings, and a few shoulders to cry on. It may help."

"It would help a great deal, sir. Thank you, I will be much relieved to know she is amongst so many friends."

"I understand your desire to set your house in order. I wish I could grant you leave."

"Please, sir—" Nathanael averted his eyes and took a deep breath. "—I fully understand and am even ashamed of myself for the momentary anger I felt in being denied the request. You have not been home in five long years. I know how much Mount Vernon means to you, and how deeply you long to return home yourself, if only briefly."

A weak, sad smile came to George Washington's lips. This friend knew him so intimately. How often had they read one another's emotions without spoken words? How often had they leaned on one another for strength and encouragement? While gazing at him, the Commander in Chief of the Continental Army realized his need through the years to keep this Quaker general close by his side. For this former ironmaster displayed much more than brute strength of body, but an enormous strength of character which proved so vital to George Washington's command. And tomorrow he would be gone.

"I do long to see Mount Vernon," he replied through a raspy throat. "I fully expect you to pay a visit on your way through Virginia. Lady Washington will be highly insulted if you do not make a point of it."

"It will be an honor to lodge in your home, General."

George Washington nodded, smiling affectionately. Then, turning his attention to a pile of papers on the table, his expression became grave.

"I cannot say for certain at this point, but it would appear your suspicions that the British intend to turn their full attention to the South may be well founded. Intelligence reports indicate that General Clinton is deploying an undetermined number of troops south. Rumors, only rumors at this time, indicate that King George has commanded Clinton to turn his attention in that direction in an attempt to cut off the Southern states."

"What is the estimated number of enemy troops presently in position?" Nathanael asked.

"Between South Carolina and Georgia, Lord Cornwallis has some 8,000 troops under his command."

"And Continental troops?" Nathanael asked certain of the grim reply.

"With the surrender of Charleston, we lost 5,000 men. With the defeat at Camden, we lost close to 1,500. There are scarcely 2,000 troops at present, and as many as half are in no condition for active service."

Nathanael stared at him in shocked disbelief, and then slowly dropped his eyes downward. "—I feel like David must have in viewing the Philistine army from a distance," he replied somberly.

George Washington nodded. "Organized government in Georgia and South Carolina no longer exists—North Carolina is weak." The Commander handed Nathanael various intelligence reports. As Nathanael scanned the papers, the General continued.

"The problem of supplying troops is quite different in the South. There is little produced in the way of manufactured goods. Because of this, there are few artisans to be found. Vast stretches of wilderness separate the populated areas. Though there is ample amount of food and forage, the lack of transportation will render it difficult to obtain.

"Because I am not certain at this point of the enemy's intentions, I cannot risk sending any troops South at this time. Clinton may very well be luring us to make just such a move—only to attack when our force is weakened. We cannot risk him getting a stronghold here. You must build your force from the Southern states themselves."

"In all honesty, sir, it sounds rather hopeless—" Nathanael was visibly disconcerted.

"With one single act, David sent the Philistines to flight," George Washington reminded him of the Biblical warrior, hoping to encourage his friend.

"I do not possess the unwavering faith of David."

"David's faith was present when needed. Take courage—a few partisan bands are still very active and successful in their sneak attacks against the British. Francis Marion, Andrew Pickens and Thomas Sumter command them. Contact these men as soon as possible."

"These bands are made up primarily of horsemen, aren't they?" Nathanael asked.

"They are. Their surprise attacks are swift and deadly."

"As I see it, sir, I will need to depend to a large degree on horsemen to keep the enemy from overrunning the country."

"William's cavalry is awaiting you in North Carolina," George Washington said referring to his cousin, the able cavalry commander, Colonel William Washington. "And Colonel Lee and his boys are there as well. Both gentlemen, I am sure, will be delighted to be of service to you."

Nathanael smiled envisioning the young Virginian, Colonel Henry Lee. Lee had become a close friend of Anthony Wayne's prior to his transfer South; and though no one would have thought it possible, the zealous cavalry commander, affectionately referred to as Light-Horse Harry, was even more dapper and vain than the Pennsylvanian swashbuckler.

"Well," Nathanael said, his smile now a wide grin, "Colonels Lee and Washington will have the opportunity to really put their boys to the test."

George Washington chuckled, for he was quite fond of them both. "They certainly will. And General Steuben will have ample opportunity to once again put his great talent to use turning raw troops into a disciplined force."

"Von Steuben is going with me?"

The gratitude in Nathanael's eyes stirred George Washington. He paused for a moment and reached out to the younger man, empathizing with the fear and self-doubt now wrapped in heartfelt gratitude in learning that such a dependable comrade and friend would be at his side. His own thoughts quickly reflected on his taking command in Boston. That rag-tag bunch of provincial soldiers had to have been the sorriest excuse for an army that ever assembled. How hopeless—how utterly inadequate he felt at the time—how frightened with the immense responsibility before him.

"From Delaware to Georgia you are in command, and there is not a man in this army I have more confidence in for accomplishing what needs to be done," he said, his hand on Nathanael's forearm. "Weaken them and break the grip they now have on the South. The fate of this country may depend on it. I want detailed reports of your movements. If the war does in fact turn Southward, I will plan my moves in accordance with yours."

"It may take six weeks for any intelligence to reach you," Nathanael reminded him.

"And six weeks for my return. Your warranted concern regarding this is well founded, one of the reasons you were my choice for this command." George Washington removed his hand from Nathanael's arm and leaned back in the chair studying his subordinate officer. "Your counsel has been sought by me for every engagement this army has made, save White Plains, and then only because the distance between us prohibited it. There is not a general officer in this army whose military ability and knowledge I respect more. I have received and acted on your counsel on many occasions, and save for one incident of misjudgment, I cannot remember regretting it," he said, gently referring to the blunder at Forts Lee and Washington.

"I am familiar enough with your strategic reasoning to feel comfortable in determining your probable tactics in a given situation—and you with mine. On this may depend our ability to possibly snare the British between our two armies. I will study your moves, General, and I will respond in accordance."

"You may rest assured that dispatches will be frequently issued, sir."

George Washington nodded his approval. "I can see that you are tired, my friend. You got little sleep last night worrying about Catharine and the children," George Washington said knowingly. "I had a servant prepare the chamber across the hall for you. Go rest until dinner. I have invited Generals Lafayette, Knox, Wayne and Stirling to join us—it will give you the opportunity to get their counsel and say good-bye. Von Steuben will also join us."

"Thank you, sir," Nathanael said as he stood, preparing to take the Commander up on his offer of rest.

George Washington nodded in response, and then watched affectionately as the younger man limped toward the door. "Nathanael." He called out.

"Sir?" Nathanael said, slowly turning to face the General.

"What of Major Ward? Will he be joining you and your aides southward?"

"I am leaving that up to the major, sir. He has been serving me on a voluntary basis these past few months. He has a sweetheart back in Rhode Island who would like nothing more than to have him come home and settle into married life," Nathanael smiled. "I guess I would feel pretty good about having him close at hand for Caty and the children. I will miss him terribly, but that, at least, will be a comfort."

Nathanael appreciated the gathering of such close and trusted friends more than words could ever express. Their wise counsel, verbal encouragement, genuine affection and jovial humor were greatly treasured; and he knew, even as the moments passed, that his mind would frequently fall back on this evening for comfort in the challenging weeks and months to come. However, as the hours ticked by, the inevitable occurred—time to bid farewell.

"I have a letter here for Harry Lee. Would you be so kind as to deliver it for me, sir?" Anthony Wayne asked as Nathanael escorted his friends outside.

"I would be happy to."

Anthony pulled the letter from the coat beneath his cape and handed it to Nathanael. "Colonel Lee sings the praises of the South's beauty—the climate, the flora, the women!"

Nathanael rolled his eyes and grinned as Henry Knox grunted and the others laughed. It was so like the bachelor Light-Horse Harry Lee to make such a comment, and so like Mad Anthony Wayne to repeat it.

"I discern that Horatio Gates is not keeping our young cavalry commander busy enough." Lord Stirling commented.

"I agree, your Lordship, and I intend to have Light-Horse Harry at such a continuous gallop he will only sweat in the climate, eat the flora, and never have time to notice the women." Nathanael stated with a chuckle.

"Do not count on it, General. He may be at a continuous gallop, but Harry Lee will always find a way to be a true gallant with the ladies." the Marquis de Lafayette jokingly commented.

"Spoken like a true Frenchman, my dear Marquis!" Baron von Steuben bellowed, patting the young French general on the back. "I shall be on my vay, General Greene. I have much to attend to still."

"I will see you in the morning, Baron," Nathanael said.

After each man bid farewell to the baron, Anthony continued, "Henry Lee paints a lovely picture of the Southland, but perhaps one has to be a native

Southerner to fully appreciate it. I fancy myself that, and therefore I should adapt nicely to the deep South."

"A Southerner? By what stretch of the imagination do you view yourself as a Southerner? You are from Pennsylvania, man! And central Pennsylvania at that!" Henry Knox chided.

"In my heart I am a Southerner." Anthony announced, laying his right hand on his chest.

"I am glad to hear it. If troops are deployed to me, I will be certain to request you personally, General Wayne." Nathanael assured him with a grin.

"Do so, General Greene, for it will be an honor to serve under you once again," he said coming to full attention and saluting.

"Take care of yourself, Nat," he added, patting his friend on the shoulder; then turning to the Marquis he said, "Will you ride back with me, sir?"

Lafayette nodded, and then directed his full attention to Nathanael. "I shall miss you, my friend—what can I say?"

"You do not have to say anymore than that, Fayette, for the feeling is certainly mutual."

Without warning the young Marquis grabbed hold of his upper arms and proceeded to kiss him on both cheeks, a European custom that Nathanael had fallen victim to on more than one occasion, and had not yet become comfortable.

After Lafayette and Wayne departed, Lord Stirling hesitantly announced his need to get back to camp. He looked at Nathanael. "God's speed to you, General. You will favor me with a letter on occasion?"

"Eagerly anticipating a response," Nathanael smiled, grasping hold of his upper arm. The earl reached across with his other arm laying his hand on top of his friend's. They held one another's gaze for a moment. After exchanging a sad smile, they released their hold. Lord Stirling took a step back, saluting his superior officer and receiving his in response.

"Well, your Lordship, the command post at West Point is still under consideration. Perhaps you will be blessed with the appointment," Henry offered as Lord Stirling mounted his waiting horse.

"I hope you put a good word in for me with His Excellency, General Greene." Lord Stirling chided.

"I have been doing little more than singing your praises since I arrived, your Lordship." Nathanael replied with a wide grin.

"I can well imagine; nothing more to occupy your thoughts, hey?" he said knowingly. "There is talk starting of a new commander being appointed to the Northern

Department—"

"I did not think you had any interest in that post with your rheumatism." Henry commented.

"I do not, but neither did Nat have any interest in the Southern Department. The way I see it: if he is being banished to the South, then the North is bound to be my nightmare."

"Not much we can do about it, your Lordship," Nathanael offered with a weak smile.

"No, not much at all—your servant, General Greene," Lord Stirling tipped his hat.

"Your servant, General Stirling."

"I will see you around, Henry." Lord Stirling called after him.

Though surrounded by the night's covering the soft light reflecting from within Headquarters, joined by the illumination of the moon above, offered enough light for Nathanael to view Henry's mournful expression.

"When this is over, I will bring my Caty and the children up to Boston. We will spend a week or two—Caty and Lucy can do all the expensive things Caty and Lucy enjoy doing when they are together. The children can play the days away in care-free innocence. As for me I would enjoy nothing more than passing the hours between pleasant conversation and browsing through your bookstore."

"Just like in the old days, hey?" Henry asked with a smile.

"Not quite," Nathanael corrected.

"No, I suppose not. We did not have wives spending all of our money then, or little ones scampering about our feet." Henry chuckled.

"No, we did not, and because of this my selection of books would be very different."

Henry folded his massive arms across his chest and inquisitively studied his friend. His interest was sparked in that livelihood he once enjoyed so much—and the drive of the bookseller was to meet the need of this customer. "What would your interests be?"

"No military books—nothing like that for a long time. I would want books for the children. Their education is very important to me."

"I could easily accommodate you there. What else?"

"Poetry."

"Really?"

"Yes." Nathanael's countenance was quite serious. "As I see, it I have a great deal of courting to do to make up for all of Caty's present heartache and distress."

Henry smiled sympathetically. "Anything else?" he asked.

"Gardening. Would you have anything on gardening?"

Henry nodded. "Flowers? Herbs? Or is it vegetables you are interested in?"

"Flowers and shrubbery—I long to surround myself with the beauty of God's creation after witnessing all this death and carnage. Caty could never get a thing to grow on that hill of ours. Maybe, working together, we can figure out what needs to be done. An herb garden would be nice too," Nathanael said as an afterthought.

"When all of this is over—when I am a bookseller and you are an ironmaster once more—I will be delighted to see to your needs, Mr. Greene."

There was a smile on Nathanael's lips, but Henry saw beyond it. It was the bleakness in his eyes that held Henry's attention. Though his friend joined in the conversation throughout the evening, even laughing with the others, there was a sense of humility in his behavior, and this dark, dismal reflection in his eyes. They had shared many experiences—supported and strengthened one another often through the years; but never, for all their intimacy and honesty, never had Henry witnessed the reflection of such distress.

"You have some fine officers awaiting your arrival, Nat," Henry offered as a means of encouragement. "Baron von Steuben will have your army fit for battle in no time."

Nathanael looked at him, mulling the words over for a brief moment. "I do not have an army—I do not even have a division—I barely have two regiments to face Cornwallis with."

"Then he will have your two regiments fit for battle in no time." Henry's smile prompted a weak one from his friend.

"I will do my best, Henry, and pray for Heaven's blessing, but the outlook is rather gloomy. What remains to be seen is: shall I lead my little army to shameful defeat, as did Horatio Gates, or shall I be forced to surrender, as did Benjamin Lincoln? What do you think, General Knox?"

"Methinks, sir, that neither shall be your fate. You may face defeat, but the shameful flight of Horatio Gates would never be your reaction. As for Lincoln's capture, you are too coy to be caught in such a predicament. But, if you are captured," Henry added, raising a concerned brow, "if you are, you have your rank in your favor; you would be exchanged in no time. Why look at Ben Lincoln. He is back home in Massachusetts surrounded by family and friends." Judging by Nathanael's perplexed gaze, Henry realized he was not offering much encouragement by his words; and, rather than dig himself deeper in this faulty attempt, he decided to remain silent.

"But what of his men?" Nathanael finally asked. He knew the answer—they both knew the answer; there was no need to speak it. General Lincoln's men were languishing in a prison camp—it was the officers and then only those highest in rank, which had any hope of being quickly exchanged.

"I am already responsible for the imprisonment of the 2,000 men at Fort Washington, and I pray God I will never lead men down that path again."

Void of a response, Henry looked down at the ground, kicking a stone with his boot.

Nathanael gazed into the darkness, his mind quickly moving away from reflecting on his imprisoned men—a thought, which caused much personal grief.

"I know it is odd, but I have been thinking a lot about my father these past few days—I long for his counsel. It does not make any sense, a military commander wanting the counsel of such a pious Quaker. He could give a great sermon; maybe that is where I came by my fascination for the military. My poor Quaker father. He would die a thousands deaths to hear me say it, but I tell you, Henry, he could preach the most awe-inspiring sermons about Joshua battling the Canaanites; David and the Philistines; Sampson; Gideon; Josiah. He always had a sermon in his heart. What I would not give to hear one now—how did we get to this place, Henry?"

"By the Divine hand of Providence, Nat. That and that alone."

"Then I will confess to you and before God, that I am frightened."

"There is nothing wrong with that—you are only human. You have pointed that out to me a time or two in the past. We have all been there—"

"No, it is not like that—I have never been so frightened or felt so totally inadequate to any task," Nathanael confessed.

Henry's eyes drifted to the light illuminating from Headquarters as he sought for the words needed to encourage his friend.

"Do you know what the prevailing attitude throughout the camp has been upon hearing of your appointment?" he asked after a moment.

Nathanael shook his head.

"Among the officers it is agreed that if anything is to be expected from the abilities and exertions of an individual, no one will be more likely to carry it through. Many have been spouting that Congress' delay in appointing you has been prejudicial and dangerous to our cause. They and I included have stated that we would stake our reputation on the outcome if you were given the opportunity.

"The respect the men have of you has been evident in that from all ranks I have heard reports that, though they know our hope in saving the South lies in you taking command, there is a universal regret among the troops at the idea of parting with you."

Henry fixed his gaze on Nathanael. "Nat, there is no disagreement on the subject—no debate. From those in Congress who stood in opposition to you more often
than not; the very ones who only a few weeks ago were ready to demand you be discharged—to the Commander In Chief, who has the utmost opinion of your character and ability—to the men who have served under you, and have been fed, clothed
and cared for because of you. These say Nathanael Greene is the man for this task.
No other has been called to this place; no other can accomplish what lies before
you. From childhood, this Divine call has been on your life—a hunger for military
knowledge in a strict Quaker environment. You explain it, Nat. You told me about
the hours you toiled over geometry despite your father's attempts to discourage
you. To what end? To forge iron? What was the drive?

"How much did you have to sacrifice to purchase your collection of military
writings? Nat, I was there. I remember the frequent visits to my bookshop over the
years, the long trips, the expensive purchases. And even then, even then, so many
years ago—a lifetime ago when we were little more than mere lads, I remember
thinking—wondering about this Rhode Island Quaker with his religious ideology
and dress being driven, so it seemed, to that which seemed so unnatural to his station in life."

Henry paused and again turned his eyes toward Headquarters. "How did either
of us come to this place? God called us here, and we simply obeyed. Now you are
being called into that particular position for which you have been so thoroughly
trained. God is Sovereign, my friend. Your training was completed through serving as quartermaster general. You will need to apply every aspect of that special
training as commander of the Southern army. You will need to raise funds and
make the connections necessary to feed, clothe, supply and pay your troops. You
will need to fall back on the knowledge gained in forming the Kentish Guards, and
encouraging the reenlistment of your Rhode Island troops so long ago. You will
need to apply every bit of military knowledge you have attained through books,
counsel and first hand experience. You will be responsible for life and death decisions—the life or death of these United States perhaps, with none other to turn to
for support and guidance save God alone. You have been called to this place, and
you do not have to feel adequate to the task, just be obedient. If the good Lord has
gone to such trouble to train you, then He will certainly be there with you every step
of the way."

Henry paused, suddenly aware of the relaxed smile on his friend's face. "A bit
preachy, hey?" he asked sheepishly.

"My father could not have done better. I thank thee." Nathanael placed his
hand on Henry's shoulder. "Promise me one thing, friend."

"What is that?" Henry asked with a smile, noting the glimmer in Nathanael's eyes.

"See that His Excellency remains obedient to his call and holds things together here. Give him a similar talk every now and again. For if the main army falls, my rank will be on no value except to get me executed in short order."

Henry chuckled. "I do not think we have any worry in George Washington losing sight of his call. Oh, he may get discouraged every now and again like you and me; but like you and me his heart is to remain faithful to the bitter end. And if the end is our defeat, then let us make sure we all hang together, hey?"

There was a brief silence as both contemplated saying good-bye.

"You should get some rest. You have a long ride ahead," Henry offered with a weak, affectionate smile.

After a warm embrace, they bid one another farewell, prepared to face the uncertainties of the future.

The stacks of cotton diapers seemed immense to Caty as she stood staring at them upon the bed, with little Natty comfortably situated upon her hip.

"I do not know, Peggy. It seems like an awful lot of diaper changes to me."

"Thee have no choice, Sister Caty. It will take all of a week to get there, and with two in diapers that's how many they will need."

Contemplatively looking from Cornelia, who was playing at her feet, to little Natty, Caty then turned her full attention to Patty, who was sitting upon the bed surrounded by yet-to-be packed clothing. Suddenly she began to laugh, "Praise be given that Patty and George are potty trained or there would be no room for people in the coach!"

Then turning to her sister-in-law she added, "Cornelia and Natty will just have to make do with less diapering!"

"Perhaps thee should reconsider and take Mother Greene up on her offer to keep the babies. It's a long, hard trip for such little ones."

"Please, Peggy, we've been over this before. Nathanael requested that all the children come with me, and so they will."

"It seems that Brother Nathanael is being quite unrealistic—" Peggy replied just as Sam Ward came into the room.

"What on earth are you doing here, Sammy? Checking up on me, no doubt, to see if I will be ready to go by morning!" Caty exclaimed with a glowing smile. "Though it might not appear so, I promise you I will!"

She walked to her cousin's side and kissed him on the cheek. "Dear, sweet Sammy. I have tried your patience to the limit by insisting on my little shopping venture, but I assure you the children and I now have everything we need. Actually I am glad you are here," she said walking back to the piles of clothing on the bed. "Please explain to Peggy that I cannot arrive in camp without the babies. I cannot make her understand how determined Nathanael is to have them all present."

Sam did not respond. Surprised by his odd silence, Caty turned to face him.

"We need to talk," he said softly.

"Oops! I am in trouble," she said with a sigh. "It's the coach, isn't it? I know it is over-packed, but I do not know what I could possibly do without. I have some baked goods I might be able to leave behind, but how could I arrive at headquarters without sweet cakes and such for the men?

"There's some tea for the ladies' gatherings, but it is not so much. Nathanael requested a few books—dare we leave them behind?" she asked then broke into a grin. "If we do, you'll have to be the one to break it to him."

"It's not the coach, Caty. Mrs. Greene," he said turning to Peggy. "Would you mind taking the children out for a few minutes?"

"No, not at all," she replied with a concerned glance for her sister-in-law. Taking Natty from his mother, she reached down for Cornelia's hand as Sam lifted Patty off the bed. Sam closed the door behind them.

"What is it, Sam? You are not acting yourself—are you ill? Of course! That is it! You picked something up before you left headquarters—Nathanael mentioned in his last letter that he was down with a mild fever. We will just wait until it runs its course—is that it, Sam, you are ill?" The color drained from Caty's cheeks as she spoke. Her eyes searched his for an answer.

Slowly Sam shook his head, unable to tell her what he knew he must.

"Has something happened to Nathanael?" She placed her hand over her lips, terrified by his silence.

"No—no, Caty, it is not that—" He reached into his pocket and pulled out a sealed letter. "This just arrived with a letter for me—I—" Sam was at a complete loss for words.

"—Maybe you should just read it—it would probably be better if you just read it," he said, trusting that Nathanael would be better able to break the news to her.

With a trembling hand, Caty reached for the letter. Sitting down on the bed, she opened the seal. Quickly the tender words became a blur as silent tears fell from her eyes onto the paper in her hand. She seemed to gasp for air as she finished reading it.

"Dear God, why?" she cried, holding the letter against her heart. "Why?" Her sobs were uncontrollable. Sam was no longer at a loss as to what to do. Going to her side, he held her in his arms.

"I am sorry, Caty. I am so sorry."

"If—if I had only—left right when you—got here—if I—had only left then—I would have—been able to—to say—good-bye." she sobbed. "When will—I see him—again, Sam? When will—the children—see their papa?"

Sam continued to hold her, listening to her pain and fears, unable to offer more than an occasional, heartfelt, "I am so sorry—"

"I have but the Shadow of an Army without clothing, tents and provisions...It is also without Discipline..."
(Nathanael Greene to Robert Howe)

CHAPTER SIXTEEN

THE JOURNEY SOUTH had started out with promise. The sense of camaraderie in the traveling companions made for hours of meaningful conversation and merriment. The Baron von Steuben's accounts of life in Prussia, and service as aide-de-camp to Frederick the Great fascinated his audience. His aide, the near-sighted Pierre Duponceau, offered much hilarity in telling of the many blundering episodes that he so often seemed to find himself in. Nathanael's stories of life in Rhode Island were filled with country wit. In addition, with Lewis Morris' natural clumsiness, and Rob Burnet's insatiable need for a factual and logical explanation of every story told, the opportunity for kind-hearted jesting was ever available.

The stopover in Alexandria, Virginia to visit the Commander's home was a welcome repose. Martha Washington's motherly smile and warm hospitality were a comfort to each of them. Her questions and comments about Caty and the children proved to ease Nathanael's lonely heart.

Nathanael retired to the guest chamber late that evening, and rested in the stillness of the majestic mansion, thinking on the one whose own heart ached to be there. Would he ever forget the final charge George Washington gave him just prior to his departure? The warm embrace? With this thought, his weary body lapsed into peaceful slumber only to be startled awake a few short hours later by a servant, as per his request. Surrounded by the blackness of the early morning, Nathanael put on his breeches, shirt and waistcoat, and made his way to the small desk in the corner of the room. Before their departure that morning, letters had to be written—there were always letters to be written. He glanced over his shoulder at the inviting bed, and quickly turned away, taking up the familiar quill pen, and by the flickering light of a single candle set to work. His first letter was to George Washington updating him on his attempts to procure supplies, and commenting on his pleasant visit at Mount Vernon.

As the journey continued, the scene before Nathanael became bleaker than even he had imagined. He was forced to leave General Steuben in Richmond, Virginia to train the promised number of new recruits, and oversee the forwarding of supplies to Southern Headquarters. Then, with his faithful aides by his side, he began the last leg of his journey.

Charlotte, North Carolina within the day. After six weeks of hard travel, it was a welcome thought, but somehow unbelievable—they would finally be at the Headquarters of the Continental Army's Southern Department within a few short hours.

Nathanael glanced at his traveling companions. Both were quiet, pensively considering what lay ahead so it seemed. *Ahead?* His thoughts rested on it briefly. There seemed to be little to gain in considering what lay ahead—the reality of it all would hit soon enough. He considered his recent pleadings before the governors of Delaware, Maryland, and Virginia. Little to nothing was given in the way of supplies—and promises of next to nothing beside. In such a ravished, war-torn state of affairs, what in truth could the governors offer?

The three weary travelers rode into the camp, guided by a young officer who had been appointed to await their arrival. Slowly the soldiers turned from their work, curious to get a glimpse of their new general. Ragged and half-starved, these pitiful creatures began to line the road.

They appear more an assembly of scarecrows than warriors. Nathanael thought. A shiver ran up his spine as he gazed at the sunken faces staring up at him. Their spiritless eyes studied his passing form. Nodding every now and again, he smiled weakly, though compassionately, at the men—his men.

As he rode, Nathanael took in the condition of the camp. The experience of having been responsible for the encampment of the Continental Army as quartermaster general gave him the ability to quickly size up the situation. The huts were poorly constructed, offering little more than basic shelter against the elements. The layout of the camp was ill fated, offering poor drainage and a probable sanitation catastrophe.

He twisted in the saddle to get a view of what lay behind the camp. As he suspected—the entire area offered little natural protection from a possible attack. *These men must be moved,* he thought as the riders approached Headquarters.

Nathanael dismounted, his aides following his lead, and walked toward the house only to be greeted by Horatio Gates and his military family just outside the front gate. All of the officers in attendance watched with anxious anticipation of the initial meeting of these two foes.

"General Greene, welcome," Horatio Gates received Nathanael's formal salute. "I hope your journey was uneventful in the way of hazard or health."

"Thank you, General Gates. Indeed it was, though we are relieved to finally have arrived."

"Please come inside, General, and let me offer you some refreshment." Horatio Gates gestured for Nathanael to precede him into the house where a servant was busy setting the table for a meal. "While things are being prepared, perhaps you would care to wash up. Let me show you and your aides to your chambers."

After dinner, Nathanael allowed minimal time for idle conversation, for the desperate state of the army required his immediate attention. A mutually respectful attitude prevailed throughout the week between the two general officers as the one leaving attempted to provide all the necessary information needed to the one taking over.

Nathanael not only studied in full the problems he faced, but he studied his officers as well. Carefully he appointed qualified, reliable men to vital supply posts: quartermaster, commissary, wagonmaster, forgemaster, superintendent of boats, clothier, commissary of prisoners, commissary of hides, and the appointments went on and on.

Special notice was taken of three brilliant young officers, each optimistic in nature with a keen insight and enthusiasm in every task undertaken.

The mild-mannered, soft-spoken, handsome Marylander, Otho Holland Williams, had drawn Nathanael's affection from the start. The twenty-seven year old colonel had served under his command four years previously during the disastrous defeat of Fort Washington. Otho suffered as a prisoner of war for two years, eager to resume his post upon release.

The appointment of adjutant general was given to Otho Williams. He quickly became a familiar and welcome face at Headquarters, and a regular guest at the General's table. When talk during dinner turned toward home and the domestic tranquility each man longed for, Otho freely joined in the conversation. The second of seven orphaned siblings, Otho had an apparent paternal affection and concern for his sisters and brother. The better acquainted Nathanael became with his adjutant general—with his solid moral character and sincere humility—the more attached he became. Before long, Nathanael found himself confiding in the young Marylander much the same way George Washington had done with him.

Next was William Washington— six-feet tall with broad shoulders and long arms. The white coat, leather breeches, and steel-plumed helmet, which identified his cavalry unit of 100 men, added definition to his already massive form. William had been studying for the ministry before the outbreak of the war. His piety and kind-heartedness were character traits both his cavalry unit and commander greatly admired. Though kin to the Commander in Chief, William never sought advantage of this close tie, but rose to his rank solely through acts of bravery and proven leadership. Nathanael came to refer to the burly cavalry officer as his "right arm", keeping him close to the main body; for the infantry seemed fearless under Colonel Washington's protection.

Then there was the dapper, swashbuckler Light-Horse Harry Lee—without a doubt the most colorful of the three—fearlessly leading his legion of 300 men, half-mounted cavalry, and half-light infantry. His legion was adorned in tight-fitted green jackets, white leather breeches and plumed steel helmets. Harry commanded respect from friend and foe alike. He was but twenty-four years old when Nathanael took command. A born soldier, Harry never seemed content unless anticipating danger. Harry's insatiable desire for danger earned him the honor of frequently being sent out to skirt the enemy in order to collect intelligence. Thus, Light-Horse Harry was referred to by the commander as his "right eye".

Confined to his desk a good deal of the time, Nathanael saw to it that order after order flowed from his pen as he attempted to organize the chaos he had inherited. His ability to quickly stabilize the confusion rekindled a sense of hope and patriotism in the men.

He made contact through letters with his partisan generals—Marion, Sumter and Pickens—introducing himself, praising their conduct and requesting them to continue as they had been.

He ordered a prison be built, and made the offer of a prisoner exchange to Lord Cornwallis. He followed this with orders for a hospital to be built in the same location, ever aware of the desperate need. He made plans for forming two magazine sites, which were to be stocked with one month's provisions; and sent out a team of men to map the various rivers in the area, that supplies might be moved by water whenever possible.

With the transfer of command complete and the reconstruction of the army well under way, Horatio Gates waited for Nathanael to instruct him concerning the court of inquiry into his conduct at the Battle of Camden. Yet, as the day of Gates' departure drew near, not a word about it was spoken.

"I have been informed that an inquiry into my conduct has been called for," Horatio said after requesting their aides leave them. "I welcome an investigation that I might clear my name."

Nathanael looked across the dining room table at the fallen hero. "Then I wish it were within my power to accommodate you, General, but at present it is impossible."

"I do not understand."

"My orders were to have General Steuben preside over the court, and though I do not necessarily feel bound to that literal order, I do not presently have any major general readily available to preside in his place. This requirement of military code, as well as the fact that many of the witnesses are not present, leaves me no choice but to deny your request. I am sorry."

"Are you, General Greene?" he asked, his steady, searching gaze fixed on Nathanael.

"I have inquired on my own as to your conduct. The officers that I have spoken to are in support of your actions throughout. And I am satisfied that the flight which followed the battle was general in nature—officers and soldiers alike taking care of themselves."

Nathanael paused, considering with great sympathy how this blot on Gates' reputation would probably never be removed even though the army's flight was beyond his control. "I am convinced, sir, that reports to the North of the battle have been misrepresented."

"I thank you for your confidence, General Greene; but, unfortunately, it will not be enough to clear my name."

"No sir, it won't; but I intend to share my opinion in the matter with both Congress and General Washington."

Horatio nodded his head in silent appreciation. "I can ask for no more under the circumstances; and, with this business out of the way and the transfer of command complete, I see no reason to stay on. If it is acceptable to you, General, I will plan to leave on the morrow."

"I see no reason to detain you, General"

Horatio nodded then stood from the table. He gazed at Nathanael for a moment. Not a word was spoken, but a keen sense of appreciation shone forth from his eyes. Still without a word he turned, slowly walking out of the room.

"Excuse me, sir, but General Morgan is here," Lewis Morris reported. Even before the announcement was complete, Dan Morgan's thunderous voice was heard as he greeted the men downstairs. Rarely did this man wait to be announced.

"Show the general up, Lewis," Nathanael said with an amused grin.

"Yes, sir," the aide replied; but before he could make his way to the top of the staircase, Dan Morgan was ascending, each step creaking under his enormous weight.

"The General is ready to see you, sir." Lewis informed him, gesturing to the open door.

"Well, I figured as much, lad, since he sent for me. Now you have yourself a good afternoon, Morris, you hear me?" Dan Morgan said, patting the aide on the shoulder as he passed.

"Thank you, General. I hope to, sir."

Ducking to avoid hitting his head on the doorframe, Morgan stepped into Nathanael's chamber, straightened up and saluted.

Nathanael was still smiling as he gestured to the chair opposite him.

"Please sit down, General."

Silently Nathanael studied this long-time acquaintance while he vainly attempted to comfortably seat himself in the chair, which seemed miniature in comparison to his frame. Dan Morgan was a giant of a man—solid and powerful, with an open, friendly face. He was an extremely likable fellow whose former profession as a teamster rendered him quite rough around the edges and notorious for his temper.

Dan Morgan's independent and sometimes irrational behavior had been a challenge for George Washington. When Congress continuously failed to honor his proven ability by promoting him to brigadier general, Morgan, in a huff, resigned his commission entirely and retired from the army. Despite George Washington's pleading, the determined teamster refused to reconsider.

Morgan returned to serve only after the disastrous outcome of the Battle of Camden. Finally, with a congressional commission of brigadier general, he assisted Horatio Gates in his pathetic attempt to hold the Southern Department together.

Like Washington, Stirling and Putnam, he was a veteran of the French and Indian War. It was during that war that a deep-rooted bitterness for British authority developed when a dispute and the subsequent striking of a British officer brought him the cruel sentence of 499 lashes. His muscled back still bore the scars, and with them a firm conviction that the lash was an inhumane form of punishment, which he refused to ever use to discipline troops.

The men adored him—this general who would mingle with the ranks. Few generals found it easy to chance that delicate balance of commander and friend by indulging in the pleasure of being among their men: Israel Putnam, Anthony Wayne and Dan Morgan were known for it. George Washington, too, did on occasion, and would more if given the opportunity. Nathanael always held that while in command situations, his own rank should be given full respect and honor; but when at ease he considered himself but a friend of the men he commanded.

Dan Morgan's superb military ability was fully recognized by Nathanael. He had proven himself repeatedly in the Canadian campaigns, and now Nathanael planned to utilize his genius. Being a keen observer of human nature, the new commander realized that he must relate to this man on an individual basis. He made it a point to study his character, his strengths and weaknesses—as he was attempting to do with various key subordinate officers, thus bringing out their full potential.

"How are things going since General Gates' departure?" Morgan asked.

"We are staying busy," Nathanael replied, leaning forward.

Thunderous laughter erupted from Morgan. "I can well imagine." He brought his huge hands down upon the table with a thud, rattling the ink well and penholder. "You have done a wondrous thing with this army these past two weeks—wondrous indeed. And I hear Tommy Jefferson sent us 300 of America's best. I would be happy to take those dear boys off your hands, General, and include them in my brigade." the proud Virginian offered, certain that this was the very reason he had been summoned.

Nathanael leaned back. "I ordered them to return this morning."

Morgan was visibly confused. "Ordered them to return to where?"

"Virginia."

All trace of humor was immediately gone from Dan Morgan's expression. "You did what?"

Nathanael locked his eyes on General Morgan's and held him under an unyielding, stern gaze. This was a command decision, and his rank would be honored. No answer would be given without proper respect shown.

After a moment, Morgan yielded to the silent challenge. Breaking eye contact, he spoke showing respect as best he could under the circumstances.

"Begging the General's pardon, but why, sir? What on earth possessed you to send those men back home?"

"We are in need of fighting men, General Morgan. What Mr. Jefferson sent us were 300 men in need—improperly clad, entirely without supply and absolutely no provisions. The conditions here may have greatly improved these past few weeks; but I can assure you, General, that we remain on very shaky ground in regard to supplies, food, and clothing. At present, we have a hand-to-mouth existence. I must be certain that the shadow of an army I now command can face the enemy if need be. To take on 300 troops without supply would prove our death sentence should the British attack. I will hold intact what little I have and not jeopardize their safety because of the ignorance of Mr. Jefferson or any governor lacking enough common sense to equip the men he sends."

"Did you explain the situation to Governor Jefferson?"

"Thoroughly."

Morgan rolled his eyes and smiled. "Isn't Tommy in for a surprise!" Again, the thunderous laughter erupted. "Lonely at the top, isn't it, General?"

Nathanael smiled reservedly, aware that what he had yet to tell this man had the potential of igniting a much greater response than what he had already witnessed.

"Orders will be given tomorrow to prepare to march." Nathanael reached for a scrolled map before him. Standing, he unrolled it holding down the corners with various items on the table. Morgan stood, studying the map.

"I have already spoken to you about relocating the camp. The engineer's report of this location meets with my approval," he said pointing to an area thirty miles south of the existing encampment. "We are in need of rest. Many of the men are in desperate need of a chance to recuperate. Our wagons are in want of repair. We must find suitable horses. And, once the men are on their feet again I need time to properly train them." He paused, staring at the map. "Yet I am concerned that in moving our entire force southward Lord Cornwallis will consider us to be in retreat and feel compelled to follow."

Morgan looked up at him. "I agree, sir. General Cornwallis will most certainly follow us."

"Yet, if troops were to simultaneously move westward—" he said, pointing to a spot on the map.

"Divide the army, sir?"

When Nathanael turned to face him, he saw the concern on Dan Morgan's face. Immediately Nathanael made eye contact.

"General Greene, are you aware that 2,500 troops from New York have been sent to reinforce Cornwallis?"

"Yes, I am aware of that, General Morgan."

"Cornwallis has 8,000 troops against our pathetic few—"

Nathanael nodded in response.

"To divide an army, especially one so small and weak—begging the General's pardon, but have you forgotten the maxim of war—divide and conquer. Sir, it would be military suicide!"

"It is military suicide to do otherwise," Nathanael calmly responded. "The stronger elite troops—the bulk of our regulars—will be sent westward, including Colonel Washington's Cavalry. The division will confuse Cornwallis. It has been reported to me that he believes our numbers are much greater than they are. From all I know of him, he is a cautious man; I do not believe he will risk a full-scale attack. He will send a scouting party to be sure, perhaps even a small force to engage in a frisk; but the troops heading westward can handle that."

"What if he does not check the westward movement, but decides instead to focus on the weaker troops?" Morgan asked.

"He will not be worried about them," Nathanael replied, moving his finger further westward on the map to a British stronghold known as Ninety-six. "His concern will be that Ninety-six is our goal."

General Morgan hesitated, aware that Nathanael Greene was right. "I have never heard of such a tactic being successful, but it is true, sir, Cornwallis is a rather cautious man. A full-scale attack is not probable unless he gets wind of your plan."

"The very reason I have not shared it with anyone but you, General Morgan."

"And why me, sir?"

"Because I want you to command the men to the west."

A slow smile came to Dan Morgan's lips as his eyes brightened. "He is bound to send Benny to me!" he began with a chuckle. "Cornwallis always sends Benny and his monsters to check things out."

"Benny?" Nathanael queried.

"Colonel Banastre Tarleton," he replied, his voice suddenly filled with notable contempt. "Certainly General Gates told you of Tarleton."

"He did," Nathanael replied, moving back to his seat and gesturing for General Morgan to do the same. *Banastre Tarleton*, Nathanael reviewed what he remembered as he comfortably positioned himself. *A young, ambitious dragoon officer who formed and led a legion of Tories.*

"Why don't I fill you in on what Horatio Gates may have left out," Morgan suggested.

"What makes you think he left anything out, General Morgan?"

"Well, they are both English-born and both came to their rank in the British army by the same means—"

Nathanael's brows were cocked as he studied Dan Morgan.

"Let's face it, sir, British officers, including men like Gates and Charles Lee, bought their rank. One must be very well bred to bear an officer's title in the

British army. Therefore, there is bound to be a sense of loyalty present between them even still—you know, one aristocrat protecting the honor of another before us lower-class amateurs who came by our rank in such an unorthodox manner—by proving ourselves. Imagine an iron master and a teamster with the rank of general—never mind our Commander in Chief being a mere farmer."

A brief silence elapsed as Nathanael considered the words. "Tell me what you know of Colonel Tarleton," he finally said.

Dan Morgan took a deep breath as though he needed a moment to emotionally prepare himself. "—If Lucifer possesses the souls of men, then I would dare say that he is presently in possession of Tarleton's soul. Save for Judas Iscariot, and perhaps Benedict Arnold, there has not been a more evil man.

"Tarleton has formed Tory bands. They follow him around to do his every wicked bidding. There is reference up North to the horror of this war being a civil war—Englishman against Englishman. Down here it is a gruesome reality of which the North has little concept. Here it is a civil war—Patriot against Tory; neighbor against neighbor; brother against brother; father against son."

He paused for a moment, looking down at the table then quickly back at Nathanael. "Tarleton leads his bands of Tories against those who side with us: beating, then hanging the men in front of the womenfolk. He burns their homes, and then that son of Lucifer gives his dragoons permission to have their way with the women. He is a heartless monster lacking any conscience whatsoever. And there is many a man in this army who has vowed to see him dead, and long to have him rot in hell."

Nathanael remained silent, uncertain of what to say.

"Don't underestimate the hatred of the men in your militia units for their Tory kin. I am not sure, General Greene, that even if we should win this war if this hatred between neighbors and kinfolk will ever be abated—and Banastre Tarleton will go down in infamy for it. And another thing, sir—"

Nathanael nodded for him to continue.

"Like the ruthless Hessians, Tarleton's quarter is no quarter. Remember that, sir, and you would do well to make sure your men realize it so that they fight with every ounce of strength when put against him. For to fall prisoner to Tarleton means certain death. I was told of how Tarleton once overtook a force of our men some 350 strong—Virginians they were. A fierce battle ensued, but our boys did not stand a chance. Their commander, a Colonel Abraham Buford, was forced to surrender. Quarter was denied. Tarleton ordered every one of those brave souls to be cut down in front of their commander—then—" Dan Morgan struggled to continue. He cleared his throat and stared straight at Nathanael. "Fifteen minutes after the slaughter, that devil ordered his monsters back over the field to plunge their bayonets into anyone that exhibited any signs of life.

"Oh, General, I welcome the thought of meeting Benny Tarleton on the battlefield; and, unlike poor Abraham Buford, with the help of the Almighty, my boys and I will be fully prepared to take him on!"

My Dear Caty,

I received two letters from you in the last dispatch from Headquarters, and am delighted to hear that you and the children are in good health. I am quite sensible to the fact that your happiness will not be complete until I return, as you must understand the void in my heart as well.

We are settling into our camp of repose—though comfortable is not a word I would use to describe the situation here, it is far more tolerable than our former state.

Might I wish you a belated Christmas blessing? Little thought was given to the day as we were en route at the time, but I have reminisced on it some since—fondly remembering the warm celebrations we have shared in the past with so many good friends.

News from General Washington and various officers arrives on a regular basis. Though you feel deprived in not being at Headquarters this winter, I have reason to be grateful for it. The situation there is far worse than even last year. I have been informed by numerous correspondents, including His Excellency, of the mutiny of the Pennsylvania Line. Reports are that one officer was killed and many wounded. A general carnage was prevented when Anthony Wayne came upon the chaotic scene; and, after a volley was fired over his head as a warning to him, Mad Anthony tore open his clothing, exposing his chest, and yelled, "If you mean to kill me, shoot me at once!" No shot was fired, and the troops calmed down enough to make their plan known to their commander. Determined to present their grievances to Congress in person, they set out for Philadelphia—over 1,000 suffering men. General Wayne went with them, hoping for an opportunity to negotiate.

His Excellency fears the New England Lines may follow suit. If a general mutiny should occur, all are in danger, for the British will swoop down on the encampment, doing infinite damage.

You are safe in Rhode Island, and that is where I want you to stay. You questioned whether you could come Southward in your last letter. My answer is nay. Nay, because of my great love for you! The trip is long and hazardous. The South provides many enemies—there would be little safety as you traveled.

Beyond that, our conditions are quite deplorable. Moreover, my orders are to weaken Cornwallis; therefore, I must be ready to do battle whenever the opportunity presents itself.

I cannot risk you being here under these circumstances—and shall not waiver in my deci-sion no matter how agonizing the separation is at present.

Benedict Arnold has proven himself as committed to the enemy as he once appeared to be to us. His wickedness is beyond comprehension. He now holds the British commission of brigadier general, and is presently in Virginia causing much havoc along the James River in an attempt to cut off supplies and troops headed my way.

General Lafayette has been ordered to Virginia with three regiments to aid General Steuben and squash Arnold's attempts.

In the meantime, I still await news of General Morgan. I received intelligence three days ago that some 1,000 enemy troops were fast approaching General Morgan's position. I have yet to hear of the outcome of that battle, and cannot rest until I do. It is 2 AM, yet sleep will not come. My restless mind finds solace in writing to you as to none other.

My love to my dear children. Kiss each one for me. (General Washington wants to know if Natty has learned to fire a musket yet.)

Because your letters are coming from Headquarters, I receive them with those of many others—including His Excellency's. I will freely confess that any orders or urgent matters of a military nature must wait until I have had the heartwarming pleasure of hearing from you first.

With my sincere love and affection,

Nathanael

After reviewing the troops, Nathanael returned to headquarters, his temper noticeably short. Being greeted by a roomful of officers awaiting private confer-ence for their various problems did not help, but this was a common scene, Rob Burnet determined, and not likely to be the reason for his mood.

"Was the drill a disappointment, sir?" Rob asked following Nathanael into his private chamber.

"No, on the contrary, quite encouraging. They're looking good." He handed Rob his cape and hat and sat at the table thumbing through the pile of papers that had accumulated in his brief absence.

"This camp is no Egypt in the way of provisions, but the discipline of the troops has greatly improved. We have militia units we can work with now." He put the papers down and began rubbing his eyes with his right hand. "Why haven't we received word from General Morgan yet?"

"Have you been able to sleep, General?" Rob asked certain of what the answer would be.

"A bit."

"Can I get you anything? Maybe a cup of coffee, sir?"

"Please—and whom do I see first?" he asked looking through the papers again.

"The Deputy Quartermaster General, sir."

"Show the poor man in if you would, Rob," he said with a weak, empathetic smile.

"Colonel Carrington, the General will see, sir." Rob announced, and then disappeared into the kitchen.

When he returned, he sat at the table alongside Nathanael, prepared to take notes on the reports, requests and grievances of the various officers.

Nathanael rarely took notes during such meetings. Instead, he had developed a rather peculiar manner of receiving reports. Comfortably resting in the chair, his head back, his eyes closed and his arms crossed upon his chest, he listened to the men. Often it appeared he was sleeping, and the humiliated officer who was experiencing this for the first time would become silent looking to the aide for assistance.

The aide would gesture for the man to continue, usually confusing the bewildered officer all the more. For often, before the aide could fully make known the meaning of his hand gestures and facial expressions, the general's eyes would pop open with a stern, unrelenting fix on the man presenting the report.

Shocked by the general's apparent alertness, and more so by his obvious annoyance that the report had come to a sudden halt, the officer would attempt to pick up where he left off, usually with the general repeating the last sentence for him. Then, with a trembling voice and wobbly knees, the officer would continue.

Today, even Rob suspected that Nathanael might be sleeping a time or two, and was surprised to see the usual scenario play out again when the officer ended his monologue. It never ceased to amaze Rob, and especially today, when, after the report was completed, Nathanael would immediately come to life. Then with great detail and precision he would lie out, point by point, the way to solve the problem.

A commotion in the foyer was heard as Nathanael was completing his response to the report from the commissary of hides. Lewis Morris' knock was quickly heeded.

"Sir, General Morgan's aide has arrived."

Nathanael stood, his face full of anticipation. "Show him in." A sudden fearful silence came over every man within headquarters as a mud-splashed major stepped into Nathanael's chamber and offered a salute. His face was aglow even through the smudged dirt. "General Greene, I got here just as quickly as I possibly could."

Nathanael dared not trust the bright countenance—he needed to hear the words.

"General Morgan sends his compliments, sir, and his congratulations. We did Tarleton infinite damage—the victory was complete, sir. Only Tarleton and a handful of his cavalry escaped. We counted 110 British dead, and took 700 prisoners. Our booty consists of two cannon, 800 muskets, 100 horses, thirty-five wagons of baggage, a great quantity of ammunition and even sixty slaves."

"Our losses, Major?"

"Only twelve killed and sixty wounded, sir."

The silence continued as Nathanael slowly lowered himself into his chair. He gazed at the major; his own face somewhat contorted as if in a state of utter shock. He opened his mouth to speak, but nothing came. Taking a deep breath, he tried again.

"Praise be given." He uttered just above a whisper. A jubilant smile took hold of his face. "God bless Dan Morgan!" he exclaimed with joyful laughter; then leaning his head back, he closed his eyes and cupped his hands over his face, repeating the words quietly—passionately.

"Gentlemen, there is great cause for celebration!" he yelled, giving permission for the pent-up excitement in them all to explode.

In anticipation of Cornwallis' retaliation, Dan Morgan's aide informed Nathanael that the army was quickly put to march to assure a safe distance between the opposing armies. General Morgan respectfully requested assistance as a major confrontation was inevitable.

Though the grand celebration of Morgan's victory continued throughout the camp, within headquarters it was short-lived. The army needed to reunite as quickly as possible. Plans were put into motion to decamp. A route of march was mapped out. Officers were summoned to receive their orders. Supply wagons were made ready. Orders were given to the Quartermaster's Department to retrieve boats and find a safe place to hide them on the various rivers that might be crossed. Finally, the call went out to the militia.

It was estimated that there were well over a thousand men in North Carolina alone who had joined a local militia company. Few companies would commit themselves to any enlistment time with the Continental Army. Yet, when the call went out in a moment of desperation such as this, they were duty-bound to turn out. Shaky and undisciplined as they were—their numbers had the potential to offer great assistance.

Within a matter of days, the army was in readiness to assist General Morgan. After putting the march under the command of Brigadier General Isaac Huger,

Nathanael set out with Lewis Morris, a guide and a sergeant's guard of dragoons, determined to reach the militia rendezvous point without delay. From there he would lead the assembled militia companies to Morgan and await the arrival of General Huger and the remainder of his men.

Though implored not to make the dangerous 125-mile trek, virtually alone, through Tory-infested country, Nathanael felt he must risk the journey to save the army. Therefore, he set out for the rendezvous point of Salisbury, North Carolina. The journey was hard pressed as the bleak clouds of January threatened that which those native to the southlands had warned him of—the torrential winter rains.

Twenty-four hours later, he arrived in Salisbury only to discover that the call for militia, a call that should have brought forth over a thousand fighting men, went unheeded. The consuming fear of leaving their homes defenseless to Tory invasion paralyzed the members of the militia companies leaving Nathanael in a deadly predicament.

Without the anticipated militia companies, the downcast, anxious commander and his small company trudged on, the threatening clouds finally unleashing their torrents of rain.

Nathanael had studied numerous maps the previous night putting to memory the vast area from where Morgan's men waited, northward to the Virginia border. Now, as they rode, he questioned his guide thus taking in every bit of information the maps failed to relay. He made mental plans for the only move that could save his desperate army from total disaster—a retreat that would cover approximately one hundred miles. A retreat that must be carefully planned and skillfully maneuvered through these torrential downpours, in ankle deep mud at times, and across four swollen rivers with the promise of Cornwallis' vultures at their heels. A retreat that must be providentially protected or it would bring absolute destruction.

The gloomy winter sky turned black as night fell. The rain continued to plummet down upon the cold and weary travelers offering no show of mercy.

"The tavern is just ahead, sir," the guide informed Nathanael, pointing to a dimly lit house in the distance.

A place of sanctuary, Nathanael thought, longing for the warmth the sight of it promised. The guide had assured him that it was owned by a family devoted to the cause of liberty.

We can rest, he thought, already relaxing in anticipation of the temporary haven this oasis offered. As they dismounted before the front gate, Nathanael ordered the dragoons to tend to the horses. He then followed the guide through the gate toward the front door with young Lewis Morris at his side.

The three stepped into the warmth; their bodies shivering uncontrollably as water steadily dripped from their capes and hats.

"Mr. Clemens, we have been expecting you," an elderly, though robust, man called to the guide from across the room. A small, hunched, white-haired woman stood at his side.

"General Greene, may I introduce you to Mr. Benjamin Steele and his wife. Mr. Steele, this is General Nathanael Greene and his aide Major Morris," the guide announced as he removed his waterlogged tricorne.

"What! You are alone, General Greene?" the astonished tavern keeper exclaimed.

"Yes, tired, hungry, alone and penniless," was Nathanael's soft reply.

"Please, General, come! We will make ready a hot bath for you," the tavern keeper gestured to a room behind him. "Please, sir, you must get out of that wet clothing before you catch your death!"

Nathanael caught a glimpse of Lewis Morris. There was uncertainty in the aide's countenance. It was his duty to protect his commander, and he was not comfortable with this situation. Lewis looked over his shoulder toward the door, no doubt anxious for the guards to appear.

"You are safe here, General. I assure you," the trustworthy guide said softly, aware of the hesitancy.

"Please, General. Both you and your aide. We have two tubs and more than enough hot water prepared," the old man urged.

Nathanael sank down in the tub, limp within the warmth of its healing power. He closed his eyes allowing his mind to rest for a moment—if only for a moment. *There is no rush*, he told himself, *nowhere to go—of course, there are letters to write—there are always letters to write.*

His thoughts wandered to a time long, long ago; a place that existed no more. He envisioned a crackling hearth, and seated close to its warmth was his mother. The dancing flames threw shadows upon that face of which he loved to look. And, except for the small boy snuggled close by her side, she was alone. *How rare to have her all to yourself*, Nathanael thought, remembering in detail the wonder of that moment in time when all the things that could ever frighten so small a boy seemed not to matter. For in her arms there was comfort. One could be forever content therein—and suddenly she was gone. It had been weeks months since he stole a thought of her. He was eleven-years-old when she died—eleven and confused and frightened. Never did he experience that all-encompassing sense of comfort again. Never had the security he had known prior to her death been felt in his life—until now.

Here in this place, for some reason, he knew he was safe. It went beyond the kindness of this old man and woman—beyond the watchfulness of his aide and guards. It went well beyond their abilities and strength; and, though he sensed in his being that great personal danger lurked ever so close, there was a confidence in Nathanael that celestial troops had been called out to do that which human capability could not.

"The horses are ready, sir," the dragoon officer announced. Nathanael nodded and turned to his host.

"Mr. Steele, how can I ever thank you and your gracious wife for your warm hospitality?"

"There is no need, General Greene. It is the least we can do."

"Might I ask one last favor of you, sir?" Nathanael asked, a twinkle in his eyes.

"By all means, General. What is it?"

Nathanael looked at the portrait of King George III above the dining room mantle. "Might I leave my mark on the back of that?"

Mr. Steele smiled, for the portrait was only kept as a measure to pacify the many Tories that came through the tavern. "Please do, General."

Rising, Nathanael walked to the hearth and removed the portrait. Carefully laying it face down on an empty table, he turned back to the fireplace and grabbed a piece of cold charcoal. With it, he wrote on the back of the canvas, "O George, hide thy face and mourn."

Lifting the portrait, he replaced it with the king's face to the wall. "Feel free to turn it when I leave, sir." Nathanael said with a smile of satisfaction.

"No, General. I think it looks much better as is."

Grinning, Nathanael reached out to shake his hand.

"God bless you, General Greene."

"And may He abundantly bless you and your wife, sir." Nathanael spotted the old woman near the door, obviously amused by the new placement of the portrait. In her hands were two small sacks.

"What might that be, Mrs. Steele?" Nathanael asked, certain it was food; for her husband had informed him that she had prepared victuals for the day's journey.

"Money—not much, a piddling in fact, but I want you to have it."

"Money?" Nathanael was astonished.

"Last night you said you were tired, hungry, alone and penniless. We were able to fill your stomach, offer a warm bath and bed, and even ease your loneliness with our poor company. But as to your being penniless?" she held the bags out to him.

"Dear lady, I cannot take your savings. Nay. I should pay thee, and intend to urge Congress to do just that. Thee have warmed us, fed us, and offered us a restful night's sleep. My uniform has been washed and pressed—even missing buttons replaced on this thread-worn waistcoat," he exclaimed glancing down at the many buttons on his vest. "I do not know when we shall again enjoy the comfort and luxury we experienced here. Nay. It is I that am indebted to thee, my friend."

"Please take this, General." she replied, her eyes glistening with tears. "It will give our old hearts great joy to know you and your traveling companions have it should you be in such need again."

Nathanael looked at her husband who nodded his approval; then taking the bags from her hands, he bent to kiss her wrinkled cheek. "Pray for me and my men, Mrs. Steele." he whispered.

"I have, and I will continue to. On that you may depend," she softly replied. Then reaching up and cupping his cheek with her hand, she added, "And now it is no longer just you and your men, but your sweet, lonely Caty and your four precious babies."

He smiled affectionately at her. She had captured his heart with her motherly attentiveness in much the same way Martha Washington had—ever sensitive to the things dearest to him.

"We must be on our way," he said taking the cape Mr. Steele now held for him and draping it across his shoulders. "Thank you both again." He took his tricorne from Mr. Steele, placed it on his head and stepped out into the cold, misty dawn.

"General Greene," Lewis Morris immediately called to him, stepping away from the dragoon officer. "Sir, a rider just passed through—one of our operatives. It seems that last night Tarleton and his dragoons scattered 300 of our militia marching toward the rendezvous point, General."

"Don't fret, Lewis. Three hundred militia is 700 short of what we need to face Cornwallis. I would have had to send them home anyway." He moved toward his waiting horse as he continued speaking. "Between you and me, who can blame the others for not showing up? They have suffered too long with the army unable to even defend their homes. They do not believe we can stand against Cornwallis; and, the sad thing is that without them we cannot."

"That is not it, sir—I mean that is not what has me concerned."

Nathanael turned away from the horse. "What has you concerned, Lewis?"

"The place where Tarleton intercepted the militia was but five miles from here. As we slept, sir, Colonel Tarleton and his dragoons were but five miles away! Had he known you were here—"

Nathanael laid his hand on the shaken aide. "In what direction did they head?"

"West, sir. Back toward the British main force."

"Very good. No doubt you have read the story of the prophet Elijah praying that the Lord might open the eyes of his apprentice."

"Yes, of course, sir."

"And do you remember what the apprentice saw when the Lord granted that request?"

"The army of the Lord surrounding them."

"That is right. Know this, Lewis, and never doubt it—we have experienced that same protection and will again, I am sure." Nathanael smiled, patted his shoulder and then mounted his horse, gesturing for the awestruck aide to do the same.

The moment he entered the room Dan Morgan and William Washington understood the gravity of the situation. Not a breath was wasted as Nathanael threw his hat on the table, received their salutes, then offered a heartfelt, though hasty congratulations to his victorious officers, and immediately turned to the maps Lewis Morris laid out on the table before them.

"We are heading to the Dan River," he announced, tracing the river, which separated North Carolina from Virginia. "Boats await us, and Cornwallis will not be able to follow. General Huger's troops should reach Guilford in two days," he said, pointing to the town on the map. "We will set out by dawn of the following day."

"Begging the General's pardon, but this is madness, sir!" Dan Morgan blurted in astonishment.

"I do not see that we have any choice."

"We certainly do have a choice, General. Look here." Morgan exclaimed, pointing to the mountains to the west. "Take the army here, and they will be safe from Cornwallis."

"To what end, General Morgan? It is not my intention to achieve a permanent retreat from the enemy. I intend to fight, but I cannot do that without reinforcements. The mountains will not achieve that goal, but Virginia will. I received word from General Steuben that General Lafayette is en route to Virginia with three regiments. If we deploy men from Lafayette, and convince the Virginia militia companies to join us—"

"If we can get over the Dan River without Cornwallis destroying us first. It is a most dangerous scheme, General!" Morgan argued.

"If we do not gather strength, we cannot do battle with Cornwallis; and he will move into Virginia himself, cutting off the South from the rest of the country. We must act boldly now, or hand Virginia, the Carolinas, and Georgia over to the British."

"I will not be answerable for what might happen in this race to Virginia." Morgan warned, fire in his eyes.

Nathanael met his fiery gaze with one of solid, confident determination. "No, you will not, for I shall take the full responsibility upon myself."

"Many men have staked their reputations on your ability to save the South, but this scheme—"

Nathanael brought his fist down hard on the table startling both Dan Morgan and William Washington.

"That is enough, General Morgan! I am not concerned about the rash gamble of their reputations—or for my own at the moment. I am concerned with the lives of my men, and the liberty of the South. You may not agree with my decision, but it stands just the same."

"—I suppose it is of no concern to me anyway," Morgan muttered almost defiantly, avoiding Nathanael's gaze. "It is not even my place to comment, sir, as it is my intention, and has been prior to your arrival, to request leave."

"For what reason?" Nathanael asked, seemingly in control of himself, though fuming within.

"Sciatica, sir. I am afflicted so badly at present that I can barely sit upon my horse for the sheer pain."

Nathanael was astounded by the sudden request. "Sciatica—" he echoed the word.

"Yes. It has plagued me off and on for a few years, triggered by the cold."

"Have you seen a physician?"

"Nothing they can do. Only time and rest will mend it."

"I need you, General Morgan," Nathanael stated through clenched teeth.

"I will be of no value to you as is, sir. I will not be able to keep up with the troops."

"I can deny you leave," Nathanael threatened.

"You can certainly do that, sir, but that will not change the fact that I will be unable to ride with the army. Colonel Washington can verify my condition, as can the camp doctor."

Nathanael turned to the burly William Washington.

"I have witnessed his discomfort since our encounter with Tarleton. I know the doctor was summoned, and I know General Morgan was forced to ignore his recommendation for bed rest in order to get the men to safety," the colonel stated.

Nathanael remained silent for a moment. "Please leave us, gentlemen," he finally said to William Washington and Lewis Morris. Visibly troubled by Dan Morgan's announcement, he positioned himself by a window that overlooked the encampment, and gazed silently at the activity outside.

"I was depending on your assistance—" he finally uttered softly, controlled but somehow unpredictable.

"I am aware of that, sir. Though I question your strategy, General, I would put my all into it if I could stay, and I wish I could stay—it will be some challenge to beat Cornwallis to that river."

Nathanael offered him a blank stare and no more.

"I have some advice which I think will be helpful, sir."

There was no response, just the same distant, empty stare. Undaunted, Morgan continued.

"You have some fine officers in Harry Lee, William Washington and Otho Williams—colonels all three, but they will out general any brigadier you presently have in your command. I suspect you are already sensible to that fact—" He suddenly seemed uncomfortable under the steady, deathlike gaze. Morgan cleared his throat and continued. "—As for the militia—we know they are not dependable under fire. They are never dependable under fire, but we have a number of former Continentals presently in the militia ranks. I was able to take advantage of these seasoned men in my frisk with Tarleton. Put the former Continentals now in the militia with the regulars to strengthen their line. Be sure to spell out what you expect from the militia—three volleys then they can fall back. If you make them understand that is all you want from them, they somehow find the courage to endure. Do not get me wrong—you will probably only get two volleys—but two solid volleys from a militia line is remarkable." Morgan smiled weakly and shrugged, choosing now to be amused by the cowardly performance of the militia lines than infuriated, as he and so many field officers were in the heat of battle.

Nathanael did not share the smile.

"It proved highly effective against Tarleton," he added.

"I will keep it in mind, General." There was a distance in Nathanael's tone.

"I intend to help you get the troops under way before I depart," Morgan offered. "Will you need an escort?"

"No, sir. I will not trouble you for such. I will move slowly, but I will manage."

"This is a temporary leave, General Morgan."

"I understand, sir. I will report for duty just as soon as I am able."

Nathanael took a deep breath. "I have much to attend to," he said, and walked past Dan Morgan toward the door, picking up his hat as he passed the table.

"General Greene." Morgan called as Nathanael reached for the doorknob. Nathanael stopped, but did not turn.

"I admire your determination, sir, and I am sorry to be leaving you under such conditions."

"So am I, General Morgan—so am I—"

"...Without baggage, necessaries, or provisions of any sort for officer or soldier...it was resolved to follow Greene's army to the end of the world."
(British General Charles O'Hara)

CHAPTER SEVENTEEN

THOUGH AWARE THAT the figures lay before him were accurate—having doubled checked every fact presented—still a disquieting, lingering doubt continued to trouble him.

"I have got the rebel," he muttered to himself, staring at the map; but no smile of satisfaction accompanied the victorious statement—only an uncertainty in it all.

He stood and, slowly moving from the table, limped toward the door, considering for a brief moment how this miserable, cold, damp winter made his knee stiffer than usual. When he reached the threshold, he impatiently—uncharacteristically—yelled at his aide, "Where is Colonel Tarleton?"

Startled, the young officer jumped to his feet at full attention. "He has been summoned, your Lordship. I should expect him—"

Even as he spoke, Banastre Tarleton entered the room, his plumed hat carefully tucked under his arm. He immediately saluted his commander.

General Cornwallis considered him for a moment—the musty odor of his wet, wool cape, his muddied boots, cheeks and nose red from the crisp winter air. Cornwallis received the salute. "What have you to tell me, Colonel?" he asked, noting the usual gleam—the sadistic gleam that Cornwallis so often saw reflected in the eyes of this twenty-six year-old aristocrat had dimmed.

"The rebel has managed to get his troops, baggage, and even a fair number of civilians, including the governor of South Carolina, safely across the Yadkin River, sir."

"Governor Rutledge is with Greene? Why?"

"I am not certain, sir, but I imagine the rebel governor, like the civilians that have attached themselves to Greene, fear our retaliation."

"How is it possible that they have already crossed the river?" Cornwallis demanded.

"It would seem, your Lordship, that he had boats awaiting them."

"And have you ordered boats gathered?"

"I have, sir, but it will do us little good at present. This rebel seems to be the child of fortune. His timing was perfect. The rain has caused the river to swell to the point of being unfordable. If the rain ceases, we may be able to cross by morning."

Frustrated, Lord Cornwallis turned and walked back into the room. He stood at the table mesmerized by the map before him.

"The remainder of Greene's troops are en route to rendezvous with him. The call for militia went unheeded. He cannot chance a confrontation—he would not risk a confrontation under the circumstances. So what is it he has planned?" He grew silent, his attention still fixed on the map. "—He is headed for Virginia." he muttered, the sudden realization chasing his former uncertainty away.

"If that is so, my Lord, he has a five-to-six days' march to the Dan River. Then he will have the river itself to contend with, bringing him to a dead halt while boats are gathered. And if it has risen as much as the Yadkin presently is, then you will have your prey, my Lord, with his back to the river." The sadistic gleam had returned to Tarleton's eyes.

"A desperate man could make the march in four days," Cornwallis softly replied.

"I do not believe that would be possible, sir." Tarleton replied.

Slowly Lord Cornwallis looked up at him. "If I were Greene, I would do everything in my power to make it in four days."

"Let us hope that Greene does not think like you, your Lordship, for it will not be possible for us to follow in full force at that speed."

"If we were not burdened with baggage—if our entire force moved as light troops."

"What do you propose we do with our baggage, sir?"

"Burn it."

Tarleton was taken aback by the order. "—Begging the General's pardon—burn our baggage, sir? We are over a hundred miles from our supply base—"

"What do you know of General Greene?" Cornwallis asked determinedly.

"Not much, sir. He is among Washington's intimates; he served two years as quartermaster general; he was a blacksmith by trade and a Quaker by religion," he snickered.

Cornwallis held his subordinate under a stern gaze. "He is an ironmaster. He is Washington's favorite. Moreover, he successfully commanded a division in six major battles—even while serving as quartermaster general. Know your enemy,

Colonel—always know your enemy. This man Greene is a master strategist and dangerous to us. He proves to be my nemesis. I have faced him in various encounters—and once, early on, I devastated him."

Tarleton's curiosity was obviously stirred.

"I laid siege to a fort he held on the Hudson River. It fell in short order giving up over 2,000 prisoners."

"Fort Washington, sir?" Tarleton asked with a smirk.

Cornwallis nodded.

"From what I heard the rebels did not offer you much of a fight, your Lordship."

"No, they did not."

"And Greene commanded?"

"He did."

"Well, my Lord, how masterful can he be in his strategy? I have not doubted that your abilities are far superior to that ironmaster's. Such an incident only further proves it." Tarleton boasted.

"It was a costly mistake on his part—a mistake which would naturally bring a desire for vengeance. Vengeance causes a man's thinking to be clouded at times. On this, I am depending. When Greene's need for revenge gets the better of him, then he will be mine."

Tarleton smiled. "Their encampment is within cannon range though a ridge protects them from any serious damage. Have you any orders in this regard, sir?"

"By all means, Colonel. Let us at least disrupt their rest."

"My pleasure, your Lordship." he said with a cunning grin.

The sound of the British cannonade came as no surprise to Nathanael. Detecting apprehension in some of the officers congregated, he said, "Don't be alarmed, gentlemen. The ridge to the south of us will effectively block all fire. The only thing they may hit is a roof top, and that with little damage." His tone was confident, having determined the possibility of being hit by damaging cannon fire before encamping.

"Why in the world are they wasting ammunition?" Colonel William Washington asked.

"Because they have a perpetual supply and nothing better to do than harass us." the artillery commander replied with notable envy.

"They do mean to harass us, gentlemen, but as for a perpetual supply—" Nathanael passed behind his artillery officer and patted him on the shoulder. He pulled the window open and listened for a moment. Then, turning to his officers, he continued. "As for their perpetual supply, if we successfully draw them northward, they will be distant enough from their supply base to put us on somewhat equal terms. Soon they will find themselves as low on powder, lead, canister and ball as we perpetually find ourselves. Are there any more questions or comments, gentlemen?"

The men had nothing more to ask or say.

"Very well. See to your duties. We will leave at first light—and do your best to get some sleep, you'll need it." The men filed out leaving Nathanael alone with his aides and secretary. He immediately walked to the dining room table, and sat down, picked up the awaiting pen, and, upon dipping it in the ink, began adding words to a letter already started.

"And do you suppose General Greene will get any sleep tonight?" Rob Burnet asked Lewis Morris with a whimsical smile.

"I doubt it, yet there's little his trusted aides can do to remedy that—short of being accused of nagging the man. But, the question more paramount to me at the moment is, will General Greene's staff get any sleep?"

Nathanael looked up and returned their expectant smiles.

The sudden arrival of General Isaac Huger's aide-de-camp prevented Lewis from discovering the General's thoughts on the matter.

"Word from General Huger, sir." the aide announced with a salute. "The general sends his compliments and wishes you to know that he expects to be at the appointed rendezvous point of Guilford Court House by noon tomorrow."

"Very good," Nathanael said, directing his attention back to the letter he was working on. "Ride back to General Huger and extend to him my compliments. Tell him I am pleased with the report," he said without looking up.

As Nathanael finished speaking, there was a fearsome crash on the roof above. Huger's aide and the secretary jumped as Rob and Lewis dashed off, aware that a cannon ball had made impact. One bound up the stairs to determine the damage as the other ran outside to ascertain the situation.

Nathanael went back to writing, seemingly undaunted by the hit. Rob quickly reappeared in the room. "Sir, there is no damage to the second floor." Even as he spoke, another ball hit the roof sending shingles flying to the ground.

Lewis ran into the room gasping for breath. "Could they possibly know you are in this house? How could they know, General?"

"We simply chose a house that's a perfect target, gentlemen," Nathanael replied as another ball hit.

Freedom's Cost

"Do you wish another house made ready, sir?" Rob asked.

"No, I do not think they will keep this up too much longer. No sign of fire, is there?"

"No, sir. But I have men standing by just in case."

Nathanael nodded. "Go reassure the owner of the house that only minimal damage is expected," he said to Lewis. Then turning to the letter on the table, he spotted General Huger's aide. "Is there something more you need, Major?" he asked.

"No, sir. I will be on my way now, General," the Major said, astonished with the calmness displayed by the commander.

As the major walked out of the room, stopping in the foyer to accept some bread, a wedge of cheese and a mug full of steaming coffee from the mistress of the house, he heard the commander speak to his staff.

"Please make three copies of this, Captain," Nathanael said to the secretary handing him the letter he had just finished. "One marked for General Washington, one for Congress, and one for my file."

"Yes, sir." the secretary replied.

"I need post riders," he said to Rob. "I will have dispatches for Generals Marion, Sumter and Pickens. I want three separate riders. We will have Marion and Sumter keep the Tories from reinforcing Cornwallis, and work on cutting off all communications with his base at Charleston. Pickens, I pray, can pull together a few hundred militia from South Carolina to trail Cornwallis' rear and harass him while we make our retreat."

"I will get the riders, sir," Rob said with a satisfied smile.

"And have another standing by. I will have a dispatch ready for Governor Jefferson and General Steuben within the hour. The sooner reinforcements and supplies are gathered in Virginia, the quicker we can turn on Cornwallis and draw him in."

"Excellent, sir." Rob stepped into the foyer, closing the door behind him. He smiled at Huger's aide who was hastily devouring his meager victuals.

"Not much of a meal is it." Rob commented, grabbing his cape and tricorne.

"—It will keep me going for another four hours," the aide replied appreciatively.

Rob nodded, having been in his place on frequent occasions.

Both men walked outside to their waiting horses as another cannon ball flew above their heads.

"How long have you been serving as General Greene's aide, Major?" Huger's aide asked as he grabbed hold of his saddle and mounted the horse.

"Three years," Rob replied, doing the same.

The aide nodded staring at the window where Nathanael's office was. "I have been in the Southern Department for quite a while—long enough to witness defeat after defeat. Too long to have any more hope of—" He turned his head to look at Rob. "I had lost all hope that we could take back the South. General Greene has managed to rekindle the hope of many men in this department that had long given up. I am more skeptical than most, but, Burnet—do you honestly think there's a chance?"

Rob smiled—it was a weak smile, but sure. "We have an uphill battle before us. Be sure of this, Nathanael Greene has no delusions about how deplorable our situation is. But, yes, Major. Yes, I do believe there is now a chance."

Nathanael failed to hear the voice of the guards as they questioned the lone rider who appeared in the wee hours of the morning. He failed to hear them rouse Rob Burnet and explain the situation to him. He only heard the loud rap on his bed-chamber door, stirring him from a sound sleep. Groggily he opened one eye, try-ing to focus on the darkened form entering the room.

"I am sorry to wake you, sir, but one of our operatives, Mr. Clarence Davison, just arrived with intelligence from the British camp," Rob announced.

Nathanael lay still for a moment, attempting to get his sluggish mind and body to respond. By the flickering light of the single candle in Rob's hand, Nathanael could see that the aide was no better rested than he was—and like himself still fully clothed.

He struggled to sit on the edge of the bed, and then slowly ran his hand over his face. "What time is it?" he murmured.

"Three o'clock, sir. Did you even get an hour's sleep?"

"About that—show the man in—"

Rob left, and upon returning with the informant, he found the room well lit and the commander seated at the table.

"Mr. Davison, good morning, sir," Nathanael said with a warm, although tired smile as he extended his hand to the man.

Davison returned the handshake. "Good morning, General. I am sorry to dis-turb you, sir, but I must act while the British sleep."

"I understand, and you need not apologize. Please sit down and tell me what information you have discovered."

Davison sat down just as a guard came to the door with a tray carrying a mug of coffee for each man present. Rob took the coffee from him and closed the door.

Then, after serving both Nathanael and Mr. Davison their mug, the conversation continued.

"Lord Cornwallis ordered the destruction of all baggage and wagons, save ammunition and medical supplies," Davison said, then took a sip of the steaming brew.

Nathanael shared a concerned glance with Rob. "That explains the smoke reported from their camp," Rob commented.

"Yeah, there was a good deal of smoke—the baggage was burned, including General Cornwallis'." Davison informed them.

"He ordered his own baggage destroyed?" Nathanael was shocked, for it was virtually unheard of that a British general would destroy his personal belongings.

"He did, sir. Word is he means to race you to the Dan River, and force a battle."

"He already has it figured?" Rob seemed surprised by the news, though Nathanael was not.

"We are up against Britain's best, Major. I would expect him to have it figured out by now. What I did not anticipate was the baggage being destroyed this far from their supply base. Lord Cornwallis means to win this race, gentlemen." Nathanael said.

"That he does, sir. In fact, not only has he turned his entire force into light troops by burning the supplies, but all horses taken from the wagons are to be mounted with two riders," Davison added.

"How high is the Yadkin River?" Nathanael asked.

"Treacherous enough for one man." Davison replied, having just made the dangerous crossing. "It is much too high still to risk crossing an army. It does not appear to be dropping fast enough to make it fordable for another twelve to twenty-four hours."

"That is good to hear. We will be able to put a fair amount of time between us. Is there anything else I should know, Mr. Davison?"

"No, sir. That is it."

"Very well. Thank you, sir." Nathanael said standing and again shaking the informant's hand. "I am quite dependent on the information you gather, sir. Operatives, especially in such a situation as the Southern Department finds itself in, are the eyes and ears of a commander. Without you I am virtually groping in the dark."

"Thank you, General." Davison replied appreciatively.

"It is the truth, sir. Major Burnet, see that Mr. Davison is reimbursed for his trouble."

"Of course, sir," Rob said.

Lewis Morris stepped into the room just as the two men were preparing to leave. Nathanael noted his apparent confusion. "Lewis, are you well rested?" he asked, a hint of a smile upon his face.

"It is only three o'clock, General."

"Indeed it is."

"No, sir. I cannot say that I am," Lewis replied with an uncontrollable yawn.

"I am sorry to hear it, lad, because we are breaking camp."

"Now, sir?" he asked dumfoundedly.

"Get the word out, Major. Get the boys roused. I intend to march in an hour. Have all senior officers report to me at once."

"What about the rendezvous with General Huger, sir?"

"General Huger was hoping to rest his men at Guilford Court House. We will meet him there earlier than was planned. There will be no time for rest though. We will march until nightfall."

"Sir?"

"Cornwallis intends to race us to the Dan, and the very life of this army depends on who wins this race. Carry on, Major."

"Yes, sir."

"And, Lewis."

"Sir?"

"See that our civilian friends are made ready for the march. And tell Governor Rutledge that he is welcome to attend the council with my senior officers."

"Yes, sir."

After reuniting with General Huger's force Nathanael again called a council of his senior officers to fully prepare for the grueling march ahead. They had 2,000 troops, with baggage, and a following of frightened civilians to move over eighty miles of wild, rugged terrain. Speed was of the utmost importance, for they were to be mercilessly pursued.

Tents were not to be pitched—for this would require too much time. A campfire's heat was to be the only protection offered against the January nights and bitter cold rain.

The ragged, tattered condition of his men was again brought to full realization upon seeing General Huger's troops. Many had no shoes to protect their feet, and such threadbare clothing as to expose their nakedness. At night, there were only enough blankets to provide one for every four soldiers. Thus, the men would be forced to take turns tending the fire while the others slept.

Even sleep was to be rationed—three hours allotted in every twenty-four. The day's march was to begin well before dawn. Then, after being pushed hard for a few hours, they were to stop and prepare breakfast—their only regular meal during this most hazardous retreat.

Deputy Quartermaster General Edward Carrington arrived at the rendezvous point with encouraging news. As per Nathanael's order, boats were awaiting the army at the lower Dan, the deepest, most treacherous part of the river. It was hoped that Cornwallis would assume this part of the river to be unfordable—unaware that a sufficient number of boats awaited Greene and his men. Thus Cornwallis would, in all likelihood, head for the upper river in an attempt to cut the American's off from the shallower waters.

Colonel Carrington also informed Nathanael that the earthworks he had ordered his engineer, Colonel Thaddeus Kosciuszko, to build on the north side of the river were well under way, standing ready to offer protection from the British once the river was crossed.

Light-Horse Harry Lee listened attentively as the orders for the march were given, wondering in his silence if it was humanly possible to accomplish this task. Then, as the deputy quartermaster gave his report, the dapper, young cavalry officer found himself in a state of utter amazement.

Such detail—such intricate detail arranged so far in advance. He thought with an awestruck gaze for his commander. *He had to have given those orders to Carrington and Kosciuszko weeks ago—before any of us even considered the great danger we might find ourselves in and this desperate need to retreat so far. The boats on the Yadkin and the Dan—the protection of the earthworks awaiting our arrival—Jefferson and Steuben already preparing reinforcements and supplies. And Greene's knowledge of this land—a place totally foreign to him, yet he speaks of the terrain before us as though he spent his boyhood upon it. Even those native to this area are amazed.* Harry thought as he looked at the awestruck faces of the officers present who called this region home. Then came the orders pertaining to Harry's boys, drawing his full attention.

"Cornwallis will no doubt attempt to flank our left in an attempt to beat us to the upper river. He's welcome to that position, but we must let him think that part of the river is our aim." Nathanael said pointing to the map set upon a stand so that the officers could have full view of it. "Colonel Williams, you will take command of General Morgan's detachment and flank to the left of the main army. This will put your elite force between Cornwallis and me. We will move parallel to one another— you being directly behind my rear guard. Stay in front of Cornwallis, drawing him to you. Hopefully he will believe you to be the rear guard of our entire force."

Nathanael pointed to a particular spot on the map. "At this juncture I will pull off to the lower river and cross the main army while you occupy Cornwallis, leading him further off course. I will send word to you when we are safely across. Then you are to pull away, hopefully confusing Cornwallis enough to be able to put some distance between the two forces."

Nathanael stopped pointing to the map and looked at Harry Lee. "Colonel Lee, your cavalry will accompany Colonel Williams' detachment. You will guard their rear. This means that you may be in contact with the enemy on numerous occasions. And it is my intention, Colonel, that any fighting remain confined to minor skirmishes between your boys and Cornwallis' advance guard."

Harry smiled and nodded. "My boys might just enjoy this minor maneuver, General."

Nathanael smiled back. "I hope and pray, Colonel Lee, that, when it is all said and done, we think on it as having been nothing more than a minor maneuver. Let us get started, gentlemen. You know where your troops are to fall in. Colonel Lee, it will be a few hours before you will need to set out. See that your men get some rest, they will need it."

"I will, sir."

Thus began the race to the Dan, which proved from the start to be every bit as grueling as was imagined. Their hardships were numerous: the cold, penetrating rain that chilled them to the core of their beings, the miry roads by day, packing mud upon their already heavy feet. As the sun settled into the western sky, the mud became rigid, slicing the raw soles of the many unfortunate enough to lack shoes.

The horses stumbled; the wagon wheels often became stuck in the thick mud. Nevertheless, on they trudged, hour after hour; so exhausted, so hungry that their minds ceased to comprehend the pain, thus allowing their bodies to continue moving—step after step after step.

As the men dropped to the ground by the campfire's warmth for their rationed sleep, Nathanael fell back with an aide to check on Colonel Williams' situation. Cornwallis had taken the bait thus far, staying parallel and directly behind Williams' detachment. So close were the opposing forces that the British front guard was almost constantly in sight of Harry Lee—often within musket range.

Harry related to Nathanael how a strange kind of affinity developed between the two opposing forces. There was a mutual interest not to fire on each other, thus the sight of one another became so relaxed and casual that a spectator would have believed them to be members of the same army.

On the second night, Nathanael, who had not slept for more than four hours in four days, found himself too exhausted to make the trip to Colonel Williams' encampment. Sending another officer in his stead, he agreed with the advice of his aides to take shelter along with Governor Rutledge in a nearby hut.

As they rode toward the hut, Governor Rutledge lamented his prior ignorance of the sufferings the army was often forced to endure. "I had no idea men could withstand such hardships—and yet I have barely heard a complaint. Valley Forge? Morristown? Was there any comparison to this, General Greene?"

Nathanael slid off his horse, momentarily dizzy he held to the saddle until his legs felt steady. "Compared to this, your Excellency, we lived in the lap of luxury. There simply is no comparison to this—"

Rob opened the door to the hut preparing to light the candle he had in his hand with the piece of flint in his pocket.

"Do not bother, Rob. We can see well enough," Nathanael said, stepping past him.

Both Nathanael and John Rutledge moved toward the bed, falling upon it, too exhausted to even pull down the musty bedding. Rob and Lewis quickly lit a small fire in the hearth, and dropped onto the floor beside it.

Nathanael laid still, his body too weary to move. Every fiber of his being desperately longed for sleep; yet, his companion tossed and turned—this way and that—continuously going from side to side driving Nathanael to distraction. He feared, above all else, that the dust in the musty bedding would be stirred enough to trigger his asthma. *Not that, Lord, please not that!* He pleaded in silence, growing more infuriated with each movement he felt.

"Would thee please be still, sir!" Nathanael finally called out.

"Me?" the governor immediately shot back, equally irritated. "I will move myself onto the floor if you do not find yourself a comfortable position, General!"

"I have been still since I lay on the bed, Governor."

Even as they barked at one another, the squirming continued; then, an inhuman squeal was heard from beneath the bedding. Both the men jumped to their feet, and together pulled back the blankets. Out from beneath the bedding came a frightened, squealing pig. It jumped from the bed and trampled over poor Rob and Lewis as it attempted to find a way of escape.

"Open the door!" Rob shouted to Lewis, who flying to the door threw it open, freeing the frantic animal.

Nathanael threw John Rutledge a bewildered glance, not completely certain in his state of total exhaustion whether this had really happened, or whether he was simply dreaming. Apparently, the other men were equally uncertain, for no one spoke a word. All four resumed their former positions, and almost immediately were fast asleep.

A dispatch from Colonel Williams reached Nathanael, well after darkness set in on the third day, informing him that Cornwallis was showing no sign of encamping for the night. The river was within a day's march; and Cornwallis, so it seemed, would offer the Americans no respite in his determination to trap them against the water.

Nathanael called for his senior officers, including Colonels Williams and Lee, and informed them that the march must continue through the night.

"The cover of darkness will offer us double protection for pulling off to the lower river. By morning light, we should reach the Dan. Colonel Williams, stay with Cornwallis until I instruct you to pull off."

"I will, sir."

"Colonel Lee, I need to have a word with you," Nathanael said as his officers walked to their waiting horses. Harry had been unusually quiet and noticeably distracted throughout the meeting. Perhaps he was only tired—he certainly had reason.

"Is something troubling you, Harry?"

Harry took a deep breath, grimaced and shrugged. "We encountered Tarleton and his demons today."

"Colonel Williams informed me. Only one casualty?"

"Yeah " Harry took another deep breath. "They got my bugler, General. He was brutally sabered and taken captive. They intended to hang him, but we managed to distract them and rescue the lad. He died in my arms—we were forced to leave his body in the woods "

"How old was he?" Nathanael asked, obviously moved.

"Sixteen, sir. He has been riding at my side for a year. He was a fine lad—a brave boy. No time to think on it now—we have a long night ahead. With your permission, sir, I will get back to my men."

Nathanael nodded, and watched his sad, young friend disappear into the darkness.

In the early hours of the morning of February 14.th, Nathanael Greene led his troops southward along the Dan River. The young Marylander, Colonel Otho Williams, with his detachment of 700 elite regulars, including the spirited help of Light-Horse Harry Lee's cavalry, continued to draw Cornwallis away.

Around noon of that same day, an eager messenger approached Otho Williams with the joyous news that General Greene was safely across the Dan. He immediately passed the word on to his weary men, that they might find strength. The pace increased as they changed direction, allowing them to miraculously put distance between themselves and the British front guard.

At dusk, they came upon the lower ford. Otho was delighted to find Colonel Carrington and the appointed oarsmen standing in readiness.

"How much time do we have, Colonel Williams?" Carrington called as he approached.

"I would say we have an hour's advance on them—not much more. Colonel Lee is hanging back to hold them off while we cross."

Carrington wasted no time, as he took charge of crossing the men and horses just as he had done that morning. Among the first passengers was the messenger Nathanael had sent to Otho with a return message that the remaining troops were now fording the river.

Upon receiving the news, Nathanael hurried down to the river's bank, anxiously watching—nervously anticipating the sound of musket fire signaling Cornwallis' approach.

No guns had yet fired when Otho Williams came across with the last of his men, after having sent word to Harry Lee to come forward.

Nathanael and Otho silently paced the river's bank together; ever fearful that time was against them. How far off could Cornwallis be? The two men watched in breathless silence as Harry and his boys galloped to the water's edge and immediately proceeded to tear the saddles from their horses' backs. Then slapping the animals hard upon the rump, they sent them into the water to cross on their own.

Encouraged on by Colonel Carrington, the men threw the saddles and their gear into the boats, and hurriedly tumbled in themselves shouting excitedly for the oarsmen to move out.

Now, especially, they found themselves utterly vulnerable should Cornwallis come upon them. Equally disturbed for their horses' safety as for their own, the men, including Light-Horse Harry and Colonel Carrington, urged the exhausted beasts on as they fought against the treacherously deep water.

When the boats pulled along the safety of the bank, Nathanael watched as though in a paralytic state while the men disembarked, most of them turning and running waist-deep into the frigid water to assist the animals up the embankment.

Partly from sheer exhaustion—mostly from utter joy and gratefulness, tears began to stream from Nathanael's eyes. "We made it—praise be to God, we made it!" he said just above a whisper.

He caught Otho Williams' glance, and smiled affectionately upon seeing the free-flowing tears from his Colonel's eyes. Reaching out, Nathanael laid his trembling hand upon Otho's shoulder.

Harry Lee sat down before a single flickering candle, determined to complete the entry in his journal before partaking in a well-deserved sleep. His stomach was full—the first time in four days. His mind was at ease, delighted in the fact that Cornwallis came to the river an hour after Harry's own boys crossed, only to find his sought-after quarry gone.

Harry thought back on the four-day march and marveled. It certainly was more than a minor maneuver, he thought with a sense of awe; and he suspected that it would go down in the annals of military history as a masterfully maneuvered retreat.

'*Generaling*,' he wrote in his journal, '*begins with infinite attention to detail! Only then can courage and brilliant tactics play their part. Thus ended this long, arduous and eventful retreat—Happily for these states, a soldier of consummate talents guided the destiny of the South—Destroy the army of Greene, and the Carolinas with Georgia inevitably become members of the British empire!*'

On the opposite bank of the river sat the arrogant Banastre Tarleton before a candle's light. His thoughts on the four-day ordeal were quite different. *Our baggage and wagons burned, our tents destroyed, our food supply non-existent—all the long, weary miles for what? Here we sit, two hundred miles from our supply base—any reinforcements well over a week's march off!*

He picked up his pen and dipping it in the ink began to write in his journal, '*Every measure of the Americans, during their march, was judiciously designed and vigorously executed—*'

"If I am indispensable, and no man is that, the hand of the Lord will cover me." (Nathanael Greene to his senior officers)

CHAPTER EIGHTEEN

A JOYFUL, EXHILARATING spirit enveloped the camp, and was encouraged by the commander. Yet at headquarters the business of recruiting more men, gathering supplies, and preparing to pursue Cornwallis in an attempt to weaken him, consumed every waking hour—and left precious few for sleep. Meals were eaten on the run. Sleep, when it was obtained, was only when the mind was too over wrought to consider another thought. Then, still fully clothed, the general and his staff fell onto their cots to be awakened a few, short hours later and take on the monumental task once more.

General Lafayette, encamped further north in an effort to drive Benedict Arnold out of Virginia, was ordered to immediately march 400 of his regulars to General Greene.

Colonel Lee, and his legion of 300, after a brief rest, was ordered back across the river to block all of Cornwallis' communications, and prevent any reinforcements from joining him.

General Steuben, Governor Jefferson and former Governor Patrick Henry worked tirelessly with Nathanael to draw out the militia.

Within two weeks, Nathanael Greene had under his command 4,500 men. Though the vast majority of this number was unstable militia, Nathanael still felt confident that it was time to face Cornwallis. Writing to George Washington, he exclaimed in regard to the anticipated battle, *'When both parties are agreed in a matter, all obstacles are soon removed!'*

Nathanael Greene agreed now that it was time to meet on the field of battle. The timing was of his choosing, as would be the site. He retraced his steps southward, through a series of elaborate maneuvers, intended to confuse Cornwallis of his intentions. Then Nathanael finally made his encampment back in the tiny village of Guilford—the exact spot from which he had begun his retreat. He had taken note that this was an ideal place to do battle—especially with as many militia companies as he now had.

The senior officers filed out of the courthouse, which served as temporary headquarters. Each one was desperate to steal a few hours' sleep before the dawn—before the battle line was drawn. William Washington quickly reappeared at the threshold, searching the room. When his eyes settled on an object in the corner, his face broke into an immediate smile.

"Light-Horse Harry is all in." he said softly.

Nathanael and his staff looked in the direction that held his attention. There sat Harry Lee, slumped over and seemingly unconscious. Nathanael smiled affectionately at the younger cavalry officer, and then turned the same smile on William. "He certainly has good cause. See if you can rouse him, boys."

Lewis walked to the chair and gently nudged Harry's shoulder. A firmer nudge was necessary.

Startled, Harry opened his eyes, obviously disoriented by his surroundings and especially the amused gazes of those around him. His bewildered gaze settled on Nathanael. "Did I fall asleep? Please forgive me, General—" he drowsily exclaimed, staggering to his feet.

"You were on patrol for more than twenty-four hours; then sat half the night through a council of war. I do not consider it an offense for you to fall asleep under such circumstances, Colonel."

"Thank you, sir. I guess I am a bit tired; a couple hours of sleep and I will be ready to ride." Harry assured him as he took his cape from Rob Burnet and wearily draped it about his shoulders.

"Would you see me to my camp, William? I do not seem to have my wits about me at present."

William chuckled. "I will carry you if need be, Harry. Come on." William placed his hand on Harry's back and guided him out the door.

Nathanael watched until they disappeared from his view. *There are no finer cavalry officers then these two—no braver men!* His thoughts were full of emotion, a common occurrence on the eve of a battle—especially when he was so in need of sleep himself. Such sentimentalism could interfere with sound judgment, and unsound judgment could lead to the needless death of many.

However, for now Nathanael decided to indulge a bit, aware that these two officers faced continual danger. For the cavalry were his scouts, keeping him informed of the enemies' position, and harassing them whenever possible. They had already faced skirmishes with the enemy in the last twenty-four hours. It was Harry that brought the news in that the entire British force was preparing to attack on the morrow. When the battle lines were drawn, Harry and William would be in the heat of it from start to finish. Warfare for the cavalry was hand-to-hand combat—phys- ically gruesome and thrillingly dangerous.

"Can we be of further assistance, sir?" Rob asked, interrupting Nathanael's thoughts, and drawing his immediate attention.

"No, gentlemen. You had better turn in."

"And will you be turning in, sir?" Lewis asked.

Nathanael smiled at his ever-attentive aides. "I will turn in soon," he replied.

Lewis' gaze remained on his commander. He cleared his throat and said, "Begging the General's pardon, but, sir, you've had very little sleep these past few nights. In all truth, sir, you have slept little for the past few weeks. Might I respect- fully suggest to the general that he go lie down—" The young aide appeared a bit unnerved by his own boldness.

Nathanael's smile was warm. "Thank you for your concern, Major. I will take your council under consideration."

Lewis nodded his head, embarrassed by the entire scene and sheepishly left the room.

Rob Burnet remained, his own stern gaze fixed on the general.

"Is there something wrong, Rob?" Nathanael asked.

"Yes, sir, there is."

"Would you care to share it?"

"Yes, sir, I suppose I should—General, I feel it is my duty—my responsibility to tell you how concerned we are for your health. You are not eating well—sir, I firm- ly believe that your table should have priority in being supplied instead of your habit of seeing that the men receive their rations first and then partaking in what is left. In the present mode, your allowance is often scantier than that of the oth- ers, compelling us to request food from the troops that you might be adequately nourished."

"I am sorry, Rob, I was not aware. This must cause you embarrassment—have the men been annoyed?"

"No, General, to the contrary. The men are in awe to think that their command- er would deprive himself so for their sake, and are always eager to sacrifice a por- tion of their own meager rations for you. As for Lewis and me—we would lay down our lives for you, sir. Surely you know this."

Deeply moved by his words, Nathanael remained speechless.

"General, your eye has flared up—it is obvious that it is troubling you," Rob con- tinued, causing Nathanael to instinctively reach up and brush his hand over the offending eye. "Lewis is right; you have not had a decent night's sleep in weeks— why you have not even had the opportunity to take off your clothing in that time."

"Few in this camp have," Nathanael, pointed out softly.

"None in this camp is under the intense strain you are under, sir," Rob's immediate reply came. "General, we cannot afford for you to become ill."

As he lifted his head, Nathanael met the unyielding gaze of his friend. "—I cannot will myself to sleep anymore than I can will another to."

"I understand that, sir. Will you at least lie down and rest?"

With a slow nod he replied, "Yes, Rob. I can promise you that much." True to his word, Nathanael trudged into the next room where his cot stood. Fully clothed he lay upon the bed, his mind repeatedly churning over the words spoken in the council of war. Reviewing the validity of the tactics he had settled on, he played out the endless torture of imagining every possible scenario.

Finally tiring of the infinite possibilities, he turned his thoughts toward home— so natural when alone in the stillness of the night, especially on the eve of a battle. These thoughts proved pleasant for a short time, as they always did. Then the agony of this lengthy, distant separation from his family took hold. It had been nine months since he last saw Caty and his sons — two years since he had seen his small daughters.

Two years! The reality of it hit very hard. Tiny Cornelia—he pictured the small creature in his mind. A month premature at birth, she was the smallest baby he had ever seen. Now she was two-years old—

He tried to shake the grievous thoughts of the years lost with his children. Their childhood was whisking by with precious few memories. Tossing and turning, he was unable to escape, and decided he must get up and write a letter to Caty. He walked into the next room then sat at the table and reached for a clean sheet of paper. Suddenly the realization hit that in his present frame of mind he could not write this letter. Too much of his heart would be shared with the pen and ink, and the risk of the enemy intercepting his personal letters was too great. The thought of his family being publicly humiliated through the publication of his most intimate correspondence to his wife was enough to squelch his desire.

"Another torture of this separation." he groaned, laying his head in his hands. "Even my heart's longings cannot be shared. My attempts to comfort her are so miserably feeble. There is so much more I wish to say—so much more—"

He stood, uncertain of what to do. Sleep was unobtainable; hence, his restless mind demanded activity. He walked into the foyer, and found his cape. Throwing it about his shoulders, he reached for his hat, then opening the door, stepped outside.

"—General Greene, sir." The startled guard came to full attention.

"At ease, Captain, at ease." Nathanael took a deep breath of the cold night air. The sweet fragrance of honeysuckle still lingered as a reminder that spring was fast approaching. Though seemingly preoccupied throughout the day with details of the topography, planned placement of troops and geometric positioning of artillery, he did enjoy the spring-like warmth, and the beauty of the dogwood and redwood against the pine and oak forest.

Now the earlier warmth was gone, and in its place was the realization that winter had not quite released its grasp. "That's all right," he murmured. "Moderately cool air is best to fight in. Keep it dry, Lord, just keep it dry"

"Sir?" the guard said.

"Nothing, Captain. I would like to make rounds."

"Will your aides attend you, sir?"

"The are asleep."

"Very well, sir. With your permission, General, I will get the horses."

Within a few minutes, they were on their way. The General stopped occasionally to speak to a sentry or offer a restless soldier a word of encouragement, but for the most part the camp was quiet.

They moved through Harry Lee's camp where Nathanael noted that, save for the sentries, there was not a soul stirring. Otho Williams' camp was the same; Isaac Huger's, William Washington's—and on he passed, working his way to the outpost commanded by Colonel John Greene.

Nathanael fully expected the officer to be awake and watchful having been posted in such a vulnerable location. As he approached the colonel's tent, he saw a lamp burning dimly within; but the only sound he heard was the deep, restful snore of a content man.

It was from a sense of sheer amazement that Nathanael dismounted, walked to the tent, and threw back the flap. Then squatting to enter, he stood by the cot peering at the stirring form.

The colonel focused on the darkened figure looming above. Upon recognizing it to be the commander, he quickly jumped to his feet.

"General Greene. What? —Um—is something wrong, sir?" he exclaimed somewhat disoriented.

"You were asleep, Colonel." Nathanael uttered in awe.

"Yes. Is there a problem, sir?" The colonel was obviously confused.

"How can you sleep when this post could suddenly find itself under attack?"

The colonel shrugged. "Why, General, we all knew you would be awake—" the ready reply came.

Stunned, Nathanael continued to gaze at the officer. Then, walking toward the doorway, he said, "Go back to sleep, Colonel. I am sorry to have disturbed you."

"Do you intend to remain awake, sir?" the colonel asked.

Nathanael turned to look at him, his hand grasping the side of the tent opening. He slowly nodded in reply.

"My sentries are posted, sir. The pickets are out there, watchfully alert. We know you are awake and watching as well. This adds to our sense of security—much like a father watching over his household. My remark was meant as a compliment, sir; but please, General, let us watch for you throughout the night."

Nathanael's gaze remained on him for a moment as he struggled within for a proper response. He never doubted that the colonel's initial remark was a compliment—it was, in fact, the greatest compliment he had ever received.

"—I thank you, Colonel," he finally uttered.

The strain of his insomnia was beginning to tell; and the test of his command ability in the Southern Department was yet to come.

"Let my mind be clear tomorrow, Lord," Nathanael silently prayed as he and the guard retraced their steps. Slowly making their way back to the courthouse, he reviewed the battle plans one more time. Dan Morgan's winning tactics would be implemented; the front line would be composed of the weaker North Carolina militia units, which numbered over a thousand men. They would have no cover, save a rail fence, and therefore would be forced to perform. Two rounds would be all that was expected—two rounds and then they could fall back to safety. To flank them on both sides would be Colonels Lee's and Washington's solid cavalry.

Behind this line and a cover of trees, would be the steadier Virginia militia about equal in number as the first line—those who had already been tested. Morgan suggested that this second line be given orders to shoot any man that ran from the first line, Nathanael reflected, turning the idea over in his mind briefly. He might scare them into thinking he had given such an order. Even George Washington had used this threat a time or two, but to actually call for it?

He had ordered the execution of a few men after a fair trial. In fact, upon taking command of the South he had ordered by way of example, such an execution for pillaging. But to shoot your own men in the back, even though their panic might cause a general rout? Within himself, he could not do it, so how could he demand it of another?

The second line will hold even if the first utterly fails—I pray God that the second line will hold! However, he was not at all sure—there was never any assurance where the militia was concerned.

Once the British make it past the militia lines, then their mettle will be put to the test. The third line is the strength of the Southern Department. Here the 1600 Continental troops will boldly take them on!

Nathanael's confidence suddenly waned. For within this third line was a regiment of new recruits from Maryland—every bit as untried and unpredictable as the front line of militia. *They will hold up!* He assured himself. *Flanked on both sides by veteran Marylanders and Virginians accompanied by the strength of artillery—trained by General Steuben himself! Of course, they will hold!* A deep sigh accompanied this thought causing the guard to look in his direction.

If the front line does not hold? I cannot risk the destruction or capture of this army. I cannot repeat General Lincoln's or Gates' mistakes! Lord God, give me a clear mind tomorrow—that is all I ask—give me a clear mind!

Before the sun's appearance in the cold, March sky above Guilford, William Washington and Harry Lee had roused their boys, and disappeared into the early morning's darkness. It was their job to locate Cornwallis, and report his progress.

Reveille sounded soon after the cavalry's departure, suddenly bringing the camp to life. Hurriedly the soldiers attended to the immediate duties of downing the tents and preparing the supply wagons to be moved to safety. With these necessary duties complete, and still no word from the cavalry, Nathanael ordered a hot breakfast be prepared to carry the men through the day.

Leisurely the soldiers sat about the fire's warmth, serenaded by the song of the cardinal and wren. Though many among the newly recruited militia and Continental units were unable to eat, the others slowly savored their meal, aware with each bite that it might be their last.

It was not until noon that the sound of gunfire was heard in the distance. Soon Harry Lee's courier arrived with news that the colonel had encountered the British front guard four miles out, and marching toward the American encampment. It was time.

The senior officers were called to the courthouse once more. Though a sense of confidence prevailed, the faces around the council table appeared grave. The men hesitated when Nathanael ordered them to return to their commands.

"Is there a problem, gentlemen?"

Otho Williams slowly stood to his feet and cleared his throat. Silence filled the room. The young colonel avoided Nathanael's gaze as he began to speak.

"Sir, it is our most urgent wish that you not expose yourself in this battle, as is your custom. Might we remind the general how much depends on his remaining at his post? There is not one of us who could not be replaced; but if we were to lose you, sir, this army would crumble."

Stunned by Otho's words, Nathanael remained speechless for a moment.

"I thank you, gentlemen. Your concern is greatly appreciated, and truly touching. But, if you want a general who commands a battle from behind the lines, then you should have hung on to Horatio Gates   If I am indispensable, and no man is that, then the hand of the Lord will cover me   To your posts, gentlemen."

By the time the cavalry returned, the troops were already in battle formation. They took up their positions on the left and right flanks of the front line, and then eagerly devoured the food that was prepared for them as their senior officers reported to headquarters.

The ease and confidence of Harry Lee's legion fascinated the frightened militia units. The troops close enough to observe them were in awe of their carefree manner. Unhurriedly they watered, and some even brushed down, their horses. Then, tired from their early morning ride, many of them sprawled out on the ground next to their beloved beasts, undaunted by the enemy's approach. Indeed, Harry's legion knew exactly how far the enemy was, and had already calculated in their minds how long it would take them to arrive. Beyond that, they had already bloodied their sabers this morning—had, in fact, bloodied them on numerous occasions these past few weeks. Since they patrolled as frequently as they did, an encounter with the enemy was a common occurrence—nothing to waste a worried thought on.

The approach of riders from the rear did not disturb the slumbering cavalry in the least, though it drew the attention of the militia line. Six riders approached; and the sight of a general's flag, the flag carried into each battle to identify the particular general officer on the field, revealed to the militia that their commander was paying them a visit. Suddenly looking alert, they awaited him, their hearts pounding in anticipation.

Nathanael reined in his horse before the senior militia officer and received his salute. After briefly speaking with him, he turned the horse about and accompanied by his aides, as well as Colonels Lee and Washington, and the militia officer, he rode down the line, smiling confidently and encouraging the men.

"Hold this line, men, and the day is ours! Three rounds, boys! Give them three rounds and then you may fall back!" he yelled to them—in truth only expecting two. Then he rode off with his aides and standard-bearer as William Washington returned to his own troops on the right flank, leaving Harry Lee to calm the militia's fears as he moved back along the line.

"Stand firm boys, and do not be afraid!" he shouted. "I tell you I whipped the British three times this very morning, and we can do it again!"

Then Harry and his brilliant confidence were gone; and the frightened men stood peering toward the spot where the road opened, solemnly contemplating their fate.

The appearance of the familiar scarlet coats sent the American field pieces into action in an attempt to harass the enemy's formation. Soon the British cannon returned the fire. Though the cannons affected no casualties on the militia front line, the continuous, thunderous blasting was enough to unnerve the shaky companies.

Harry watched from the flank, his own men mounted and eagerly awaiting the encounter. The militia did not look good, he noted, and glancing over his shoulder, he made certain that his courier was close by. Should the front line break, word must immediately be sent to General Greene who waited with the Continental line. A commander's counter orders were only as effective as the swiftness and accuracy of the couriers' reports, and Harry was well aware of this fact.

Suddenly the thunderous cannon fire ceased, bringing on an eerie silence. The sweet songs of the cardinals and wrens were no more—all fowl and animal life had wisely fled. That which remained under the clear, blue sky on the outskirts of this quaint North Carolina village were but the two opposing forces, momentarily stupefied by the nerve-rending cannons, and the thick cloud of smoke that lay between them. As the blinding smoke lifted, the militia gasped to view the sight they dreaded—the scarlet line of British troops approaching, their bayonets glistening against the sun's brilliance.

Harry watched from his position on the flank. The militia remained in neat formation, and when the order was given, positioned their muskets on the rail fence before them and awaited the word to fire. He turned to view the British advance, still some 400 feet out, and as he did, he heard the sound of the first round being discharged by the front line.

"They are too far out!" he yelled above the lingering musket fire, as he pulled hard on the reins to steady his startled horse. "Why in God's name are they shooting?"

"I do not believe an order was given, Colonel!" Harry's second in command shouted back.

Then, as was expected by Harry, the British quickly narrowed the gap before the militia had time to reload, took aim, and fired. Miraculously not one bullet hit its mark.

"Reload! Hurry and reload! Now you have them, boys!" Harry found himself muttering, but even as he spoke, the dreaded fear every senior officer held now came to light. One after another, the terrified front line began to drop their muskets.

Harry witnessed militia officers attempt to regroup, but to no avail. Setting the spurs to his horse, he raced to the fleeing line, taking a quick account of the enemy's advance. Then pulling a pistol from beneath his green dragoon jacket he yelled, "Halt and regroup, or I will order my own men to cut you down!"

Canteens and knapsacks fell to the ground to make the cowardly rout less cumbersome. Harry fired the pistol into the air, which only caused the men to run faster. He wheeled his horse about, and galloped back to his men, cussing beneath his breath,

"Tell General Greene we have a complete rout here, save Captain Eaton's brigade," he called out to his courier. The courier glanced toward the field where a lone brigade now stood at the mercy of the approaching British line.

"Tell the General that we'll attempt to inflict as much damage as we can before allowing them to pass to the second line." Again setting his spurs to the horse, he galloped off. The thunderous hoof beat of his legion followed, their sabers held high, and a fearsome war cry sounding to announce their charge.

Six hundred yards behind the front line, Nathanael waited. His hat was in one hand, his gloves in the other as he paced back and forth before his mounted staff officers. A wooded thicket blocked his view of the front line. Though he longed to oversee the initial attack, the third line was where the onslaught would be most severe, and thus he must remain.

He studied his Continental line, which stood in alert battle formation before him: the Maryland regiments to the right, the Virginian's on the left. They were firm and steady, undaunted by the rumbling twenty minutes of artillery fire. Even the new recruits appeared sure. "Good work von Steuben." He whispered as he walked behind the new recruits noting their proper stance.

A round of musket fire echoed back toward the courthouse. Nathanael's heart lightened. "They are holding up." He said aloud to no one in particular.

A return of musket fire came as no surprise. Then there was a silence—a long, distressing silence.

Nathanael stopped pacing. *The second round should have been fired!* He shouted within. As he glanced up at Rob Burnet, every fear, disappointment and uncertainty he felt in that dreaded second of time was communicated. He slapped his gloves hard against his thigh in frustration before shoving his hands into them. Then moving to the left of his horse, he prepared to mount. "The front line has fled," he said knowingly to his staff. As he pulled his body upon the horse, Harry Lee's courier approached and the sound of gunfire sounded once more.

The courier was gasping for breath as he threw a quick salute. "We have a general rout on the front line—all have fled save Eaton's brigade."

William Washington's courier reined in his horse alongside Lee's as the report was given.

"Colonel Lee tried to regroup them, sir, but to no avail. The colonel ordered his legion forward to support Eaton's brigade and inflict as much damage as possible before the enemy reaches the second line."

"Colonel Washington?" Nathanael asked the second courier.

"He has joined Colonel Lee and Major Eaton on the field."

"Return to your commanders and tell them to inflict their damage with caution. They are to take note of their own casualties. I am not willing to sacrifice my cavalry. Tell them to fall back with Eaton's brigade to support the third line at their discretion."

The couriers wheeled their horses about and raced away.

Without a word, Nathanael brought his horse into a canter, crossing the dirt road and turning in front of the Continental line. Up and down the line he moved, offering his men encouragement.

William Washington's cavalry finally fell back along with the lone militia brigade and artillery pieces. Nathanael immediately sent the militia behind the third line to safety, praising Captain Eaton for the extraordinary courage shown.

William gave a full report: a fair amount of damage had been inflicted to the enemy; they were now regrouping to move on the second line.

"Where is Colonel Lee?" Nathanael shouted as musket fire sounded once more, indicating that the second phase of the battle was underway.

"Last I heard he was engaged in hand-to-hand combat with a Hessian regiment in the wooded thicket on the far left."

"How long ago?" Nathanael asked noticeably concerned.

"It's hard to say, sir. Twenty minutes—a half-hour—"

"I have heard nothing from him." Turning to Lewis Morris, he ordered him to locate Harry Lee. He then ordered William Washington's cavalry to the right flank of the Continentals.

Soon reports began pouring in from the second line. The action was severe, but the militia was holding strong. From behind the cover of trees, the men were able to keep up a steady fire with great execution. In an attempt to break through, all British troops were engaged, except those of Tarleton's dragoons.

Orders were sent back through the couriers in response to their reports. The present outlook—except for Harry Lee's unaccountable absence—encouraged Nathanael.

Once more, he passed before the third line. "It will be our turn to welcome them soon, boys! Let us welcome them with the finishing blow! You can bring them down. Bring Cornwallis down here, lads, and all we need do is escort the remainder from Charleston and Savannah, and your homes and families are safe! The South will be forever free!"

"And then General Washington will drive them from New York!" one of the men excitedly called from the ranks.

"That is right, my friend; and, once we are rid of them, we can return to our wives and sweethearts; and we will beat our swords into plowshares and our spears into pruning hooks—neither shall we learn war any more!"

A resounding huzzah echoed as Nathanael made his way back down the line. He took up his position with his staff, and made a quick visual search for Lewis Morris, eager to hear of Harry Lee's situation. The aide was nowhere to be seen. Nevertheless, news soon arrived from the battlefront that the enemy had broken through and were being led forward by Lord Cornwallis himself.

As soon as the British were within artillery range, Nathanael gave the order for the cannons to open fire, thus briefly disrupting their formation. Though the earth shook about them as the cannons boomed, the Continental line, unlike the militia, remained firm. When the artillery fire ceased, the British determinedly made their approach. The onslaught was fierce as men on both sides fought for the very life of their army.

Seemingly able to be everywhere at once, Nathanael effectively maneuvered his troops.

"Colonel Lee is about a half mile to the east of us, sir," Lewis Morris shouted breathlessly above the gunfire, having suddenly appeared from nowhere. "He and Colonel Campbell's unit are engaged with a Hessian regiment and unable to break free."

"How are they faring?" Nathanael yelled back.

"They are holding their own, sir."

"How did he let himself get trapped like that?" Nathanael exclaimed in frustration; then, turning back to Lewis, he yelled, "I want a report on the Maryland Second Regiment. They may need support." He was still concerned that these new recruits might not hold up. Wasting no time, Lewis raced off.

"General Greene." William Washington's courier saluted. "Sir, the First Maryland have driven a sizable British force back across the ravine. Colonel Washington is concerned the enemy may be reinforced and requests permission to pursue them with his cavalry."

"How sizable a force, and under whose command?"

"About 400 men, sir, under Colonel Webster. Colonel Washington is confident that, if you take Webster and his brigade down, the enemy will be routed!"

Nathanael removed his right glove, and holding it in his left hand, he began to rub his upper lip with his forefinger. It was a tempting proposal; but to chance the remainder of his cavalry, thus leaving his entire force exposed without their protection, was simply too hazardous. Had Harry Lee been here—had he more troops to depend on, more of an army than the mere 1,600 now struggling on the field—

"No, Captain. Tell Colonel Washington that he is not to pursue Colonel Webster at this time."

"Yes, sir." The courier dashed off.

Nathanael removed himself to a spot where he could view the British colonel's position, and watched as the enemy recovered from their encounter, and regrouped—with numbers now added to their strength, they moved back into action.

Frustrated by his inability to act on William Washington's proposal, Nathanael turned his attention to the reports arriving from the right wing—the Virginia brigades. Moving in that direction, he sought to personally see to their situation just as Lewis Morris approached from behind.

"General Greene, the Second Maryland is under the attack of Colonel Webster's Brigade. They are not holding well. Colonel Williams is bringing the First Maryland forward to counterattack." Lewis called.

Nathanael jerked his horse about, his own face suddenly pale. Setting his spurs hard, he raced off with Lewis, Rob, and his standard-bearer in hot pursuit.

Troops were engaged in combat near the Second Maryland's original post. Nathanael was confused as he peered through the dust and smoke. Though he tried to evaluate the situation, he found it impossible to determine which American regiment was presently engaged and how they were faring. In an attempt to get a better view, he pressed forward, shutting out the pleadings of his aides to turn back.

On the edge of the ensuing battle, the commander obtained a clear view. Too enthralled to be sensibly concerned for his own safety, he observed the exhilarating scene. Colonel Washington's cavalry, along with Otho Williams' steadfast First Marylanders, had fearlessly engaged the British brigade in hand-to-hand combat—swiftly and mercilessly cutting the enemy down. And through the clamor—the excited battle cry of the warriors, the agonizing death cry of those slashed by the relentless sabers, the muskets popping, the beating drums and cavalry bugles, and the orders shouted in every direction—through the enticing, nauseating, spellbinding mingled odors of wasted gun powder, horse flesh, human sweat, fresh streaming blood and lacerated bowels, Nathanael sat upon his steed, momentarily mesmerized.

Then through the smoke, he caught a glimpse of a British field piece. He peered in the direction of the cannon; and, as the battling soldiers scuffled out of his way, Nathanael found his eyes simultaneously locked on to those of the officer mounted beside the cannon—General Charles Cornwallis.

In the split second of time that their eyes met, Nathanael was aware of every fact he had learned of this man—his superb military record, his thorough command of his troops, and the absolute respect and honor they felt toward him. Though he sympathized with the political complaints of the Americans, he was a British patriot through and through—a gentleman in every sense of the word with an unusual, open love and devotion for his invalid wife and family. A limp plagued him and an eye aliment, which even now, Nathanael could see, was fully inflamed as was his own.

His spellbound attention remained on this man, who, no doubt, might have become his friend in another time and another place. However, here they were enemies—enemies to the death. And all the aggression and hostility, all the frustration experienced between their two opposing countries, which led to these last six years of hate and horrendous destruction was completely embodied in their persons with such magnitude and force that it sent a piercing chill through Nathanael's body.

He hated him completely, yet he utterly respected him. He had no doubt that it would not be wrong to shoot him down—if he could get his arm to respond and take hold of the pistol beneath his jacket. Yet he knew with equal assurance that, if he did this, he would greatly mourn the death of this man.

The ambivalence of the moment was more than he could endure—as was true, so it seemed, for Lord Cornwallis as well—for each remained transfixed on the other.

"General Greene, you are in grave danger!" Rob Burnet frantically shouted, grabbing hold of Nathanael's bridle in a daring act. Without another word, Rob set his spurs to his horse and taking his commander in tow hurried off the field.

As they raced away, the cannon thundered. Nathanael yanked hard on the reins, jerking the horse's head back and almost pulling Rob from his saddle.

"You cannot go back, General! Please do not go back!" Rob pleaded as Lewis, his own face as pale as his companion's, positioned his horse to prevent Nathanael from returning.

"That son of Lucifer is firing on his own men!" Nathanael exclaimed. "Is it utter lunacy or bravery that would cause him to gun his own men down with ours?" His gaze remained fixed on the carnage below. Then turning to Lewis, he growled, "Thee will remove yourself from my path, Major!"

Lewis glanced at Rob, and then boldly fixed his eyes on Nathanael's.

"I cannot do that, sir."

"Will thee disobey a direct order, Major Morris?"

"My standing orders are to protect you, sir, with my life, if need be. General Greene, we cannot allow you to return!"

Nathanael looked back on the scene below. The American forces were being led out of the range of the deadly grapeshot. Through the smoke, he viewed the horrid sight of mangled bodies—American and British alike, many still writhing in agony from the grapeshot's ghastly impact.

"How can I defeat an enemy such as this? How can I stand against a man so dark and sinister that he will not hesitate to kill his own men in order to win a battle?"

The sound of approaching riders drew Nathanael's attention. To his great relief he discovered it to be Harry Lee and his aide.

Taken aback by the general's ghostly appearance, Harry hesitated to speak. "Sir—have you been injured?" he asked with noted concern. Nathanael did not answer, but turned his attention back to the scene below.

"He is all right," Rob said, though his expression offered little assurance.

Harry appeared confused, but chanced to speak.

"You have fared well without my boys, sir. You have done the enemy infinite damage."

"Not so!" Nathanael shouted, shaking his head. "If your boys had not been detained, I would have chanced a cavalry charge on Webster, and this melee would never have played out!"

Harry was noticeably shaken by the lacerating remark. Immediately aware of the damage his words had inflicted, Nathanael took a deep breath. "—It was either a brilliant tactic on Cornwallis' part to tie up my cavalry unit, or simply a fortunate turn of events. Regardless, it doesn't really matter now—"

Two more riders approached. "Sir, British infantry are working around to our rear." General Huger's courier reported, pointing back toward the right wing.

"And we are down to five rounds, General; besides what the reserve unit has in order to cover a retreat." Deputy Quartermaster Carrington added.

A brief silence elapsed as Nathanael toyed with the temptation of attempting one final blow. Quickly he abandoned the thought, for the risk was much too great.

"Disengage the troops. Let's get our men to safety."

The already established plans for retreat were immediately put in motion with the reserve unit of Colonel John Greene—the very officer who had slept so contentedly on the outpost the night before—coming forward to draw the enemy's attention as the battle-worn Continentals pulled off the field.

The retreat was orderly as the men pushed three miles back to the appointed rendezvous point. Here, along the banks of the Ready Fork, they rested as their commander received reports from his various units, and waited to see if Cornwallis wanted to continue the contest.

Casualty reports were disheartening at first. Although only 200 men were killed or wounded, not too surprising a number for a two-hour battle, the bulk of these were Continental—the backbone of his army. And to make matters worse, among the wounded were two of his general officers.

The artillery pieces were abandoned on the field—the artillery horses having been shot down. Though stragglers continued to wander into the temporary encampment, reports indicated that more than 1,000 men were unaccounted for—most of them from the front line of the North Carolina militia.

As evening came upon them, and with it the threat of rain, Nathanael gave up his ordered search for deserters and the anticipation of Cornwallis' pursuit. He had hoped to rest the men overnight and contemplated taking Cornwallis on again come morning; but, with the threat of rain, he knew that such an encounter would be deadly. With the powder wet, muskets would fail to fire. The British would not flinch at resorting to the bayonet, but the Americans, save for the cavalry and Otho William's men, had not yet emotionally mastered this gruesome aggression, even in the face of imminent death.

As the cold, pelting rain began to fall; Nathanael set his men on a ten-mile trek, which lasted the entire night. With the morning's light, they came upon the position of their new encampment in a wooded area beside an ironwork on the banks of Troublesome Creek.

Nathanael Greene, Mezzotint published by V. Greene
National Archives and Records Administration

Daniel Morgan, painting by Alonzo Chappel
National Archives and Records Administration

Otho Holland Williams by Charles Willson Peale
Courtesy, Independence National Historical Park

Light-Horse Harry Lee, painting by Charles Willson Peale
Courtesy, Independence National Historical Park

William Washington, painting by Charles Willson Peale
Courtesy, Independence National Historical Park

Cornwallis, painting by Sir W. Beechey
National Archives and Records Administration

Banastre Tarlton, painting by Sir Joshua Reynolds
National Archives and Records Administration

Caty Greene and Eli Whitney perfecting the cotton gin.
Century Magazine, January 1878

Catharine Littlefield Greene Miller, c. 1809
Attributed to James Frothingham (American, 1786-1864)
Oil on panel 32 3/4 x 25 3/4 inches
Telfair Museum (Museum purchase, 1947.2)

"In this critical and distressing situation I am determined to carry the war immediately into South Carolina."

(Nathanael Greene to George Washington)

CHAPTER NINETEEN

"GENERAL—GENERAL GREENE." Rob nudged him three times, affecting no response. The fourth time he opened his eyes. "General—excuse me, sir. Mr. Davison is here."

The eyes shut again. "General Greene, the operative is here with news from the British camp." Nathanael mumbled something, stirred a bit, and went back to sleep. Rob stepped out of the marquee where Lewis waited with the American spy.

"I cannot seem to wake him," Rob said with a shrug, sharing a concerned glance with Lewis.

"We have no choice but to wake him, boys; I have no time to dawdle if I am to return safely behind enemy lines before daybreak!" Mr. Davison protested.

"I understand that, sir. Perhaps you could give the message to us, and we will see that the General gets it—" Rob suggested.

"Impossible. I must see that the General receives it directly."

"We fully understand your situation, Mr. Davison. It is standard practice that the commanding officer receive an operative's report directly; but, please try to understand ours," Rob began firmly. "The general has been under immense strain these past several weeks; and, since arriving in this camp yesterday, he has literally collapsed twice. Our chief surgeon has ordered complete bed rest—this is the first decent sleep he has obtained in weeks. You will be paid for your trouble as usual—"

"It is not the money, Major!" the operative exclaimed. "Who is second in command?"

"That would be General Huger, sir," Lewis replied.

"Then bring me to him—"

"General Huger was injured in the battle and is presently indisposed, as is our third in command, General Stevens," Rob informed him rather smugly. "Colonel Williams, the adjutant general, would be next in line—"

"Then bring me to Williams."

"What is the problem?" Nathanael's drowsy voice took them by surprise. Rob went into the marquee where the General sat on the side of the cot, and informed him of the situation. Slowly Nathanael rose from his bed and walked to the camp desk as Rob escorted Davison in.

"I am sorry to disturb you, General," the operative said, stunned by Nathanael's appearance. Like his aides, his hair was filthy, slicked back in its natural oil; his uniform dingy and worn; the golden epaulets having little luster. His face was in need of a shave; and the body odor, emitting from everyone the operative met in camp, was most unbearable.

But beyond the repulsive dirt and odor was the general's physical appearance. His face was drawn and pale with dark circles hanging below blood-shot eyes. His right eye being noticeably swollen and crusty.

"No need to apologize, sir. I have been anticipating your visit. Please, sit down," Nathanael said pointing to a stool. "How is Cornwallis faring?"

"His army has been dealt a severe blow. By the dictates of war, he may have won the battle—the ground is his. But, General Greene, in truth you are the victor. Cornwallis suffered 550 casualties—a quarter of his fighting force, and a fair number of officers. Being so far from his supply post, he is in desperate need; and the country-side, astounded by the result of the battle, is offering little to him by way of supplies or reinforcements."

"Will he attempt to regroup and attack?" Nathanael asked.

"No, General. He is utterly inapt to face you again under the present circumstances. He must be resupplied, yet realizes he has little chance of escaping your attack should he head south to regroup with Lord Rawdon. His only hope, so he believes, is to head northward to Virginia."

Rob pulled out a map and placed it on the desk before them. Mr. Davison traced the proposed line of march with his finger.

"General, you could easily crush him if you pursue. His march to Virginia will be slow," Davison commented.

Nathanael's attention was on the map. "In your opinion, Mr. Davison, do you think General Lafayette's force, combined with General Steuben's recruits, can keep Cornwallis in check?"

"In Cornwallis' present state, yes; I have no doubt of it—but you could destroy him right now, sir."

"The temptation to finish Cornwallis off is strong; and perhaps stronger still is the desire to join with Generals Lafayette and Steuben to pursue the black-hearted

Arnold. I have never felt such need for vengeance—and the greatest gift I could give General Washington is Arnold's head."

Mr. Davisons' eyes were fixed on the bloodthirsty general, whose entire countenance had changed, revealing the intense struggle within.

"But, nay, Mr. Davison. No matter how tempting or how righteous a pursuit it would be, my duty lies to the South. I cannot chase this crippled quarry northward and turn my back on some 6000 enemy troops well entrenched in the South. Is there anything else I should know, Mr. Davison?"

"No, sir, nothing more."

"Very well. Thank you, sir, for your valuable assistance." Nathanael extended his hand to the operative. "Major Morris, see to Mr. Davisons' reimbursement," he called to Lewis, and then grabbing a sheet of paper, he dipped a quill in the inkwell in a single, graceful movement, which had become as natural as breathing.

"Sir, the doctor is of the strongest opinion that you need to rest," Rob urgently reminded him after the operative left.

"I know; but I must inform General Washington and Congress, as well as warn Generals Lafayette, Steuben and Governor Jefferson."

"Sir, might it wait until morning?"

Nathanael looked at him, a hint of irritation in his expression. "These dispatches must be ready to go by first light. Come morning we will have the business of preparing militia to be deployed to shadow Cornwallis."

Rob studied his commander's face as he busied himself at the desk. *He has noticeably aged since taking command of this post,* the aide thought. *What is it exactly? He is graying, but it is more than that—it is his countenance. Beneath the smiles his countenance is grave; even the smiles are becoming more and more infrequent. Even now—with the news of Cornwallis being crippled, there is no excitement. There is not so much as a hint of satisfaction.*

"Might I assist you in writing the letters, sir?" the concerned aide asked.

"Thank you, Rob, but no. They must be in my hand to fully relay the gravity of the situation."

"Sir, I am concerned for your health. Isn't there some way?"

There was a mixture of appreciation and frustration in Nathanael's gaze. "What would thee have me do, my friend? I have a war to fight and my general officers are down. What can I do?" the question was asked in all sincerity—Rob even detected a pleading in his tone.

"—I do not know, sir. I wish I knew—"

"You and Lewis get some sleep. There will be much to do come sunup."

"Sir, how can we sleep knowing you are here working?"

Nathanael put the quill back into its holder and gave his full attention to the aide. "Rob, hear me well. My health is very poor at present; I am not denying that fact, but at this moment, I have no choice but to press on. I may need to depend on you more than ever in the next day or two; and the truth is your health and that of Lewis is not much better than my own. To lose your service now would be more detrimental than having lost the service of my general officers. Do you understand me?"

Tears formed in Rob's eyes in response to Nathanael's words. There was no greater compliment he could receive. "—Yes, sir, I understand."

"You can do me one thing," Nathanael said.

"What is that, sir?"

"Awaken the poor secretary. I will need his services in copying these letters."

"Of course, sir."

"Any further word on the missing militia?" Nathanael asked, the pen already busy scratching words on the paper.

"A few stragglers have come in—nothing more."

He stopped writing and stared blankly at the tent wall before him. "What am I to do with troops such as these? And are the other militia units still threatening to walk out?"

"Yes, sir. Nothing has changed. They still claim their term of enlistment includes whatever time it takes for them to march home, and they are determined to allot themselves plenty of time for the return trip."

Nathanael began to write once more, mumbling as he wrote. "It is impossible to command men that refuse to submit to authority. Maybe we will be better off without them—less mouths to feed. I will try to reason with them in the morning—"

As he stepped into the marquee, Nathanael was surprised to find the chief surgeon awaiting his arrival.

"It is a beautiful day, isn't it, General?" the physician's greeting came, thick with a Southern drawl. He remained seated on a stool, casually leaning his body against Nathanael's small field desk.

"That it is, Dr. Johnson," Nathanael's dry reply came.

"I hope you are not offended at my taking the liberty to wait for you, sir."

"No, Doctor, I do not see any harm in it." Nathanael slowly, almost painfully, made his way to the desk and sat down.

"I imagined you might be down at the creek washing up. Since the order was posted this morning for the men to take this time of repose to bathe and scrub their clothing, the entire camp has the sudden fragrance of spring rather than the rancid odor of men who have not removed their clothing for over a month's time. But, it would appear that you and your staff have not followed through with today's general orders. And it would appear that you have chosen to ignore medical orders as well—unless, of course, your riding about the camp is an indication that you have made a miraculous recovery since my visit yesterday."

Dr. Johnson was well known for his brusqueness and his rather unorthodox military manner, neither of which disturbed Nathanael, for he genuinely like the man. There was a hint of glimmer in Nathanael's good eye as he reached his left hand across his chest and rested it upon the dingy epaulet on his right shoulder. "I was under the impression that this indicated that I give the orders here," he said wearily.

"Rex lex?" the doctor asked.

Nathanael threw him a weak smile, immediately recognizing the Latin phrase, *the King is law.* "Something like that," he replied. "The truth of the matter is that in this little world of the Southern Department I am somewhat of a dictator." He began to rub his weary eyes with his hand.

"That you are, General Greene, but no one seems to mind because it is well-known that you, like General Washington, are a benevolent dictator. Word is that you have never taken advantage of or abused any man under your command."

"I endeavor to do my best to be fair," Nathanael replied with a rather blank stare.

"Now, as for my order—oh, but let me rephrase that," Dr. Johnson said with a smirk. "My pointed recommendation that you rest—"

"I have pressing matters to attend to, Doctor," Nathanael protested.

"Do you, General?" Dr. Johnson asked, his brows cocked. "Dispatches have been sent to the necessary individuals; today's general orders have been posted; the cavalry is instructed to ride at first light on the morrow; the militia unit is preparing to march; and Colonel Williams has been informed of our present situation. Quite honestly, sir, all seems to be under control. As your personal physician, I do have some authority. Might I strongly implore the general to bathe in the creek with the assistance of your guards, for I am of the firmest opinion that you are presently too weak to be safely left unattended in the water. Then, I recommend you lie upon your bed and stay there for the next forty-eight hours."

"Forty-eight hours?" Nathanael echoed.

"At the very least, General. It is obvious, sir, that you are on the verge of a physical breakdown. You are not in a position to question my diagnosis, recommended treatment or prognosis."

"Forty-eight hours? That's absurd."

The doctor sighed; then with a smile, which his eyes did not reflect, he mumbled, "I have heard tell of this New England stubbornness, but never believed it to be true—until now." Then more directly, he added. "I will not compromise on the forty-eight hours, sir, and will even dare point out to the general the grave danger ahead if he does not heed my advice and obtain rest."

There was no longer a smile, only a look of deep concern. "The weather is lovely now, sir, but remember it is only March. By June, the gentle breezes we now enjoy will be occasional—by July, they will be but a memory. Oh, I have no doubt that in New England you have bouts with severely hot weather; but down here it will last for weeks on end, and you will wonder if hell itself could, in truth, be any hotter."

"I have been warned of the summer's heat, Doctor. I do not seem to grasp your point," Nathanael replied, his forehead resting upon his hand.

"My point is, dear General that should you presently neglect your health—somehow managing to stay on your feet by sheer will-power, the summer months may literally kill you. Few escape the diseases it brings—the weak are choice victims. Even in your most robust state quinine will be a daily supplement to your diet in the hope of escaping putrid fever."

"I have had putrid fever."

"And you have lived to speak of it? How fortunate. Unlike the pox, putrid fever can recur," the doctor said matter-of-factly. "I understand you are plagued with asthma?"

"—I am," Nathanael hesitantly admitted.

"The term 'plagued' will take on an entirely new meaning this summer. It is considered a curse down here—a curse that has the power to kill."

With a weak, forced smile, Nathanael met the doctor's steady gaze. "I am beginning to wonder if you are working for the British, assigned the duty of frightening me from this post?"

"No, General, I am simply your physician; and, I hope, your friend; who desires to keep you alive. The struggles we face here are enough to contend with—little to eat, less to drink, and this smoke-filled air to breath." Dr. Johnson said referring to the constant smoke emitted from the nearby iron works.

"I am more accustomed to breathing this smoke than I am fresh air." Nathanael remarked, the same weak smile upon his face.

"Excuse me, General," Lewis said as he entered the marquee. "A post rider just arrived from Headquarters. There is a letter from Mrs. Greene, sir!"

An immediate glow came over Nathanael's face. Even with 700 miles between them, Caty had the ability to bring joy to his life. Quickly rising to meet Lewis' approach, quicker than he had been accustomed to moving these past two days, Nathanael reached for the letter. Upon grasping hold of it, he felt the room spin about him. His legs buckled under his weight, and in the sudden darkness, he heard the shouts of Doctor Johnson and the aides as they scrambled to his side. Then there was nothing—

Nathanael woke to the sound of men conversing outside. Momentarily disoriented, he lay still for a few minutes. He had collapsed, that much he remembered, but how long he had been unconscious, he had no idea. As he reached for the watch in his waistcoat pocket, he was surprised to find his entire uniform had been replaced with a clean pair of breeches and a linen shirt.

It is Long Island all over again, he thought, remembering the odd, unnatural confusion of waking up after a week of semi-consciousness. *Ah, but Henry was there to greet me then.*

He turned his head to face the door of the marquee, imagining he heard Henry's voice. He listened—hoping against hope that it could be true, but quickly realized that it was William Washington's voice he heard as he conversed with Rob Burnet.

Gently pushing himself to a sitting position on the edge of the field bed, he called out to Rob. The response was immediate.

"Sir, please. Dr. Johnson will have my head if he finds you sitting. You are on complete bed rest, General—no sitting, no writing—" Rob grabbed hold of his shoulders and gently guided him back down.

"That confounded man thinks he is the commander of this post. What sort of army do I have? The physicians order the generals about, and every member of the militia believes he is a general, submitting to no one's command."

Rob nodded sympathetically.

"How long have I been asleep?"

"About eighteen hours, sir, and all is running as smoothly as one could expect under the circumstances. Colonel Williams has taken temporary command; and, with the assistance of Colonel Washington, he is managing."

"What about the dispatches from Headquarters?" Nathanael asked, positioning himself on his elbow and searching the tent for the bundle of envelopes.

"Not to worry, sir. Colonel Williams took the liberty to read the official correspondence. Nothing was of such an urgent nature that it could not await your attention before being responded to. Your personal letters are here." Rob walked to the foot of the bed and opened Nathanael's trunk, pulling the sealed letters out. "Your uniform has been washed and is presently drying outside," Rob informed him as he handed him the letters.

Nathanael's expression communicated his confusion. "I do not remember a thing."

"No, I am sure you do not. The doctor said the human body is created to protect itself in a state of such extreme exhaustion by going into a comatose state. He is the one that removed your clothing and cleaned you up—why that man even shaved your face and shampooed your hair all in that bed. I have never seen such proficiency in it—juggling bowls this way and that and never spilling a drop," he said with a chuckle. "Doctor Johnson felt certain that your state of untidiness would deter from your recovery, and he felt that the opportunity to clean you up in a comatose state was advantageous, for then, as he put it, sir, he would not have to endure your verbal protest and New England pride."

"Remind me to speak to that man about his insubordinate attitude," Nathanael said with a smile. "And where's your uniform, Major?" he asked.

"Out drying along side yours and Lewis', General. If we were ever to come under attack now, no one would know the militia from the enlisted men and either of them from the officers. Oh, but doesn't it feel good to be clean, sir?"

"That it does." Nathanael took Caty's letter from the top of the pile, smiling at the sight of her handwriting.

"Why don't I go get you something to eat while you read your mail," Rob offered. Eagerly scratching the seal to the letter, Nathanael only nodded in response.

Rob turned to leave, calling back, and "I will send word to the doctor. He wanted to be notified when you awakened."

"Belay that!" Nathanael shouted.

Rob spun around. "Sir?"

"Do not notify the doctor just yet. Send instead for Otho Williams. I want a complete report on what has transpired in the last eighteen hours. Send, too, for Colonel Carrington—I must know how the Quartermaster's Department is faring—"

"Sir, Dr. Johnson may not approve—"

"What the good doctor does not know—"

A frown was Rob's response.

"He said I must stay in this blasted bed for forty-eight hours—no sitting, no writing. He said nothing about receiving reports, giving orders, dictating letters or reading did he?"

"—No, sir, but I am sure—"

"When I give orders they are very explicit, are they not, Major?"

"They are, sir, but—"

"And when I receive orders that are not explicit, I am left to interpret them as befits the situation. The doctor gave his vague orders—now it is up to me to interpret them." There was a definite twinkle in Nathanael's eyes as he turned his attention back to Caty's letter.

"New England stubbornness—the doctor is right." Rob mumbled loud enough to be heard by his beloved commander. "God bless you and your New England stubbornness."

Activity at headquarters changed very little except that reports were made, and orders given at the general's bedside. Under his instructions, maps were brought in and propped in such a way that Nathanael, supporting his upper body weight on one elbow, could view them from a semi-prone position.

He studied the maps for hours, speaking little of his plans. The engineer, deputy quartermaster general, cartographer and scout were called in separately on more than one occasion. Both Washington's and Lee's cavalry were sent out and promptly made their reports upon returning to camp.

Doctor Johnson watched the hubbub in agitated disbelief at first. Then, with a sigh, he threw up his arms in defeat seeing that the general's health was indeed improving even with the persistent activity all about him.

When his time of confinement ended, the aides were amused to see Nathanael bound out of bed and immediately call for his uniform. Then, fully adorned, he walked to the desk, hesitating for a moment before sitting down. He quietly returned to the field bed, and reached under the pillow, pulling a folded letter from beneath it. Then walking back to the desk, he sat down, placing the letter in one corner of the small desk; and taking a fresh sheet of paper and quill in hand, he began to write.

Rob and Lewis shared a glance, amused by the retrieval of the letter. As Rob walked past the desk on the way to his own, he stole a peek at the letter, fully assuming it was Caty's recent letter to him. Surprised, he discovered the writing to be in the general's hand, and addressed to 'Mrs. General Greene, Coventry, Rhode Island.'

"Sir, you just got out of bed this minute. How is it that you already have a letter prepared for Mrs. Greene?" he asked pointedly.

Nathanael looked from the letter to Rob with the appearance of a disobedient child.

"General, Dr. Johnson's orders were explicit in that you were not to write—for to write, you would, in fact, have to get out of bed and sit at this desk."

"Perhaps I dictated it." Nathanael suggested, a coy smile on his face.

"A letter to Mrs. Greene? Never. And the writing is obviously in your hand. See here, Lewis, is this not the general's hand?"

Lewis stepped behind Nathanael's chair and glanced at the letter on the desk. "Appears to be your writing, sir," he said with a grin, as amused by the general's mischievousness as by his humorous address of his wife as 'Mrs. General Greene.'

"What can I say, gentlemen? I have been caught." Nathanael said, laying his right hand over his heart.

"Confession is good for the soul, sir. How many more did you write as we slept?" Rob asked, placing his hand on the commander's shoulder.

"I promise that this was all—I do promise." he assured them. Neither appeared convinced. "See here—I am writing to His Excellency," he said pointing to the paper he was working on. "Surely if I were to indulge in writing, I would have taken the opportunity to write General Washington."

"If it were not for the fact that Doctor Johnson was holding us personally responsible for your every move these past two days, I might feel compelled to report the matter to him," Rob said with pretended annoyance as he moved to his desk.

"But what is the good of it?" Lewis asked, doing the same. "He will just take it upon himself to lecture us—and to what end? The general will still do what he is determined to do."

Nathanael grinned at both of them, and then returned his full attention back to the letter before him. Stopping in mid-sentence, he began to mumble to himself; then, grabbing the paper, proceeded to crumble it in his hand.

"Lewis."

"Sir?"

"Get me a post rider—the most trusted among them—Martin, I should think. Is Mr. Martin in camp?"

"Yes, sir. He returned yesterday from a run to General Lafayette's camp."

"Send for him."

"Right away, sir."

Taking a fresh sheet of paper, Nathanael wrote a brief letter to George Washington, then a lengthier one to Henry Knox, and yet another to Lord Stirling. As he finished the salutary address to Anthony Wayne on the next one, the post rider arrived.

"Mr. Martin, I need you to ride to Headquarters. You will be carrying the usual correspondence, and bringing back the same; but the letter to General Washington is not the entirety of what I must tell him. I cannot entrust my words to paper for fear the enemy might intercept it; and, therefore, must ask you to put it to memory."

"I understand, sir."

Nathanael instructed Lewis to retrieve the maps he had been studying.

"You will leave at first light on the morrow. This will give you the opportunity to put to memory all I have to tell you," Nathanael said as he rolled out the first map. Lewis and Rob gathered about, having eagerly anticipated a tactical plan in the making.

First, the militia units already deployed would continue to shadow General Cornwallis, with the hope that he would believe that the entire Southern force was on his heels. Cornwallis would continue his march into Virginia thus utterly cutting himself off from his Southern troops. The only feasible way of reuniting with them would be to rendezvous with the British fleet, and then be transported back to Charleston. In the meantime, Cornwallis would be in a weakened, somewhat paralytic state, and at the mercy of any harassment Generals Lafayette and Steuben could bring his way. Leaving Cornwallis in such capable hands, Nathanael intended to turn his attention further south; and, with the joint effort of his partisan generals—Marion, Sumter and Pickens, he would carry out a series of sequentially planned attacks on the British posts in South Carolina. With these posts captured, the British would remain only in Charleston and Savannah.

Mr. Martin was sent off even before Nathanael conferred with his senior officers. Various responses were shared as the plan was revealed to them; and, as was his habit, Nathanael, showing the utmost courtesy to their ideas, allowed each man to put forth any opposing view or suggestion. Then, in response, he answered their every apprehension, convincing them in the process of the soundness of his plan.

"Virginia is presently our supply source, sir. Heading thus into South Carolina, won't we find ourselves in the same predicament we enticed Cornwallis into?" Harry Lee asked.

"Not at all, Colonel. The posts we are attacking are not proportionately manned to hold us back. We will cut off their communications with the other posts and prevent any reinforcements or food supplies from arriving. A surprise attack will ensure us that their present food supply is not adequate to withstand a siege. They will fall in short order, and all the military supplies in their possession will become ours with the compliments of his majesty King George III!" Nathanael said with a grin.

"Shouldn't General Cornwallis be our focus, sir?" General Huger asked, his bandaged arm gently supported in a sling around his neck. "True, we did him substantial damage, but he is not yet defeated—shouldn't we see this through?"

"General Lafayette will be only too happy to give his Lordship a proper greeting. Between Lafayette and Steuben, Cornwallis will be dealt with. And General Washington is fully aware—" His words drifted off. "Our attention is best directed southward. If we capture these posts," he said, running his finger along the line of British forts on the map, "then we break their stronghold on the South. The British cannot rule for long a land they do not occupy. In capturing these posts, we will gain the support of the frightened civilians, thus increasing our numbers and adding to our own strength."

"What if Cornwallis should get word of your plan, General? What if he turns on us, and we find ourselves trapped between his army and Lord Rawdon's 6,000 men?" Otho Williams asked.

"A fair question—a possibility, but highly improbable. Cornwallis must know that his present army would never successfully complete such a march. As for the frightful sound of General Rawdon's 6,000 troops, keep in mind, gentlemen that he is spread out between two states. Such numbers cannot be easily rallied. We will never face 6,000 on the field. Facing half that number is possible, but in a defensive position, that's reasonable."

With all opposing arguments soundly answered and the senior officers in support of his plan, Major General Nathanael Greene led his ragged army toward South Carolina.

It had been a rather extraordinary day—even by Harry Lee's standards. As he gazed out the window of the Motte mansion, he contemplated the day's events, preparing in his mind the verbal report General Greene would expect upon his arrival.

For more than a week Harry's legion had been united with the hard-fighting horsemen of the elusive Francis Marion. Through the window pane Harry caught a glimpse of the partisan general sitting on the stump of a tree near the edge of the wood, his close companion and second, Colonel Peter Horry at his side.

Colonel Horry was obviously carrying on a conversation, Harry noted with a smile, as he watched the shy militia general nod now and again between sips from the canteen of his daily ingestion of vinegar water.

'Swamp Fox' was the name Banastre Tarleton had pinned on Marion. For his uncanny ability to evade the enemy in the lowland swamps between his deadly attacks, had driven Tarleton to distraction on many an occasion. Harry had been privy to spend a night at Marion's hidden camp on Snow Island where he came to 'know' this humble, almost reclusive man, through the amazing accounts of his ability and daring as told by his men.

A more troublesome bunch Harry had never met; but Marion had their respect and devotion. Marion's men also related their commander's apprehension in meeting General Greene; for Horatio Gates had shown little regard for the partisan general's work—even publicly displaying an attitude toward Marion and his men that caused them a great deal of embarrassment.

But General Greene was different, Harry tried to explain. Greene had the utmost respect for the feats they performed. Had General Gates ever given Marion the assistance of the cavalry? He asked them. Though their answer was in the negative, they still had their apprehensions, along with Marion's, as to how this commander of the Southern Department would respond to them.

On this present mission, Harry had been sent to assist Marion in taking a British depot known as Fort Motte. Though the fort was no more than a plantation house, which had been occupied by the enemy, it had been strongly fortified.

Mrs. Motte, the unwilling hostess of the British garrison, refused to occupy a room in her own home—opting instead to live in her overseer's house on a hill just north of the mansion. She welcomed the arrival of Lee's and Marion's troops, giving the senior officers permission to do what they must to bring about the surrender of the garrison.

After much deliberation between Colonel Lee, General Marion and their officers, they came to the hard decision. The quickest means of accomplishing their task was to implement an old Indian tactic of shooting flame-tipped arrows into the dry timbers of the roof of the house, thus setting it on fire over the heads of the enemy.

It was further decided that the charming, debonair cavalry commander should disclose to the widow Motte their destructive strategy. And so he did.

Then, much to Harry's surprise, not only did the old woman fully approve the plan, declaring herself willing to sacrifice her home and possessions for her country, but she even supplied the arrows for its implementation.

With one of Marion's marksman setting the roof aflame with the arrows, another stood ready with a fixed rifle to frighten any British soldier who attempted to extinguish the flames.

Soon a white flag was shown, and without a drop of blood being shed the garrison surrendered. The fire was quickly extinguished with minimal damage incurred.

Now, strange as it seemed, dear Mrs. Motte was stewing chickens from her own coop to serve the hungry officers, American and British alike. How would the general respond when Harry informed him that this wonderful old lady fully expected them to sit down and dine with the enemy?

The sound of approaching hoof beats distracted Harry's thoughts. Though Harry could not see the riders, he watched as Francis Marion stood, indicating that it was indeed the general and his party.

The young cavalry commander made his way outside to greet the general and give his rather unusual report. Nathanael made little comment beyond an occasional smile, or chuckle—even to the bizarre dinner invitation.

As the report ended, Harry fully expected a question or two in regard to details, but instead the general said, "I am eager to meet this brave Daughter of Liberty, and apologize for the necessary damage done to her home, but first, where might I find General Marion?"

Harry escorted Nathanael to the edge of the wood where Francis Marion remained. Delighted, Harry made the introduction.

Marion and Horry immediately saluted the superior officer. Nathanael responded, by taking off his hat and extending his hand.

"General Marion, I am honored to finally have the privilege of meeting you. Might I take your hand, sir, for I am a great admirer of yours?"

Stunned, Francis Marion placed his hand in that of Nathanael Greene's, and for the first time Harry Lee witnessed a smile on the face of the 'Swamp Fox'.

The final battle, fought on September 8th at Eutaw Springs proved so fierce that few came off the field unscathed. Finally stealing a moment two days after the battle was fought to write his wife; Nathanael praised the gallantry of his brave men. Even now, tears welled as he shared with her how many a valiant man died at Eutaw Springs. Images of this most bloody and obstinate battle continued to haunt his mind.

The summer's heat was grueling, bearing relentlessly upon the wounded whose agony was intensified by the blistering rays of the sun. The clear, cold water of the springs located on the edge of the battlefield began to run red with the blood of the wounded who managed to drag themselves there to quench their violent thirst.

So exhausted were both sides in the end that Nathanael proposed to the British commander, under a flag of truce, that the armies unite in moving the wounded and burying the dead. Then abandoning the field to his victorious though shattered enemy, Nathanael Greene led his own crippled troops to safety. Rough liters were devised to transport those unable to walk while the walking wounded were supported by staggering comrades who proved faithful to the task.

Both Rob and Lewis incurred minor wounds, he informed her, but the new aides taken on during this chaotic summer campaign—Captains Nathaniel Pendleton, William Pierce, and Thomas Shurbrick—came off the field without a scratch.

After finishing the letter, he placed the quill pen in its holder and reached for the pocket watch, which lay on the desk. He opened the timepiece. *One o'clock— early still*, he thought as he leaned back in the chair, momentarily enjoying the stillness of the camp and the pleasant music of the night creatures. The only distracting sound was that of his own labored breathing. To wheeze had become a constant condition in this taxing heat—just as the good doctor had predicated. And, as predicted, the asthma attacks were more frequent and severe.

Nathanael leaned forward and folded Caty's letter. After carefully addressing it, he put his seal on the back; then, almost as an afterthought, he reached for the delicate locket, which lay, beside his watch and the medallion Lafayette had given him.. He opened the locket, and gazed at the small miniature of his wife—a recent gift for her lonely, homesick husband. Nathanael smiled affectionately at the picture, and then carefully placed the locket back beside the watch and medallion.

Standing, he walked to the tent opening. The guard, alert at his post, quietly greeted his commander.

"A bit warm, isn't it, Captain." It was more a statement than a question.

"That it is, General."

"Feel free to take off your coat, Captain. You will be much more comfortable, I am sure," Nathanael, said, his own coat and waistcoat long ago removed, and even the first few buttons of his shirt undone.

"Thank you, sir. I think I will. I find myself missing the hills of the Santee on nights like this."

Nathanael smiled. During the stifling heat of August, he had rested his men in the cooler, healthier region of the Santee hills. He, too, missed the soft breezes the higher altitude provided—and the temporary relief from wheezing.

"I think I will walk down to the creek—might sit there for an hour or so," Nathanael informed him.

The guard nodded as he pulled out a pocket watch to check the time. The general was free to have an hour's private solitude; but a guard must be aware of his whereabouts, especially during the night while his aides slept. "Enjoy the quiet, sir."

It was a bright night. A dazzling, full moon illuminated the well-worn path to the creek. Nathanael squatted by the water's edge; and, cupping the water in one hand, he sipped the cool liquid. Then placing both hands in, he splashed some upon his face and neck letting the refreshing fluid drip down onto his chest and back.

He comfortably positioned himself by the moving water, listening as it gurgled past. *Such a peaceful sound,* he thought.

"Peace," he whispered the word. He had not given thought to that idealistic, dreamlike state of being for some time—certainly not since he took the Southern command. Nevertheless, here it was in the forefront of his mind. It still seemed unobtainable in a very real sense, but the intense longing remained.

Such peaceful moments were so far and few between anymore—today was an exception. He smiled remembering the letter from Henry found in a duplicate mailing of dispatches from Headquarters.

Henry's letters always brought him up-to-date on the goings on in the military family: General Washington's frustration in regard to British Commander in Chief Clinton's dormancy in New York was evident. He was helpless to draw him out to fight.

"Clinton has held that town for years—we should have burnt it to the ground when we had the opportunity." Nathanael muttered to himself with disgust, remembering Congress' absolute refusal at the time to hear of such a violent act against the town. "War is violent, gentlemen!" he added aloud in response to the memory of their absurdity, which in turn gave the perfectly situated haven of New York to the British.

Henry assured him, without offering any detail that His Excellency was seriously considering Nathanael's recent suggestion in regard to Cornwallis—indeed, might he be trapped?

Anthony Wayne, delighted to lead his restless troops into action again, was ordered to assist Lafayette in putting a check on Cornwallis and in seeing that Nathanael's supplies were not intercepted by the continued treachery of Benedict Arnold.

The recent discovery of Arnold's destructive raid on his own hometown of New London, Connecticut, prior to his present pillaging in Virginia, stirred in Nathanael a deeper thirst for his blood. Never had he felt such intense hatred for any man.

Henry's letter went on to inform him that Lord Stirling had been given the long dreaded orders to head to Albany, New York and take command of the Northern

Department. "No doubt his Lordship will seek your consolation with his pen—" Henry remarked. Nathanael smiled as he considered his friend's plight. "I will offer him a trade off—all of my many problems for his few. This accursed heat for the climate I am more accustomed to. You can only remove so many articles of clothing to cool off, your Lordship, but you can bundle up to your heart's content to keep warm. That is if there is still enough compassion and human decency left in the Northern states to see that your men are properly clothed against the elements. The Southern Department, in our continuous state of want for basic clothing, would die in short order to such exposure." Nathanael whispered to himself.

'Have you heard of Colonel Hamilton's falling out with His Excellency?' Henry questioned in his letter. Yes, Nathanael had received a personal letter from Alec, and a brief mention from General Washington. Their relationship had been strained since the execution of John André. It seemed to Nathanael that Alec had lost a degree of respect for the General. Indeed, the odd circumstances of his abrupt resignation indicated as much—even an attitude of self-pride and arrogance, which had gotten completely out of hand. To resign because the Commander in Chief supposedly inconvenienced Hamilton by making the aide wait upon him? Nathanael did not fully understand Alec's complaint, nor did he see how he could. It was the duty of an aide-de-camp to wait upon his commander. As for General Washington—even in his brief mention of the affair, it was clear that he was still grieving the incident.

Henry shared how Nathanael's recent response to the accusation from a member of Congress that he had not mastered the art of retreat, was so enjoyable that he took the liberty to relate it to many in camp who relished it as much as he: *'There are few generals that have run oftener, or more lustily than I have done. But I have taken care not to run too far, and commonly have run as fast forward as backward, to convince our enemy that we were like a crab, that could run either way!'*

But Henry had learned of another remark Nathanael made in a letter to a mutual friend: *'We fight, get beat, rise and fight again!'* It was written, Henry felt sure, in a moment of courageous determination—a trait Henry knew so well in his friend and admired exceedingly. Many an empathetic sigh was the response of his comrades and friends upon hearing that statement, Henry informed him. Though his suffering and that of his men was intense, and seemingly endless—the extent of which most in the main army had never experienced—Henry assured him that the respect for his ability and the praise for his magnificent accomplishments echoed throughout America, and had even been shouted abroad to the European allies.

We fight, get beat, rise and fight again. Nathanael remembered writing the words. It so aptly described this Southern Campaign. In four battles, the Americans had, by the strictest dictates of war, been the victors only once. But victory on the battlefield was not his main objective—weakening the British stronghold was, and that they had done. In each and every battle—each and every siege, though the last against Ninety-six seemed disastrously ineffective, they had, in fact, gained the advantage as though the blessings of Heaven were upon their every effort.

He had even been informed that a British officer, frustrated by the fact that Britain's finest commanders were being held at a standstill by a Quaker ironmaster, had declared, *"The more Greene is beaten, the farther he advances in the end. He has been indefatigable in collecting troops and leading them to be defeated!"*

Nathanael smiled as he remembered the account; and, though tempted to gloat, he quickly dismissed the thought. "I am hardly indefatigable, Lord; we both know that only too well." he whispered the prayer, aware of his own deplorable health and that of his army. Between the accursed fevers, which had befallen his men, and the recent casualties at Eutaw Springs, his strength had greatly dwindled.

"Eutaw Springs." he whispered the words, his throat suddenly choked with emotion. "One hundred forty of my boys dead and four hundred wounded. Ah, but, such undaunted courage—Lord, I am so proud of them—so very proud."

He considered Otho Williams. *Could a commander have more admiration for a subordinate?* he wondered with a true sense of awe. In a moment of utter desperation, when all seemed hopeless, he turned to the gentle Marylander. "Sweep the field, Colonel!" he shouted. Without so much as a blink, Otho rallied his regiments forward; bayonets fixed, and savagely did what needed to be done in order to offer his commander the opportunity to pull the remainder of the troops off the field to safety.

Then there was William Washington. In the previous battle at Hobkirk's Hill, Nathanael had been extremely disappointed with his performance, and reprimanded him for it. *Perhaps too severely,* he thought with a deep sigh. William had proven himself exceedingly effective and courageous at Eutaw Springs, remaining on the field to cover the retreat—many of his men being slaughtered and finally William, himself, falling captive to the enemy.

"I need a clean trade off for him, Lord. Please—I cannot afford to have him paroled and sitting out the rest of this war."

As for Harry Lee—'Light-Horse Harry' had gotten a bit too bold of late, and was reined in on several occasions. "There is a limit to the endurance of your men, Colonel." Nathanael had sternly warned him. "Pay heed to your quest for glory, Harry. Ambition is an admirable quality, but excess, under these circumstances, can dull sound judgment and lead many a man to his death."

Nathanael was worried about Harry. There was a change in him—a restlessness, as if he were searching for something beyond his reach. Though Harry now made frequent mention of physical ailments, Nathanael wondered with concern if the physical problems did not have their origin in his disturbed mind. Like a father observing the struggles of a beloved son, Nathanael tried to help the distraught, young Virginian.

His thoughts turned to the needs of the cavalry. The need for good horses was growing desperate. He had always made certain his cavalry was superiorly mounted to the enemy. Now, with Cornwallis entering Virginia, Governor Jefferson and the state legislature, falling victim to the greatest enemy—their own fear—refused to let Lafayette and Steuben purchase the desperately needed animals as ordered. Nor would Mr. Jefferson send the agreed-to-quota of units to Nathanael's aid— fearing both the militia and horses would be needed against Cornwallis. Now, to Nathanael's utter frustration and Jefferson's shame, Cornwallis was taking the horses at will; and the militia remained in Virginia.

He sighed. *There is nothing more discouraging than to have your own people put obstacles in your way. If they would only do what was required, what was agreed upon, then that which I am expected to do might even be possible—*

He lingered on the thought, feeling the despair take hold inside. "Is it even possible, Lord?" he asked. "I knew from the start it would be an uphill battle—that I can deal with. But I am not sure I can fight my way up a mountainside. If it were only the British we were fighting against, my job would be simple," he whispered.

The hatred throughout the South of Tory for Patriot and Patriot for Tory was unfathomable. The potential of the Southern states being depopulated was very real through frightening, bloody skirmishes, out-and-out murders, and the frequent flight of families fearing for their lives.

He had watched on many occasions as families paraded past him in their desperate attempt to find a safe haven. Men, hindered by physical limitations or the emotional turmoil of killing a brother, cousin or life long friend—leading their frail wives on foot, their horses having long been confiscated by one side or the other. Small babies sat upon their mother's hips as the other children scampered about her skirts, scarred forever in the tenderness of youth by the horrors of this civil war. Nathanael longed to call to them— and somehow make them understand that in time, by the grace of God, he hoped to push the enemy from their shores. He wanted them to understand that, once the real enemy was gone, they could find a way to end this civil strife through forgiveness.

Even Martha Washington had been forced to flee her home when it was discovered that a raiding party was en route to Mount Vernon. Nathanael took a deep breath, lowered his head and shuddered as he considered this outrage. He sudden-ly remembered his own wife's fears when British and Hessian troops occupied Rhode Island. "Thank you for protecting them," he whispered to Heaven.

Caty and the children were safe and well now—at least they were six weeks ago when her last letter was written. *So much can happen in six weeks,* he lamented.

Her letters had been full of encouragement and delightful tid-bits of home life. But of late, there had been a change. Her unhappiness was easily detected between the lines. She begged him to send for her. No doubt, the words were written as her tears fell—his own heart broke as he read them.

How could he send for her? Though his heart ached to have her with him, he could never expose her to this extreme danger and hardship. The journey itself, through Tory-infested country, was life threatening. He could not allow her to come here. If the danger of attack was not enough, then the danger of living amid the disease-infested swamps, as they were often forced to do, or the semi-starva-tion conditions, which reduced them to turn to snake or alligator meat for suste-nance, was more than enough reason to keep her safe at home.

"Dear God, the snakes and alligators themselves are enough of a danger," he muttered aloud. "I cannot allow her to come here," he said determinedly. "Nor can I adequately relate my many reasons to keep her away. No doubt, my reprises to her pleadings seem harsh and cold, though I try my best to reveal my heart in the mat-ter. What can I do, Lord? Please help her to understand that it is because I love her so, that I say no."

Glancing at the brilliant moon, he realized it was time to get back. He took a deep breath aware that he must shake the depression that was threatening to take hold. His men must sense an unwavering confidence in their commander. Heaven alone would know his fears, Heaven alone—

He stood, and began walking back to the camp, turning one last time to glance at the moonlit sky.

Frustrated by her inability to sleep, Caty gave up the attempt. She climbed out of bed, and took hold of the oil lamp. After scraping the flint to light it, she grabbed the lamp with one hand and a shawl with the other. As she passed the children's chambers, she peeked in. All four were sleeping soundly.

Caty stepped into the girls' room and pulled a blanket over Cornelia and Patty's small bodies. *How angelic they are,* she thought with an affectionate smile as she pushed back a lock of curls from Patty's face. *If only they were so angelic throughout the day.* She remembered the frequent episodes of bickering over whom would play with what—and if it were not for the girls disputing which one had the doll first, then it was Natty getting in their way or George delighting in teasing them both. Now all was peaceful—and they certainly were precious to behold.

With the bedchamber doors left open Caty, made her way to the front door. Upon discovering the brilliance of the full moon, she decided that she would not need the lamp. Carefully, she placed it on the foyer table and made her way to the front door.

There was a pleasant breeze stirring, warm enough for comfort, yet brisk enough to drive any annoying mosquitoes away. It was a perfect summer's night, as those in early September so often proved to be. She found her way to the garden, and leaning against the old, majestic maple tree, she gazed into the night sky.

Suddenly, as though it had jumped at her from the darkness, an overwhelming sense of loneliness enveloped her. Lifting her arms, she wrapped them tight about herself in a secure embrace.

"God, I am so alone. Do you see me here?" she whispered breathlessly.

She had insisted on moving from Coventry after various business upsets forced the Greene brothers to divide the family properties. Because of Nathanael's continuous absence from the ironworks, his beloved 'Spell Hall' was given to Jacob; and this farmhouse, which stood thirty-five miles southwest of the homestead in Potowomut, and further still from the ironworks in Coventry, became Nathanael's inheritance.

Nathanael accepted, with dignity, his lot; but he thought it best that Caty and the children remain with Jacob or his stepmother. However, as he so often did, he left the final decision with Caty, *'Whatever is your pleasure'*, he wrote.

Caty sighed at the thought of his written words. At the time, she felt desperate for a change. The first weeks were pleasant with various projects in decorating the house and tending to the much longed-for flower garden to occupy her, not to mention the welcome escape from the endless clamor of the ironworks. Before long, a few of Nathanael's comrades made their way to her new home for brief social calls: Cousin Sam, Billy Blodget—the now retired Navy chaplain, and even Nathanael's former Commissary General, Jeremiah Wadesworth. None came empty-handed.

Jeremiah, who now served as supply agent to the French fleet assembled in Newport, always paid a visit with full crates of staples and produce for the family of his absent friend.

Such visits were pleasant and a Godsend, as Caty's sole income was Nathanael's military pay, which had not been arriving of late. But even these simple, innocent pleasures were to be whisked away, Caty feared. Rumors had begun to circulate that mischief was brewing with the young, vivacious, and very lonely general's wife entertaining male callers in her husband's absence.

Caty was appalled and humiliated—never fearing her husband's trust would wane for a moment should the vicious rumors reach him, but fearing that such evil-minded people could rob her of one of the few pleasures left.

She had no doubt that it was Jeremiah Wadesworth's visits that caused the most gossip. He was handsome—Caty could hardly deny that fact—and every bit as arrogant and flirtatious as Anthony Wayne; and, like Anthony, his loyalty to Nathanael Greene was sure.

"The old biddies in this town are simply jealous that Colonel Wadesworth is not sharing a cup of tea with them." Caty muttered with a satisfied smile. "Ah, but it hardly matters now—with the French fleet leaving Newport, the colonel will leave as well."

Caty had just been informed by Sam of General Washington's plan for a joint move on Lord Cornwallis in Virginia. "The main army and the French fleet against Cornwallis? Why so much effort against such a weak force?" she had asked Sam.

"Haven't you heard, Caty? Cornwallis has been reinforced with troops from New York. Generals Lafayette and Steuben's limited force cannot meet the challenge," Sam said.

"Then those that criticized Nathanael were right. He should have pursued Cornwallis into Virginia—"

"No. What Nat did was brilliant. Look at what's happened here, Caty." He said, requesting a piece of paper and quill pen. With diagrams, he explained the reports of Nathanael's success in forcing the evacuation of the British outposts as Cornwallis slowly marched toward Virginia.

"He knew that, between Lafayette's obstinate persuasion and Cornwallis' attempt to be reinforced or rescued from the sea, the earl might find himself in a vulnerable position."

"I still do not understand," she repeated.

Sam smiled. "General Washington has been hoping for an opportunity to entice the French fleet into action. This setup is perfect. Nat forced Cornwallis north into Lafayette's lap. The French fleet, ever aware that their young nobleman is sparring with the British earl, must respond to their sense of national pride and come to the aid of the Marquis. The French will prevent the British fleet from coming to Cornwallis' aid while the main army makes its attack."

"Nathanael was aware of all this when he battled Cornwallis at Guilford Courthouse?" Caty asked in awe.

"No, not exactly—but I am sure he considered it. He put all the pieces together and hoped."

"How could you possibly know this, Sam?" Caty asked, full of wonder.

"I was his aide for a fair amount of time. When you work that closely—that intimately with a man in such intense circumstances, you come to think like him; you must learn to think like him." Sam looked up at her. "And, Caty, if such a sizable British strength is defeated here, this war might just be coming to an end."

"Could it be true?" she asked breathlessly.

"Yes, dear Cousin. Only three port towns will remain occupied—New York, Charleston and Savannah. A siege can be laid on the Southern towns with the aid of the French fleet, thus cutting off all food supplies and communication with New York. New York will be abandoned if the Southern towns fall, and then we are free!"

"Then this battle in Virginia is most important," Caty said softly, her eyes fixed on Sam's diagram.

"Yes. Very important."

"But Nathanael will miss it, won't he?"

"He will not only miss it, he may not even hear of it until days after it is fought."

Caty looked up at him, a tear slowly running down her cheek. "He's worked so hard for this. How very sad that he will not take part in it—how very sad."

A tear sprung forth even now, as she remembered the conversation with Sam. Lifting her hand, she wiped it from her cheek.

"It does not seem fair that others might wear the laurels he so plainly deserves to share in," she whispered to Heaven. "I may not understand his mind in military matters as Sam and his many aides and comrades do; but I know his heart like none other. Though he will shrug off the intense disappointment at not being a part of this coming battle in light of selfless duty, the pain and loneliness he experiences when he learns of it—though mingled with overwhelming joy—will be very real indeed. Oh, Lord, take care of him if you would." she prayed, the familiar fear threatening to terrorize her as it so often did at moments like this with doubts of his safety, his health, or worse. How could she know with the numerous skirmishes, ambushes, sieges and battles being reported from the South? How could she be sure from day to day that he was even alive?

With steadfast determination, she looked into the heavens. "I will not fall victim to such frightening thoughts!" she exclaimed. "Continue to care for him as you have, Lord. Assure him of my love. Would that I could envision him as he is at this very moment. Might he be asleep? Tattoo has long sounded." She smiled at the foolishness of her thought. Nathanael was always awake long after tattoo, and out of bed before the sound of revelry.

A sudden chill ran through Caty's body. She pulled the shawl snug about her shoulders, and began to walk toward the house. As she walked, she remembered a recent letter from George Washington. *No doubt, General Washington will inform Nathanael of this particular correspondence, himself.* Caty thought with a grin. Suspicious that her husband was being overprotective, Caty had written to His Excellency requesting that he advise her as to whether a trip south was safe. The Commander refused to become entangled in the middle of this conflict between his friends, telling Caty that her husband, who had a clear view of the circumstances of such a trip, could alone determine the propriety of it.

"Nonsense!" she said under her breath remembering his words. She was certain to receive a written lecture from her husband in response to George Washington's report of her attempt. *His husbandly duty,* she thought, a grin still upon her face; but between the lines she would sense Nathanael's pleasure in her desperate boldness—the very reason His Excellency would report the matter at all— to bring his friend a moment's pleasure.

"We have hundreds of men almost as naked as they were born, and it is painful to the last degree, to behold their deplorable situation. The Southern army seems to be doomed to sufferings. I wish it were otherwise; but it is not in my power to help it."
(Nathanael Greene to Peter Horry)

CHAPTER TWENTY

SITUATED AGAIN IN the High Hills of the Santee, Nathanael waited. First, his men needed to recuperate from their strenuous campaign. Injuries and illness were so prevalent that he had set up a chain of hospitals extending from the High Hills northward to Charlotte.

After personally making rounds of the hospitals, Nathanael reported to Congress the deplorable conditions. Medical supplies from Virginia had long been cut off by Arnold's continued treachery. Many of the army physicians themselves fell victim to the diseases of the South. And to his utter shock, he witnessed the haunting scene of his brave, dying soldiers—lying helpless, often in their own excrement, for lack of medical attendants to care for them. The sight and smell of their festering battle wounds, filled with maggots, was more than Nathanael could endure. What could he do but plead for volunteer help in the hospitals; plead for more medical supplies; pray that Arnold could be stopped; and offer a brief word of encouragement and praise, being certain to touch each one of his brave fellows as he spoke to them. What more could he do?

Not only were the medical supplies cut off, but soon all dispatches from General Washington ceased to arrive. It was discovered that Banastre Tarleton had been assigned the task of intercepting this correspondence to and from Greene. And, as was Tarleton's way, he accomplished it with great zeal, leaving many a post rider for dead and throwing Nathanael Greene into a state of absolute uncertainty.

Aware that a joint effort was to be carried out against Cornwallis by General Washington and French Admiral DeGrasse, Nathanael did not know if he was expected to join the main army in the forming attack, or stay situated to prevent the numerous British troops around Charleston from possibly reinforcing Cornwallis in Virginia. The latter seemed most likely; but, wanting to be certain, he sent Harry Lee with orders to find General Washington.

Nathanael explained in his correspondence to General Washington his quandary due to Tarleton's perseverance, and requested an update and any orders. He then boldly suggested that, should the General be successful in defeating Cornwallis, might the main army, combined with the force of the French, consider Charleston as their next target. All reports indicated that 9,000 British, Hessian and Tory militia troops were gathering in that area.

Within a week of Harry's departure, dispatches began arriving from General Washington's Headquarters near Yorktown, Virginia. A siege was under way, which promised ultimate victory.

Ever aware of his favorite, most trusted subordinate's great sacrifice in subduing the enemy in the South—and sorely missing his dear friend's companionship, especially at this decisive moment of the long, arduous war—General George Washington took the time to assure his general of his delight in him. As he read the words, Nathanael's heart longed to be among them: Washington, Knox, Wayne, St. Clair, Lafayette, Von Steuben. Lincoln   how desperately he wished he could share this extraordinary event with them!

Harry Lee came bounding into camp on the afternoon of October 22nd. Leaping from his horse, he raced into Nathanael's marquee; and with a sharp salute, unable to contain himself any longer, he breathlessly blurted, "General Washington's compliments, sir. And he wishes you to share in the celebration of America's glorious victory over General Charles Cornwallis! Cornwallis has surrendered, sir!"

A more enthusiastic audience could not be mustered, as Nathanael's staff speedily gathered about him, each hanging on Harry's every word.

Harry Lee, noted for his descriptive drama, left nothing to the imagination—from the lengthy, frustrating siege, to the grand, though solemn, parade as the enemy surrendered. Nathanael's somber expression revealed his empathy at hearing Harry's description of the Commander in Chief's day-to-day struggles. Henry Knox and his men had, as usual, performed superbly with their guns. "Mad" Anthony Wayne had led his boys fearlessly in battle as expected. He took a musket ball in the leg.

Two surprising tidbits shared by Harry were the fact that Alec Hamilton rejoined

General Washington and was actually given a command of his own during the battle. And, to Nathanael's utter astonishment, the old Wagoner, Dan Morgan, joined in the fray as well.

By the time Harry finished his enthralling account, there was not a dry eye in the group. As the immediate, almost riotous celebration wound down, Nathanael detected somberness in his young cavalry officer's countenance.

"You must be tired, Harry," Nathanael remarked as the others busied themselves with various assignments in relating the joyous news to the troops.

Harry shrugged. "I suppose I am, sir."

Nathanael gestured to the stool alongside his desk, and reached for the dispatches Harry extended to him as both men sat down.

"Is something troubling you, lad?" he asked, pulling a letter from General Washington out of the pile and breaking the seal.

"It was a glorious battle, General—glorious indeed! But, as your emissary, General Washington offered me no part in it. I was strictly an observer."

Nathanael put down the letter, directing his full attention to his friend, but did not respond right away. Harry's extreme change in mood, from exuberant excitement to near despondency, was disturbing.

Light-Horse Harry Lee was a born soldier; and at the youthful age of twenty-six, had perhaps experienced more danger and displayed more daring than any man in the Continental Army. And now, with the surrender of Cornwallis, this war might finally be entering its death throes—and what would a man like Harry Lee do with no danger to face, no enemy to subdue?

The jubilance in most at the prospect of peace was a source of distress in Harry. It was not the death and carnage that he found fulfillment in, but the desire to do that which he did so masterfully—lead men in desperate combat.

"I am sorry that your great abilities were not put to use at Yorktown," Nathanael's compassionate words came. "Had I known the situation there, I would have strongly recommended to His Excellency that he assign you as he saw fit. My sincere apologies. But take heart Harry," he said leaning forward and placing his hand on the young man's arm. "Do you have any idea how much I envy you in having witnessed it?"

"You are right, sir. I did get to witness the battle and the surrender. And I also was granted a short leave during the siege to visit my family."

"Your parents must have been delighted to see you." Nathanael commented with a knowing smile. Leaning back in the chair, he studied the dispatches on the desk before him.

"I am keeping you from reading your mail, General."

"I will get to it soon enough," Nathanael replied. "I sense that there is still something on your mind—What is it, lad?"

"General, I spent a great deal of time being entertained by various officers while at the camp in Yorktown. The truth is, sir, their mode of living appeared quite luxurious compared to that of the Southern army. There were nightly feasts and comfortable accommodations for the officers—why a lieutenant in the army of the North enjoys comforts denied the commander of the Southern Department. Intimately acquainted with your many hardships, sir, I found it extremely distressing to witness the vast contrast—"

"Well, Colonel, I appreciate your devotion. But, please, do not burden yourself on my account: for I am a firm believer that an individual will store up treasure for himself in Heaven for sacrifices he may be called upon to make here," Nathanael said with a warm smile.

"Then you shall have much treasure awaiting you, sir."

Nathanael turned his attention back to the letter on the desk, and proceeded to read. It began with General Washington's expression of personal sorrow that Nathanael was not able to participate in the battle.

As Nathanael proceeded to read, his heart sank. His request for the full force of the main army, along with the French troops and naval support to take out Charleston and Savannah was denied. Although General Washington assured Nathanael that he supported the plan, French Admiral DeGrasse declared that his fleet was due in the West Indies. French General Rochambeau planned to return to France with his troops after resting them in Virginia for the winter.

Without the French support needed to effectively subdue the South in quick order, and with New York still occupied by the British, General Washington felt constrained to return northward. Aware of Nathanael's discouragement in receiving the disappointing news, George Washington assured him that his small army would be reinforced with veteran troops under the command of General Arthur St. Clair and General Anthony Wayne.

Nathanael tried to hide his own disappointment. He placed the letter down and turned his attention toward Harry.

"Did His Excellency share the contents of this letter with you?"

"No, sir, he did not."

Nathanael forced a smile as he comfortably leaned back in the chair. "Close to a thousand veteran troops are being deployed to us under St. Clair and Wayne."

"Wayne and St. Clair?" Harry asked incredulously, a sudden smirk upon his face. The intense, open animosity between these men was common knowledge. "And some say the General does not have a sense of humor—"

Nathanael let out a short, grunt-like laugh. "A dry sense of humor at times   What did I do to deserve this, Lord?" he said with a slight smile. "Let's hope it is true—," he added, momentarily overwhelmed by the fact that troops he depended on—troops he desperately needed, never seemed to arrive for one reason or another.

"Their numbers will even things up a bit, sir. Have any plans, General?" Harry asked, unaware of his tormenting doubts.

"Yeah, if they reach us, I plan to separate Wayne and St. Clair as soon as they get here. God knows we have enough civil strife about us. I will send General Wayne to Savannah to keep an eye on things there. Then we will do the only thing we can with the numbers we have—box the British in at Charleston."

Unable to await the lengthy march of Wayne and St. Clair's troops, Nathanael moved his army toward Charleston. Fully expecting a confrontation with the enemy, he was surprised to learn that all British and Hessian troops in the vicinity, along with a large number of militant Tories, had fled before him to the safety of the port town. Immediately the British began working on fortifications and stocking food provisions in preparation to be laid to siege, without a fight.

Somewhat confused by the fact that British General Alexander Leslie offered no fight, though his force was presently double that of the Americans, Nathanael decided to take full advantage of the situation and encamp his men in the most strategic positions possible.

In the lowlands, thirty miles south of Charleston, Nathanael encamped his main force. The cavalry settled in closer to the town where they could keep a watchful eye on the goings on while the partisan generals continued patrolling the area surrounding the two armies. When Wayne and St. Clair arrived, the siege would tighten: but for now, the situation was quite comfortable.

Nathanael's men had never been this far down in the lowlands. Once the dark, forbidding swamps, masterfully hidden beneath towering cypress trees, were forded, the men stood amazed at the beauty about them. It was an almost mystical land of live oaks and Spanish moss. Along the rivers lay the magnificent rice plantations—many now abandoned—others in desperate need of repair. Here food was abundant; rice, fruit, vegetables, poultry and fish. The army fattened itself on the richness of the land.

Suddenly the social graces of Nathanael and his officers were once again called upon as the grateful citizens of the lowlands extended their hospitality. The general was amused with the gallant spirit, which prevailed among his many bachelor officers as they vied for the attention of the young ladies present. And, as he watched them enter into the early stages of courtship, his mind wandered back to the days when he was the young gallant pursuing the blushing Caty Littlefield—and his heart ached more than ever to have her at his side.

She was free to come to him, he plainly told her in a letter after one such gathering. With the surrender of Cornwallis, and the siege of Charleston, passage South was safe. Though many of the militant Tories were tucked away with the British and Hessians, those, which remained in the countryside, were hiding out in the swamps for fear of being persecuted.

Nathanael, who implored the vengefulness to stop, deemed reports of barbarous persecution inhuman. Such acts would only fuel the fire of hatred; and this, he said, was alien to the interests of the nation. *'Persecution only strengthens the cause it intends to destroy,'* he warned. He beseeched the governors of the Southern states to devise a way of making peace with their Tory brothers.

Arrangements for Caty's trip South were quickly set in motion. Billy Blodget was to escort Caty as far as Philadelphia where Rob Burnet, who had been sent North on medical leave, was to meet her and see her safely to camp.

Pleased with the present conditions facing his army—and the brilliant prospect of being reunited with his wife—Nathanael finally allowed himself to relax, though the wondrous state was short-lived. Informants soon reported that General Leslie was expecting reinforcements from New York and Ireland—as many as 5,000 troops.

With the realization that he would be hopelessly outnumbered if the information were accurate, Nathanael sent out desperate pleas for help. He ordered St. Clair and Wayne to hasten their march and begged General Washington for more troops, now stationed in Virginia, to be deployed to Charleston. He pleaded for French General Rochambeau to come to his assistance, and begged the recruiting officer to get troops on the march.

George Washington denied his request, reasoning that it was best not to weaken Virginia's present military strength, as it was feared the enemy might attempt to re-enter the state. Rochambeau sent his apologies and excuses for why he would not be of assistance. And the recruiting officer informed him that the South was war-weary, apathetic and without money; thus he was finding it impossible to raise troops.

Desperate, he wrote to Governor Rutledge of South Carolina, proposing a plan to recruit soldiers from among the slave population. But prejudice against black troops was too strong in the deep South, and Nathanael's proposal was promptly rejected.

Discouraged by the sudden turn of events, Nathanael considered his plight: his ammunition supply had been effectively cut off leaving him desperately low. Should the British discover his short supply he would not be able to stand against them—even if the rumored reinforcements did not arrive.

Then there were the threatened resignations of his partisan generals—Sumter had altered the commander's orders to his liking more often then not; and, finally, coming under the verbal thrashing of the superior officer, the militia general quit the service in a huff.

Pickens, too, began thinking himself privileged to pick and chose his orders. He made his threat of resignation known upon being reprimanded for his insubordinate attitude.

Even Marion! Francis Marion—the epitome of military discipline had felt put out by the Southern commander—sending his commission along with a disgruntled letter to Nathanael.

And with all the patience he could muster, implementing all the diplomacy he had attained, Nathanael Greene attempted to woo his partisan generals back into service, pointing out to each that he expected no more of them than that of his own officers. Gently, though firmly, he reminded them that his own service had been as painfully sacrificial, if not more so, to aid his bleeding country.

Sumter could not be persuaded—Pickens was, though reluctantly so. Only Marion was able to shake the discouragement, and return selflessly to the task yet ahead.

But the constant struggle to stay afloat left Nathanael Greene in the midst of his own, seemingly hopeless, despair. He replied to General Washington's latest denial to his desperate plea for substantial help; his words remained characteristically subordinate to his beloved Commander. Desperately he wanted to believe that George Washington's reasons for denying him assistance were sound, yet inwardly he doubted. Tormenting thoughts lingered, but who was he to blame? Congress? Rochembeau? General Washington? Or was it the Southern governors, or the thousands of men in these Southern states, paralyzed by their own fear?

"Lord, I am sinking!" he cried out in earnest prayer. "I cannot stay afloat beneath this enormous weight any longer. I feel as though we have been abandoned. Why must it come to this? The blood of so many valiant men shed in vain. Forbid it, Almighty God!"

British ships from New York and Europe did arrive, and the commander of the Southern Department anxiously awaited the report, holding his breath as the numbers were given. Only 560 troops had disembarked.

"I thank thee, dear Lord," he whispered as he lifted a trembling hand to his perspiring brow.

"I was never frightened," he told his staff officers with a weak smile. "But, I was confoundedly scared!" They joined their beloved commander in joyous laughter as the immense tension, which had built for weeks, found its release.

The announcement that General Wayne's troops were fast approaching the camp sent Nathanael out on horseback to greet his long-time friend. Yet from a distance, Nathanael detected that Anthony was not well. With every step of the horse, his body slumped forward as though struggling to stay upon the saddle.

Concerned, Nathanael quickened his own pace, hastening to his friend's side. No attention was given Anthony's officers and aides who formally saluted the commander.

"My compliments, your Excellency." Anthony said just above a whisper. Though his eyes shone forth his delight in seeing this friend, his smile was noticeably forced. "Forgive me for not saluting, General Greene, but I have no doubt that if I make the attempt I will fall from my mount—." And with that, he toppled toward Nathanael who, reacting quickly was able to catch his friend's body and gently lower him to the ground.

Nathanael closed the book he was reading, laying it upon his lap, and turned his full attention on Anthony's stirring form. Within a few moments, the younger man's eyes were open; after briefly studying their surroundings, they settled on Nathanael.

"Not exactly a proper military greeting, now was it, General?" Anthony chided, embarrassed by the entire scene.

"Some things cannot be helped. You gave me quite a scare. How are you feeling?"

"Death seems appealing at the moment."

Nathanael offered him a sympathetic smile as he reached out to touch his feverish arm. "Can I get you something? Are you hungry—or perhaps thirsty?"

"A drink of water."

Nathanael stood, and stepping over to the nightstand he laid the book upon it, and picked up a mug filled with water. He placed his arm under Anthony's shoulders, and gently lifted him, bringing the mug to his parched lips. When he had had enough, Nathanael carefully removed his arm, and placed the mug back on the nightstand. Anthony attempted to shift position in the bed; the intensity of the pain caused him to moan quietly.

"I am sorry, but we have no laudanum, or even rum to deaden your pain," Nathanael said as he sat back down. "My chief surgeon was by; he lanced the wound and cleaned it. Did General Washington realize that wound had not healed before he sent you out?"

"General Washington broke camp before I did. I thought it was healed. The truth is the ball is still in my leg. The surgeon said it would cause more damage to cut it out—just got aggravated by the march I suppose— Are you aware that Lady Washington's son took a post as aide-de-camp to the General?"

Nathanael nodded. He was aware of George Washington's frustration with his adult step-son. Jack Custis was somewhat of a prodigal, and proved to be a constant source of irritation and concern to his parents. No doubt Jack's decision to serve as aide-de-camp both surprised and pleased his step-father.

"Jack came down with camp fever in Yorktown. He did not survive."

"I heard," came Nathanael's sad response.

"Lady Washington is greatly distressed."

"No doubt. She has now lost all four of her children. Jack leaves behind four children himself. Perhaps these will bring joy to her life."

"Perhaps—" Anthony paused, then added, "It is good to see you, Nat. You have aged some since taking this command, but I suppose that is to be expected given the circumstances."

"I feel as though I have aged twenty years in two years' time," Nathanael replied.

"Hardly! And the truth is the gray hair is comely. It befits a commander in chief." Anthony smiled reassuringly. "You have become quite a hero up North—the only man able to free the South from British domination! How loudly they sing your praises, your Excellency."

"The war is not over yet, my friend," Nathanael reminded him.

"No, but the fact that Charleston was reinforced with only minimal force—and talk of possible peace talks in France—lead me to believe that it is just a matter of time—"

"Peace talks?" Nathanael asked.

"Yes. Haven't you heard? Our foreign ministers are meeting with those of Great Britain."

A glimmer of hope suddenly appeared in the commander's dull eyes. He leaned back and gazed at his friend, savoring the words.

"And Congress is appointing a Minister of War. Word is they want you."

"—Me?" Nathanael asked, noticeably surprised. "Will wonders never cease. Congress is desirous that former Quartermaster General Nat Greene take up politics?" He broke into laughter. Then becoming quite serious he added, "They will have to find someone else for that post. I am going home when this is over. I am going to be a husband to my wife, and a father to my children." He paused, and upon focusing his attention on the book of military tactics on the table, his expression suddenly became somewhat contorted, as though repulsed by the book.

"I do not like politics; nor do I relish the thought of working with a Congress that does not have proper powers. The truth is, the more I am acquainted with human nature, the less fond I am of political life. They think I am fond of army life—how they mistake my feelings. I just want to go home."

He paused again, staring straight ahead as though deep in thought. Then turning to Anthony he added, "I have come to envy those of the world who live in pleasant obscurity. Let's face it, General Wayne, the soldier and the politician die living in order to live after death!"

A weak, sad smile was Anthony's only response. He turned his face from Nathanael and gazed at the ceiling. "So what will you do after the war? Go back to forging iron?"

"I cannot do that—business has drastically declined. The forge simply cannot support all our families any longer."

"What of all the investments you made with your commission while quartermaster general?"

"I have little to show for any of them—the profiteering ventures were a failure. I purchased a sizable tract of land off the coast of Georgia on Cumberland Island. I should think the timber reported to be there would be marketable. The citizens of the Carolina's and Georgia have proved themselves more than generous."

"What do you mean?" Anthony asked.

"To show their appreciation the governors of each state have bequeathed to me certain land holdings."

Anthony was surprised by the announcement, and his inquisitive expression led Nathanael to continue.

"It is property that was abandoned by loyalists who have fled to England—and a piece of land on the frontier as well," Nathanael explained, attempting to shrug the whole thing off.

"Sizable pieces of property?" Anthony queried, aware of the vast land holdings in the South.

Nathanael shifted position, suddenly uncomfortable with the conversation. "Yes, they are fairly sizable—"

"How sizable?"

"Well, acre wise the piece on the North Carolina frontier is the largest—um, I was told it was about 25,000 acres—"

"Twenty five thousand acres!" Anthony exclaimed.

"It is not useable—not to me anyway. But I trust that as the country grows we will be forced to expand westward. Perhaps someday my children or grandchildren will put it to good use."

"What of South Carolina's and Georgia's gifts?" Anthony asked.

"South Carolina and Georgia have graciously given me abandoned plantations, each consisting of around 2,000 acres."

Anthony's face broke into a wide grin. "Bless my soul! Nat Greene will be a gentleman farmer like George Washington!"

Nathanael looked at him, the smile in response to his friend's excitement quickly waning. "I do not know about that. If I could find a way, I would simply go back to Rhode Island. It is home—it will always be home."

He took a deep breath and threw Anthony a weak smile. "You know me—I am a New Englander through and through. What will you do after the war? Is the family tannery still in operation?"

"Productive as ever." There was no emotion in Anthony's tone or expression. "I cannot imagine a more depressing future. Look at us, Nat. After all, we have experienced in these past seven years—how can we possibly be content going back to being a tanner, an ironmaster or even a gentleman farmer? How?"

Nathanael's warm smile met Anthony's perplexed gaze. "I will have no problem being content. As long as my family is provided for and happy I would return to the forge, or take up farming, or do whatever it is I can."

"Not me. I do not think I can go back to the tannery," Anthony lamented.

Nathanael leaned forward and placed his hand on Anthony's shoulder. "Even in time of peace we will need a well trained army, and, therefore, some of us will have to remain to oversee it. You and Harry Lee should consider such a post."

"Harry Lee will return to Virginia and his plantation." Anthony scoffed, moaning softly as he changed position again.

"If Harry hangs up his sword he will wither away—as will you. You were both born to this station, like it or not." Nathanael said with a chuckle as he rose to his feet. "I have recommended to Congress and His Excellency that Harry be promoted to brigadier general—Otho Williams as well. What do you think?"

"I think their promotions are over due. Do they know?"

"No. And I do not intend they should. Congress is notorious for denying my recommendations."

"Ah, but wanting you as Minister of War as they do, they may grant your every wish to win you over."

"One can always hope," Nathanael said with a smile, and added, "You need to get some rest, my friend. I have much yet to speak to you about in regard to our situation here—and am greatly desirous to hear your account of Yorktown and all the news from camp."

Anthony nodded, grimacing from the pain as he moved. "Has St. Clair arrived?"

"Three days ago."

"Do you suppose he is losing sleep tonight worrying about my condition?" Anthony asked with a playful grin.

"No, I do not suppose he is." Nathanael replied reflecting Anthony's expression. "But Harry is anxious to see you—and William Washington."

"William? I thought he was in prison?"

"He was never really in prison—because of his rank the British housed him with a family not too far from here, as he recovered from his wound. It turned out to be a family of patriots—they turned out to have an attractive, young daughter who took it upon herself to nurse our dear colonel back to health."

"Awe, don't tell me. Has William gone and fallen prey to a woman?" Anthony exclaimed with a grin.

"I could not manage an exchange for him; therefore I arranged to have him paroled. He was released just the other day and reported to headquarters with this pretty, little thing on his arm and introduces her as Mrs. Washington!"

Anthony began to laugh. "He has gone and got himself married?" he bellowed.

"He certainly has—and you have never seen a couple as starry eyed as these two are." Nathanael assured him, smiling affectionately at the thought of his young cavalry officer and his new bride. "Are you sure I cannot get you anything?" He asked once more.

"No. Nothing right now, but thank you, sir."

"Then you had better get some sleep. If you should need anything call out—I am across the hall, and my aides are in the chambers on both sides of yours." Nathanael blew out the candles in the room and walked to the partially open door, turning once more to face his friend.

"Good night, General Wayne. I am delighted to have you with me."

"Good night, General Greene. I have hoped for the opportunity to serve under you once again."

The visits to Anthony's bedside were frequent in the days to follow. Soon the two friends were seen walking together—short walks at first, with the subordinate general leaning on his commander for support. But before long, the daring swash-buckler was restless to return to active duty.

The situation at Charleston was at a stalemate. Though the food supply was abundant, Nathanael saw no sense in over taxing it. Savannah, Georgia was presently occupied by the enemy, and presently unchecked. To send a portion of his troops further south to lay siege to Savannah seemed a most sensible move. Such a move would lessen the threat of a possible British stronghold developing; prevent a rapid depletion of food for his troops; and last, but certainly not least in the Southern commander's mind, this move would provide the perfect opportuni-ty to separate the archenemies, Arthur St. Clair and Anthony Wayne. More famil-iar with Anthony's strategic ability, Nathanael was comfortable with him taking the post. Though he would miss his friend's company, he had no doubt that the situa-tion in Savannah would be in good hands.

After deploying the Pennsylvania troops south, Nathanael turned his full atten-tion to the situation at hand. He had encouraged Governor Rutledge and the General Assembly of South Carolina to once again convene, thus reestablishing civil authority in the state, and relieving himself the duty of maintaining martial law. Though Nathanael assured the governor that all was relatively safe in regard to the legislature reassembling, he urged him to exercise caution just the same, and meet within a close proximity of the army, which would protect them from any sur-prise attack. He continued steadfastly guarding the assembly throughout their ses-sions.

Before long, his men became restless. A threatened mutiny was quickly squelched with the swift, public execution of the ringleader, and the exile of others involved to a nearby arsenal where they were forced into hard labor under guard.

Rice, fruit and vegetables were plentiful, but meat was scarce and rum non-existent. Though the southern winters were temperately mild, one still needed the protection, and decency of clothing against the elements. And always there was the nagging fear that in their lengthy absence, their families were left without any tan-gible means of support.

Rumors of possible peace talks in Paris still prevailed; but, as far as Nathanael was concerned, until official word was given, the war continued. Until the last British soldier sailed from the American shore, General Washington and General Greene both agreed that their posture would be defensive, and their guard would remain up.

Thus, when British General Leslie sent Nathanael a proposal for a truce, begging that his foraging parties be allowed to collect provisions without the risk of attack, Nathanael immediately declined. General Leslie argued that there was no need for the shedding of anymore blood—with peace talks soon to get underway, why not make concessions on both sides that the two armies might enjoy more tolerable conditions until official peace was declared?

Without the consent of Congress, Nathanael could not agree to a truce, he told the British commander. But, beyond that, he did not truly believe that peace was at hand. The recent, disheartening news, of a glorious English naval victory over French Admiral DeGrasse's fleet left both George Washington and Nathanael Greene apprehensive of the possibility of the British being inspired to try once again to subdue America by reinforcing New York, Charleston or Savannah.

No truce—no compromise. Therefore, minor skirmishes continued as British foraging parties attempted to gather food supplies.

"The exalted talents of General Greene have been amply displayed in North and South Carolina — without an army, without means, without anything he has performed wonders."
(Henry Knox to John Adams)

CHAPTER TWENTY-ONE

AS THE BLEAKNESS of the winter months settled in with the various, endless concerns of command, Caty's frequent reports of her travels arrived, brightening Nathanael's existence.

Severe winter conditions in Philadelphia prevented her and Rob Burnet from proceeding southward for almost a month. Though delighted to be staying with the Washingtons, Caty became anxious to be reunited with her husband.

Illness again forced a delay as they moved further south, but in early April, three months after setting out from home, a dispatch from Rob Burnet arrived at headquarters announcing that they were in Salisbury, and expected to arrive at camp by mid-afternoon the following day.

The temptation was great to ride to Salisbury that night and surprise her. However, immediate responsibilities prevented such impulsiveness on Nathanael's part.

"Go ahead, General. Things will be fine here for a day," Harry Lee coaxed, having been present, along with William Washington when the announcement arrived.

Nathanael turned his attention to his young friend, a whimsical expression upon his face. "I have no doubt that you could handle things here, Colonel Lee, but you see, I would have to leave the command to one of my general officers—and none are as capable as you." He said with a wink.

Harry smiled at his own impetuosity.

"Rob said they encountered Otho Williams in Salisbury," Nathanael read from the dispatch.

Harry and William nodded, a definite sadness falling upon their faces. Otho Williams had left camp only a few days previous, having been granted temporary leave by Nathanael to return home in the hopes of restoring his failing health. His presence was already sorely missed.

"Otho has updated Rob on the news of the family, and thrilled Mrs. Greene with the accounts of her—" Nathanael stopped reading.

"Thrilled Mrs. Greene with the accounts of what?" Harry asked. Both men wore a grin, noting the general's obvious embarrassment.

Nathanael looked up, smiling sheepishly. "With the accounts of her brave knight's daring—" he said softly.

"Well, it is true!" William exclaimed, still smiling.

Suddenly serious, Nathanael glanced again at the dispatch, then folding it; put it in the inner pocket of his jacket.

Harry and William glanced at one another. "—What's troubling you, General?" Harry finally asked.

"Probably Otho's leaving—I am concerned about his health."

"No doubt you are, sir, but I find it hard to believe, with Mrs. Greene arriving tomorrow, that Otho Williams is dominating your thoughts!" Harry commented with a smirk.

Nathanael looked at his officers; both had become very close to him—very intimate. Taking a deep breath, he contemplated sharing his concern.

"—I—," he began, hesitated, and looked away. Then determinedly, as if in dire need of their support, he directed his attention back to them, and took another deep breath.

"—I am sensible to the fact that I have aged well beyond my thirty-nine years since taking this post. My wife is quite young still—quite beautiful. What would a beautiful, young woman want with such an old man?"

Again, Harry and William glanced at one another, both apparently stunned by the question.

"You are as strong as an ox, General, and as fit as any man I have ever seen." Harry began. "So you have a few extra gray hairs—I hear that women find gray hair on a man to be attractive—it lends a more distinguished appearance."

Nathanael smiled at Harry's honest attempt. William rolled his eyes at Harry, and shaking his head he began to speak.

"General, I did not have much opportunity to spend time in the company of you and Mrs. Greene, but from what I heard others say—especially General and Mrs. Washington, your wife is openly in love with you. The risk she is taking in coming this great distance only proves it. Such love is not diminished so easily—on the contrary, sir, I fully expect the sacrifice you have made will endear you all the more to her."

Nathanael studied William for a moment, and then smiled weakly. "I am sure you are right. Forgive me, gentlemen. I have never considered myself a vain man, but—"

"It is not vanity, sir. It has been two years since you have seen one another. Such apprehensions are to be expected, I should think," William said with a comforting smile.

With an escort of aides, guards and his two cavalry officers, Nathanael set out from camp at noon the next day to meet his wife. About ten miles out the party heard the rumble of an approaching coach. Beckoning the men to halt, Nathanael waited breathlessly for the coach to come into view, and then setting his spurs to the horse, he galloped forward to meet it.

"General!" Rob called with a salute from the driver's box. "I did not expect to see you this far out, sir!"

"You are looking well, Rob. How are you feeling?" Nathanael asked as he dismounted and pulled off his gloves.

"I am feeling much better, sir, thank you," Rob replied as Nathanael handed his gloves, along with the horse's reins to an attentive aide, though he did not take notice of which aide it was, nor of Rob's reply, for the coach door suddenly swung open.

Before he had the opportunity to step forward and offer his assistance, Caty was standing on the ground alongside the coach.

Nathanael said nothing, nor did he do anything. Transfixed, he gazed at his wife. She smiled softly in response to his apparent awe. Then slowly—ever so slowly—Nathanael reached up, and taking hold of his tricorne, removed it from his head, again staring in silence.

"—Thee are more beautiful than I remembered—," he finally said, almost in a whisper.

Her smile widened, clearly revealing her dimples. "And look at you with your skin so bronzed and wisps of gray. You are more dashing than ever!"

He stepped forward, refraining from taking hold of her too quickly, but gently placing his free hand on her cheek, he tenderly caressed it.

"This is not your usual greeting, General. Have two year's separation made you feel the part of a stranger?" she asked, her dark eyes purposely attempting to draw him out of his awkwardness.

"I am not sure if it is that, or the fear that I am dreaming once again, and shall momentarily awaken to continue the torment of being separated from thee—"

She cupped his sun-tanned face in both her hands, disturbed by the dullness she found in his eyes.

"It is no dream, Nathanael. I am here—and your men are waiting, your Excellency." Her face was aglow.

He turned his head, briefly looking over his shoulder at his mounted escort. "What do you mean?" He asked with a smile.

"They are waiting for you to properly welcome me to camp, aren't they, Rob?" She called out to the aide atop the coach, who could not help but overhear the conversation.

"That they are, General!" he called back.

"I do not like to try the patience of my men," he said with a smile, though his eyes still lacked the glimmer of which Caty was accustomed.

Gently taking her into his arms, Nathanael proceeded to kiss her with the cheering approval of his men led by Colonel's Lee and Washington.

The glory of spring had gone virtually unnoticed by Nathanael until his wife's arrival. Then suddenly, as though her very presence initiated nature's renewal, he too came to life—and the glimmer, long absent from his eyes, slowly returned to its full luster.

Tea frolics and dinner parties became commonplace at headquarters, where Caty's flowing conversation and glowing countenance quickly won her the affection of all. And Nathanael, who never doubted that her popularity would be immediate, was amazed at the enormity of it as he found his own seemingly diminishing in comparison.

"Might I sit with you, General?" Harry Lee asked, surprised to find the commander sitting by himself in a quiet corner of the parlor as the others socialized.

"Make yourself comfortable, Colonel." Nathanael took a drink from the mug in his hand, peering contentedly at the gathering.

"How is it that you are managing to escape the continuous chatter, sir?" Harry asked, apparently worn out by the evening's activities.

Nathanael shrugged. "They do not seem to notice me anymore," he said, a pleasant smile coming to his lips. "I believe I could walk up those stairs and climb into bed, and if it were not for Lady Greene or one of the aides seeking me out no one else would notice my absence."

Harry appeared skeptical as he turned from Nathanael to the men and women passing before their seated forms. Once the center of attention at such social functions, few even seemed to notice the general now as they scampered to get close enough to Caty to partake in her conversation.

"Amazing!" Harry uttered.

"Isn't it? She has always had this effect. Ca not say I blame them—her flowing tongue and cheerful countenance quite triumph over my grave face." He took another drink from the mug. "I am rather enjoying this turn of events." He added with a smile.

"Well, seeing we are alone, so to speak, might I have a word with you, General?" Harry asked, still staring at the gathering before them.

"What is on your mind, Harry?"

"Have you given consideration to my request to return home, sir?" He turned to face his commander.

Nathanael met his determined gaze, hesitating for a moment. "—Yes, Harry, I have."

Harry waited for him to continue—it did not seem he would. "Your decision, sir?"

Again, he hesitated, turning away from Harry's gaze, and fixing a blank stare on the gathering.

"General St. Clair has also requested medical leave, which I was forced to grant."

"I was not aware of that, sir."

"An officer is of little use to me if he is bedridden, and I am keenly aware of the strain this war has put on the health of many. Harry, I understand your health is poor—but there is more to it." Nathanael was smiling as he turned his head to look at Harry. "There is a woman."

"I beg your pardon, sir?"

"You are going home to get married—isn't her name Matilda?" he asked knowingly.

Harry appeared dumbstruck, and failed to answer.

"The cousin you went to visit while in Yorktown—isn't the girl's name Matilda?"

"Yes, sir, I did see my cousin Matilda on that particular visit."

"And you have been writing her since and even proposed marriage—"

"Has a man no secrets in this camp?" Harry asked playfully.

"If it is a secret, boy, you should not have revealed it to as many as you did."

Nathanael studied the younger man for a moment, a gentle smile upon his lips. "As far as granting you leave—I am praying your poor health is the result of simple lovesickness, and, considering the immense strain you have been under these past years in the line of service, I will gladly grant you leave—temporary leave." he emphasized. "Do you hear me, Colonel? I will not hear of you resigning from the army. I fully expect, that should I need you, you shall immediately return."

"Of course, General—thank you, sir. When shall I be able to head home?" He asked excitedly. It was the most excitement Nathanael had seen displayed by him in quite some time.

"Within the week I should think."

"Then will you excuse me, sir, for I have much to do to prepare."

Nathanael nodded.

"Might you extend my gratitude to Lady Greene for her hospitality—I do not believe I could get near her with the throng about her."

"I will see to it, Harry."

"Thank you, sir." Harry stood.

"General Wayne will be disappointed to find you gone when he returns," Nathanael stated.

"Savannah has not been evacuated yet—and perhaps I will be back before it is, sir."

"Perhaps," Nathanael said, though somehow he knew Harry's departure would be for good.

"I promise you, General, that I will name my first son after you!" Harry exclaimed, a grateful smile upon his lips. "By your leave, sir."

Nathanael nodded his approval for Harry to go.

With the onset of summer came intelligence that the British were to evacuate Savannah. Confident of the source, and concerned that those leaving Savannah might only be transported as far as Charleston, Nathanael ordered Anthony Wayne to return with his troops as soon as the evacuation was complete.

By the end of July 1782, the enemy abandoned Savannah. Wayne's men were reunited with the main force of the Southern Department. Ready for a possible conflict, Nathanael waited, but Charleston remained subdued. The transport ships passed the South Carolina coast, heading northward—New York would be their destination.

Within days, Nathanael received intelligence that General Leslie was under orders to evacuate Charleston, and had only to wait for the transport vessels to arrive. Though the source again was reliable—though the failure to reinforce Charleston with the British troops from Savannah certainly indicated as much—Nathanael still refused to heed General Leslie's pleas for a truce in order for his men to forage food.

"If his men need food would it be so terribly wrong to call a truce that they might supply themselves without the risk of being attacked?" Caty asked at the dinner table after Nathanael announced the arrival of General Leslie's latest request to Anthony.

"I will take no chances, and not relax until the British are gone," he replied dryly.

"They are intending to leave, and shall do so as soon as the transports arrive. He promises a truce on his end—a definite peaceful gesture I should say." Caty said matter-of-factly, causing those of Nathanael's aides, unfamiliar with her ease at questioning some of her husband's decisions, to raise a cocked brow.

"Oh, Caty. Dear, naive, Caty." Anthony began with a chuckle. "Let me speak in defense of your wise husband. May I, General?" He asked, turning to receive Nathanael's smiling approval.

"No general worth his commission would risk his reputation on the enemy's promises or peace gestures."

"Really, General Wayne?" She asked, obviously upset with his laughter and condescending remark. She held his grinning stare under a stern gaze for a moment, and then broke into a smile herself. "You are as arrogant as ever."

"More so, I should think." he replied.

"Indeed." She turned to her husband who was clearly amused by the conversation. "Now tell me, General Greene, does he speak for you?"

"In reference to you being naive—never!" He exclaimed with a playful wink for Anthony. "But beyond that I most certainly agree. If General Leslie's army needs food badly enough he can surrender, and then I will be happy to accommodate him. Have you forgotten so quickly his attempt to capture me?"

Caty cast her eyes downward, embarrassed by the fact that she had momentarily forgotten the attempt at a recent dinner party given by a local, prominent family.

Just prior to sitting down to eat, a man barged into the mansion, loudly insisting that he speak to General Greene. Nathanael went to see about the commotion, and was astonished to discover that the man—an operative from Charleston, had word that General Leslie was en route and intended to take captive Nathanael and his staff. He further indicated that their host and hostess were in on the plot.

Sending the operative off, Nathanael returned to the dining room, immediately ordering his men out, and taking Caty by the arm he quickly followed. Within twenty minutes, the mansion was surrounded by British dragoons shouting for the "rebel" general to surrender, only to discover that Leslie's sought after quarry was safely back at camp.

"I would be a fool to trust Leslie—and were the tables turned, I would think him a fool if he were to trust me."

Leslie's attempts for a truce continued as the weeks passed; and Nathanael's response was always the same—cordial but firm. And, as the stifling summer heat engulfed the lowlands, the merciless fever found its victims. By August, the fever was spreading rapidly throughout the camp. So frequent were the deaths that funeral services were omitted. Those native to the area claimed this to be the sickliest season in thirty years.

So far, Nathanael was faring well—religiously taking his daily dose of quinine. But a few of his aides were displaying early symptoms of the disease, and then Caty, too, showed signs of succumbing to the fever.

Determined to get his wife out of the suffocating, bug-infested lowlands before the fever took hold, he immediately wrote to General Leslie for permission to send her, and the aides, to an island off Charleston's coast, and presently under British control.

To Caty's utter astonishment, General Leslie quickly consented, and Nathanael began with the arrangements for their stay on Kiawah Island.

"Aren't you concerned?" Caty asked from the bed as Nathanael wrote orders preparing for their supply.

"I am greatly concerned, and the quicker you get to that fresh, sea air the better I will rest," he said, dipping the quill and continuing to write.

"I mean, aren't you concerned that General Leslie will not let us pass, but instead take us captive?"

Turning to face her, Nathanael was surprised by the apprehension upon her face.

"There is nothing to fear. The British will let you pass."
He said.

"How can you be so certain? Are you now forgetting how he tried to capture you only a few months ago?"

"No, I have not forgotten, and if I were going to the island he may make the attempt again, but I am not." he said with a smile.

"But taking me captive would directly affect you—as would taking your aides—"

"Yes, it would greatly affect me, but Leslie's situation is such that he cannot be burdened with prisoners—save me. I promise that you and your party will be safe."

"I do not understand, Nathanael." she remarked, visibly perplexed. "You refuse him safe passage to gather food supplies time and again, and yet he is trusted to grant us safe passage. Why should he?"

Nathanael rose from his seat at the desk, and walked to the bed. Sitting next to her, he took hold of her hand. "I do not want you to be frightened. I would never

send you if I had the slightest apprehension that Leslie would not honor his word."
He paused. "Let me see if I can explain. Foraging supplies for an army sustains the
army. To allow them to do this unencumbered is no different, in a sense, than
agreeing to a truce that their ammunition be restocked. We are laying siege to
them, and the purpose of laying siege is to force a surrender or evacuation. To offer
passage to a handful of sick individuals—including a woman—hardly compares. It
is the duty of an officer and a gentleman to do so."

"Then you would do the same were he to ask?" Caty queried.

"I would." His immediate answer set her at ease.

"You rest, Angel, while I finish making arrangements," he said, standing and
walking back to the small desk in the corner of the bedchamber. "Mrs. Connolly
has agreed to go as your companion and nurse. I have also requested that Dr.
Johnson go; he is feeling rather poorly himself."

After scratching a few words on the paper, he turned to her with a bright smile.
"And you will be happy to hear that Colonel Washington and his bride will be joining you as well."

"Good. I will finally have the opportunity to be acquainted with the girl. The
way William dotes on her I have had no time alone with Jane!" Caty began to laugh.
"Oh, Nathanael, they are too funny, hugging and kissing as they do. I do not believe
they ever let go of one another's hands! Were we ever so madly in love?"

Nathanael turned to face her, appearing astonished by the question. "I still
am!" he said. "Maybe I should let General Leslie capture me, then, when I am set
free, unable to take command under the terms of my parole, I will have all the time
in the world to dote on you, hold your hand, hug and kiss—"

Caty smiled. "—Really? What a wonderful thought. How long do you suppose
General Leslie would keep you before granting parole?" She asked playfully.

"There is no telling. He may torture me for information, or send me to New
York to be interrogated, or even send me to England to be executed by way of example."

"But then, again, he may not—" she said, drawing him in with her alluring
smile.

"—Then again, he may not—" Nathanael agreed, standing and walking back
toward her. "Are you willing to take the chance?" He asked, sitting beside her, the
glimmer in his eyes delighting her.

She laid her hand on his arm, playing with the fabric of his shirt. "—I have been
neglected for great spans of time, Nathanael, months—years alone. The way I see it
I deserve such doting—don't you agree?"

"Most certainly, my lady," he said, lifting her hand to his lips and kissing it. "And I will gladly risk my neck to the gibbet or ax—or both, for I understand King George takes pleasure in performing both acts on those found guilty of treason. But for you Catharine Littlefield Greene, it is well worth the risk!"

Caty met his smiling gaze, "I shall miss you terribly—"

"On the island?" he asked. Caty nodded. "Nay! I will not hear of it! Once you start breathing that fresh, salt air, and bathing in the sea water, you will feel much better."

"And I can return?"

"Nay. You will stay there until this deadly heat breaks and the fever has run its course in the camp —about six weeks I should think."

"Oh, Nathanael, so long?"

His smile was more forced than ready Caty noticed. "It will be a brief separation for us, considering," he replied.

Caty only sighed. It was apparent that her mood had changed. Nathanael raised his hand to her soft cheek, and gently caressed it.

"You miss the children," he stated.

"Very much," she said, her eyes wandering from his.

"It is not fair to you, always deprived of the company of either children or husband."

"When will it all end?" She asked, fixing her gaze back on his.

"Soon, Angel—we will be a family again soon."

Letters passed frequently from Kiawah Island to headquarters throughout the hot month of August as Caty and the aides sent detailed accounts of their stay. All had made a rapid recovery, just as Nathanael had predicted.

The daytime activities of the group were reported to include horseback riding and races in the sand. The men indulged in body surfing, while the women cautiously waded in the shallow water. At night backgammon, card playing and games of wit occupied their time. Caty was reported to be the picture of health, observing and laughing at all about her. And humorous stories of William and Jane Washington's inseparability were frequently mentioned.

Nathanael's responses to all their joyful reports were prompt, until the fever forced him to his sickbed. When Caty discovered that her husband was ill, she insisted that one of the aides accompany her back to camp. To her great surprise, and relief, she arrived only to find that her husband had overcome the worst of the fearful disease, and was perpetually seated at his desk sending dispatches, writing orders and receiving reports.

Fearful of the possibility of her being re-infected, Nathanael assured her that he was well. He then speedily sent her back to Kiawah Island for the remainder of the summer.

The summer months proved trying beyond the threat of depleting the army by way of the fever. With the enemy quietly subdued in Charleston, and their imminent evacuation expected, the army of the Southern Department had little to do but wait. With the danger of enemy attack removed, the civilians now viewed the encamped troops as more of a nuisance than a Godsend. And the troops, unappreciated and tired of the deprivations of army life, developed an almost obsessive longing to return to their homes.

A minor mutiny was discovered in the plotting stage, and instantly squelched. Plundering, a crime, which the commander would not tolerate, and had quickly brought under control upon taking command of the Southern Department, was again being acted out. Once more, the gallows received soldiers found guilty of such violations, and once more, the commander in chief of the Southern army prayed that it would not take more than one or two examples to put an end to the mischief.

Yet, in his heart he knew the plight his men faced was bleak. If the sickly season had not been enough to discourage them, then the neglect of the states for their provision certainly was—especially with the cold, wet, winter months fast approaching.

Meat and spirits were already scarce—clothing was non-existent. With a good part of his army thread-barren and shoeless, Nathanael realized he must act on his own for their provision, trusting that Congress would back his decision.

Finding but one man who would consider supplying the army on a promissory note, Nathanael entered into an agreement with John Banks. If the commander of the Southern Department could provide, up front, $1,500.00 in hard currency, Mr. Banks would deliver the desperately needed food and clothing, billing the Superintendent of Finance in Philadelphia for the remainder.

There seemed no choice. Nathanael could provide for his men through Banks' offer, or turn them loose on the civilians to forage for themselves. The money needed for the down payment of provisions was borrowed, and the agreement finalized. As promised, the supplies began to arrive, alleviating the apprehensions of the troops and most especially of their commander.

"Excuse me, General. Mr. Banks is here to see you, sir," Lewis Morris announced, disrupting the conversation at the dinner table.

"Is he?" Nathanael asked, having no expectation of a visit from the sutler. "Show him in, Lewis."

"Have you eaten yet, Mr. Banks?" Nathanael asked, gesturing for him to sit in an empty chair at the table.

"Yes, I have, sir."

"Then join Lady Greene, General Wayne and myself in a cup of tea." With a simple nod of his head, the aides were dismissed from the table.

"Thank you, General," Banks replied, preparing to take the seat vacated next to Caty.

"Is this a social or business call, Mr. Banks?" Caty asked pertly.

"Unfortunately, my Lady, it is business."

"How dull," she said with a smile.

"Indeed you are right, Lady Greene, as all my visits here tend to be. I am looking forward to the gala celebration you are planning for Charleston's evacuation. Have you received the fabric you requested for the gown?"

"I have, Mr. Banks, and it is exactly what I had in mind. You were very attentive to my description."

"You said the gown was to fashionably reflect your husband's uniform—the colors with which I am well acquainted. But, my Lady, I am afraid I have had no success in locating the epaulets you requested."

"Epaulets!" Anthony Wayne exclaimed then burst into laughter.

Nathanael turned a quiet, expressionless gaze on his wife. "Epaulets?" he muttered.

"—Small ones, very, very small ones—," she hesitantly replied, demonstrating the size with her forefinger and thumb. Then a slow, brilliant smile broke out upon her face. "General Washington would certainly appreciate them!" she boldly stated.

Cocking his brow, Nathanael's expression became inquisitive. Caty noted the gleam in his blue eyes in anticipation of her answer to his unspoken question.

"He once told me that Lady Washington wore the epaulets in his home!" She smiled sweetly and stood. "If you will excuse me, your Excellency, I have matters to attend to in regard to the ball. Good evening to you, General Wayne, and to you, Mr. Banks."

"Good evening, Lady Greene," Anthony and John Banks replied.

Nathanael watched in silence as she left the room, quietly closing the door behind herself.

"It shall be a grand celebration with Caty as the hostess," Anthony said with a grin.

Slowly Nathanael turned his gaze on his friend. "Yes and the thought of it terrifies me," he softly replied. Then looking at John Banks he said. "And what can I do for you, Mr. Banks?"

"We have a slight problem, General Greene," he said, reaching for the teapot and pouring the steaming brew into a clean cup. "It is nothing to worry about really, just a minor problem."

"What is it, Mr. Banks?"

"Well, I am actually embarrassed to relate it to you, sirs—" He threw a quick, timid glance at Nathanael and Anthony then focused his attention on the teacup. "I have somewhat overextended myself in another business venture —nothing serious, I can assure you," he said, fixing his dark eyes on Nathanael's. "But the merchants presently supplying me are pressing for immediate payment. And, unfortunately, sir, my hands are tied. I have no such cash flow, and am dependent on those in Philadelphia paying me that I might pay them. You understand how it goes, General Greene—"

Nathanael's expression was blank. "Did your suppliers not realize that you were working on a promissory note?"

"They did, sir, and were content with the situation until rumors began to circulate that my credit was on shaky ground. Now it seems they fear I will spend the money due them on creditors from the other business venture. I can assure you both this is simply not true. Certainly, General Greene, after similar experiences as quartermaster general you understand how these rumors get out of hand."

"—I can empathize with such a situation," Nathanael said hesitantly.

"Of course you can. And we must keep in mind, gentlemen, that most of our suppliers are not committed to our cause—they stand in the middle, seeking only to make a profit from whichever side is willing to pay their price. With the transport vessels docked, and the British actively evacuating Charleston, many merchants are sensible to the fact that their supplies will go to waste if not sold to the Continental Army."

Banks paused, and took a sip of the tea, his gaze steadily fixed on Nathanael.

"Because these merchants have no loyalty to your army, General, they feel no duty, or compassion, in supplying you, and would just as soon cut off the supply as send it without cash in hand."

"I have no access to the cash needed—certainly there must be a way of negotiating."

"Yes, General, they are willing to continue the supply under one condition."

"What condition?"

"Though these scoundrels are not loyal to either side, they are wise enough to understand the tide has turned. You, General Greene, are the hero of the South, and they believe you to be a man of integrity. They will continue supplying your army if you will personally become surety for me by endorsing my bills on Philadelphia."

Dumbfounded, Nathanael failed to respond.

"Do you doubt that Congress will honor this debt, sir?" Banks asked.

"No. They are sure to honor it."

"Then what is the problem, sir?"

Nathanael threw a quick glance at Anthony. "The thought of personally becoming surety for such a vast debt is a bit unnerving, Mr. Banks."

"Indeed it would be, sir, but as you said, Congress is sure to honor this debt, so your signature is only a means of quieting the murmuring of these scoundrels—and of caring for your suffering men, General."

Again, Nathanael looked at Anthony, who appeared just as uneasy over the turn of events.

"I understand your concern, sir. It is only natural. But, if you delay, I fear these merchants will interpret it as doubt on your part that Congress will, in fact, honor the debt. Thus you risk them permanently cutting off supplies."

"Do you have the papers on you?" Nathanael asked.

"I do, sir, right here." John Banks reached into his pocket for the contracts as Anthony began to speak.

"Might I have a word with you in private, General Greene?"

"Of course, General Wayne. Mr. Banks, would you excuse us for a moment, please?"

"Certainly. I will go into the next room and find a quill and ink for you, sir." He said, and stood to leave.

"This does not feel right, Nat. Something does not seem right here—," Anthony whispered as Banks left the room. "It is too rushed. You should have time to consider it."

"I agree, but he is right. They probably will view any delay as uncertainty on my part. I cannot chance our supply source drying up."

"What do we know of this man, Banks?" Anthony asked.

"I have received word that he is reputable. Rob Burnet is confident of his character, and has been offered a position in his firm after the war."

"Burnet's checked him out then?"

Nathanael nodded. "And one of our operatives in Charleston as well—'upright and obliging' is what he reported."

Anthony sighed. "It seems you must trust the man, General."

"It seems so."

When Banks' returned, Nathanael promptly placed his signature on the papers.

On the morning of December 14, 1782, the sound of reveille over the British encampment in Charleston was heard for the last time as the evacuation of 8,000 enemy troops entered its final scene. For weeks not only had the troops crowded the harbor wharves, but refuges as well. The Tories abandoned their homes and possessions fearing the possibility of retaliation by their countrymen when British protection was withdrawn.

An agreement was made between General Nathanael Greene and General Alexander Leslie stating that the British would inflict no damage on the city prior to departing; and that the Americans would allow them a peaceable evacuation. The Continental Army would take possession of Charleston as the British rear guard marched out. When word was received from General Leslie that the last of his troops were ready to march, Nathanael offered General Anthony Wayne the honor of being the first to enter the city with a vanguard of American troops.

A few hours later the remainder of troops marched into the emancipated capital of South Carolina, led by their commander in chief and the newly elected governor, John Mathews. American flags and hastily contrived banners draped the balconies welcoming the victorious troops. Cheering crowds comprised of Patriots, who for years were forced to suppress their loyalties, wept for joy at the realization that Nathanael Greene had accomplished, that, which was deemed impossible.

To the delight of Charleston's citizens, and Nathanael's soldiers, immediate preparations were made for Caty's victory ball. Though refreshments would be scant, she made up for it with the help of Nathanael's engineer, Thadeus Kosciusko, by festively decorating the ballroom with festoons of magnolia leaves and flowers.

As the army band prepared to play the opening number, Nathanael led Caty out onto the dance floor. When the minuet began the eyes of all in the room focused on the commander in chief and his lady. Following the dance, with the delightful applause of a captive audience, Nathanael affectionately kissed his radiant wife on the cheek, then summoning his second in command, General Anthony Wayne; he turned the vivacious Caty over to him, aware that he would prove a more graceful and enduring dancing partner.

Though Nathanael had balked at his wife's insistence in hosting this gala event, as he entered into the festivities about him, he realized she was right. His men, who had fought long and hard for this triumph, seemed to gain a sense of dignity in the celebration. Moreover, the citizens of Charleston, who had patiently endured their captivity, were enlivened with this joyous occasion marking their release.

In the countenance of South Carolina's former governor, John Rutledge, Nathanael saw the reflection of his own inner state. A sense of contentment and joy—emotions long forgotten now boldly embraced his soul. The fears, anxieties and desperation of the two years he commanded the South suddenly gave way to peace.

Though his orders were to occupy Charleston until the rumored Peace Treaty with Great Britain was signed, Nathanael was finally convinced in his heart that the war was truly over, and soon his men could go home.

Though he attempted to carry on conversations with various individuals, his focus continued to fall back on Caty. Partner after partner had vied for her attention on the dance floor. As always, she had captivated her audience with lively conversation and a glowing countenance.

He found himself laughing aloud as he watched her—the blue and gold gown, with its small, delicate epaulets was flowing gracefully about her swaying form. *Yes, General Washington would appreciate the gown,* he thought, suddenly remembering how Caty had once boldly challenged the Commander in Chief of the Continental Army to a dancing marathon. Neither would concede, until finally, after three grueling hours on the dance floor, they both agreed to mutually call an end to the contest.

Even while dancing Caty caught a glimpse of Nathanael's humorous, attentive gaze. Her responsive smile was all the invitation he needed. Walking across the ballroom floor he politely dismissed her present dancing partner, chivalrously presenting himself in his place.

"Two dances in one evening, General! And to what do I owe your favoring me thusly?" Her face was aglow.

"I have been watching you—"

"I am well aware of that fact!" Her immediate reply delighted him.

"I found myself envying the attention being given the others—" he confessed.

"Really?" She asked incredulously.

He smiled at her response, pulling her closer to himself. "Lady Greene, this certainly is your finest hour. Thank you for insisting on this ball."

She looked up at him, her dark eyes shining. "A victorious people must celebrate; and their illustrious leader must be duly honored. In truth, your Excellency, this is your finest hour. Were you a Roman general the laurels would be waist deep about your feet I should think!"

Nathanael continued to smile—a smile of contentment, which she had not witnessed for years. "What is it you are thinking?" She asked.

"How very happy I am. It will not be long now, Caty, and we will be able to go home and be reunited with the children—all of us together, with no more trying separations. There will be time enough for me to make up for my long absences."

He paused and chuckled a bit, pulling her closer still. "We will spend our summers in Rhode Island—blessed little Rhode Island. And our winters will be spent on our plantation here in South Carolina."

"Would you consider such a trip back and forth?" She asked with wide-eyed wonder.

"Why not? It is but a two weeks sea voyage from New England to Charleston. We will have the best of both climates! And we can visit General Wayne's estate in Savannah!" he exclaimed, speaking of the plantation adjoining his own property on the Savannah River, which had been presented to Anthony in appreciation of his service there.

"And what of your plantation in Georgia?" She asked.

"I will hire some people to get it back into production—rent the house out maybe—"

"Hire people? Do you mean Negroes?" she asked, aware of his repulsion to slavery.

"—No. I mean overseers—As distasteful as it is I will be forced to purchase a number of Negroes for both plantations to get things started. I am told the fields have lain dormant for years, and the houses and outbuildings are in dire need of repair."

Though his smile had waned at the prospect of such a repulsive purchase, the newfound tranquility remained. "I will not keep men enslaved. We will get things under way, begin to turn a profit, and I will free them. I intend to offer them room, board and a fair wage to work for me—Caty do you have any idea the profit that can be made from these properties?"

Slowly she shook her head, enthralled by his excitement.

"The potential prosperity the South has to offer is beyond comprehension. Finally—finally, a break in the clouds—a hope, a true hope for the future. Finally, Angel, we can get on with our lives."

Headquarters was established in the stately mansion of John Rutledge, and the Greenes found their friendship with the former governor and his wife growing deeper with each passing day. On many an evening an informal social gathering formed in the Rutledge's parlor offered much opportunity for various discussions. Nathanael and his aides were often prompted to tell and retell accounts of the Southern campaigns.

Anthony Wayne was especially fascinated with the one hundred mile retreat to the Dan River, and the recounting of the many battles and sieges. He, in turn, added his own tales of subduing Savannah, even sharing, with a definite air of confidence, the story of the surprise night attack by Indians, which had allied themselves with the British. When Anthony first reported this attack to Nathanael, he lacked all confidence, even expressing the doubts he felt in his own ability to command—this, having been the second surprise attack he experienced, for the Paoli Massacre would always haunt him.

Nathanael set out for Savannah and spoke to Anthony, bringing an immediate healing to the swashbuckler's hurt pride.

"The fact that a surprise attack was made against you during the night is not my major concern," Nathanael told Anthony. "For such an attack is the nightmare of all commanders. What concerned me was whether you were able to form your troops readily enough to counter this attack. You did so, with resounding results. Such a situation is a grave test of command—and you, dear sir, have done exceeding well!"

Caty, aware that the civilians among those gathered struggled to follow talk of tactics and strategies, was quick to focus on the more humorous tales of the arduous campaign. She related to the gathering, with great drama and hilarity, the story of how the commander in chief of the Southern army and the governor of South Carolina once shared a bed with a pig!

And how could she not retell the story told her of the time Harry Lee's men reported hearing the enemy's movements about their camp one night. Harry, concerned by the urgency of their reports, ordered his legion to take up battle formation, anticipating throughout the long night the enemy's attack. Yet, when daylight finally came the enemy turned out to be a pack of wandering wolves attempting to pass along their usual route, upon which Harry's men had encamped.

Enjoying Caty's accounts Nathanael attempted to offer his own in telling the story of how William Washington, though badly outnumbered, forced the surrender of a strong Tory outpost. When those familiar with the story began to laugh Nathanael could not control his own laughter enough to speak.

"What happened?" Anthony asked eager to hear the account. Nathanael only pointed in William's direction. The cavalry colonel, with his adoring bride at his side, hands clasped as usual, greeted Anthony's eagerness with a wide grin.

"I summoned for them to surrender, and received a very rude response," he said with a shrug, causing those already amused to laugh even more.

"Not strong enough to storm the stockade I ordered my men to appear to be laying siege, and busied myself with carving the trunk of a tree in the shape of a cannon. We mounted it on wheels and brought it to the edge of the woods in proper military style!" He chuckled at the remembrance of it.

By now, Nathanael was able to speak. "Our ingenious colonel then sent a messenger under a flag to warn the garrison of their impending destruction unless they surrendered."

"And?" Anthony queried further.

"And they surrendered, sir, without a shot being fired!" William replied sending Nathanael and the others into hysterics once more.

"Good man, Washington!" Anthony exclaimed with an appreciative smile for the resourceful officer.

"You did me proud, Colonel." Nathanael commented, still grinning.

"We had a good bit of fun with it, sir. And what of Captain Pendleton's capture of the enemy at Eutaw Springs, sir?" William asked with a smile of approval for the young aide-de-camp.

"Please, Captain, tell me of it." Anthony coaxed, delighted with such stories of unorthodox daring.

Captain Pendleton sought the commander's approval, which was immediately granted in the form of a smile and nod.

"In the midst of the battle I discovered that a detachment of the enemy was flanking our rear. Finding the general on the field, I informed him of the situation. Being understandably preoccupied, for he was, as usual, in the line of fire," the captain commented with a whimsical smile directed to the other aides present who had frantically endured the general's fearless behavior. "Without even a glance in my direction he ordered me to ride to the enemy and inform them that they would be cut to pieces by his cavalry if they did not immediately surrender."

Anthony turned an incredulous gaze on Nathanael who met it with a confident smile. "He obeyed my order and the detachment surrendered," he said.

"Unbelievable!" Anthony exclaimed. "And what is the story behind Harry Lee capturing a detachment of Tory horsemen by pretending to be a British officer?" He asked, determined to learn the truth of the incident.

"While on patrol, Colonel Lee's legion came upon what appeared to be militia horsemen," Nathanael began. "The colonel, thinking they were Patriots, gave little thought to them joining up with his legion until their senior officer made a request to one of Harry's officers to speak with Colonel Tarleton."

"The infamous Banastre Tarleton?" Anthony asked.

"Indeed, for it was a Tory detachment, and the quick thinking cavalry officer kept them thinking they were with Tarleton's legion while he sent word to Colonel Lee explaining the situation. The colonel, aware that Tarleton was in dangerous proximity, knew he must try to avoid a noisy engagement with this detachment. So, he met with their senior officer putting on a British accent, and pretending all the while to be Tarleton."

"Their uniforms are so similar—if you did not know Harry Lee from Banastre Tarleton you could easily be fooled," William Washington interjected.

"And so they were, for a time anyway, but Harry knew the façade would not last, so he sent word through his officers for his legion to surround the detachment, hoping to force a quiet surrender."

"Because Tarleton was so close?" Anthony asked.

"Close enough to hear a ruction. Harry's issued orders were to take them prisoner if possible, but, if they were determined to put up a fight, they were to be quickly and quietly put to the sword."

"And, from what I understand they insisted on a fight," Anthony said.

"They did."

"Tarleton never heard it?"

"Nay. It was masterfully executed, though the repercussions were loud. I received complaints demands and threats from the British for weeks of how it violated the maxims of war."

"And how did you answer their charges?" Anthony asked.

"With truth. It was an unfortunate situation, but quite necessary—Tarleton has committed heinous crimes without any cause—how dare he censure Colonel Lee. I quickly reminded them of the invalid and elderly Patriots they took captive in Georgia, forcing them to stand in the front lines in British uniforms, that their own sons and brothers would unwittingly fire upon them." Nathanael took a deep breath, visibly disturbed. "And I reminded them of the militia officer they took captive, executing him with no justifiable reason except to put fear in any man who was considering taking up arms against them.

"The law of nations does not seem to apply to British conduct here in the South. Oh! But how they cry out when they imagine the least violation against them."

"General Greene, you have put a damper on the evening by telling of these barbaric accounts!" Caty scolded. "And you!" She continued, facing Anthony. "You asked the question that led to this morbid discussion!"

Anthony grinned in response to her scolding. "Forgive me, madam. Perhaps I can redeem myself and brighten the conversation with a humorous occurrence at Yorktown."

Caty appeared doubtful.

"Oh, you will enjoy this, I promise. General Knox and Colonel Hamilton, with their men well entrenched in preparation for an attack, began to discuss whether it was soldierly to call out when a shell was spotted. Knox believed so—Hamilton disagreed.

"Their argument continued, each one becoming annoyed with the other when suddenly two shells were fired into the redoubt. The men about them instantly cried out, 'A shell! A shell!' and scrambled for better cover.

"Knox and Hamilton, too, sought cover—Hamilton safely barricading himself behind Henry Knox! Now, those who know this pair can fully appreciate this scene—our dear General Knox as enormous as he is, and Alec Hamilton's smaller frame!" Anthony bellowed above the hysterical laughter, which already gripped his audience.

"Well, General Knox, annoyed by Hamilton's previous argument, attempted to force the colonel to release his hold on him, and in the struggle lost his balance, fell over, and rolling on the colonel accidentally knocked him loose near the shells. Hamilton quickly scrambled back to Knox's side, none too soon, for the shells then burst.

"As soon as the immediate danger was abated, General Knox turned to Hamilton, steaming mad, and shouted, 'What! Tell me what you think now, Mr. Hamilton, about crying 'shell'? And let me make this clear—you, sir, are never to make a breastwork of me again!'"

"Henry never mentioned it to me!" Nathanael exclaimed through his laughter.

"No. Nor will he, for he was totally humiliated by the entire scene! And, certainly Hamilton will not utter a word!" Anthony assured them.

"Did you witness it, sir?" William Washington asked.

"No, to my great sorrow, I was not there to see it, but one of Hamilton's officers took great delight in telling me, and I promised, on my life, that I would never reveal my source!"

"Poor Henry!" Nathanael exclaimed.

"Henry?" Caty cried with a grin for her husband. "I know you love him, as do I, but consider Alec Hamilton's plight! Can you imagine having Henry fall on you?"

"Another unusual story worth telling would be the scene I encountered coming off the field after the battle at Hobkirk's Hill," William offered. Then looking at

Nathanael he paused, shaking his head as though he still could not believe what he had witnessed.

"—We had lost two field pieces at Guilford Courthouse because the artillery horses were killed. We could not afford to lose another. But after this battle, it was discovered that the artillery horses were again shot down, and the artillerymen would have to leave the cannon to the enemy, or drag them off themselves. Being in retreat, with the enemy on our heels, the artillerymen fell into a state of panic.

"General Greene came upon them, and jumping from his horse he threw the bridle to an aide and grabbed hold of the dragrope pulling on that cannon with every ounce of strength in his being; encouraging the men with his words as he pulled. As Providence would have it, I came upon the scene at that moment. My men had captured a fair number of dragoons which were quickly forced to dismount that we might save the guns with their horses."

William stopped speaking, though he remained visibly awestruck by the account he related. His gaze was fixed on Nathanael. "It was because of such displays of humility, selflessness and genuine concern for your men, General Greene, that you won the devotion of your troops, and thus, when faced with impossible odds have been able to regain the South!"

Caty poked her head into the open doorway of the sitting room. She was surprised to find only John Rutledge and Anthony Wayne.

"Excuse me, gentlemen, but I was certain I would find General Greene with you."

"He was with us earlier, but received mail from Philadelphia and went upstairs to read it," John Rutledge replied with a warm smile. "Has Mrs. Rutledge returned?"

"Yes, she is in the kitchen checking on dinner preparations."

"And how was your tea frolic, Caty?" Anthony asked with a grin.

"Absolutely delightful! Now, if you gentlemen will excuse me, I must find my husband."

"To fill him in on all the latest gossip, I will wager." Anthony said with a chuckle.

"It is not gossip—anyway I have to make it appear like it is not gossip or Nathanael will scold me." She said with a giggle.

She hesitated as she turned to leave. "—Do you know if the news from Philadelphia is good?" she asked.

Anthony responded with a weak, sympathetic smile, understanding her apprehension. News from Philadelphia was usually mingled—the good with the bad. On rare occasions, it was humorous, as the recent announcement of Alec Hamilton's marriage to General Phillip Schyler's daughter proved to be. With that announcement, light-heatedly related by numerous friends in Philadelphia, Caty was quick to remind Nathanael and Anthony how Alec had once declared to them both that he would never marry a general's daughter.

However, since that last piece of joyful tidings, two accounts of tragedy arrived. First was the sad news of General Charles Lee's unexpected death. He had been removed from command following his questionable conduct at the Battle of Monmouth. He spent the remainder of his days as a recluse in his Virginia home.

As sad as the news of this pitiful man's death was it did not compare to the emotional devastation that would follow. For with the next dispatch came the tragic word that General Lord Stirling had passed away.

George Washington attempted to break the news gently to the earl's friends by telling them of his lordship's ongoing bout with a cold in the frigid climate of northern New York. He told Nathanael, Caty and Anthony of how he had sent a crate of lemons to Albany, hoping Lord Stirling's health would improve by ingesting the tropical fruit. However, pneumonia had set in, claiming the beloved warrior's life.

The news proved a great blow to all—but especially to Nathanael, and especially when the war was so close to a victorious end. For weeks, Nathanael mourned his friend's death—and only recently had he seemed to overcome the emotional setback.

"I do not have any idea whether the news is good or bad," Anthony stated. "He went upstairs about an hour ago. I should think the fact that he has not come down yet means he is busy making responses, and therefore the news, one way or the other, is not of enough interest to immediately relate to us." Anthony tried to sound reassuring.

With that small bit of encouragement, Caty made her way up the stairs. Upon opening the door, without prior warning to her husband that she was about to enter, she found him sitting at the small desk, his forehead resting in his hand. Slowly, ever so slowly he looked up at her, his countenance twisted as though wrought with intense pain.

"—What is wrong, Nathanael?" Caty gasped. A chill ran through her body in anticipation of his response.

He tried to reply; she saw his lips move, but no words came.

"Has something happened to the children? Or to the Washingtons?" She cried, lifting a shaking hand to her breast, her heart seemingly stopped beating.

"Nay. Nay, everything is fine." He said with a forced, comforting smile. Caty did not appear convinced. "Here is a letter from Jacob," he said, holding an envelope up for her to view. "The children are doing wonderfully, except that they miss their mama. And here is one from General Washington," he said, grabbing hold of another envelope from the desk.

Walking to his side Caty lay her hand on Nathanael's shoulder and gazed into his troubled eyes. He immediately turned from her gaze, busying himself with the mail.

"There are some letters for you, Angel; one from Lady Washington; another from Lucy Knox and still another from—"

Caty took her other hand and placed it on his cheek, gently forcing him to look at her.

"What has happened?"

"Nothing."

"You are not telling me the truth."

"It may amount to nothing."

"What, Nathanael? What may amount to nothing?"

"Oh, Caty, I do not want to trouble thee with it—" he said, pulling away from her and standing.

"Have the British come against General Washington?"

"No. It is nothing like that." He shot back, his own distress becoming more evident.

"Please tell me," she softly pleaded, her concerned gaze locked on him.

He nervously looked around the room, sighing deeply. "—Stories have begun to circulate in Philadelphia that I have entered into a secret business partnership with John Banks in order to make a profit off the sales made to the Southern Department."

"How absurd!" Caty quietly exclaimed. "You have dealt with these types of malicious rumors in the past. Your character and reputation are well known. Your friends will quickly silence those guilty of such mischief."

He looked directly at her. "Many in Philadelphia are already questioning my integrity. Only those intimately acquainted with me see it as a monstrous lie."

"Perhaps the situation seems exaggerated in your mind right now," she gently suggested.

"Hurt pride? I wish that is all it was. A letter from John Banks was discovered in which he made claim that Rob Burnet has already entered into a partnership with him—"

"Not yet—after the war," Caty corrected him.

"Nay. The letter stated that Rob agreed to this business arrangement prior to Banks becoming sutler to the army. The letter insinuates that I, too, am involved as a secret partner. Such involvement by Rob, if it is true, certainly puts me in a questionable light as far as Congress is concerned. I have been ordered to make a deposition of my conduct. General Wayne and Colonel Carrington are under orders to do the same."

"What does this mean, Nathanael?"

"—It means that Congress may not honor the debt until they are satisfied that I am innocent—and that may take years—they many never believe it. It also means that I must see that any money that might be forwarded from Philadelphia be sent directly to me. I cannot trust John Banks to pay the merchants—there's simply too much at risk here."

"How much money are you responsible for?" she asked, bracing herself for the answer.

He looked at her; straight through her it seemed.

"No less than $200,000.00." Walking to the window, he gazed out upon Charleston's busy street.

"If I can cultivate the plantations their value will increase, I will sell the property in South Carolina—it will bring more money, being the better of the two. We will live on the Georgia estate for now. I could sell the farm in Rhode Island—it will not bring much, but—the sale of timber on Cumberland Island will earn enough to support us, and little by little perhaps we can build a house on the island, sell the property in Georgia, and live there."

"Congress will support you, Nathanael. After all, you have accomplished here, certainly they will believe you!" A small tear streaming down her cheek betrayed her weak smile of encouragement.

"I am sure you are right," he said, though in truth he was not at all sure. Walking to where she stood, he pulled her into his embrace. "Do not worry, Angel, it will work out somehow. Now, I want you to ask Anthony to come up. Give me about ten minutes to inform him of what is going on, and then tell Rob I want to see him."

She looked at him, his expression full of pain in response to the apparent betrayal on the part of the trusted aide.

"There must be a misunderstanding—Rob would not have knowingly taken part in profiting off the army. God, I pray that he did not take part." He said with a sigh, resting his head upon Caty's.

Despite Rob's claim to innocence, despite John Banks' public statement that his letter was misinterpreted, enough questions had been raised in the minds of many against the character of Nathanael Greene. Officers, including Anthony Wayne and Edward Carrington filed depositions in an attempt to clear their commander's name. However, many in South Carolina had grown weary of supporting an army with no enemy in sight, and, wanting to be rid of the burden, choose to believe any negative rumors to justify their own lack of character.

With a new governor, and the uncertainty of the state's current civil standing, military and civil authorities clashed. With former militia officers taking seats in the state legislature, Nathanael's troubles intensified. Some of these militia officers, still nursing grudges against their former commander for one frivolous reason or another during the campaign, stood opposed to him now.

Charleston merchants began pressing Nathanael for the payment of clothing supplied to Banks. Putting them off for as long as possible, Nathanael was forced to find a way to temporarily satisfy them when judgments against him were handed down in the South Carolina courts. Forced to turn to two wealthy friends for financial assistance—Jeremiah Wadesworth and the Marquis de Lafayette, he borrowed heavily to quiet his creditors.

The longed for news of an official peace with Great Britain arrived on April 16, 1783, almost eight years to the day that the Battles of Lexington and Concord were fought The war for American independence was over. Celebrations broke out up and down the American coast. Those in Charleston, soldier and civilian alike, rejoiced with a grand display of fireworks and dancing. Though Nathanael's men were elated with the glorious news and celebration, they were issued neither rice nor bread that day, for the commissary had none.

It was a bittersweet victory. Those who had sacrificed the most had the least to show for it. The spirit of unrest among the Southern troops was understandable— and word was that George Washington's men were faring much the same as they awaited New York's evacuation.

At last, Nathanael received orders to disband his army, with a fraction of their overdue pay sent along with the order. The North Carolina and Virginia regiments were the first to break camp, marching to their home states. Those of Pennsylvania and Maryland anxiously waited for transport ships, fearing with each passing day the deadly fever that would engulf the low country with summer's arrival.

When the ships finally came into port, Nathanael informed Caty that she, too, would sail for Philadelphia with the first of the Pennsylvania troops.

"You promised that we would go home together and be reunited with the children—no more lengthy separations you said!" Caty protested as he continued to lay out the items he wished to send home with her.

"That was before the Bank's scandal. Certainly, you can see things have changed. I must see to the condition of the plantations and do what I can to get them in operation."

"Then let me stay with you—please let me stay with you," she pleaded.

When Nathanael looked up at her, Caty was taken aback by his stern expression. "Nay. I will not hear of it. You have been away from the children for too long. It will be another three or four months before I arrive home, and the summer fever will be threatening soon—"

"You are not immune to the fever, and may very well end up in your sickbed, or worse!" She firmly replied. "I am expected to leave knowing full well the immense strain you are under in regard to this debt?"

"I will be fine, Caty," he shot back.

"I hate sea travel—you know that!"

"Colonel Kosciusko will be traveling with you. I spoke to him of your fear, and he promises to look out for you."

"What good is your engineer to me if the depths of the sea are to swallow me up?" She exclaimed.

"What good am I to you if the sea is to swallow you up?" He asked with a reserved chuckle, only proving to infuriate her.

"And what of the fact that I am carrying your child, and wondering if you really will make it home at all!" Tears began to stream down her cheeks.

"—Another child?" He asked hesitantly, knowing he should be elated by the news, yet finding it hard with the enormous financial burden upon him to welcome the added responsibility. Closing his eyes, he took a deep breath. He was silent for a moment as he wrestled with the guilt of his own inner response to this news, and the fact that a part of him truly wanted to escape all responsibility at the moment.

He opened his eyes looking upon his wife, who trembled as she wept. Walking to her, Nathanael held her in his arms, unable to offer any words of comfort though tormented by the sound of her sobs.

"—I want so desperately to go home with you," he finally managed to say. "I want nothing more than to greet our children together and to quietly anticipate the arrival of this precious one—but I must see to our land holdings for our family's sake." He held her tighter. "I will be home. Four months and I will be home."

"I am worried about you, Nathanael." She sobbed, looking up at him through tear stained eyes. "Beyond the pressures of this debt; beyond the fear of your becoming ill—Nathanael, your army will be entirely disbanded within the week, including the departure of Anthony. How will you cope with suddenly being so alone?"

"I will have two aides with me."

"That hardly counts!" she protested.

"—I shall, no doubt, feel like Sampson after losing his strength," was his sad and honest reply.

"The vast, I had almost said the enormous, powers of his mind...qualified him not less for the Senate than for the field."
(Alexander Hamilton in reference to Nathanael Greene))

CHAPTER TWENTY-TWO

UNACCUSTOMED TO SUCH cold, crisp air so early in the season, Nathanael pulled the collar of his cape snugly about his neck as a chill ran through his body. He considered, with a smile, the absurdity of it—a native New Englander freezing on a relatively mild October night.

That southern climate thinned my blood, he thought, and remembered the temperature on a night, seemingly very long ago now, when the Continental Army made a surprise attack on Hessian troops only a few miles from were he now rode. The brutal cold on that memorable Christmas night had been seared into the mind of every man who made that sacrificial march on Trenton, New Jersey.

As they directed their horses around a bend in the road, Nathanael and his aides had their first glimpse of John Cox's house in the distance. His former assistant quartermaster had remained an intimate friend through regular correspondence. In his last letter, Cox insisted that Nathanael spend time at his home before presenting himself in Princeton, where Congress was temporarily presiding. Grateful for the invitation, and especially the opportunity to rest after almost two months of traveling, Nathanael had promptly replied to the gracious offer.

Not wanting to catch his host off-guard, Nathanael had dispatched a message the day before to inform John of his close proximity. Reining the horses in at the tethering post, the men dismounted. As the aides tended to the weary beasts, Nathanael, equally weary, limped toward the front door.

He raised a tired arm to lift the iron knocker and banged it loudly, waiting for a servant to respond. The door flew open, and John Cox stood before his friend, his own countenance aglow. They grasped hands in a firm shake. Nathanael stepped into the foyer as they excitedly greeted one another.

Out of the corner of his eye, Nathanael caught the form of another man standing quietly in the shadows by the staircase. He was a tall man of a commanding form. Drawn to the shadowed figure, Nathanael forced his eyes to focus, all the while engaging verbally in the joyful reunion with John Cox.

"—Your Excellency?" Nathanael gasped; suddenly aware of whom he was viewing.

George Washington did not move; nor did Nathanael. Seemingly paralyzed, both men gazed at one another, tears welling in their eyes.

The Commander tried to speak, cleared his throat and tried again. "—Words cannot adequately express my joy, Nathanael!"

Unable to offer a verbal response Nathanael walked toward George Washington, falling into his open arms in an emotional embrace.

The hours passed quickly as these intimate friends, whose hearts had beat in unison for the very life of their beloved country, shared details of the triumphs and tribulations of their three-year separation. After engaging in much reminiscing of past, mutual experiences, and commenting affectionately on their many friends, their conversation turned to the grief still felt in the loss of Lord Stirling.

Nathanael went on to relate the gratitude of the citizens as in town after town he was honored with grand dinners and festive balls. So frequent were the celebrations that he was forced at times to make only a brief appearance in order to keep to his travel itinerary.

"I imagine that you did not mind missing a few." George Washington said with a smile, knowing Nathanael's dislike for such social functions

With the realization that dawn was fast approaching; their host and the aides having long before made their way to bed, George Washington apologized to Nathanael for keeping him from much needed sleep.

"We can continue our conversation as we ride to Princeton," the Commander commented as both men raised their weary bodies from the chairs. "What is it, Nathanael? Your countenance has changed."

"Indeed, has it, General?"

With a comforting smile, George Washington nodded.

"It seems that whenever I go before Congress I feel most uneasy—it has never been a secret that we lack affection one for another. They employ me, but they do not love me." He said with a forced laugh.

"I believe Congress will come through for you in regard to the Bank's affair." The General said.

"I wish I had your confidence, sir—"

The sight of the victorious commanders riding abreast of one another, with a trail of staff officers following close behind, brought the activity of many a townsman to a halt. They stopped to gaze at the passing forms of the officers, some removing their hats out of respect, while others loudly cheered Washington and Greene—the only general officers to serve continuously from the earliest days of the war to its glorious end.

Word had been sent by Nathanael to Congress of his desire to address them. Though they anticipated his arrival, no formal reception was accorded to the man, who, next to General Washington, had done most in the field to achieve independence. Nathanael had anticipated the somewhat cold and discourteous reception, and took it in stride, but George Washington was noticeably disturbed. After being introduced by the president of Congress, with a gratuitous word of thanks for his service in the South, and the promise that two field pieces taken from the British during the Southern Campaign would be presented him at some future date, Nathanael was given the opportunity to speak.

With a formal, emotionless salutation, Nathanael began, and then paused. How he wished this moment could be different—vastly different. That this august body, which he had put himself in sacrificial subjection to, could fully realize the agony of his time of service, and the sincerity of his patriotism. Rather than holding him at arms length in questioning his character because of the rash statement of a disreputable man; that they might instead be welcoming him back in a warm embrace as a persecuted brother, having suffered long for their common cause.

He searched the faces before him seeking the warm gazes of the few friends seated among them: Phillip Schulyer, Jim Varnum, John Sullivan, Robert Morris, and William Duer. Nathanael drew strength from their unspoken support.

He cleared his throat and continued to speak, his voice and countenance now filled with emotion. "Gentlemen, I left my home in Rhode Island more than eight years ago, having visited my family and friends but once in that span of time. Having successfully completed my assigned task in the South; and having obtained permission from General George Washington, I now humbly ask of you permission to resign my commission as major general in the Continental Army of the United States of America."

As was customary in such matters a response from Congress was not immediate, forcing Nathanael to postpone any definite plans for the trip home. He spent the time completing all official military business in regard to his Southern command, as well as to enter a written claim in Congress for the debts incurred on behalf of the army.

The main army had not yet disbanded, for the British had not completed their evacuation of New York. Though Nathanael's commission remained active, he had no command, and therefore none of the responsibilities that came with it. Free to come and go as he pleased, he visited with his old friends: Lafayette, Von Steuben, Anthony Wayne, Charles Pettit, John Cox, Thomas Paine, and of course Henry Knox and the Washingtons.

Henry handed Nathanael a mug of grog and seated himself opposite his friend. Nathanael smiled, enjoying the solitude of the moment—the Knox family had retired for the night, and though an autumn wind howled outside, the mood in the dimly lit parlor was warm.

"What is this I hear of you heading North by week's end?" Henry asked.

"Congress granted me permission this afternoon to return home."

"We will be marching into New York within two week's time. Surely you will stay and ride with us!" Henry exclaimed. "How could you miss such a grand moment, Nat? The last of the British to leave America—the crowning event of our victory!"

Nathanael continued to smile. "I have a family in Rhode Island which I dearly love." He took a sip of the grog.

"I know that—and I know you are eager to see them, but for the sake of partaking in such an event will two weeks longer make a difference?"

"I promised Caty I would be home by the end of November, and so, I will."

"Considering the state of your marriage, I guess it is best you do get back as promised—."

"My marriage? What are you talking about, Henry?"

"That you and Caty had a falling out."

"What are the rumors?" Nathanael asked.

"Well—it is common knowledge that your marriage is on very shaky ground. Caty's indulgence while in Philadelphia was witnessed by all, and reportedly met with a sharp reprimand by you. And you should know that some have hinted that Anthony Wayne's attention to her while she was here was an attempt to take advantage of the situation."

Nathanael began to laugh. "How do these stories get so out of hand?"

"Then it is not true?" Henry asked, obviously relieved.

"Of course not."

"I am happy to hear it. I must confess that I have been rather distant to Wayne because of it."

"For Heaven's sake, Henry, you know me well enough to ask rather than speculate. Caty was upset with me for not coming straight home with her. You know how women can get."

"Only too well—" he muttered.

"She failed to respond to my numerous letters. Then, when I received word of her spending, my anger for her lack of correspondence was unleashed in a letter. I regretted writing it as soon as it was sent, and dispatched another on its heels filled with apologies."

"And?" Henry asked.

"And she was gracious enough to forgive me and ask my forgiveness as well."

"That does not explain Wayne's attention."

"I asked him to attend her at social functions and keep a protective eye on her in my absence. Come now, Henry. I would ask the same of you, and you know it— or was his behavior toward her unseemly?" Nathanael asked.

"No. Now that you have explained it, it seems innocent enough. It is obviously no more than idle gossip, which led many to false conclusions—I am sorry, Nat. It seems I owe an apology to Wayne." Henry said contritely.

"Do you plan to return home before taking on the post as Minister of War?" Nathanael asked, anxious to change the subject.

"Are you certain you do not want the post? When Ben Lincoln announced his resignation the name of Nathanael Greene was the only one mentioned by Congress to replace him." Henry stated with a steady gaze on his friend.

"I have turned down that position twice. I am going home—you are welcome to it, and God bless you. So, are you returning to Boston?"

"Yes. Lucy and I would like to spend about a month in Boston."

"Good. Then we will have time to visit while you are there."

"Of course we will. You promised to bring your family to Boston, remember?"

"I remember," Nathanael replied softly, a smile of contentment upon his lips as he recalled their having made plans for the event prior to him heading southward to take command.

"I will not be running the bookstore, but I am sure my brother will be happy to see to your needs: the children's education, poetry and gardening, wasn't that your interest?" Henry said with a chuckle, ever the attentive merchant.

"I ran into Charles Pettit today. He said he had some disturbing news for you about this scoundrel Banks, but said no more than that. What's going on?" Henry asked.

"Banks was sent money from the Financial Secretary before word arrived from me to stop payment to him. The money was designated to pay those that supplied my troops. Word arrived today that the merchants were never paid. The money was instead used to pay off his other business debts."

"Leaving you with the legality of the debt," Henry stated.

"So he thinks. I have been informed that Banks owns a substantial amount of property. I intend to see if we cannot force its sale to cover the debt."

Henry nodded. "What of Major Burnet, Nat? Many feel you should have dismissed him immediately to prove your innocence."

"Why? The man claimed that he was not involved in any dealings in regard to the army contract."

"And did you believe him?"

"Do you really need to ask, Henry? Rob Burnet was my aide for six years. He proved his devotion to me, and his country, repeatedly. Yes, I believed him."

"And do you still believe him?" Henry asked softly, aware of the evidence that pointed to the fact that both Burnet and another officer had entered into partnership with Banks when the army contracts were being negotiated.

Nathanael remained quiet for a moment, clearly distraught by the situation. "He has confessed it to me since—"

"And?" Henry asked.

"And I have forgiven him, for how could I do otherwise Henry. He was facing the same situation many of us were—the war was coming to an end, and we had no means of support awaiting us. Banks tempted him with the promise of a lucrative position—and Rob fell."

Henry studied Nathanael for a moment. "Isn't his name actually Icabod Burnet?" he finally asked.

"Yeah, it is. Why?"

"Strange—do you recall the name in Scripture?" Henry asked.

Nathanael nodded, but offered nothing more.

"The Hebrew for Icabod means, 'to fall from glory'. How aptly this long-time aide-de-camp's name fits. How very strange—"

He was gone, and the emptiness the Commander experienced three years prior, when sending his second in command to the Southern Department, was upon him again. Thoughts flooded George Washington's mind of their years of service together—precious thoughts such as their initial meeting in Massachusetts when the Quaker general, his militia units displaying superior discipline, formally greeted his Commander in Chief. George Washington's affection for the young Rhode Islander was almost immediate.

Lack of deceit was one of the outstanding character traits of this dear friend—honesty, integrity, loyalty, determination, and humility. He was a trusted subordinate, a wise counselor. Now, with his commission resigned, he had returned home.

Prior to Nathanael's departure, a promise was made at the prompting of George Washington that the Greene family would spend time now and again with the Washingtons at Mount Vernon when they sailed from Georgia to Rhode Island.

Even now, he smiled at the thought of these future visits. *How delightful it will be for both Patsy and me to have them all under our roof—how delightful.*

However, his smile began to wane as his thoughts fell back upon Nathanael's departure. George Washington had offered his blessing, and tenderly embraced his friend. Then, stepping away from one another, Nathanael, fully uniformed for his trip home, came to full attention saluting his former Commander one last time.

"A final farewell," the General whispered, staring at the flames dancing within the hearth. He was desperate to shake the ominous feeling. "No." He quickly corrected himself. "It was only good-bye. We'll share a joyous reunion again." He attempted to reassure himself.

Opting for sea passage from Philadelphia to Newport, Nathanael took full advantage of his carefree time aboard ship. Books were borrowed from the captain's berth as he indulged his mind in nautical tales of exploration and adventure, naval accounts of various battles, and even tackled a volume on navigation. Except for reading, sleeping and a bit of conversation with the crew, he found little else to do to occupy his time, and no desire for any activity beyond that.

The day and approximate time of his arrival in Newport had been relayed not only to Caty, but to various relatives and friends as well, thus he fully expected to be greeted by a few familiar faces. Climbing to the upper deck upon hearing the announcement that the ship would soon be docking, Nathanael was greeted with a rather odd question by the captain.

"Have you a speech prepared, General Greene?"

"A speech, Captain? I hardly think my family and friends require a speech." he replied with a chuckle.

"Well, sir, I am aware you have a large family, and do not doubt that your circle of friend's is sizable as well, but—take a look, General," he said pointing toward the dock with one hand while handing Nathanael the spyglass with the other.

"It would appear that all of Rhode Island has assembled to welcome her illustrious son home." The captain said with a warm smile for the stunned major general.

Nathanael stepped onto the dock amid a cheering crowd, and was immediately greeted by the governor, members of the state congress, and the commander of the Kentish Guards—the militia unit he had helped organize nine years before. Escorted by the governor they walked to a nearby staging platform where speeches were to be made. With his attention drawn in various directions due to the activity all about him, Nathanael failed to see Caty as he approached the platform. As he climbed the last step, his focus immediately centered on her beaming smile.

"Welcome home, General Greene!" she said loud enough to be heard above the throng.

Nathanael smiled, and reaching up, slowly removed his tricorne. "It is very good to be home, Mrs. Greene."

His attention was drawn to a boy half her height, dressed in a sharp continental blue jacket and buff breeches. The youngster stepped forward, and, looking up at Nathanael, raised his hand to offer a neat, military salute. Shadowing the boy was a small, chubby fellow, dressed in an identical outfit, who mimicked the older boy's every move.

Before Nathanael had time to respond to them, two little girls called timidly from behind Caty, "Welcome home, Papa," and with Caty's prompting they made a sweet curtsey.

Dumbfounded, Nathanael suddenly realized he was gazing at his own children. Upon returning the boys' steady salute George quickly ran to his father, followed close behind by little Natty. Squatting down, Nathanael eagerly received them into his arms.

Coaxed by their mother, the girls slowly moved toward their father. With George and Natty still in his embrace, he looked upon the small girls, their pretty faces peering at him beneath ringlets of dark curls flowing from beneath matching white bonnets. Their large eyes reflected their apprehension.

He released his hold on George, and reached out, gently touching the arm of the older girl. "My, Patty, how pretty this dress is on you. Did Mama have it made special?"

Patty smiled weakly and nodded. "It is red, white and blue, just like the flag!" She sweetly replied, lifting her little cape to expose more of the dress.

"Indeed it is the same color as the flag." He said with an affectionate smile. Then turning to the younger girl, he caressed her cheek.

"Corneila, did Mama make your pretty curls?"

"—No, sir. God made my pretty curls!" she beamed.

Though tears began to well in his eyes, Nathanael fought to contain the sobs, which threatened to break forth. Sobs of grief in having his own children, save perhaps George, view him in the only way they could, as an absolute stranger. And, sobs of joy as well, in viewing their innocence and beauty at last.

In Caty's gaze, he found the strength he needed to control his pent up emotions. Standing, with Natty still in one arm, he pulled her close with the other, and softly kissed her cheek.

"Forgive me, Angel, for such a reserved greeting, but all eyes seem to be upon us at the moment," he whispered.

"You are forgiven, General," she replied with a content smile. "Do you see who is here?" she asked, directing his attention behind where his former aides, Sam Ward and Billy Blodget stood in full uniform. They saluted their friend, and then exchanged a warm embrace.

"Your brothers and Cousin Griffin are here, right out in front," Caty whispered to him as the governor began to address to the crowd. "I wanted them up here with you, but I was told there was a limit to how many could be on the platform."

Nathanael nodded as his eyes locked on the beaming faces of his brothers and cousin—eager to be done with the formalities that he might be able to greet them properly.

One speech after another was given, and finally Nathanael was asked if he might care to address the people, which he did with eloquence and ease.

His former aides were then asked to stand alongside him as the Kentish Guards presented themselves. Sam and Billy stepped forward and joined him in a review of the militia unit, which proved as emotionally stirring as any he had ever made. Nathanael took a deep breath in an attempt to control his innermost feelings. He vividly remembered that April morning eight years previous when being denied an officer's commission because of his limp; he willingly, and proudly, prepared to march in their ranks to the aid of their fellow colonists in Massachusetts.

As the members of the Kentish Guards began to discharge their muskets into the air in a thirteen-gun salute, Nathanael found he could no longer contain his tears. Rhode Island's honored son had indeed returned

Festivities, which lasted throughout the week, left the Greene family exhausted, though delightfully so. As per Nathanael's request, Caty had rented a house in Newport, and here he made his initial adjustment to civilian life, carefully storing away his uniform in a trunk and donning non-military attire once more.

His attention was first focused on becoming acquainted with his children. George, whose familiarity with his father was the strongest due to his many visits to camp, showed little apprehension or shyness. The eight year old asked question after question. Three-year-old Natty, who admired his brother exceedingly, was eager to welcome this stranger whom George so adored.

The girls proved harder to win over. Patty, now six, and Cornelia, five, had no recollection of this man who had seen them only as infants—and then only briefly.

Patiently, Nathanael allowed them to keep their distance, tenderly smiling in their direction, speaking softly to them; and slowly, but surely, seeing signs of gaining their trust and affection. Finally, the hugs, which his own arms ached for, were given as they freely, and excitedly, joined George and Natty in calling him papa.

Frequently visitors dropping in on the Greene home found themselves disrupting a family game of Puss in the Corner, or discovered the general on the floor with all four children attempting to tie him down as they acted out their favorite bedtime story, *Gulliver's Travels*.

Numerous trips were made to visit family in Potowomut and Coventry. Military friends corresponded regularly. A trip was made to visit the Knoxes, and many came to stay with the Greene's including Jeremiah Wadesworth, Colonel Kosciusko, the Baron Von Steuben, and the Marquis de Lafayette.

The marquis' visit proved most enjoyable to Nathanael and Caty. Enthusiastically requesting to meet Nathanael's brothers, he was taken to the homestead and Spell Hall, leisurely touring the mills and iron works. And, taking a special interest in the children, he prompted them to call him, "my dear marquis," delighting in the sound of their sweet voices. On more than one occasion, Lafayette suggested that Nathanael consider sending George to France when he became of age that he might complete his education there under the marquis' guardianship.

Before leaving, he presented Nathanael with a gift of attractive leather riding gloves. "For any occasion in which you might don your uniform again," he said, having noticed in Philadelphia the worn condition of Nathanael's gloves.

Rarely was there an evening when the Greene's were not entertaining or being entertained. However, as Caty's pregnancy progressed, Nathanael determined that his wife needed more rest, and gladly limited their social activities.

Various offers were made to entice Nathanael back into public life. Congress requested that he consider taking on a commission to enter into peace negotiations with the Indians.

No! was his firm, though polite, reply.

Fully enjoying the sweet repose of domestic life, he had hung his sword above the mantle, and was content with reminiscing on military exploits with Billy, Sam and Jim Varnum when the later was free to leave Congress and make a trip home.

Even George Washington and Henry Knox could not coax him to briefly don his uniform and meet them in Philadelphia to attend a meeting of the Society of the Cincinnati. The society, which was formed by Continental and French officers who served in the American Revolution, was an attempt to keep them united. Requesting that Jim Varnum appear in his stead as the second officer of rank from Rhode Island, Nathanael stayed home with his family about him, and failed even to attend the local, more convenient meetings of the Rhode Island chapter of which he was elected president.

Though he was determined to stay out of public life for a time, his correspondence to his many friends showed a keen interest and sharp understanding of the vital questions being put to the new nation. He still supported a temporary state tax to pay the war debt—including the money owed officers and enlisted men alike. Each state, he believed, should be required to cover their expenses. Thus, he hoped the six years back pay owed him would provide for his family's living expenses until he could get situated in Georgia.

A state tax would also cover the expense of feeding and clothing the Continental Army, thus offering the means to reimburse him for the staggering sum he was being held personally responsible for in supplying his Southern troops.

Their fifth child made her appearance in February, being joyously welcomed into the family circle. Though little Louisa Catharine was strong and healthy, Caty was weakened by the delivery and slow to regain her strength. Aware that she would be confined to home, Caty became distraught when word arrived from Anthony Wayne urging Nathanael to join him in a trip South that they might see to their properties.

"I do not want any more separations!" Caty pleaded after Nathanael shared with her his proposed trip. "Do you realize that in the nine years we have been married we have been together for less than half that time?"

"I do not like it any more than you, Angel, but I do not see how I can avoid it."

"You have men overseeing the plantation in Georgia! You said yourself the sale of the property in South Carolina is imminent. What great need have you to go now without us?"

He hesitated. Having held some information from her for fear of her frail health being further threatened, he now wondered if she was strong enough to hear it. "—A recent storm destroyed a good portion of this year's rice crop. I need to see what, if anything can be salvaged. Some damage to the house was sustained as well. I must be sure it is in proper repair before I can move you and the children down."

"Oh, Nathanael! Can't Anthony assist you by overseeing the situation—or even Nathaniel Pendleton?" she asked, referring to her husband's former aide-de-camp who had set up a law practice in Savannah.

"—If it were only that, yes, I would request their help, but—"

"But, what?" She braced herself for the answer.

"I have received word that squatters have set themselves up on Cumberland Island, and are selling timber from our property."

"Can't the authorities be informed?"

"I have done so, but received no response. I am depending on the sale of that timber to support us, and am doubly dependent on it with the rice crop being destroyed."

"Is there no end to it all?" She asked, turning away from him in her frustration.

Nathanael went to her, and taking her into his arms held her in silence for a few moments.

"I absolutely dread the thought of leaving you and the children again. However, because I love you so I must go south and see to my only means of providing, and temporarily satisfying the creditors of this enormous debt I find myself under. I have never owned so much property as now, and yet never felt so poor—I have no desire to stay beyond what is necessary."

"Then it will be a short trip?" she longed for a promise that would make it somehow more endurable.

"Very short. Anthony and I will sail down and back. I will stop in South Carolina to see to the sale of that property, then to Savannah and Cumberland Island—and a brief stop in Virginia—"

"Virginia? Why Virginia?" she asked, noting his sudden discomfort in having mentioned his plan to stop there.

"I received intelligence that John Banks is presently residing there."

Caty could not help but smile in response to the fact that her husband apparently still had spies working for him.

"Intelligence?" She echoed.

He nodded, returning her smile.

"And what is it you propose doing when you see John Banks?"

His smile suddenly disappeared. In its place was a look Caty had never witnessed before—anger so intense that, for the first time, she felt momentarily frightened of him.

Nathanael took a deep breath. "—I do not really know," he said with the pretense of being calm. "Somehow I intend to force him to free me of this debt. How I will do that I do not know, but do it I will."

True to his word, Nathanael returned to Rhode Island within three months time, immediately lavishing attention on his family to make up for the brief separation.

He had managed to accomplish all he set out to do. The repairs to the house were underway; the squatters on Cumberland Island had been removed, and a portion of that valuable property, as well as the plantation in South Carolina had been sold.

All that remained undone—forever undone— was forcing John Banks to bear responsibility for the debt that was rightfully his. Nathanael never had the opportunity to reveal, even to himself, what drastic length he might go to in forcing John Banks' hand. For upon arriving in Virginia he discovered that the embezzler was dead, having fallen victim to a fever only a few days before.

"He was the most finished villain that this age has produced. Save for Benedict Arnold I have never hated a man as I did him," Nathanael confessed to Caty. After a brief pause, a sudden fear was reflected in his eyes, and he added, "I verily believe that if I had met him, and he did not favorably respond to my predicament, I would have put him to death myself—may God forgive me."

With yet a spark of hope still alive Nathanael submitted another claim to Congress for the debt incurred on behalf of the army. However, when he discovered from his friends in Philadelphia that an investigation into his prior conduct as Quartermaster General had been undertaken, and that a private, coded letter written five years before between former Commissary General Jeremiah Wadesworth and himself had been discovered, even this minute spark was extinguished.

Never, in their vengeful state of mind, would certain members of Congress believe the letter to be innocent; the code having been used only to protect the private affairs of himself and Jeremiah from just such meddling. If the sworn depositions stating his innocence by the officers of the Southern Department; the sacrificial record of his military command; and the great effort put forth as Quartermaster General were not enough to stir certain members of Congress into giving him the benefit of the doubt, then he was certain that in their evil imaginations there was nothing he could say or do that would alter their declaration of his guilt.

Accepting the fact that he was in fact solely responsible for the crippling debt, he resigned himself to pay it off as he could. Yet, even still, he dared to hope against hope that one day Congress would consist of a majority who would have regard for him, and reimburse him for the supply of his troops.

"He was great as a soldier, greater as a citizen, immaculate as a friend..."
(Anthony Wayne in reference to Nathanael Greene)

CHAPTER TWENTY-THREE

AS AUTUMN APPROACHED, Nathanael and Caty put into motion their plans to move south. Certain furnishings, Nathanael's library, and various personal belongings were shipped ahead to Georgia. Loose ends were tied up in regard to business with Jacob and Griffin, who intended to involve themselves in transporting to market some timber and rice aboard merchant ships they owned. The old farmhouse in Westerly was rented out, and finally a tutor for the children was hired to travel and live with the family. After receiving the blessings of family and friends Nathanael and his family boarded the ship bound for Savannah, Georgia, promising to return come spring.

The voyage began with great enthusiasm. The older children considered it an adventure, and eagerly accompanied their father or new tutor, Mr. Phineas Miller, onto the quarterdeck whenever possible. Caty, too, though frightened of sea travel, was excited by the prospects, which lay ahead.

Caty chose to stay below deck with one-year-old Louisa, venturing above only for a breath of fresh air. To view the vast ocean about the small ship was terrifying. Only within their small cabin did she feel any sense of security.

"I must overcome this foolishness," she told herself time and again, realizing that such voyages were now to be undertaken four times a year. Therefore, it was with a keen sense of determination that she forced herself to join the family above deck. Strengthened by her husband's encouraging smile she clenched his arm tightly, frequently scolding the children to stay away from the rail, or to stop running for fear of a tragic mishap. In response, Nathanael reached over with his free arm and gently squeezed her hand, softly assuring her that the children were safe.

Noting her improvement day by day, Nathanael was dismayed when the ship sailed into a fierce gale, which forced the passengers below deck. The winds pounded against the ship's hull, roughly tossing its occupants about. Concerned for his distraught wife, Nathanael protected her from the knowledge that the strength of the wind had caused the sea to rise tremendously, and that a crewmember had actually been lost overboard.

The tempestuous sea caused Caty and the children to become ill. Ignoring his own queasy stomach, Nathanael huddled his family about him on the floor of the dark cabin. He placed one arm about his wife's trembling body as the children scampered upon his legs or into the secure embrace of his other arm.

As the vessel continued to pitch and reel, battered by the winds about them, Nathanael attempted to draw the attention of his frightened wife and children with a whimsical tale. He encouraged each of them to come up with a tale of their own. Thus, the hours passed with each taking a turn at story telling. But, secretly, Nathanael wondered if this very night, his family was destined to pass into eternity together.

Baby Louisa was the first to awaken, crying hungrily, and immediately causing the others to stir.

"It stopped," Caty's relief was evident even in the softness of her tone. Lifting her weary head from Nathanael's shoulder she stood, and carefully stepped over the sprawling forms of the drowsy children to chance a look through the porthole. The sun warmly glistened upon a calm sea.

"When did it end?" She asked Nathanael, whose eyes remained closed, his head awkwardly resting against the cabin wall behind his seated form.

"Before sunrise. I do not know what time it was. It was still pretty dark."

She turned to face him, and smiled at the precious scene of the children, having used their father's body for their security against the storm as a sailor might tie himself to a mast.

"You must be sore!" Caty exclaimed as one by one the children moved away from him.

"My arms and legs fell asleep hours ago; my neck is so stiff I do not believe I can move it from this position, and my backside—let's just say it is beyond agony. But the worst of it is that Louisa wet through her diaper and soaked me to the skin as you can plainly see; and I have been seated in a puddle of vomit all night—"

Caty burst into laughter, bringing a smile to Nathanael's lips. His eyes finally opened.

"Praise be to God—we are alive." he spoke the words softly though his face was suddenly aglow.

"Praise be to God!" Caty echoed. Then stepping toward him, she offered her hand to help him to his feet.

Finally reaching the safety of the Savannah River, the ship sailed past the river forts to the docks of Georgia's capitol. Nathanael escorted his family down the gangplank, relieved to find Nat Pendleton waiting to greet them with two coaches standing ready to escort the family to their plantation, *Mulberry Grove*.

The children, filled with energy after being cooped aboard ship for two weeks, were given permission by their father to run about the open fields as the coach pulled to a gentle halt before the two-story brick mansion standing amid a grove of mulberry trees.

"Mr. Miller, would you please see that the children stay away from the water," Nathanael asked the tutor as the children dashed away.

With Nathanael's assistance, Caty stepped out of the coach. Instinctively she looked back toward the river and let out a sigh. Nathanael squeezed her hand.

"We had a river flowing past Spell Hall," he reminded her.

"It was not so large, nor so close as the Savannah."

"I will teach them well to respect it, and keep their distance—do not worry. Now, come and let me show you our home."

"I will help Mr. Miller keep an eye on the children while you look about, sir," Nat Pendleton offered, sensible to the fact that the couple might want to be alone.

"The trees need to be cut back," Nathanael remarked as he led his wife along the paved path toward the pillared doorway.

"Why so many mulberry trees?" She asked taking in the imposing trees, which lined the pathway.

"I understand they were planted with the hopes of promoting a silkworm farm which, unfortunately, proved unsuccessful."

They took their time exploring the house. Caty was impressed with the size of the rooms, and especially the large glass panels in the parlor, which offered a breathtaking view of the Savannah River below.

Typical of Southern homes, the kitchen was set apart from the main house thus protecting the inhabitants from excessive heat of the cooking fire during the warmer months. Yet, two massive brick chimneys stood at either end of the Georgian mansion to service the many spacious fireplaces built within to warm and dry the rooms during the rainy winters

"Our furniture seems rather insignificant in this large house." Caty commented, remembering how the pieces seemed to fill Spell Hall.

"By and by we will add all the furniture you could want for. In fact, there are quite a few fine pieces, which were moved into one of the outbuildings when the house was being refurbished. You can look them over and have them brought back in if they're to your liking."

Nodding, Caty wandered out of the room and back to the parlor. Gazing through the glass panels, she watched the children play in the clearing with the river scenically flowing past them in the background.

Surprised by her sudden silence Nathanael assumed she was disappointed. "I am sorry it is not to your liking, Angel," he sadly remarked.

She turned to face him, a slow smile coming to her lips. "Not to my liking? General Greene, it is absolutely beautiful! Why in the world do you think it is not to my liking?" she asked incredulously, her wide eyes revealing her surprise at his assumption.

He shrugged his shoulders, confused by her surprise at what seemed to him a most logical conclusion. "You are so quiet."

Caty let out a quick laugh and walked to him, wrapping her arms around his neck. "I was contemplating all I could do in decorating this magnificent house—and the flower gardens! Nathanael, did you see the many flowers still in bloom?" She excitedly asked. "And just imagine the grand balls we could have here! Why this room is huge!" She exclaimed, freeing him from her hold and gracefully twirling about the room. "Wouldn't General Washington enjoy dancing in this room?"

"Indeed he would." Nathanael said with a chuckle, delighting in his wife's sudden exuberance.

"When, Nathanael? When can we have our first party?" Her twirling stopped as she eagerly awaited his reply.

He began to laugh, realizing she had, as usual cornered him into condoning yet another social event. How could he possibly say no when it gave her such pleasure?

"We will need a bit of time to settle in, and it would probably be polite to wait until General Wayne arrives. Why don't you plan your event for a month from now. Would that meet with you approval, Lady Greene?"

"Indeed, it would, your Excellency!" she said with a graceful curtsey.

Though restrained in her spending, Caty's ball proved as festive as she could have hoped. More social gatherings were soon to follow be they at the Greene mansion, or the fine home of a newly acquired friend. Even Anthony Wayne fell into suit in hosting a dinner at his own estate known as *Richmond*.

Patty, Cornelia and little Louisa would often wait outside their parents' bedchamber as their father and mother prepared themselves for just such an evening out. When their father would exit the room, the girls would come to attention, and wait for his unspoken permission to go in, which was always given with a playful smile and the wink of his eye.

Dashing into the bedchamber the girls would plop themselves upon the fluffy feather mattress beneath the delicately laced canopy. The rich, floor length draperies of royal blue, and the thick pile of the woolen, Oriental rug gave the room an air of regality. The scent of their mother's sweet perfume added to the fairy tale imagery.

Caty would grin at the three cherub-like faces peeking out over the feather mattress, as they followed her every movement. Delightfully, they watched as she finished arraying herself, her blue-black hair flowing about her delicate shoulders. Her tiny shoes sparkled with diamond buckles, and the intricate lace on her stunning gowns of silk set her in a dream-like fantasy. In their minds their mother was a beautiful princess being taken to the grand ball by the prince they all openly adored—their papa.

Aside from the evenings' frequent activities, a daily routine quickly took shape at *Mulberry Grove*. No stranger to hard work, Nathanael experienced a true sense of satisfaction in the exhausting weeks of planting. His hope for the spring of 1786 was to have sixty acres of corn in, and one hundred thirty of rice.

By mid-March, Caty was enthralled with spring's array of beauty on her paradise estate. Nathanael shared her excitement, and more so as the increasing warmth of April quickly brought to maturity their vegetable garden and fruit orchards.

Phineas Miller set to work with the children's studies, delighting Nathanael not only with his talent in regard to the education of his sons and daughters, but by inspiring in Caty a desire to expand her own knowledge as well. Contentedly she would sit for hours with her books. Often, as the family sat down to the evening meal, with Phineas and their regular dinner guest, Anthony Wayne, Caty would begin the evening's conversation by discussing the book she was presently reading.

With planting complete, and the ghastly heat of summer not yet encroached, the Greene's basked in the luxurious beauty of their Southern estate. Late afternoons were spent playing with the children. As the older three would attend their studies, Nathanael would bounce Natty and Louisa on his knees amusing them with humorous tunes from his days in the army. And they in turn would delight him by performing for their mother "Papa's funny songs", and begging for more.

George, Patty and Cornelia, would scamper from the classroom the moment Phineas dismissed them. Upon finding their father with the younger ones, they would drag him by the hands into the yard for a game, or a long hike along the river's bank. Caty joined them on occasion, but more often watched from the comfort of her portico rocker as the children's gleeful screams filled the afternoon sky.

Visits to Nat Pendleton's, who was acting as legal council in regard to the Bank's affair were frequent. Occasionally Caty would accompany her husband, giving her the opportunity to visit with Captain Pendleton's wife. However, for Nathanael these visits were becoming more and more distressing, a fact, which he attempted to mask. The Charleston merchants, dissatisfied with the time span in which Nathanael could pay them back, were pressing him for more money

I am looking forward to the voyage home," Caty said with a sweet smile for Nathanael as she reached across his lap placing her hand on his. In response, he turned his attention away from the passing scenery as the servant directed the horse-drawn open carriage along the dirt road.

"You are dreading the voyage," he said with a knowing smile.

She laughed. "I am dreading more the stifling heat of the southern summer. Feel how hot it has already become. And I am absolutely delighted with the thought of seeing General and Lady Washington."

He nodded in reply, and although he still wore a smile, it was more forced than ready, she noted. The meeting with his attorney had had its usual effect and this particular meeting more so, it seemed, for one of the Charleston creditors was there as well.

Nathanael turned his attention back to the passing scenery.

"You should put your hat on," she reminded him as he squinted his eyes against the bright sun. He failed to respond, and the tricorne remained on the seat next to him.

"Captain Pendleton seems to have adapted nicely to married life. He's almost as doting as William Washington was!" She said trying again to distract him from his secret thoughts. "Do you suppose William and Jane are as starry eyed two years into their marriage?"

"By the sound of his letters it would appear so," he replied without looking at her.

"Nathaniel Pendleton has a most negative effect on you," she bluntly stated.

He turned a blank stare on her. "Nat Pendleton is a fine man and trusted friend."

"I agree, but he still has a most negative effect on you."

"As my legal counsel, in this most negative matter, it cannot be helped, I am afraid. His assistance has been invaluable in keeping things under control—I pray I can one day repay him."

"Are things under control, Nathanael?"

He failed to answer, and though his gaze was fixed on her face, he seemed to be lost in his own thoughts, not seeing Caty at all.

"—Do you mind if we stop at the Gibbon's estate?" He suddenly asked, seemingly unaware of her question. "Mr. Gibbons has a substantial portion of his land in rice and invited me to stop by at my convenience to examine his fields."

"No, I do not mind."

He gave instructions to the servant to stop at the home of Mr. Gibbons. The carriage pulled to a gentle halt before the entrance of the grand estate. Nathanael stepped down from the carriage, and then assisted his wife.

"You left your hat on the seat," Caty reminded him.

"I don't need it."

"Nathanael, the sun is strong. It will shade your face and protect it from burning."

"You know I find them to be an annoyance except in the cold or rain. I will send for it if I find I need it," he assured her as he walked toward the mansion door.

After a bit of refreshment William Gibbon, proudly led Nathanael out to the vast fields of rice while his wife and Caty entertained one another. Two hours passed before the men returned—Nathanael's face reddened from the sun.

Except for a few brief comments about his tour, Nathanael remained silent for the remainder of the trip, even appearing to be napping with his eyes shut tight. As they approached *Mulberry Grove*, Caty nudged him gently.

"Nathanael, we are home," she softly said.

Slowly he nodded his head though his eyes remained closed.

"Is something wrong?"

"I have a headache."

"Too much sun," she said, mildly annoyed at his stubbornness in not wearing the hat. "Let's get you inside. A good night's sleep should cure the problem."

A restless night failed to reduce the pain, and, with the sun's rising, the dull ache lodged over his eyes. Unable to obtain any relief by remaining in bed he forced himself to join the family for breakfast, eating little.

Aware that their father was not feeling well the children heeded their mother's warnings to let him rest, satisfying themselves with brief visits beside his cot on the cool portico. Confused by her papa's passive behavior, three year old Louisa gently climbed upon his lap seeking to sooth his discomfort by resting her little head upon his chest, and softly patting his shoulder with her tiny hand. Touched by the selflessness of her love, Nathanael placed his arm about his youngest child's small body, holding her close to himself until she fell asleep.

"Might I pour you another drink, Papa?" Patty's sweet voice was heard asking.

He opened his eyes and turned his head to face his daughter, only to find her brothers and sister sitting with her on the portico floor beside his cot.

Though the brightness of even the shaded portico increased the pain in his head, he smiled at the precious faces staring up at him.

"Yes, pumpkin, I will take another drink," he softly replied, trying not to disturb Louisa's nap.

"And shall I dampen the cloth again, Papa?" Cornelia asked, wanting to be as helpful as her older sister.

"I would appreciate that, sweetheart," he said, reaching up and pulling the partially wet cloth from his forehead and handing it to his little girl.

After taking a sip of the water, and thanking Patty for it, Nathanael turned his attention to Natty, who now quietly hovered at his side.

"What did you learn in your studies today?" he asked the six-year-old.

"I can cipher real good—Mr. Miller says so!" Natty proudly reported.

"So I have been told. And how goes your reading?"

"I am trying real hard, Papa, but I like to cipher out best!"

Nathanael lifted his hand, and placed it on the boy's head, tousling his hair a bit as Cornelia gently placed the cool, wet cloth back on his forehead.

"Thank you, sweetheart," he said. "Are you excited to be sailing back to Rhode Island?" he asked them all.

"Yes, Papa," each one replied, some with great enthusiasm, their excitement in being reunited with their kin, and seeing the wonders of the ocean worked to overcome their fear of possible storms, and a lengthy confinement aboard ship.

"And shall Mr. Miller go with us?" George asked.

"Of course he will, son," Nathanael replied, aware how attached the children had become to the kind-hearted tutor. Nathanael, too, had grown fond of Phineas Miller, finding him to be a brilliant young man. In time, he intended to improve his own Latin skills under Phineas' tutelage, and perhaps even attempt a study of Greek.

"And we shall have a fine visit in Virginia, won't we George?" he asked.

"We will, Papa!" The older boy replied, eagerly anticipating their trip to *Mount Vernon*.

The girls appeared skeptical.

"Is Mama still drilling you on how to behave when you are at the Washingtons?" he asked, aware of Caty's determination to have the girls appear just so.

"Yes, sir," both girls replied, their faces suddenly downcast.

"What is it your mama expects of you?" He tenderly asked

"Our most graceful curtsey, and then we should be certain to smile always, and keep to the background—speaking only when questions are put to us," Patty promptly replied.

"And is that so much?" He asked, smiling at his daughters who still appeared troubled.

"—Our curtseys are not always so graceful, and though neither of us have trouble keeping quiet, it is awfully hard to smile all the time, Papa." Cornelia complained. "We have met lots of generals, and never had to be just so. We are afraid General and Lady Washington may not like us, and that will spoil your visit, Papa!"

"Come here, Cornelia," Nathanael said, holding his arm out to touch the child. "It's true that you have met many generals who have stayed in our home—"

"Not all of them, Papa!" Natty corrected him, shaking his small head from side to side. "We went to visit Uncle Henry, remember?"

"That is right, Natty. Do you remember the other general's names?"

"Yes, sir! Uncle Anthony is a general, even with a sword like you—and so is my dear marquis!" he said, referring to Lafayette just as the marquis had prompted during his visit, bringing a smile to Nathanael's lips. "And there was Baron bon Steuben," he stumbled over the name, "And General Varnum—he is the only one that has general with his name I think! That is all of them, but George says you are the most powerful!"

"I did not say most powerful, Natty! I said Papa was in charge of them!" George corrected.

"My rank was higher than theirs, but General Washington was in charge of the whole army. That is why your mama is concerned that you behave just so. But I will tell you a secret," he said, caressing Cornelia's cheek, and looking beyond her to her sister. "If you should not do well on your curtsey, or not be able to smile all the time—why even if you get excited and happen to speak out of turn, General and Lady Washington will love you just the same. I promise."

"What is it you are promising them?" Caty asked as she stepped onto the portico.

"I once promised George that I would teach him to fire a musket when he turned eleven. That day is fast approaching." Nathanael said with a wink for the children. "And I also promised that I would take the older ones out in the row boat before we left for Rhode Island."

"Then you had better get well quickly so you can fulfill that promise." she said. "It is time for your father to rest children, go off and play. And look at this baby asleep on your lap. Patty. Tell the servant to come and put Louisa in her bed. You must be firmer with them, Nathanael or you will not get any rest," she said, taking Louisa into her arms.

"They are wonderful, Caty. I love having them about."

After handing Louisa to the servant woman, Caty said on the cot next to her husband. Reaching out Nathanael took hold of her hand as he closed his eyes.

Caty took the cloth from his head with her free hand and examined his forehead.

"It still appears to be swollen. Nathanael, I have never heard of a sunburn causing such swelling. I really feel that we should send for the doctor."

"Nay, Caty. It will go down. A touch of sunstroke is all—I do not want them draining my blood for a simple case of sunstroke," he said, gently squeezing her hand.

She dipped the cloth in the basin of cool water and reapplied it, then offered him the cup Patty had filled.

"I forgot to tell you that Captain Pendleton will be stopping by this evening with a paper for me to sign," he said after taking a sip of the water, and closing his eyes against the sunlight once again.

Caty sighed, anticipating more dealings with the Bank's affair.

"It is in regard to the timber on Cumberland Island," he reassured. With his eyes closed, he again reached out for her hand. "See that I am notified when Pendleton arrives—and that he is made comfortable for the night. Is Anthony staying away because I am ill?"

"He does not want to disturb you."

"Pendleton may enjoy his company. Perhaps you should send for him when the captain arrives."

"If Nat Pendleton wants to socialize with Anthony Wayne then he can go over to *Richmond* to see him. We are not responsible for entertaining them tonight. You, sir, are to rest and regain your health. And I am to see that you do just that." Caty scolded.

"Yes, ma'am," he said with an amused, though strained, grin. Then squeezing her hand he added, "Angel, when was the last time I told you I loved you?"

"Two days ago," she promptly replied.

"And do you believe it is so?"

"With every fiber of my being," she softly replied aware that he was beginning to doze. "And be sure that I love you as well, General Greene," she whispered gently, lifting his hand to her lips and kissing it.

By the time Nat Pendleton arrived, the swelling in Nathanael's head had become more noticeable. At the sight of the general's condition, the former aide-de-camp instantly sent a servant to Savannah to find the doctor.

After applying the standard treatment of blistering and bloodletting, the doctor assured Caty and Nat Pendleton that Nathanael needed only to rest—that his condition was certain to improve by morning. With that, he left.

As the night wore on, Nathanael's pain steadily increased. By dawn, his suffering was so intense that Caty ordered all the curtains in the room to be drawn tight to block the sun's rays. She then made plans with Nat Pendleton to take the children home with him that the house might remain as quiet as possible. Frightened by their father's grave illness, and their mother's obvious concern, the children wept as Phineas Miller helped the young attorney load them into the waiting coach.

Sending for Anthony, he and Caty took turns sitting by Nathanael's bedside. As hour passed into hour, Anthony noted Nathanael's condition beginning to deteriorate, for not only did the tormenting pain and swelling remain, but also the few words he occasionally managed to utter were becoming incoherent. Finally, the moaning stopped as he mercifully lapsed into a stupor.

Anthony summoned Nat Pendleton, telling him to find another doctor to tend to the general. Again, the standard treatments were applied, with the doctor concurring that the diagnosis was sunstroke, and assuring them before he left that rest was the only true cure.

"This is not merely sunstroke." Anthony protested to young Pendleton after Caty led the doctor out of the darkened bedchamber.

"You were with him during the Southern Campaigns. This man spent hours under the grueling summer sun, often in a weakened state with little food, a perpetual lack of sleep and his body constantly fighting asthma or the blasted fevers this climate brings."

"If it is not sunstroke, what is it, sir?" Pendleton asked, gazing at the still form of his beloved commander.

"I do not know." Anthony walked to Nathanael's side; keeping a sharp eye on the door should Caty return. "Johnson would know—why couldn't Johnson be here with us?" he cried out, desperately longing for the expertise of the former head surgeon.

"His speech became incoherent—perhaps its apoplexy," Anthony thought aloud as he lovingly studied the face of his friend.

"He is only forty-four years old, sir. He is too young for apoplexy!" Pendleton protested.

"Young? Nathanael Greene sacrificed his health and youth in the war. And what the war failed to rob him of in terms of health or peace of mind, an ungrateful people did in not coming to his support when he was in need, as he so readily did for them time and again!"

Anthony paused, sighing deeply. "I am not really a praying man, Captain, but I will tell you this, I have prayed that that scoundrel Banks, met with his just reward. And I have prayed that the people of this nation—those in Congress and those in the Southern states who most benefited by this man's enormous sacrifice— would come to their senses and free him from this burden. And, now—what now, Captain? May God have mercy on their ungrateful souls!"

He gently took one of Nathanael's limp hands into his own, and gazed into the eyes that vacantly stared back at him. "Nat, squeeze my hand if you can hear me—if you can understand what I am saying." There was no response.

"I am afraid that a part of him, a very vital part of him, has lost the will to live." Anthony mournfully commented.

"But what of Mrs. Greene and the children—he loves them so—he would keep on fighting for them!" Pendleton exclaimed.

"If he could—but between his broken body and his broken spirit—perhaps he convinced himself that Congress would certainly come to the aid of Caty and the children if she were made a widow and them fatherless—"

"Do not even speak it, General Wayne, please!" Pendleton begged.

Anthony looked up at the younger man, his own face contorted with grief. "General Greene was a casualty of the War for Independence—his wounds were hidden, like this piece of lead in my leg, but it is impossible for him to escape their deadly effects. No man could escape the slow, agonizing death of his wounds. And few men would have endured so long—"

"Get some sleep, Caty, you must get some sleep—" Anthony said, stepping beside her seated form at Nathanael's bedside. Half her body lay sprawled upon the mattress, her hand tightly clasping that of her husband's.

"I must stay with him," she groggily replied.

"It will do you no good to get sick too. The children need you—"

"I cannot go!" she protested, desperately grabbing hold of the feather mattress as Anthony tried to guide her out of the chair.

"Caty, Nat will have my hide if he discovers I let you stay up night after night like this."

She looked up at him, latching onto any words, which offered hope of his recovery. A sad, exhausted smile came to her lips. "He will be angry with you, won't he?"

"Most certainly! Now come on and go sleep for a few hours."

"You will call me if he awakens?" she asked, staring at her husband.

"Of course I will call you—"

Anthony fought back the tears as he watched Caty kiss her husband's lips and pitifully bid him a good night's sleep. Then she slowly staggered out of the bed-chamber.

He then sat alone at the bedside, and took hold of his friend's hand, recalling how Nathanael had sat with him day after day as he recovered from the festering wound in his leg.

"Do you remember when I was ill, Nat? I could see the concern in your eyes. And now it is my turn to be concerned." He lowered his head momentarily, taking a deep breath.

"Nat, you have to fight. You once said during your Southern campaign, 'We fight, get beat, rise, and fight again!' It is not over yet, General Greene! You must rise and fight again! This country has so much to face yet – so much need of you." He took another deep breath, wiping a tear from his cheek as he looked at his friend. Through vacant eyes Nathanael's gaze remained fixed on the ceiling. Anthony squeezed his hand.

"Do you remember when we first met, General Greene? It was at Valley Forge—" And with that Anthony recounted their common experiences, from their first days together at Valley Forge to the disbanding of the army in Charleston. Then, still determined to keep his unresponsive friend company, he told the stories of his campaigns in Canada, the massacre of his men at Paoli, of the daring attack at Stoney Point, and finally the glory of Yorktown. Exhausted himself, General Anthony Wayne fell asleep in the chair at his former commander's side.

The sun's appearance in the June sky was not the cause of his stirring. Instead, the labored, erratic breathing startled him from his sleep. Still grasping Nathanael's hand, Anthony watched in fearful silence—helpless to do a thing but offer his feeble comfort to this dear friend and comrade as he quietly slipped away.

The most heart-rending task he had ever undertaken was accomplished—and now Anthony sat alone in the parlor giving Caty time alone with her husband.

With the realization that many friends in Savannah must be notified in order to make the necessary funeral arrangements, Anthony picked up a quill—Nathanael's quill—and with a trembling hand began to write:

"My dear friend General Greene is no more. He was great as a soldier; greater as a citizen; immaculate as a friend. Pardon this scrawl; my feelings are but too much affected, because I have seen a great and good man die."

Together Anthony and Nat Pendleton dressed Nathanael's body in full uniform, placing on his hands the gloves the Marquis de Lafayette had presented to him. Carefully lifting the body from the bed, they placed it gently in a waiting coffin. Then, coming to full attention General Wayne and Captain Pendleton saluted their former commander as the mournful sound of Caty's uncontrollable sobs filled the room.

George Washington placed his hat on the foyer table, and walked quietly toward the parlor in search of his wife.

"Back so soon, General?" Martha asked, laying her knitting in the basket at her feet. "Are you feeling all right? It is rather early for you to call it a day."

"Finished up a project and did not see the point in starting the next this late in the afternoon."

"The supper table is not even set. Would you prefer to eat early?" She stood, preparing to instruct a servant to see to the meal.

"What? No company tonight?" He asked incredulously, for it was a rare evening that a guest did not dine with them.

"No company tonight," Martha echoed.

"Speaking of company—have we received any word from General Greene? I cannot imagine what the delay is. Perhaps farming has gotten into his blood, and he is hesitant to leave with the promise of such a bountiful crop."

"I will be greatly disappointed if they do not come!" Martha replied.

"As will I—as will I. But no word from him? It is unlike Nathanael not to keep me abreast—"

"There is no word from General Greene, but there is a letter from Colonel Lee. His letter is in your study on the desk. Are you hungry?" She asked again as he headed in the direction of the study.

"No, not just yet," he called back. Within a few minutes, Martha heard him calling for her.

"I cannot seem to find Colonel Lee's letter," he informed her.

"It is right on the desk," she said, walking to his side and immediately laying her hand on the desired item.

"I am sorry, Patsy," he said contritely.

"I suppose it cannot be helped," she returned with a smile, having discovered through the years that most men seemed unable to locate items laying right before them in obvious view. "Do you think Light-Horse Harry is stirring things up in Congress?" Martha asked, as her husband sat in his chair.

"The boy has always enjoyed a good fight, and there are plenty to be had on the Senate floor." He said with an affectionate smile as he broke open the seal.

Martha lingered for a moment, straightening a few things on the desk, and then turned to leave the room.

"Dear God, no—" She heard her husband utter. The intensity of his pain sent a frightening chill up Martha's spine.

Turning to face him, she was taken aback with his ghost-like appearance. "What is it, George?" she whispered, afraid to hear his reply.

He only looked at her, a tear slowly running down his cheek. Martha could see his chest rise and fall as he struggled with the shock of Colonel Lee's words.

"What is it, George?" she repeated, her eyes already glistening with tears.

He held the letter out to her, his hand shaking. Taking hold of it with her own trembling hand, Martha forced herself to read the words:

"Your friend, and second, the noble General Greene is no more. Universal grief reigns here. How hard is the fate of the United States to lose such a man in the middle of life. Irreparable loss! But he is gone, and I am incapable to say more!"

Martha gazed at her husband as he stared across the room through empty eyes.

"Dear Lord, not Nathanael—!" George Washington called out with a choking sob.

Martha moved to his side and slowly knelt beside his chair, laying her head upon his lap. Lifting his hand, he gently placed it upon her. Together they wept.

"Resolved that a monument be erected to the memory of Nathanael Greene . . . the late Major General in the service of the United States, and commander of their army in the Southern Department . . . in honor of his patriotism, valor and ability, . . ."
(United States Congress, August 8, 1786)

APPENDIX

CATY GREENE, widowed at the age of thirty-two, continued on at Mulberry Grove. The young tutor, Phineas Miller, immediately stepped in taking charge of the shattered household. Seeing to the daily task of running the plantation in Nathanael's stead, Phineas provided stability in the management of the estate throughout the crisis.

A year after Nathanael's death, Caty presented to Congress a claim of indemnity in behalf of her late husband's estate—nothing was resolved. It was during this trip north that **Cornelia Greene** relates, in the memoirs of her childhood, her delightful encounter with George Washington:

"The eventful day came. We were graciously welcomed by Mrs. Washington; but my heart was so thick with fluttering, and my tongue so tied, that I made but a stuttering semblance of response to her kindly questions. At length the door opened, and General Washington entered the room. I felt my mother's critical eyes, and advanced with the intention of making a courtesy and declaiming the little address previously taught me; instead of which, I dropped to my knees at Washington's feet, and burst into tears.

"All the resources of dramatic art could hardly have devised a more effective coup. Washington stooped and tenderly raised me, saying with a smile, "Why, what is the matter with this foolish child?" The words do not have a tender sound, but language may not convey the gentleness of his manner and the winning softness of his voice, as he wiped away my tears with his own handkerchief, kissed my forehead, and led me to a seat as he might a young princess. He sat beside me, and with laughing jests, brought down to the plane of my appreciation, banished my sins from my eyes, rescued me from humiliation, and brought me back to composure. He guarded me from my mother's outraged eyes, kept

me with him while in the drawing room, had me placed beside him at the dinner-table,
and with his own hands heaped all of the good things on my plate. After dinner he took
me to walk in the garden, and with an intelligent stooping to my intellectual stature, and
a sympathetic understanding of my emotional state and need, he drew me into talks on
the themes of my daily life, and won me into revelations of my hopes and fears..."

As young **GEORGE WASHINGTON GREENE** neared his twelfth birthday, his education became a matter of concern to Nathanael's former comrades. George Washington had made the offer to Caty, to take on the responsibility of educating his namesake. A second offer had also been put forth by the Marquis de Lafayette, who suggested in a letter to Caty that George be educated in France under his charge, and at his expense. The marquis explained that he had discussed George's studying abroad with Nathanael, and therefore requested that Caty allow him to fulfill her late husband's wishes for the boy's education.

Caty, embarrassed by the fact that her estate was already heavily indebted to the marquis, and, no doubt, confused by the dual offer of both Washington and Lafayette, hesitated in her reply. Lafayette, therefore, turned to Henry Knox for help in persuading the young widow.

After much deliberation Caty decided to accept Lafayette's generous offer. George was sent to New York where he resided with the Knoxes until the appointed day in which he set sail for France in the company of an American diplomat enroute to that country. It was General Knox who saw the boy off at the dock after presenting him with a gift of fifty dollars.

With the continued help of Phineas Miller, along with the sale of many of her private possessions, Caty was able to stay afloat financially, even managing to divide her time between Georgia and Rhode Island, as her husband had planned to do. It was on one such trip in 1789, that Caty stopped over in New York to visit with many old friends now appointed to high governmental positions, including the newly elected President of the United States and his wife: George and Martha Washington. The widow Greene was entertained at the President and First Lady's dinner table, and accompanied them to the theater, even sitting in the presidential box.

President Washington returned the favor of Caty's visit while touring the South. He scheduled two stops at the Mulberry Grove estate, dining with Caty and the children.

It was in 1791 that Caty decided to make another appeal to the United States Government beginning the presentation of her case, in person, before the Treasury

Department. Her good friend, Alexander Hamilton, was now Secretary. The petition contained numerous documents and affidavits: including statements by many of Nathanael's former officers, the former governor of South Carolina, and even a sworn statement made by John Banks prior to his death.

Of course, Treasury Secretary Hamilton approved the memorial, stating that although Nathanael had technically erred in signing the promissory notes without the government's authority; his family should not be allowed to suffer poverty in consequence. Hamilton forwarded the petition and his findings to the House of Representatives for congressional review.

Anthony Wayne, now a member of Congress as a representative from Georgia, immediately proposed a resolution in Caty's behalf. However, former militia general, Thomas Sumter, was also a member of Congress, and still nursed a grudge against Nathanael Greene's expectation of subordination from him during the Southern Campaigns. Sumter was responsible for raising violent opposition against Caty's petition as Anthony Wayne worked frantically seeking support for it.

Once again Nathanael Greene's reputation became a matter of debate as Sumter and his cronies charged the late major general with being connected in the speculations of John Banks, despite the fact that all sworn affidavits, including those submitted by Banks and Rob Burnet, stated otherwise. The attention of Harry Lee, Otho Williams, Edward Carrington and Nathaniel Pendleton were immediately drawn to the debates. Indignant at the attack on the reputation of their 'dear, much-injured commander', as they now referred to him, they boldly responded.

When General Greene's enemies in Congress began to bring into question whether Greene exaggerated the deplorable conditions his army faced in the South, and then went on to question the soundness of his military strategies as well, the former subordinates of the Southern Commander intensified their protests. They were expert, first-hand witnesses to the army's sufferings, and the military genius of Nathanael Greene.

Encouraged by her friends, Caty waited as the tense days and weeks passed. Finally the announcement was made that the bill for indemnification was before the House for a vote. Almost afraid to hope for the best after so much hardship in her life, Caty Greene nervously awaited the roll call. It was by a margin of only nine votes that her claim had been approved.

Passing quickly before the Senate, all that was needed for her to receive the first installment of the $47,000 she petitioned for, was the signature of the President of the United States. Caty was seated in the gallery of the House when word arrived from President Washington stating that he had, *"This day approved and signed an act for indemnifying the estate of the late General Nathanael Greene."* Though the long awaited triumph had come, the words of General Greene's early biographer, William Johnson, in response to this bleak victory still resounded — *"Where was the indemnity for the sacrifices of property he had made? For the many distressing and laborious hours he had suffered? For the mortified feelings of a soldier, and the anxious cares of a parent, when approaching his dying hour?"* Historian William Johnson was keenly aware that this vote of Congress did not clear the name of the commander of the South. Even as he worked on the general's biography in 1822, there were those who still doubted the character of General Nathanael Greene.

On a return trip from Rhode Island the following year, the Greene's and Phineas Miller were accompanied by a friend of Miller's by the name of Eli Whitney. Whitney, like Miller, had accepted a position as tutor to a Southern family. Yet, upon arriving, Eli Whitney discovered that the position had been filled. Unable to afford the return voyage, Whitney was invited to stay at Mulberry Grove where he would have the opportunity to continue his study of law under the instruction of Nat Pendleton. In return for his board, young Whitney performed minor repairs on the estate and invented for his generous hostess a few household gadgets and toys for the children.

It was at Mulberry Grove that Eli Whitney invented the cotton gin. Tradition is that the vivacious widow of Nathanael Greene assisted Whitney in completing his famous invention. The ingenious Whitney became frustrated by the fact that after the seed was separated from the cotton fiber, the fibers stuck to the teeth of the gin's cylinder, clogging its action. The story holds that when Caty was made aware of Eli's impasse, she picked up a nearby hearth brush, and putting it against the cylinder, cleaned the teeth. Upon viewing her simple demonstration, Whitney mounted a coarse brush on a second revolving cylinder with great success.

Both Phineas Miller and Caty Greene entered into a partnership with Whitney to patent and then market this remarkable invention. Unfortunately word of its design had leaked out, and before the cotton gin's patent had been approved, copies of it had entered the marketplace. Before long Caty found herself tied up in yet another legal battle.

With trouble erupting in France, the Marquis de Lafayette thought it best to send George back to the safety of his own country. George, now seventeen years old, was quickly reacquainted with his loving mother, adoring sisters and brother and former tutor. Tragically the joyous reunion was short-lived. Only a few weeks after his return, he set sail with a friend on the Savannah River. The boat capsized, drowning George Washington Greene.

Well acquainted with personal tragedy and hardship, Caty managed to continue on, with Phineas Miller once again there to offer comfort and support. Though we have no portrait of Phineas, all accounts refer to him as 'gentle', 'cultivated', and 'conscientious'. And so it was this gentle man that won the heart of Caty Greene. They were married in New York, with several of Nathanael and Caty's old military friends in attendance, including President and Lady Washington.

As the legal battle over the cotton gin patent raged on, Caty and Phineas found themselves again in financial upheaval. Forced to auction off the Mulberry Grove estate for the pitiful sum of $15,000, they moved the family to Cumberland Island and began to build the home Nathanael had intended prior to his death.

The family was supported by the sale of the valuable timber on Cumberland Island. Live oak from the former ironmaster Nat Greene's property was used in the hull of the USS Constitution. The hull of the Navy frigate proved so hard that she is still referred to as 'Old Iron Sides'.

It was during this rather gloomy period of readjustment for the family that Caty received the sorrowful news that three old and dear friends had passed away. First came the tragic news of Anthony Wayne's death, followed by that of Henry Knox, and finally, and perhaps most devastating of the three, the news that George Washington was no more.

Yet, her gloom was soon temporarily relieved when word arrived that the ongoing legal battle over Eli Whitney's patent was finally resolved in favor of Whitney and his partners. Caty and Phineas received a handsome compensation, which they invested in their property on Cumberland Island.

Now having the finances available, Caty and Phineas were able to complete their mansion, which they called Dungeness. Together they enjoyed its comfort for only a year, when suddenly Caty Miller again found herself widowed at the age of forty. Always 'the good soldier', she managed to carry on. Even in her later years she continued to be the center of attention at social functions, as she enthralled her captive audience with her memories of camp life with the Continental Army.

It was during the summer of 1804 that the shocking news of Alexander Hamilton's violent death came to Cumberland Island. The fact that Nat Pendleton had served as Hamilton's second in the fatal duel with Aaron Burr only added to the shock. It was Nat Pendleton that informed the duelists of the rules, and he who gave the frightful signal to fire. It was Nat Pendleton who supported his dying friend in his arms, and Pendleton who later returned to the scene of the shooting to retrieve a bullet-pierced tree limb to prove that Alexander Hamilton purposely fired into the air, thus sparing Aaron Burr's life, and sacrificing his own.

Only a few weeks after the news arrived of Alec's death, Caty received a letter from Aaron Burr, who was now in Georgia, requesting to visit her at *Dungeness*. Because they were old military friends, Burr having served as an aide-de-camp to George Washington; Caty felt that she could not deny him the hospitality of her home. Yet, she was greatly disturbed that it was by this friend's hand that another friend—a more intimate friend— had been killed. Thus, she granted Aaron Burr permission to come to *Dungeness* and to make her home his own during his stay, but, unable to face him, she left before his arrival, and did not return until he left.

The remaining Greene children married. **LOUISA** remained at *Dungeness* with her mother, while young **NATHANAEL** chose to settle in Rhode Island. **PATTY** and **CORNELLIA**, it seems, had a serious falling out with their mother, and together with their husbands and children moved to the Tennessee frontier onto the land that had been given to their father by the state of North Carolina.

In 1811 American troops were stationed on Cumberland Island as tension mounted once again between America and England. As rumors of war became reality, Caty was advised to leave this vulnerable position. As a veteran of war she refused to be moved from her homestead, seemingly enjoying the activity of the troops about her, and no doubt the memories camp life stirred.

In August of 1814, Caty became the victim of a southern fever. At the age of fifty-nine, too tired to fight on any longer, she finally surrendered. As the British invaded the Federal City of Washington, D.C., Catharine Greene Miller was laid to rest, having never learned of the city's destruction.

THE GREENE BROTHERS were able to productively work the mills and forages once again after the war's end. Years of diligence made them quite prosperous, though they continued to live simple and modest lives.

The family homestead in Potowomut remains privately owned by a descendent of Kitt Greene. The lovely old farmhouse sits amid a serene setting, virtually secluded from the bustle of our modern day. In the stillness one can imagine the boisterous laughter and chatter of Quaker Greene's imposing brood of eight sons as they set about their daily routine of life.

Upon a hilltop in Coventry stands Nathanael's 'Spell Hall' now preserved by the General Nathanael Greene Society. The house is open to the public.

ANTHONY WAYNE: The gossips of Savannah began to wag their venomous tongues in the weeks following Nathanael's death. Outrageous tales began to circulate throughout the town. Anthony was accused of suffocating Nathanael with a pillow as he lay upon his sick bed in order to take advantage of the opportunity to have Caty for himself. Though Anthony and Caty were able to endure the painful gossip, and even prove to frustrate the perpetrators when no romantic involvement developed between them, Anthony soon showed symptoms of falling into a state of depression. Never able to make a decent profit off his Georgia plantation, nor to persuade any members of his family to join him at his southern estate, he was becoming apathetic and idle, finding his escape in drink.

Concerned for her friend, Caty suggested he return to active service. Anthony refused to consider it when he learned that his old enemy Arthur St. Clair had been appointed commander in chief. He was then persuaded by friends to run for a seat in Congress, which he did, successfully—or so it seemed.

While in Congress he diligently represented his constituents, and tirelessly worked to help Caty in her petition to be reimbursed the money Nathanael was forced to pay for the supply of his troops. Yet, before long talk in Georgia was that Congressman Wayne had illegally gained his seat. When the talk prompted an investigation it was discovered that the voting was rigged in Anthony's favor at many polling places. Though he claimed to have no knowledge of the scandal, Anthony resigned his seat in Congress.

Now, especially, Caty was concerned for her friends emotional health. When it was discovered that General St. Clair was to resign as commander of the army, she used her influence with President Washington to suggest that General Wayne be given the position. The President hesitated at first, not certain that Wayne could handle supreme command. Washington even referred to Anthony as a 'rouge', but nonetheless appointed him commander in chief.

Washington's choice proved an excellent one. Major General Anthony Wayne was effective in bringing temporary peace to the frontier, and earning the respected title of 'The chief who never sleeps' from the Indians of the Northwest.

Following the death of his estranged wife, Anthony became engaged. Though duty called him back to the Northwest, the middle-aged couple made plans to marry just as soon as he returned. But the hardships of the army had paid their toll on Anthony Wayne, and a flare-up of gout claimed his life.

Thirteen years later, Isaac Wayne, the general's son, traveled to Erie, Pennsylvania in a one horse sulky to retrieve his father's remains and bring them home for burial. When the grave was opened it was discovered that Anthony Wayne's body was in a near perfect state of preservation, and therefore could not be transported in the sulky. Confused as what to do, Isaac sought the help of an army surgeon who suggested that the body be boiled, thus separating the flesh from the bones. No doubt a bit reluctant and sickened, Isaac agreed. The bones of his father were then transported home, while the flesh was reinterred in the original grave. Thus, General Anthony Wayne has two gravesites.

HENRY KNOX, who referred to Nathanael Greene as his *'truly beloved friend'*, proved the depth of his friendship time and again in his generous care of Caty and her children.

Henry was appointed Secretary of War under President Washington, serving that post with great diligence and enthusiasm. From this cabinet position he instructed Anthony Wayne in his dealings with the Indians of the Northwest, and oversaw the potential for disaster brought on by Shay's Rebellion and the Whiskey Rebellion.

Accustomed to their own share of personal tragedies, Henry and Lucy remained very much in love despite the hardships and separations of war, and the death of eight of their ten children. (One of which, upon his birth, Henry teasingly wrote to Nathanael that he intended to name for him, but that he did not particularly care for the name Nathanael, thus he would name him for a Roman general whom he knew Nathanael admired.)

After his time of service as Secretary of War, Henry and Lucy retired to Maine and lived comfortably in their spacious mansion, *'Montpelier'*. It seems the Knoxes lived too comfortably here, for they fell into serious debt, which would plague Henry for the remainder of his life.

At the age of fifty-seven, Henry suffered a fatal throat infection, tragically brought on when the former artillery commander swallowed a chicken bone which could not be dislodged.

THE MARQUIS DE LAFAYETTE: Though the life of Lafayette is well documented in many outstanding biographies, it seems that few Americans are familiar with the remarkable story of this French aristocrat. Therefore, though I will refrain from summarizing the lives of such men as George Washington or Alexander Hamilton, assuming the reader is familiar with their great impact on history, I will make an attempt, though I fear a poor one, to summarize the life of this steadfast defender of liberty—Marie Josph Paul Yves Roch Gilbert du Motier—the Marquis de Lafayette.

Following the American Revolution the twenty-four-year-old major general of the Continental Army arrived in his native France only to find it on the verge of its own revolution. The complexities of the French Revolution are not my aim, but instead the unwavering courage, and fervent love of liberty displayed by the young marquis.

Becoming a member of the National Assembly in 1789, Lafayette took a leading role in the French Revolution, promulgating a bill of rights based on *America's Declaration of Independence*. By popular acclaim he was made military ruler of Paris, and became the referee between the crown and the representatives of the people, constantly putting forth the need for lawful, nonviolent change.

He attempted to discourage the growing influence of the violent revolutionists, known as the Jacobeans, and at the same time verbalizing his disappointment of King Louis XVI's attempt to flee the country. Lafayette found himself an enemy of both factions. (It was at this time that the marquis sent George Washington Greene back to the safety of America.)

Aware that the Jacobeans intended to arrest him as a traitor of the people because of his support of a constitutional monarchy, Lafayette fled to northern France. Unfortunately for the marquis, this area had been occupied by the Austrians who where themselves at war with France. As a general in the French army, Lafayette became a prime target for the Austrians. He was soon captured and imprisoned.

His military rank insured respectful treatment until an unexpected attempt to rescue him failed. Enraged, Lafayette's captors threw him into a rat infested dungeon cell. He was held in solitary confinement. His jailers were warned never to call him by name again. They were to refer to him with a number. At first, reading materials were allowed, though anything that mentioned the word 'liberty' was immediately confiscated. Soon he was told that all reading materials were to be withheld, and that the four walls of his dungeon cell were all he would ever see.

Tortured as he was by such acts of mental cruelty, perhaps the most devastating of all was the fact that he would receive no news of his family. Aware the Terror prevailed over France, and that all with aristocratic ties were being systematically executed regardless of age or gender, Lafayette fully expected that his own wife and children were already dead. His captors knew that their psychological abuse of complete isolation and deprivation would drive him to despair. Therefore they confiscated his eating utensils that he might not have the means to attempt suicide.

Adrienne du Motier, the child-bride of Lafayette, (an arranged marriage, performed when Adrienne was but fourteen and Lafayette sixteen), managed to sneak their son, George, out of France, and eventually to America under the guardianship of George Washington. When the political extremists came to arrest Adrienne, she was relieved that her daughters were allowed to remain in the custody of their tutor.

The barbaric systematic execution of aristocracy claimed the life of Adrienne's mother, sister and grandmother (her father and remaining sisters having managed to flee France prior to the Terror). Adrienne fully expected to follow them in death.

Through the pressure of friends, and that of the American Ministers to France, Gouvenor Morris and James Monroe, Adrienne was released after two years of imprisonment, and given permission to return to what remained of her husband's property. Yet, in an extraordinary act of selfless devotion, Adrienne decided to leave France to find her husband, thus bringing to the attention of the world the injustices of Lafayette's treatment. Her daughters, finally reunited with their mother and longing to see their father once more, opted to go with her and join their father in prison.

Having spent a year in solitary confinement, with but a single, smuggled message of his family's well-being in all that time, Lafayette one day heard the door to his cell open, and to his utter astonishment found himself face to face with his wife and daughters. Filthy, pale and terribly thin, Lafayette's appearance shocked his family. They, too, bore the telltale signs of their own horrible existence. Falling into one another's arms the family shared emotions too great to describe. After more than twenty years of marriage, the marquis, for the first time, fell in love with his courageous wife who had loved him from childhood.

They would spend two more years in cruel captivity; the marquis' family finally being released after a total of five years in prison. The family was then forced to remain in exile per order of France's new first consul, Napoleon Bonaparte, who considered Lafayette a personal threat to his popularity with the people.

Following a year's exile in Holland, which Lafayette considered *'like being dead'*, he boldly returned to France despite Napoleon's threats. Lafayette declared that if France had indeed become free again, as Napoleon boasted, then so had he! Napoleon's response was to treat Lafayette as though he did not exist. The cruelest exhibit of this was demonstrated when a memorial service was held to commemorate the death of George Washington. Lafayette was not invited, and moreover, Napoleon made certain that the orations given did not mention anything of the former French general of the Continental Army or his close friendship with Washington. In fact no mention of Lafayette was allowed whatsoever.

With the downfall of Napoleon, Lafayette once again became politically active, serving as a member of the Chamber of Deputies. As each new form of leadership in France became corrupted, Lafayette was sure to raise his voice in dissent, always standing for social equality, popular representation, religious tolerance, and freedom of the press.

Ten years after their release from prison, Adrienne, who even during the Terror proudly referred to herself as *'the wife of Lafayette'*, passed away. Her husband of thirty-four years had remained by her side throughout her illness. His devotion to her since their imprisonment had been complete, and her death proved his most difficult trial. *"Up to now you have found me stronger than my circumstances; today the circumstance is stronger than I,"* he told a friend the day he lost his Adrienne. Though she had encouraged him to remarry after her death, Lafayette had become too devoted to her memory for that. He was content to be surrounded by his children, and, as the years passed, by his grandchildren.

In 1824, President James Monroe sent an invitation to Lafayette to once again come to America. Eagerly accepting, Lafayette arrived in America with his son, George. Together they embarked on a triumphant journey through all the states of the union. Thousands turned out to greet this hero of the Revolution wherever he went. Countless dinners, official functions and formal balls were planned in his honor.

When visiting the tombs of George and Martha Washington, Lafayette was given complete privacy, later emerging in tears. He met with the aged, former revolutionaries and ex-presidents, John Adams and Thomas Jefferson, as well as, Madison and Monroe. While in Washington, D.C., he dined with newly elected President John Quincy Adams.

He took part in the Masonic ceremony to lay the cornerstone for the Bunker Hill Monument, and from that very spot and other significant places in his travels, Lafayette gathered soil to take back with him to France. For, this aging citizen of two countries realized he could only be buried in one, and though he desired to be buried in France beside his Adrienne, he longed to be buried beneath American soil.

Returning to France, he was again a member of the Chamber of Deputies. In the July Revolution of 1830, he served as commander of the National Guard. Soon he found himself opposed to the 'citizen king' Louis-Philippe's show of violence.

Following a lengthy bout with a cold, the Marquis de Lafayette died at the age of seventy-six, clutching the medallion about his neck that held Adrienne's portrait. Because the nation was still in political turmoil, and Lafayette having been in opposition to the government's stand, the strictest precautions against demonstrations during the funeral procession were enforced. He was quietly laid to rest in his American soil. In America a time of national mourning was declared upon learning of the general's death.

HARRY LEE was given leave of the Southern Department, never to return to active duty during the Revolution. A born soldier, Harry attempted to satisfy his restless spirit through political involvement. Serving as a member of the United States Congress, and as governor of Virginia, he seemingly remained content for a while.

Deeply attached to his cousin-bride, Matilda, the Virginia couple seemed to have a life of affluence and ease ahead. Three children were the gift of this union, the first son being named for Nathanael Greene.

Tragedy struck the Lee household when Matilda became gravely ill and died. Harry's reaction was one of despondency. Forced to carry on for the sake of his children and his constituents, Harry finally pulled himself together though the gleam was forever dimmed in his eyes. Three years after Matilda's death, Harry married again. His second wife bore him five more children.

When news reached Governor Harry Lee that General Arthur St. Clair was resigning as commander in chief of the military, Harry quickly applied for the position. Though highly qualified, and seemingly favored for the post by both President Washington and Secretary of War Knox, Harry was denied the position because it was feared that the act of promoting the former cavalry colonel to commander in chief would cause a fair amount of turmoil amongst the general officers. Losing this position to his friend Anthony Wayne, proved a great disappointment. Eager to return to military life, Harry volunteered his services to the French army. Though offered a commission of major general by the French, George Washington persuaded Harry to decline.

In 1794, with the Whiskey Rebellion threatening, and Anthony Wayne presently occupied on the frontier, President Washington offered Harry the assignment of marching fifteen thousand troops to Pittsburgh to put down the disturbance and round up the ringleaders. He was given the commission of major general, and for the first time donned the blue-and-buff uniform of the old Continental Line; the uniform of Harry's cavalry had been green and white. His time of active service was short, and within a year he returned to civilian life once again.

It was Harry Lee that announced to George Washington the tragic news of Nathanael Greene's death. So, too, it is Harry Lee's words that America remembers in reference to George Washington's death, as he eulogized this man he so admired as being, *"First in war, first in peace, and first in the hearts of his countrymen!"*

As the years passed, the onslaught of serious financial problems threw Harry into a severe depression. Then, by a series of unfortunate accidents, he found himself involved in a political riot in which he was attacked by a mob, suffering permanent injuries.

During the War of 1812, President Monroe, seeking superior leadership for the army, offered General Lee the command. Harry was too weak to accept. His close friends, James Madison and Monroe, raised funds to send Harry to the West Indies in the hope of finding a cure. Spending two years in the islands with no respite, and sensing that his death was imminent, Harry became anxious to return home.

He arranged for passage back to the United States, and, as his health showed signs of quickly deteriorating, he prevailed upon the captain to set him ashore when he discovered that the ship was near to Cumberland Island. Though Caty had already passed away, Harry was confident that the remaining family of his old comrade at arms would take him in. He was warmly welcomed, and cared for by Louisa, who as a child often heard his name spoken with affection by her parents.

As soon as the army garrison, now posted on the island, heard that Light-Horse Harry Lee was ill at *Dungeness*, they promptly arranged for two officers to be present at Harry's bedside, night and day, to keep this hero of the American Revolution company. The officers, feeling privileged to this assignment, treasured the tales Harry shared with them of his military experiences.

A few weeks after his arrival at *Dungeness*, General Henry Lee died at the age of sixty-two. The love of his former commander had seemingly reached beyond the grave to shelter his troubled friend in his dying hour. Light-Horse Harry was given a full military funeral. The Marines fired thirteen salvos, the proper salute to a major general. The boom of artillery followed.

Harry was laid to rest beside Caty. He left behind his second wife and eight children. Only his youngest child would venture southward to visit his grave. In his youth this son had memorized long passages from letters his father had sent to the family. This boy was only five-years-old at the time of his father's death, and had but little recollection of his gallant father as he grew to manhood. Yet it was this son that would follow in his father's footsteps, becoming one of the greatest generals in America's history—Robert E. Lee.

OTHO HOLLAND WILLIAMS returned home on medical leave just prior to the war's end. Having spent a year as a prisoner of war, and then enduring the hardships of the entire Southern Campaign, he was aware that his health would probably never be restored. Nevertheless, this young Marylander was determined to live life to its fullest in the years he had left.

Promoted by Congress to brigadier general on the recommendation of Nathanael Greene, Otho entertained the thought of returning to active command, but with the war coming to a close, there was little need for an additional general officer. Thus he settled into civilian life, taking a bride, and investing in real estate.

His marriage proved very successful, with an adoring wife, and five sons—one named for Nathanael Greene and another for Harry Lee.

His investments proved equally successful. In 1790, Otho Williams offered to President Washington a large piece of property along the Potomac River as the site of the nation's capitol. President Washington politely declined the generous offer, leaving Otho with the land, which would become the town of Williamsport, Maryland.

Offers of support were given for him to take on such positions as Secretary of Treasury, governorship of Maryland, and the rank of second in command of the army. Yet, Otho was forced to decline as his health continued to deteriorate.

With the hopes of stabilizing his condition, he sailed to the Caribbean. Little relief was found. General Otho Williams died at the age of forty-five. A year later his wife followed him to the grave, having died, so we are told, of a broken heart.

BENEDICT ARNOLD was commissioned brigadier general in the King's army, and served that post diligently. As if his shocking act of treachery were not enough, Arnold cold-heartedly led enemy troops in burning and pillaging towns in Virginia, and even his native Connecticut.

It was later discovered that Benedict Arnold had entered into treasonable correspondence with British General Clinton while serving as military governor of Philadelphia—more than a year before he was discovered to be a traitor. His wife, though successfully fooling George Washington, Henry Knox and Alexander Hamilton with her display of an emotional breakdown upon learning of her husband's treachery, was, in fact, very much involved in his treasonous act.

Peggy Shippen Arnold, whose family had strong loyalties to the British crown, vehemently supported her husband's treachery. Indeed, she may have been the catalyst in forming his decision. She and their infant son joined Arnold shortly after he fled to the British.

Arnold was to discover that few admire or trust a traitor, especially the individuals of the country you have defected to. Benedict Arnold, whose name in America is synonymous with treachery, was held in scorn by those in England. He died in 1801 at the age of sixty, pitifully requesting, before his death, that he be buried in the uniform he wore while serving as a general of the Continental Army of the United States of America.

GEORGE AND MARTHA WASHINGTON: George Washington is affectionately referred to as 'The Father of America'. Yet, if he is symbolically America's father, Martha must indeed be viewed as her mother. Her selfless character should be an inspiration to American women even today. How many young, frightened wives of Continental officers cried on her shoulders, we can only imagine. Caty Greene seemed to have won a special place in her heart. Certainly others came to her, and her motherly concern and wise counsel strengthened them throughout the difficult years of war and beyond. Martha has been viewed as the 'dowdy matron' wife of George Washington due to her more aged portraits (or even those of a younger Martha that were poorly done). The astounding work of Michael Deas, based on an age-regression image by a forensic anthropologist, shows us a youthful, beautiful woman.

Though we are given the definite impression by some historians that the marriage of George and Martha Washington was little more than one of convenience, we get a very different view from one who knew them intimately. In letters to his wife, Nathanael Greene often referred to the Washington's relationship. In one such letter, he shared with Caty that Mrs. Washington had come to camp, and teasingly told her that the General's lady was happy with her 'better' half. He then went on to say, "*Mrs. Washington is excessive fond of the General and he of her. They are happy in each other.*"

Martha, seemingly in an attempt to protect the privacy of her marriage, destroyed all correspondence between herself and her husband before her own death. Although one must respect her desire for privacy in this her most intimate relationship, we cannot help but feel the void it left. (Caty Greene, too, destroyed all her letters to Nathanael, though she kept his to her.)

George Washington has been viewed throughout the years as a cold, unapproachable man. Though many of his contemporaries may have left us this impression, it is believed to have come from their own self-consciousness. It was said by a historian of that time that "*The mind was so borne down by respect in approaching Washington, that there was scarcely play left for vivacity of feeling; and such was the commanding gravity of his air and manner, that those who had no opportunity of exploring the benevolent workings of his heart, were ready to pronounce him a cold character.*"

Certainly the deep affection that was shared by George Washington and his devoted subordinate, Nathanael Greene indicates the former's heart. This intimacy is witnessed time and again in their personal writings, letters separate and distinct from official dispatches. In these letters the Commander would, on occasion, forsake the traditional formality of ending his letters with, "your most affectionate and humble servant", and instead simply, though tenderly, close his words with, "Love...George Washington".

George Washington's concern for the education of Nathanael's eldest son, the genuine tenderness shown to little Cornelia Greene, and his visits to Caty and the children while President, are further witness of his emotional attachment to his late friend. Perhaps the most insightful and stirring of all are his comments in regard to Nathanael's death, written to the Marquis de Lafayette a full year later, stating, *"I can scarce persuade myself to touch upon it..."*

What part Nathanael Greene might have played in Washington's presidency one can only wonder. Certainly he would have had an influence, as regular correspondence between the two continued after the war, with shared views on varying subjects, but most especially politics. Many historians believe he would have served in Henry Knox's place as Secretary of War. Others feel he may have been persuaded in time, to take on the command of the army. Whatever position he might have accepted, it is agreed that this Quaker general would have continued to make a positive impact in his nation's history. Perhaps Alexander Hamilton stated it best when he wrote, *"His qualifications for statesmanship were not less remarkable than his military ability."*

Nathanael Greene, in the words of his biographer, William Johnson, *"Was distinguished by a winning kindness of manner, a spontaneous flow of feeling, which has left an extraordinary enthusiasm in the affections of all who knew him intimately."* Thus the grief experienced upon his sudden, untimely death by his close-knit family and numerous friends, was great indeed.

NATHANAEL GREENE'S body, in full uniform, was transported down the Savannah River to Captain Pendleton's house for the last honors. As the vessel passed Fort Wayne, the artillery fired minute guns. Upon its approach into the harbor, the anchored ships lowered their colors to half-mast.

The streets of Savannah were vacant, and businesses shut down as the townspeople solemnly gathered about the Pendleton home to show their last respects to the man who reclaimed the South from the British. A military guard of honor stood at attention as the coffin was carried from the boat into the house, where Caty and the children waited.

Later that afternoon the funeral procession, led by a militia regiment with muffled drums and reversed arms, headed for the cemetery at Christ Church, as a band played the Dead March from *Saul*.

The service was read in a voice trembling with emotion, followed by the firing of three general discharges by the militia regiment as the artillery simultaneously fired thirteen rounds. Nathanael Greene's body was then placed in a borrowed tomb.

As the years passed, the tomb's exact location, having no identification mark, was forgotten. In 1900, the state of Rhode Island provided funds to locate the remains of General Greene. Thus, several vaults were opened, and finally a silver coffin plate and several metal military buttons identified his remains. Beside the general were the remains of his son, George. The remains of both were removed from the vault and reinterred under an appropriate monument in Savannah's Johnson Square.

One can only hope that on occasion a passerby would stop to inquire of this monument. Perhaps an individual who has a true sense of the agonizing sacrifice which was freely offered to accomplish that which was deemed impossible, might even shed a tear over the circumstances which hastened the death of this great and amiable Patriot.